# Hypermedia and Literary Studies

## Technical Communications
## Ed Barrett, editor

*The Nurnberg Funnel: Designing Instruction for Practical Computer Skill*
John M. Carroll, 1990

*Hypermedia and Literary Studies*
Paul Delany and George P. Landow, editors, 1991

# Hypermedia and Literary Studies

edited by Paul Delany and George P. Landow

The MIT Press
Cambridge, Massachusetts
London, England

First MIT Press paperback edition, 1994

©1991 Massachusetts Institute of Technology

This book was printed and bound in the United States of America.

Library of Congress Cataloging-in-Publication Data


Hypermedia and literary studies / edited by Paul Delany and George P. Landow.
     p.   cm. — (Technical communications)
     Includes bibliographical references and index.
     ISBN 0-262-04119-7 (HB), 0-262-54073-8 (PB)
     1. Criticism—Data processing. 2. Criticism, Textual—Data processing.
3. Hypermedia systems. 4. Hypertext systems. I. Delany, Paul. II. Landow, George P. III. Series: Technical communication (M.I.T. Press)
PN98.E4H97 1991
802.85—dc20                            90-19495
                                          CIP

# Contents

# Foreword

Work on this collection began in August 1988 with a call for papers on the electronic forum HUMANIST. At every point since then our work has been advanced and mediated by computerized text-handling. More than five hundred e-mail messages passed between authors, contributors and the MIT Press, and an archive of these messages would be as large as the volume itself; all essays and illustrations were either submitted directly on disk or entered by scanning; and the final layout was assembled (to the specifications of the MIT Press) in an English Department office at Simon Fraser University by John K. Gilbert, using Pagemaker 4.0 on a Macintosh IIx and LaserWriterIINT. In "From Electronic Books to Electronic Libraries," an essay in this collection, Nicole Yankelovich examines the conditions under which a work of this kind, with two editorial centers some 2500 miles apart, might be completed entirely on-line. For the present, though, we have still found equipment from every era of literacy to be indispensable: the scanner, the xerox copier, the phone, the postal service, the library, pen and paper, and an occasional face-to-face conversation. We might assume, from this, that hypertext and hypermedia are likely to prove *supplemental* technologies rather than clear-cut *substitutions* for textual modes that then disappear utterly, like Victorian copy-clerks. To adapt a Saussurean metaphor, the arrival of hypertext causes the other occupants of the textual bus to shift position, but no one actually has to get off. We would argue, then, that text-based computing in the humanities should be able to co-exist happily with more traditional modes of textuality; and we hope to examine some of the relevant issues in a sequel to the present volume.

Paul Delany would like to thank the following people at Simon Fraser University for their moral or material support of his work on hypermedia: Tom Calvert, former Vice President for Research and Information (now President of the Science Council of British Columbia); Ross Saunders, Associate Vice President Academic; Nick Cercone, Center for Systems Science; Bob Brown, Dean of Arts; and Sandra Djwa, Chair of the Department of English. His work was funded by a President's Research Grant, a Special Research Grant, and a grant from the Center for Systems Science.

George Landow acknowledges all the past and present staff of the Institute for Research in Information and Scholarship (IRIS), with especial thanks to its founding director, William G. Shipp, and its current co-directors, Norman K. Meyrowitz and Marty J. Michel. Nicole Yankelovich, IRIS Project Coordinator during the initial development and application stages of Intermedia, and Paul D. Kahn, Project

Coordinator during the the *Dickens Web* and later Intermedia projects, have proved enormously resourceful, helpful, and good humored even during periods of crisis, as has Julie Launhardt, Assistant Project Coordinator, who created the screen dumps used in "The Rhetoric of Hypermedia." The Iris facilities engineers, Todd VanderDoes and Larry Larrivee, continue to maintain the hardware during conditions of continual change.

Since Brown University's Computing and Information Services took over responsibility for the Intermedia lab in the Center for Information Technology from the IRIS team in 1988, Steve Andrade, Chris Chung, and Vic Nair have made teaching and research with Intermedia possible. Landow owes an especial debt to his enthusiastic and talented graduate and undergraduate research assistants, particularly David C. Cody, Kathyrn Stockton, Shoshana M. Landow, and Gary Weissman, and to his students at Brown University. The development of Intermedia was funded in part by grants and contracts from International Business Machines, Inc., Apple Computers, and the Annenberg/Corporation for Public Broadcasting Project, and Landow is grateful to them and other IRIS sponsors and affiliates.

We are jointly indebted to our co-operative and intellectually stimulating contributors; to Terry Ehling, our enthusiastic and efficient editor at the MIT Press; to Edward Barrett, who reviewed the manuscript; to Georges Borchardt Inc.; and to John K. Gilbert, whose many hours in front of a computer screen generated a complex and attractive modern text in traditional form.

Several essays in this collection have previously appeared elsewhere (though most have been substantially revised in this printing). We are indebted to the following journals for permission to reprint: *IEEE Computer* for "Reading and Writing the Electronic Book"; *The Journal of Computing in Higher Education* for "The Rhetoric of Hypermedia"; *College English* for "Reading Hypertext: Order and Coherence in a New Medium"; *Academic Computing* and *Laserdisk Professional* for "The Shakespeare Project"; *Hispania* for "Hypermedia for the PC"; and *Canadian Journal of Educational Communication* for "Conceptualizing Hypermedia Curricula in Schools." Portions of "Topographic Writing: Hypertext and the Electronic Writing Space" appeared in Jay Bolter's *Writing Space: The Computer, Hypertext and the History of Writing,* and in *Language and Communication.*

Paul Delany
George P. Landow

September 1990

# Part I

Introduction

# Hypertext, Hypermedia and Literary Studies: the State of the Art

George P. Landow
Department of English, Brown University

Paul Delany
Department of English, Simon Fraser University

## Hypertext, hypermedia and the history of the text

The written text is the stable record of thought, and to achieve this stability the text had to be based on a physical medium: clay, papyrus or paper; tablet, scroll or book. (**Bolter**)[1] But the text is more than just the shadow or trace of a thought already shaped; in a literate culture, the textual structures that have evolved over the centuries *determine* thought almost as powerfully as the primal structure that shapes all expression, language. So long as the text was married to a physical media, readers and writers took for granted three crucial attributes: that the text was *linear, bounded,* and *fixed.* Generations of scholars and authors internalized these qualities as the rules of thought, and they had pervasive social consequences. We can define *Hypertext* as the use of the computer to transcend the linear, bounded and fixed qualities of the traditional written text.[2] Unlike the static form of the book, a hypertext can be composed, and read, non-sequentially; it is a variable structure, composed of blocks of text (or what Roland Barthes terms *lexia*) and the electronic links that join them.[3] Although conventional reading habits apply within each block, once one starts to follow links from one block to another new rules and new experience apply. Instead of facing a stable object—the book—enclosing an entire text and held between two hands, the hypertext reader sees only the image of a single block of text on the computer screen. Behind that image lies a variable textual structure that can be represented on the screen in different ways, according to the reader's choice of links to follow. Metaphors that can help us to visualise the structure "behind" the screen include a network, a tree diagram, a nest of Chinese boxes, or a web.

The immediate ancestor of modern hypertext was described in a pioneering article by Vannevar Bush in the 1945 *Atlantic Monthly*.[4] Bush called for mechanically linked information-retrieval machines to help scholars and decision makers in the midst of what was already an explosion of information. In the 1960s Douglas C. Englebart and Theodor H. Nelson began to design and implement computer systems that could implement some of these notions of linked texts, and today hypertext as a term refers almost exclusively to computerized hypertext programs, and to the textual structures that can be composed with their aid. Hypertext programs began to be widely available on personal computers in the late 1980s; current examples are *Guide* and *Linkway* for IBM-compatible PCs, *Intermedia* for Macintoshes running A/UX, and *Writing Space* and *HyperCard* for most Macintoshes.

Because hypertext breaks down our habitual way of understanding and experiencing texts, it radically challenges students, teachers, and theorists of literature. But it can also provide a revelation, by making visible and explicit mental processes that have always been part of the total experience of reading. For the text as the reader *imagined* it—as opposed to the physical text objectified in the book—never had to be linear, bounded or fixed. A reader could jump to the last page to see how the story ended; could think of relevant passages in other works; could re-order texts by cutting and pasting. Still, the stubborn materiality of the text constrained such operations: they required some physical task such as flipping pages, pulling another book from a shelf, or dismembering the original text beyond repair.[5] Over the centuries, readers developed a repertoire of aids to textual management; these aids operated both within a single volume, and in the relations between volumes. They constituted a *proto-hypertext*, in which we can find important models for hypertext design today—though the special powers of the computer allow us to look beyond the textual aids that evolved during the long history of writing and printing.

Within the individual volume of the traditional book we may find such *internal* hypertextual functions as tables of contents, page-numbers, chapters, verses, rubrications, footnotes, and indexes. Some of these may be assigned by the original author, others by specialists in textual organization such as indexers or printers, or by later generations of scholars. *External* hypertextual functions have traditionally been post-authorial, supplied by librarians and bibliographers. Indeed, once one extends the idea of "a text" to include a collection of volumes the object of study ceases to be bounded, linear or fixed, and some kind of implicitly hypertextual organization will always be necessary.

How does hypertext actually work? Two examples, already familiar to most scholars, will help to show its underlying principles. Take first the elementary, but not trivial question, faced by large research libraries: we have a hundred and fifty kilometers or more of shelves—in what order should the books be placed on them? The primitive solution is an accession system, like the British Library, where each new volume is simply added on at the "end" of the shelf, and volumes are classified by the *physical* address of their original placement. Modern systems try to establish a *logical* order that places related books together, independent of any particular arrangement of shelves. This creates a kind of hypertextual linking, but done on a fixed and one-dimensional basis (so that, for example, one must choose between uniting all the books on the same subject, or all by the same author).

On-line library catalogues, now coming into general use, can be thought of as coarse-grained and rudimentary hypertext systems that support a "virtual" rearrangement and retrieval of individual volumes at the terminal. However, they are usually limited to a few standardized search categories, such as author, title and subject; and they cannot discriminate between any textual units smaller than a complete book. More sophisticated systems, such as the on-line MLA Bibliography, can perform subtler searches, using more detailed descriptors and dealing with articles as well as books. But neither deserve to be called true hypertext systems, because they operate on textual classifications rather than on the actual underlying complete texts. True hypertext must be able to define textual units, and link them in various ways, within an overall textbase or, to use another term now gaining currency, "docuverse."

Our second example of the principles underlying hypertext could be any standard scholarly article in the humanities. In reading an article on, say, Joyce's *Ulysses*, one reads through the main text, encounters a symbol that indicates the presence of a footnote, and leaves the main text to read that note, which can contain a citation of passages in *Ulysses* that supposedly support the argument in question as well as information about sources, influences, historical background, or related articles. In each case, the reader can follow the link to another text and thus move entirely outside the scholarly article itself. Having completed reading the note—and perhaps some of the texts to which it refers—one returns to the main text and continues reading until one encounters another note, and again leaves the main text.

This kind of reading constitutes a mental model of hypertext. Suppose now that one could simply touch the page where the symbol of a note, reference, or annotation appeared, and that act instantly brought into view the material contained in a note or even the entire other text—here all of *Ulysses*—to which that note refers. Scholarly articles situate themselves within a network of textual relations, most of which the print medium keeps out of sight and relatively difficult to follow—because the referenced (or linked) materials lie spatially distant from the reference mark.

Electronic hypertext, in contrast, makes individual references easy to follow and the entire field of interconnections explicit and easy to navigate. Instant access to the whole network of textual references radically changes both the experience of reading and, ultimately, the nature of that which is read. If our putative Joyce article was linked, through hypertext, to all the other materials it cited, it would exist as part of a much larger system in which the totality might count more than the individual document; the article would now appear woven more tightly into its context than would a print-technology counterpart. The ease with which readers traverse such a system has further consequences: for as they move through this web or network of texts, they continually shift the center—and hence focus or organizing principle—of their investigation and experience. Hypertext provides an infinitely re-centerable system whose provisional point of focus depends upon the choices made by a truly active reader.

Hypertext thus presages a potential revolution in literary studies. However, an almost unlimited power to manipulate texts brings with it conceptual problems of extreme difficulty, which can be summed up by the questions: "What is a unit of text?" and "What are the relevant links between units?" Among traditional textual units the best-recognized and most functional ones are the word, the sentence, and the book. To think of them as commensurable units on a linear scale of magnitude is natural, but misleading. A word is a conceptual unit, a sentence a syntactical one, a book a unit whose identity is largely determined by its traditional status as a physical object. Nonetheless, they are units that can be handled by many kinds of textual aids developed over the whole period of literacy. But between the sentence and the book (in terms of magnitude) we find such units as footnotes, paragraphs, chapters and essays; these are less amenable to definition, because they are largely informal means of organizing thought.[6] For the same reason, however, they are likely to be important elements for building hypertext structures: they are the kind of mental "chunks" that we use to break a complex issue into components and make it intelligible. In addition, we are beginning to imagine new textual units, not yet codified or even named, that will be specific to the hypertext environment. They will come into being and pass away in the dynamic virtual text of the computer, products of such broad cognitive principles as identity, association and structure.[7]

These deep theoretical implications of hypertext converge with some major points of contemporary literary and semiological theory, particularly with Derrida's emphasis on decentering, with Barthes's conception of the readerly versus the writerly text, with post-modernism's rejection of sequential narratives and unitary perspectives, and with the issue of "intertextuality." In fact, hypertext creates an almost embarrassingly literal embodiment of such concepts, and several essays in this collection take up the affiliation between the computerised textuality of the present and the Continental literary theories of some twenty years before (see **Slatin, Dickey, Moulthrop, Harpold**).

Finally, hypertext can be expected to have important institutional as well as intellectual effects, for it is at the same time a form of electronic text, a radically new information technology, a mode of publication, and a resource for collaborative work. "Both an author's tool and a reader's medium, a hypertext document system allows authors or groups of authors to link information together, create paths through a corpus of related material, annotate existing texts, and create notes that point readers to either bibliographic data or the body of the referenced text. . . . Readers can browse through linked, cross-referenced, annotated texts in an orderly but nonsequential manner."[8] Such electronic linking shifts the boundaries between individual works as well as those between author and reader and between teacher and student. It also has radical effects upon our experience of author, text, and work, revealing that many of our most cherished, most commonplace, ideas and attitudes towards literary production are the result of the particular technology of information and cultural memory that has provided the setting for them. This technology—that of the printing-press, the book, and the library—engenders certain notions of authorial property, authorial uniqueness, and a physically isolated text that hypertext makes untenable. Hypertext historicizes many of our most commonplace assumptions, forcing them to descend from the ethereality of abstraction and appear as corollary to a particular technology and historical era. We can be sure that a new era of computerized textuality has begun; but what it will be like we are just beginning to imagine.

**From hypertext to hypermedia.**

Expository prose, with its linear and propositional structures, has been too much identified with the privileged form of reason itself. Hypertext provides a better model for the mind's ability to re-order the elements of experience by changing the links of association or determination between them. But hypertext, like the traditional text from which it derives, is still a radical reduction—to a schematic visual code—of what was originally a complex physical and intellectual experience, engaging all the five senses. *Hypermedia* takes us even closer to the complex interrelatedness of everyday consciousness; it extends hypertext by re-integrating our visual and auditory faculties into textual experience, linking graphic images, sound and video to verbal signs. Hypermedia seeks to approximate the way our waking minds always make a synthesis of information received from all five senses. Integrating or (re-integrating) touch, taste and smell seems the inevitable consummation of the hypermedia concept.

---

Consciousness itself is a continuous linking and re-structuring of images selected from past, present and future; from the real and the imaginary; from the internal and external realms of experience. Current hypermedia programs have taken only a few, faltering steps towards electronic representation of human memory, fantasy and cognition. Nonetheless, hypermedia is, in conception at least, a much better model of the mind's typical activities than exists in the severely restricted code of linear prose. We can argue, therefore, for a natural progression from the printed word to hypertext and hypermedia—analogous to the progression from painting to still photography, to silent movies, and now to movies with color and sound. This is not to claim that the newer media will altogether supersede the older ones. The black and white photograph remains viable, but is no longer the absolute standard of representation that it was in the nineteenth century. Similarly, the printed book will remain a central element of culture even as the new ways of interacting with texts make their own claims on our attention.

Some authors do not distinguish between hypertext and hypermedia on the basis that hypertext links one passage of verbal discourse to images, maps, and diagrams as easily as it does to another verbal one. Music and graphics are not, however, just another text, nor do they convey the same kind of information as do verbal texts. Some hypermedia programs, notably Apple's *HyperCard*, can also include launching or controlling programs that permit not just following links between units, but also the active manipulation of text, sound, graphics or video at the point of arrival. Larry **Friedlander's** *Shakespeare Project* is a good example of how information in various media can contribute to the electronic reconstruction and analysis of dramatic performance. In such cases, we would no longer speak of traversing or reading a hypertext structure; rather, each node in the web can become an active window where different processes are invoked. When the "control level" of programs is used to access remote resources and integrate information acquired there, hypermedia units become truly unbounded, and merge conceptually with the "trawlers" or "personal information managers" described below in the section on "The New Alexandria".

Recent science-fiction, such as William Gibson's *Neuromancer*, has speculated on the total reproduction of experience through a "Simstim" (simulated stimulation) medium.[9] Some experiments of this kind have been made in the world of entertainment and for military and commercial training.[10] In literary studies, however, we assume that hypermedia will be limited, for the rest of this century at least, to sight and sound.

## Reconfiguring the text

*Dispersing the traditional text*

Although in some not-so-distant future all individual texts may electronically link to one another, thus creating metatextual structures of a kind only partly imaginable at present, less far-reaching forms of hypertextuality have already appeared.[11] We already have works composed in hypertext that join blocks of text by electronic links to each other and to such graphic supplements as illustrations, maps, diagrams, visual directories and overviews. Second, there are the metatexts formed by interlinking individual sections of individual works. A third case is the adaptation for hypertextual presentation of material conceived in book technology. Such adaptations can work with textual units already given by the author, such as the individual sections of *In Memoriam*.[12] Conversely, one may, in the manner of Barthes's treatment of "Sarrasine," impose one's own *lexias* upon a work not explicitly divided into sections.

A fourth kind of hypertext puts a classical linear text, with its order and fixity, at the center of the structure. The composer then links various supplementary texts to this center, including critical commentary, textual variants, and chronologically anterior and later texts. In this case, the original text, which retains its old form, becomes an unchanging axis from which radiate linked texts that surround it, modifying the reader's experience of this original text-in-a-new-context.[13]

When compared to text as it exists in print technology, all these forms of hypertext evince varying combinations of atomization and dispersal. Unlike the spatial fixity of printed text, no one state of an electronic text is ever final; it can always be changed. Hypertext builds in a second fundamental mode of variation, since electronic links or reading pathways among individual blocks permit different paths through a text. The numerating rhetoric of "first, second, third" so well suited to linear text may appear within individual blocks of text but cannot control the unfolding of understanding in a medium that encourages readers to choose various paths, rather than following a fixed and linear one.

From a literary perspective based on book technology, the effects of electronic linking may appear harmful and dangerous. The notion of an individual, discrete work becomes increasingly undermined and untenable within this form of information technology, as it already has within much contemporary critical theory. Hypertext linking, reader control, and continual re-structuring not only militate against modes of argumentation to which we have become accustomed, but they have other, more general effects. The reader is now faced by a kind of textual randomness. The writer, conversely, loses certain basic controls over his text: the text appears to break down, to fragment and atomize into constituent elements (the *lexia* or block of text), and these reading units take on a life of their own as they become more self-contained because less dependent on what comes before or after in a linear succession.

At the same time that the individual hypertext block has looser, or less determining bonds to other blocks from the *same work* (to use a terminology that now threatens to become obsolete), it also can bond freely with text created by other authors. In fact, it bonds with whatever text links to it, thereby dissolving notions of the intellectual separation of one text from others as some chemicals destroy the cell membrane of an organism. Destroying the cell membrane will kill the cell; but destroying our conventional notions of textual separation has no fatal consequences. However, it will reconfigure the text and our expectations of it. As an individual block loses its physical and intellectual separation from others when linked electronically to them, it also finds itself dispersed into them. The necessary contextualization and intertextuality produced by situating individual reading units within a network of easily navigable pathways weaves texts, including those by different authors and those in nonverbal media, tightly together. One effect is to weaken and even destroy altogether any sense of textual uniqueness, for what is essential in any text appears intermingled with other texts. Such notions are hardly novel to contemporary literary theory, but here again hypertext creates an almost embarrassingly literal reification or actualization of a principle or quality that had seemed particularly abstract and difficult in its earlier statement. Since much of the appeal, even charm, of these theoretical insights lies in their difficulty and even preciousness, this more literal presentation promises to disturb theoreticians, in part, of course, because it disturbs status and power relations within their—our— field of expertise.

*Dismantling textual hierarchies*

Although the fundamental thrust of the printed page is to force the reader to read ahead if she is to read at all, specialized forms of text have developed that use secondary codes to present information difficult or impossible to include in linear text. The foot- or endnote, which is one of the prime ways that books create a secondary textual space, requires some code, usually a number in superscript font, that signals readers to stop reading the "main" text and begin reading some additional patch of text that is linked to that point in the main text.

In scholarly editions and criticism, such divisions of text partake of fixed hierarchies of status and power. The smaller type that presents footnote and endnote text, and its placement away from the normal center of the reader's attention, make clear that such language is subsidiary, dependent, less important. In scholarly editing, typographic encoding makes clear that the editor's efforts, no matter how diligent, are less important than the words being edited—for these appear in the main text. In scholarly writing these conventions also establish the importance of the dominant argument in opposition to the author's sources, scholarly allies and opponents, and even the work of fiction or poetry upon which the critical text focuses.

One experiences hypertext annotation of a text very differently. First, electronic linking destroys the binary opposition of text and note that founds the status relations that inhabit the printed book. Following a link can bring the reader to a later portion of the text or to a text to which the first one alludes. It may also lead to other works by the same author, or to a range of critical commentary, textual variants, and the like. The assignment of text and annotation to different "statuspheres" therefore becomes very difficult, and such text hierarchies tend quickly to collapse. Hypertext may well have to restore some of these status relations—for example, by assigning different priorities to links, or using multiple typefaces—to control this democratizing and even anarchic thrust.

Hypertext linking situates the current or "on-screen" textual unit at the center of the textual universe, thus creating a new kind of hierarchy in which the power of the center dominates that of the infinite periphery. But because in hypertext that center is always a transient, decenterable virtual center—one created, in other words, only by one's act of calling up that particular text—it never tyrannizes other aspects of the network in the way a printed text does.

*Opening textual borders*

Yet another form of democratization or absence of hierarchy: in hypertext systems links within and without a text—intratextual and intertextual connections—become equivalent, thus bringing texts closer together and blurring the boundaries between them. For example, Milton's various descriptions of himself as prophet or inspired poet in *Paradise Lost* and his citations of Genesis 3:15 create *intertextual* links. Similarly, his citations of the biblical text about the heel of man crushing the serpent's head and being in turn bruised by the serpent link to the biblical passage and its traditional interpretations as well as to other literary allusions and scholarly comment upon all these subjects.[14] An *intratextual* link, in contrast, might link a passage in which Milton mentions prophecy to other writings by him that make similar points. Hypertext linking simply allows one to speed up the usual process of making connections while providing a means of graphing such transactions—if one can apply the word "simply" to such a radically transformative procedure. The speed with which one can move between passages and points in sets of texts promises to change the way we read and write, just as high-speed numeric computing changed various scientific fields by making possible investigations that before had required too much time or risk. One change comes from the fact that linking permits the reader to move with equal facility between points within a text and those outside of it. Once one can jump from, say, the opening section of *Paradise Lost* to a passage in Book 12, thousands of lines "away," or to a French source for the opening, or to a modern scholarly comment, then, the *discreteness* of texts, which print culture creates, has radically decreased and even disappeared. One may argue that the hypertext linking of such passages does no more than copy the way one actually experiences texts in the act of reading; nonetheless, when the act of reading is given a new dimension of speed and control by electronic means, it has begun to change its nature.

Computers may re-create certain qualities of pre-literate culture more pervasively than even Walter J. Ong has been willing to admit. In *Orality and Literacy* Ong argues that computers have brought us into what he terms an age of "secondary orality" that "has striking resemblances to the old [oral, preliterate culture] in its participatory mystique, its fostering of a communal sense, its concentration on the present moment, and even its use of formulas." Nonetheless, although Ong finds interesting parallels between a computer culture and a purely oral one, he still insists: "The sequential processing and spatializing of the word, initiated by writing and raised to a new order of intensity by print, is further intensified by the computer, which maximizes commitment of the word to space and to (electronic) local motion and optimizes analytic sequentiality by making it virtually instantaneous" (136). But by inserting every text into a web of relations, hypertext systems promote nonsequential reading and thinking and hence produce a very different effect.

Since it weakens the boundaries of the text, nonsequential reading can be thought of as either correcting the artificial isolation of the text from its contexts or as violating one of the chief qualities of the book. According to Ong, writing and printing produce the effect of discrete, self-contained utterance:

> By isolating thought on a written surface, detached from any interlocutor, making utterance in this sense autonomous and indifferent to attack, writing presents utterance and thought as uninvolved with all else, somehow self-contained, complete. Print in the same way situates utterance and thought on a surface disengaged from everything else, but it also goes farther in suggesting self-containment. (132)

As Ong also points out, books, unlike their authors, cannot really be challenged:

> The author might be challenged if only he or she could be reached, but the author cannot be reached in any book. There is no way to refute a text. After absolutely total and devastating refutation, it says exactly the same thing as before. This is one reason why "the book says" is popularly tantamount to "it is true." It is also one reason why books have been burnt. A text stating what the whole world knows is false will state falsehood forever, so long as the text exists. (79)

But if hypertext fosters integration rather than self-containment, always situating texts in a field of other texts, can any individual work that has been addressed by another still speak so forcefully? One can imagine hypertext versions of books in which the reader could call up all the reviews and comments on that book; the "main" text would then inevitably exist as part of a complex dialogue rather than as the embodiment of a voice or thought that speaks it unceasingly. Hypertext, by linking one block of text to myriad others, destroys that physical isolation of the text, just as it also destroys the attitudes created by that isolation. Because hypertext systems permit a reader both to annotate an individual text and also to link it to other, perhaps contradictory texts, it destroys one of the most basic characteristics of the printed text: its separation and univocal voice. Whenever one places a text within a network of other texts, one forces it to exist as part of a complex dialogue.

Hypertext also blurs the boundaries of the metatext. Conventional notions of bounding do not apply to hypertext, whose essential novelty makes it difficult to define or describe in the established terms that derive from another information technology and embody hidden assumptions inappropriate to hypertext. Particularly inapplicable are the notions of textual "completion" and of a "finished" product. Hypertext materials are by definition open-ended, expandable, and incomplete. If one put a work conventionally considered complete, such as the *Encylopaedia Britannica*, into a hypertext format, it would immediately become "incomplete." Electronic linking, which emphasizes making connections, opens up a text by providing large numbers of points to which other texts can attach themselves. The fixity and physical isolation of book technology, which permits standardization and relatively easy reproduction, necessarily closes off such possibilities. Hypertext opens them up.

## Hypertext and the author

### Virtual presence

Many features of hypermedia derive from the *virtual presence* of all the authors who contribute to its materials. Using an analogy to optics, computer scientists speak of "virtual machines" created by an operating system that provides individual users with the experience of working on their own individual machines when they in fact share a system with as many as several hundred others. Since text processing is a matter of manipulating computer-generated codes, all texts that the writer encounters on the screen are virtual, rather than real, texts in two senses. First, according to conventional usage they only become completed texts when printed on paper in so-called hard copy. Second, once a writer places some portion of that text in the computer's memory, any textual work generates a virtual text in another sense: the original resides in memory and one works on an electronic copy until such time as the two converge when the text is "saved" by placing the changes in memory. At this point text in the reader's intention and in memory coincide. In a similar manner, the hypertext writer and reader experience the virtual presence of other contributors.

Such virtual presence is of course a characteristic of all technology of cultural memory based on writing and symbol systems: since we all manipulate cultural codes in slightly different ways, each record of an utterance conveys a sense of the individual who makes that utterance. Hypertext differs from print technology, however, in several crucial ways that amplify this notion of virtual presence. Because the essential connectivity of hypermedia removes the physical isolation of individual texts in print technology, the presence of individual authors becomes both more available and more mutually influential. The characteristic flexibility of this reader-centered information technology means, quite simply, that students have a much greater presence in the system, both as potential contributors and collaborative participants but also as readers who chose their own paths through the materials.

### Collaborative work

Hypertext demands new modes of reading, writing, teaching, and learning. In so doing it creates new understanding of collaborative learning and collaborative work. To most people, "collaboration" suggests two or more scientists, songwriters, or the like working side by side on the same endeavor, continually conferring as they pursue a project in the same place at the same time. Landow has worked on an essay with a fellow scholar in this manner. One of us, he relates, would a type a sentence, at which point the other would approve, qualify, or rewrite it, and then we would proceed to the next sentence. But probably a far more common form of collaboration (and the one used in this introduction, whose authors live two thousand miles apart) is "versioning," in which one worker produces a draft that another person then later edits by modifying and adding. Both of these models require considerable ability to work productively with other people, and evidence suggests that many people lack this quality. According to those who have carried out experiments in collaborative work, a third form proves more common than the first two: the assembly-line or segmentation model of working together, in which individual workers divide up the overall task and work entirely independently. This last mode is the form that most people engaged in collaborative work choose.[15]

Networked hypertext systems like Intermedia offer a fourth model of collaborative work that combines aspects of the three just described. By emphasizing the cooperative interaction of blocks of text, networked hypertext makes all additions to a system simultaneously a matter of versioning and of the assembly-line mode. Once ensconced within a network of electronic links, a document no longer exists by itself. It always has an active relation to other documents in a way that a book or printed document never can. From this crucial shift in the way texts exist in relation to others derive two principles that determine this fourth form of collaboration: First, any document placed on a networked system that supports electronically linked materials potentially exists in collaboration with any and all other documents on that system; second, any document electronically linked to any other document collaborates with it.

According to the *American Heritage Dictionary*, to *collaborate* can mean either "to work together, especially in a joint intellectual effort" or "to cooperate treasonably, as with an enemy occupying one's country." The combination of labor, political power, and aggressiveness that appears in this dictionary definition well indicates some of the problems that arise when one discusses collaborative work. On the one hand, the notion of collaboration embraces notions of working together with others, of forming a community of action. This meaning recognizes that we all exist within social groups, and must make our contributions to them. On the other hand, collaboration also invokes a deep suspicion of working with others, something both aesthetically as well as emotionally engrained since the advent of romanticism, which exalts the idea of individual effort to such a degree that it often fails to recognize or even suppresses the fact that artists and writers work collaboratively with texts created by others.

Most of our intellectual endeavors involve collaboration, but we do not always recognize it. The rules of our culture, particularly those that define intellectual property and authorship, do not encourage such recognition; further, information technology from Gutenberg to the present—the technology of the book—systematically hinders full recognition of collaborative authorship.   Hypertext, however, foregrounds this element of collaboration that other technologies of cultural memory suppress.  It changes our sense of authorship, authorial property, and creativity (or originality) by moving away from the constrictions of page-bound technology.  In so doing, it promises to have an effect on cultural and intellectual disciplines as important as those produced by earlier shifts in the technology of cultural memory that followed  the invention of  writing and printing.[16]

Throughout this century the physical and biological sciences have increasingly conceived of scientific authorship and publication as group endeavors. The conditions of scientific research, according to which many research projects require the cooperating services of a number of specialists in different fields, bear some resemblances to the medieval guild system in which apprentices, journeymen, and masters all worked on a single complex project. The financing of scientific research, which supports the individual project, the institution at which it is carried out, and the costs of educating new members of the discipline, nurtures such group endeavors and consequent conceptions of  group authorship.  In general, the scientific disciplines rely upon an inclusive conception of authorship:  anyone who has made a major contribution to finding particular results can appear  as authors of scientific papers, and similarly, those in whose laboratories a  project is carried out may receive authorial credit if an individual project and the publication of its results depend intimately upon their general research.   When a graduate student's dissertation appears in the form of one or more  publications, the advisor's name often appears as co-author.

Not so in the humanities, where graduate student research is supported largely by teaching assistantships and not, as in the sciences, by research funding. Although an advisor of a student in English or Art History often acts in ways closely paralleling the advisor of the student in physics, chemistry, or biology,  explicit acknowledgments of cooperative work rarely appear.  Even when a senior scholar provides the student with a fairly precise research project, continual guidance,  and access to crucial materials that the senior scholar has discovered or assembled, the student does not include the advisor as co-author.

Part of the reason for the different conceptions of authorship and authorial property in the humanities and sciences, it is clear, derives from the different conditions of funding and the different discipline-politics that result.  However, attitudes fostered by print technology are also responsible for maintaining exaggerated notions of authorial uniqueness, and ownership that often convey a distorted impression of "original" contributions in the humanities. The sciences take a relatively expansive view of authorship and consequently of text ownership, whereas the humanities take a far more restricted one that emphasizes individuality, separation, and uniqueness—often at the expense of creating a vastly distorted view of the connection of a particular text to those that have preceded it.

Whatever the political, economic, and other discipline-specific factors that maintain the conception of noncooperative authorship in the humanities, print technology has strongly contributed to the sense of a separate, unique text that is the product—and hence the property—of one person, the author. Hypertext changes all this, in large part because it does away with the isolation of the individual text that characterizes the book. As McLuhan and other students of the influence of print technology upon culture have pointed out, modern conceptions of intellectual property derive both from the organization and financing of book production and from the uniform, fixed text that characterizes the printed book. Printing a book requires a considerable expenditure of capital and labor, and the need to protect that investment contributes to notions of intellectual property. But these notions would not be possible in the first place without the physically separate, fixed text of the printed book. Just as the need to finance printing of books led to a search for the large audiences that in turn stimulated the ultimate triumph of the vernacular and fixed spelling, so, too, the fixed nature of the individual text made possible the idea that each author produces something unique and identifiable as property.[17]

## Hypertext and literary theory

### Hypertext and intertextuality

Thaïs Morgan suggests that intertextuality, "as a structural analysis of texts in relation to the larger system of signifying practices or uses of signs in culture," shifts attention from the triad constituted by author/work/tradition to another constituted by text/discourse/culture. In so doing, "intertextuality replaces the evolutionary model of literary history with a structural or synchronic model of literature as a sign system. The most salient effect of this strategic change is to free the literary text from psychological, sociological, and historical determinisms, opening it up to an apparently infinite play of relationships."[18] Morgan points to a major implication of hypertext (and hypermedia) intertextuality: such opening up, such freeing one to create and perceive interconnections, obviously occurs. Nonetheless, although hypertext intertextuality would seem to devalue any historic or other reductionism, hypertext systems in no way prevent those interested in reading by means of author and tradition from doing so. And regardless of whether these systems fulfill certain claims of structuralist and post-structuralist criticism, they surely provide a rich means of testing those claims.

By its very nature, hypertext emphasizes intertextuality in a way that page-bound text in books cannot. Scholarly articles, as we have seen, offer an obvious example of *explicit* hypertextuality in nonelectronic form. Conversely, any work of literature—by which for the sake of argument and economy we mean "high" literature of the sort we read and teach in universities—offers an instance of *implicit* hypertext in nonelectronic form. If one looks, say, at the "Nausicaa" section of Joyce's *Ulysses* in which Bloom watches Gerty McDowell on the beach, one notes that Joyce's text here "alludes" or "refers" (the terms we usually employ) to many other texts or phenomena that one can treat as texts, including the Nausicaa section of *The Odyssey*, the advertisements and articles in the women's magazines that suffuse Gerty's thoughts, popular music, facts about contemporary Dublin and the Catholic Church, and material that relates to other passages within the novel. Again, a hypertext presentation of the novel would link this section not only to the kinds of materials mentioned but also to other works in Joyce's career, critical commentary, and textual variants. Hypertext would permit one to make explicit, though not necessarily intrusive, the linked materials that an educated reader perceives surrounding the main text of *Ulysses*.

*Hypertext and de-centering*

Most first-generation computer-assisted instruction follows the model of printed workbooks, taking the user through a pre-arranged sequence of exercises. Such systems constrain anyone using them to follow a single sequence or relatively few possible sequences. In contrast, hypertext is composed of bodies of linked texts that have no *a priori* axis of organization. In other words, hypertext has no fixed center, and although this absence can create problems for the reader and writer, it also means that anyone who uses hypertext makes his or her own interests the de facto organizing principle (or center) for the investigation at the moment. One experiences hypertext as an infinitely decenterable and recenterable system.

Such capacity has an obvious relation to the ideas of Derrida and Althusser, two thinkers who emphasize the need to shift vantage points by de-centering discussion. Derrida has pointed out that a procedure he calls "de-centering" has played an essential role in intellectual change. For example, "Ethnology could have been born as a science only at the moment when a de-centering had come about: at the moment when European culture—and, in consequence, the history of metaphysics and of its concepts—has been dislocated, driven from its locus, and forced to stop considering itself as the culture of reference."[19] Derrida makes no claim that an intellectual or ideological center is in any way "bad," for as he explains in response to a query from Serge Doubrovsky, " I didn't say that there was no center, that we could get along without a center. I believe that the center is a function, not a being—a reality, but a function. And this function is absolutely indispensable."[20]

Hypertext systems permit the individual reader to choose his or her own center of investigation and experience. What this means in practice is that students are not locked into any particular kind of organization or hierarchy. The experience of Intermedia reveals that for those who choose to organize a session on *Context 32* by making use of author overviews, moving, say, from one for Keats to one for Tennyson, the system represents an old-fashioned, traditional, and in many ways still useful author-centered approach. On the other hand, nothing constrains the reader to work in this manner, and any who wish to investigate the validity of period generalizations could organize their sessions by using the Victorian and Romantic overviews as starting or midpoints; while yet others could begin with ideological or critical notions, such as Feminism or Victorian novel. In practice most readers employ *Context 32* as a text-centered system, since they tend to focus upon individual works. Even if they enter the system by means of an individual author, they tend to spend most time with files devoted to individual works, moving between poem and poem (Swinburne's "Laus Veneris" and Keats's "La Belle Dame Sans Merci") and between poem and informational texts ("Laus Veneris" and files on chivalry, medieval revival, courtly love, Wagner, and so on).

*The rhetoric and stylistics of hypertext*

Hypermedia redefines some of the basic characteristics of page-bound text, such as the rigidly hierarchical distinction between a main text and its annotation in scholarly works. Nonetheless, it still depends upon many of the same organizing principles that make page-bound discourse coherent and even pleasurable to read. In other words, this new information technology requires stylistic and rhetorical devices just as do other forms of writing (**Landow**). Authors in this electronic medium face three related problems: First, how can they orient readers and help them read efficiently and with pleasure? Second, how can they indicate where the links in a document lead? Third, how can they assist readers who have just entered a new document to feel at home there? Drawing upon the analogy of travel, we can say that the first problem concerns *navigation* information necessary for making one's way through the materials. The second concerns *exit* or *departure* information and the third *arrival* or *entrance* information. In each case, creators of hypermedia materials must decide what readers need to know at either end of a hypermedia link in order to make use of what they find there.

---

## Hypertext and cultural institutions

*The hypertextual instructor*

For teachers, a hypermedia corpus of multidisciplinary materials offers a far more efficient means of developing, preserving, and linking course materials than has existed before. Though course development is extremely time-consuming the materials developed, however pioneering or brilliant, rarely transfer to another teacher's course because they rarely match that other teacher's needs exactly. Similarly, teachers often expend time and energy developing materials that have potential use in their other courses, but do not make use of them because of the time necessary for adaptation. A hypermedia corpus does a better job of conserving the products of past endeavors because it requires so much less effort to select and reorganize them. It also helps teachers to easily and efficiently modify their curriculum to take into account new materials. For example, in response to the wishes of students and faculty, the survey of English literature in *Context32* evolved to include not just writings produced in mainland Great Britain but also writings in English written elsewhere. Unfortunately, anthologies that include writings by major African and Asian authors who write in English are difficult to come by; but with hypertext one may add selected poems by Wole Soyinka, a Nigerian who recently won the Nobel Prize for Literature, and then link his poems where relevant. Thus, his poems on Ulysses link to Joyce's novel and to poems by Tennyson and a contemporary Australian poet, A. D. Hope; while Soyinka's poems on Gulliver connect to Swift's *Gulliver's Travels.*

Hypertext also provides better support for teaching interdisciplinary courses. Interdisciplinary teaching no longer has the glamor it once did for several reasons. First, some have found that the need to deal with several disciplines has meant that some or all end up being treated superficially or only from the point of view of another discipline. Second, such teaching often requires faculty and administration to make extraordinarily heavy commitments, particularly when courses involve teams of two or more instructors. In contrast to previous educational technology, hypertext offers solid materials in each discipline and the virtual presence of teachers from other disciplines. It also allows and encourages integrating all of one's teaching, so that one's efforts function synergistically. A hypermedia corpus preserves and makes easily available one's past efforts as well as those of others. Its emphasis upon connectivity also encourages one to relate all of one's interests at those points that touch upon one another. Someone teaching an English course that concentrates on literary technique of the nineteenth-century novel can nonetheless draw upon relevant materials in political, social, urban, technological, and religious history. Teachers frequently try to allude to such aspects of context in passing, but the limitations of time and the need to cover the central concerns of the course often present to students a decontextualized, distorted view. By having related materials available, teachers can (1) simply permit students to encounter them during browsing, (2) suggest relevant areas students can investigate, or (3) create assignments that model the way a professional draws upon several approaches, disciplines, or bodies of material.

Hypertext helps to integrate scholarly work-in-progress with teaching. All of the qualities of connectivity, preservation, and accessibility that make hypertext an enormously valuable teaching resource also make it equally valuable as a scholarly tool. In particular, one can link portions of data upon which one is working, whether they take the form of primary texts, statistics, chemical analyses, or visual materials, and integrate these into courses. Such methods allow faculty to explore their own primary interests while simultaneously showing students how a particular discipline arrives at the materials, the "truths of the discipline," it presents to students as worthy of their knowledge. Such an approach, which may well emphasize the more problematic aspects of a discipline, accustoms students to the notion that for the researcher and theorist many key problems and ideas remain in flux. Hypertext also provides a particularly efficient means of carrying out one of the most important goals of teaching: to encourage both exploration and self-paced learning by linking and interweaving a variety of materials at differing levels of difficulty and expertise. The presence of such materials permits faculty members to accommodate the slower and well as the faster, or more committed, learners in the same class.

*Hypertext and students*

In the remainder of this section, we will be assuming *interactive* rather than *passive* hypertext systems. By a passive system we mean one that is designed by experts to present a particular subject-matter effectively—an encyclopedia, classical art, an income-tax code—and is then "locked" against modification by users. These users will still be free to traverse the web of blocks and links in their own way, but they cannot change either the primary texts or the way they are combined. Conversely, a fully interactive system (*Context32* is a notable example), allows users to edit, add or delete blocks of text, and also to modify the links between blocks. In practice, the freedom of interactive users will probably need to be restricted, just as there must be rules of order in a seminar or committee meeting. But it is still useful to keep in mind passive and interactive as two poles: hypertext as an aid to presentation of a fixed subject, versus hypertext as a tool that facilitates exploration and communication within an unbounded field of inquiry. **Slatin** develops this point with his distinction between "browsers," "users," and "co-authors."

---

For students, interactive hypertext promises new, increasingly reader-centered encounters with text. Experiencing a text as part of a network of navigable relations offers quick and easy access to a far wider range of background and contextual materials than has ever been possible with conventional educational technology. Students in schools with adequate libraries have always had the materials available, but as recent educational studies and theory make clear, availability and accessibility are not the same thing. Until students know how to formulate questions, particularly about the relation of primary materials to other phenomena, they are unlikely to perceive a need to investigate context, much less know how to go about using library resources to do so.

Even more important than having factual material available is learning what to do with such material when one has it in hand. Critical thinking relies upon relating many things to one another. Since the essence of hypertext lies in its making connections, it accustoms students to make connections among materials they encounter. A major component of critical thinking consists in the habits of seeking the way various causes impinge upon a single phenomenon or event and then evaluating their relative importance; and hypertext encourages such habits.

Hypertext also helps a novice reader to learn the habit of nonsequential reading characteristic of more advanced study. Scholarly and scientific writing require readers to leave the main text and venture out to consider footnotes, evidence of statistics and other authorities, and the like; they must then integrate their scattered evidence into a complex intellectual structure. The Brown experience suggests that using Intermedia teaches students to read in this sophisticated way. This effect, which first appears in students' better use of anthologies and standard textbooks, exemplifies the way Intermedia and appropriate materials together quickly get students up to speed.

In addition, a corpus of hypertext documents intrinsically joins materials students encounter in separate parts of a single course and in other courses and disciplines. Hypertext thus integrates the subject materials of a single course with other courses. Students, particularly when novices in a field, continually encounter problems created by necessary academic specialization and separation of single disciplines into individual courses. Hypertext's intrinsic capacity to join varying materials creates a learning environment in which materials supporting separate courses exist in closer relationship to one another than is possible with conventional educational technology.

Hypertext materials also reconfigure education by integrating the subject material in a single course continuously throughout a single term. In courses that use conventional educational technology—such as books, lectures, reserve reading, lecture handouts and examinations—students tend to synthesize the materials in a course only when studying for and taking examinations, if at all. The Brown experience has demonstrated that the connectedness of a hypertext corpus permits students to integrate each new bit of material as it is encountered.

Hypertext also demonstrates how a subject expert makes connections and formulates inquiries. One of the great strengths of hypertext is its capacity to use linking to model the kinds of connections that experts in a particular field make. By exploring such links, students benefit from the experience of experts in a field without being confined by them, as students would be in a workbook approach. Hypertext thus helps novices to learn, quickly and easily, the *culture* of a discipline. At the same time as hypertext materials show the student how an expert works in an individual discipline, they also familiarise the student with the vocabulary, strategies, and other aspects of a discipline that constitute its particular culture.

The capacity of hypertext to initiate the novice into a disciplinary culture suggests that this new information medium has an almost totalitarian capacity to model encounters with texts. However, the intrinsically antihierarchical nature of hypertext counteracts such a danger. An interactive hypertext system allows users to adapt materials to their individual needs, providing a customized electronic library that makes available materials as they are needed and not, as lectures of necessity must often do, just when the schedule permits, and for a mass audience.

The infinitely adaptable nature of hypertext also provides students a way of working up to their abilities by providing access to sophisticated, advanced materials. Considered as an educational medium, hypertext also permits the student to encounter a range of materials varying in terms of difficulty, because authors no longer have to pitch their materials to single levels of expertise. Even novice students who wish to explore individual topics in more depth therefore have the opportunity of following their curiosity and inclination as far as they wish; while more advanced students always have available more basic materials for easy review when necessary.

The reader-centered, reader-controlled characteristics of hypertext also allow student-readers to shape and hence control major portions of what they read. Since readers shape what they read according to their own needs, they explore at their own rate and according to their own interests. In practical terms the ease of using hypertext means that any student can contribute documents and links to the system; in this way, they can experience how a scholarly discipline evolves by a complex dialogue between its practitioners.

The combination of the reader's control and the virtual presence of a large number of authors makes an efficient means of distant learning. The very qualities that make hypertext an efficient means of supporting interdisciplinary learning also permit students to work without having to be in residence at a single and central site. Thus, the adaptable virtual presence of hypermedia contributors serves both the distant, unconventional learner and college student in a more conventional setting. For those interested in the efficient and just distribution of costly educational resources, hypertext offers students at one institution a way to share resources at another. Again, these qualities of hypermedia help dispersed students to benefit from materials created at any participating institution.

All these qualities make reader-centered hypermedia corpus well suited for use by those generally nonconventional students who pursue their learning outside the usual institutional setting, and often geographically distant from it. The very strengths of hypertext that make it such a major aid to student and teacher in conventional institutions also make it the perfect means of informing, assisting, and inspiring the unconventional student. Because it encourages students to choose their own reading paths, hypertext provides the individual, individualistic learner with the perfect means for exploration and enrichment of particular areas. By permitting one to move from relatively familiar areas to less familiar ones, a hypertext corpus encourages the autodidact, the resumed education student, and the student with little access to instructors to get in the habit of making precisely those kinds of connections that constitute such an important part of the liberally educated mind. At the same time the manner in which hypertext places the distant learner in the virtual presence of many instructors both disperses the resources they have created in a particularly effective manner and allows the individual access to some of the major benefits of an institutional affiliation without major cost to either party.

*The canon and the curriculum in hypertext*

The same factors—connectivity, virtual presence, and shifting of the balance between writer and reader—that prompt major, perhaps radical, shifts in teaching, learning, and the organization of both activities inevitably have the potential to affect the related notions of canon and curriculum. The literary canon as we know it is largely a product of book technology and the economic forces that play upon it.[21]

When a work is entered into the literary canon, it gains certain obvious privileges. This passive grammatical construction accurately describes how those in positions of power decide what book or painting will receive the stamp of cultural approval and enter this select inner circle. The gatekeepers of the fortress of high culture include influential critics, museum directors and their boards of trustees, and far more lowly scholars and teachers. Some of the chief representations of the canon appear in the middlebrow anthologies that are hangers-on of high culture. In the Victorian period these included popular collections like F. T. Palgrave's *Golden Treasury;* today the most important arbiters of canonisation are the major college anthologies. To have gained entrance to the Norton or Oxford anthology is to have achieved not necessarily greatness but what is more important, certainly, the possibility of being read. And that is why, of course, it matters that so few women writers have managed to gain inclusion.

Anyone who has studied literature in a secondary school or university in the western world knows that only canonical works are guaranteed readers, from neophyte students to supposedly expert teachers. Further, to read these privileged works is itself a privilege and a sign of privilege. It shows that one has been canonized oneself—beatified by experience of being introduced to beauty, admitted to the ranks of those of the inner circle who are acquainted with the canon and can judge what belongs and does not.

One can look at this power, this territoriality of the canonized work in two ways. Gaining entrance clearly allows a work to be enjoyed; failing to do so thrusts it into the limbo of the unnoticed, unread, unenjoyed, un-existing. Canonization, in other words, permits the member of the canon to enter the gaze and to exist. Not belonging to the canon keeps one out of view. One is in effect excommunicated. For as in the Church's excommunication one is not permitted to partake of the divine refreshing acts of communion with the divinity, one is divorced from participation in the eternal, but one is also kept from communicating with others. One is exiled from community. Likewise, one of the harshest results of not belonging to the canon lies in the fact that noncanonical works do not communicate with one another. A work outside the canon becomes forgotten, unnoticed, and if a canonical author is under discussion, any links between the uncanonical work and the canonical tend not to be noticed.

We say *tend* because under certain conditions, and with certain gazes, noncanonical works can turn up at the end of connections. But within the currently dominant information technology, that of print, such connections and such linkages to the canonical require almost heroic and certainly specialized efforts. The average intelligent educated reader, in other words, is not expected to be able to make such connections with the noncanonical work. For her they do not exist. The connections are made among specialized works and by those readers—professionalized by the profession of scholarship—whose job involves exploring the reader's equivalent of darkest Africa of the nineteenth- and early twentieth-century imagination: the darkest stacks of the library where reside the unimportant, unnoticed books, those one is supposed not to know, not even to have seen. Like the colonial power, the canonical work acts as a center—the center of the perceptual field, the center of values, the center of interest, the center, in short, of a web of meaningful interrelations. The noncanonical works act as colonies or as countries that are unknown and out of sight and mind.

That is why feminists object to the omission or excision of female works from the canon, for by not appearing within the canon, works by women do not . . . appear. One solution to this more or less systematic dis-appearance of women's works is to expand the canon to include more great women's works recently discovered or else to change standards or definitions of the canon, as some feminist critics have done by arguing for the inclusion of diaries, letters, and other forms of nonfiction by women. A second approach lies in creating an alternate tradition, an alternate canon, and a third argues that one should do away with all canons.[22]

Grandiose announcements that one is doing away with The Canon fall into two categories, resembling either the announcements, doomed to failure, that one is no longer going to speak in prose or those of the censor that in totalitarian fashion tells others what they cannot read. Equally important, doing away with the canon leaves one not with freedom but with hundreds of thousands of undiscriminated and hence unnoticeable works, with works we cannot see or notice or read. Better to recognize a canon, or numerous versions of one, and argue against it, revise it, add to it.

In fact, the entire notion of world literature, great touchstones, and studying English academically has a comparatively brief history, and that history has seen almost continuous change and flux. Nonetheless, the canon, particularly that most important part of it represented by what educational institutions offer students in secondary-school and college courses, is slow to respond to present needs. One factor in such resistance derives from sincere interest and conviction, though as we have seen such conviction can change surprisingly quickly in the right circumstances—right for change, not necessarily right according to any other standard. Another factor, which every teacher encounters, derives from book technology, in particular from the need to capitalize a fixed number of copies of a particular work. As historians of print technology have long argued, the cost of book technology necessitates standardization.[23] Although education inevitably benefits in many ways from such standardization, it is harmed by it as well. Most of the great-books courses, which had so much to offer within all their limitations, require some fixed text or set of texts. Revising, making additions, taking into account new works requires substantial expenditure of time and money, and the need to sell as many copies as possible to cover the costs of this expensive information technology means that one must pitch any particular textbook, anthology, or edition toward the largest possible number of potential purchasers.

Although hypertext provides no universal remedy for the ills of American education, it does allow one to individualize any corpus of materials by allowing reader and writer to connect them to other contexts. In fact, the connectivity, virtual presence, and shifting of the balance between writer and reader that permit interdisciplinary team teaching also permit one to preserve the best parts of book technology and its associated culture. Suppose one teaches a survey course in English literature, and wants to include more women writers. A few years ago, if one turned to the Oxford or Norton anthologies one received the impression that someone had gone through these books quite consciously excising the presence of women from them—and therefore from most beginning undergraduates' sense of literature. One could of course complain, and in fact many did complain. After a number of years, say, seven or eight, a few suitable texts began to appear in these anthologies, though Norton also took the route of publishing an anthology of women's literature in English. All this new presence of women is certainly better than the former nonpresence of women, but entering them into the canon and curriculum is taking a long time. What is worse, many of the texts that at last appear in these anthologies may well not be those one would have chosen.

A second problem is less likely to find redress as quickly as has the first: the difficulty of introducing into English literature courses works by authors of non-English ethnic backgrounds who write in English. This problem, which precisely typifies the difficulties of redefining the canon and the curriculum alike, arises because so many of Britain's major authors during the past century have not been English. In England, whose citizens distinguish quite carefully among English, Welsh, Scots, and Irish, many major figures have not been English since the rise of modernism: Conrad was Polish, James American, Dylan Thomas Welsh, and Joyce and Yeats Irish. Generally, anthologies include these figures without placing too much emphasis on their non-Englishness.

Today the situation has become far more complex, and in Great Britain's postcolonial era if one wishes to suggest the nature of writing in English—which is how we define English literature—then one must include both writers of Commonwealth and ex-Commonwealth countries and also those with a wide range of ethnic origins who live and write in English in the United Kingdom. Surveying leading novelists writing in English in Britain, one comes upon important English men and women of course like Graham Swift, Jane Gradham, and Penelope Lively. But among the novelists who have won prestigious prizes of late one must include Salman Rushdie (Pakistan), Kazuo Ishiguro (Japan), and Timothy Mo (Hong Kong); and if one includes novels in English written by authors occasionally resident in Britain, one must include the works of Chinua Achebe, the Nobel Prize winner, Wole Soyinka (Nigeria), and Anita Desai (India). And then there are all the Canadian, Australian, not to mention American novelists who play important roles on the contemporary scene. The contemporary English novel, in other words, is and is not particularly English. The contemporary novel is English in that it is written in English, published in England, and widely read in England and the rest of Britain; it is not English in so far as its authors no longer necessarily have English ethnic origins or even live in England.

The problem faced by the teacher of literature, then, is how in the case of contemporary English literature to accommodate the curriculum to a changing canon. Of course, one can include entire novels in a course on fiction, but that means that the new does not enter the curriculum very far. In fact, relying on print technology, the academic version of the expanded canon of contemporary literature will almost certainly take the same form as have inclusions of Afro-American literature: it will appear in separate courses and be experienced as essentially unconnected to the central, main, defining works.

Hypertext offers one solution to this problem. In his version of the survey course which is a prerequisite for Brown English majors, Landow includes works by Derek Walcott (Jamaica) and Wole Soyinka (Nigeria) and plans in future years to add fiction by Mo or Achebe. How can hypertext aid in conveying to students the ongoing redefinition, or rather self-redefinition, of English literature? Since Soyinka writes poems alluding to *Ulysses* and *Gulliver's Travels,* one can easily create electronic links from materials on Joyce and Swift to Soyinka, thus effortlessly integrating the poems of this Nigerian author into the literary world of these Anglo-Irish writers. And since hypertext linking also encourages students to violate the rigid structure of the standard week-by-week curriculum, it allows them to follow links to Soyinka's work when reading earlier writers. By allowing students to range throughout the semester's curriculum, hypertext permits them to see various kinds of connections—not only historical ones of influence and reactions against a precursor text but equally interesting ones involving analogy. In so doing, this kind of educational technology inserts new work within the total context.

Such contextualization, which is a major strength of hypertext, has an additional advantage for the educator. One of the great difficulties of introducing someone like Soyinka into an English literature course, particularly one that emphasizes contextualization, involves the time and energy required to add the necessary contextual information. In *Context32*, one already has materials on British and continental history, religion, politics, technology, philosophy, and the like. Although Soyinka writes in English, received his undergraduate degree from Leeds, and wrote some of his work in England, he combines English and African contexts, and therefore to create a context for him analogous to that created for Jonathan Swift and Robert Browning, one has to provide materials on colonial and post-colonial African history, politics, economics, geography, and religion. Since Soyinka combines English literary forms with Yoruba myth, one must provide information about that body of thought and encourage students to link it to Western and non-Western religions.

Such an enterprise, which encourages student participation, draws upon all the capacities of hypertext for team teaching, interdisciplinary approaches, and collaborative work, and also inevitably redefines the educational process, particularly the process by which teaching materials develop. Because hypertext corpora are inevitably open-ended, they are inevitably incomplete. They resist closure, which is one way of stating they never die, and they also resist appearing to be authoritative: they can provide information beyond a student's or a teacher's wildest expectations, yes, but they can never make that body of information appear to be the last and final word. Like literature itself, hypertext remains an open, changing, expanding system of relationships, one that allows one to read Soyinka without abandoning Homer.

*The politics of hypertext: who controls the text?*

As the capacity of hypertext systems to be infinitely recenterable suggests, they have a corresponding potential for being anti-hierarchical and democratic. As **Yankelovitch, Meyrowitz** and **van Dam** point out, in such systems "Ideally, authors and readers should have the same set of integrated tools that allow them to browse through other material during the document preparation process and to add annotations and original links as they progress through an information web. In effect, the boundary between author and reader should largely disappear." Moreover, readers rather than authors decide how they will move through the system, for the reader can determine the order and principle of investigation. Interactive hypertext has the potential to be a democratic or multi-centered system in yet another way: as students who use the system contribute their comments and individual documents, the sharp division between author and reader that characterizes page-bound text has begun to blur and threatens to vanish. By contributing to the system, student users become authors and designers as well; and they thus establish a community of learning, demonstrating to themselves that a large part of any investigation rests on the work of others.

Mixed with the generally democratic and even anarchic tendencies of hypertext is an opposing principle: that hypertext readers have more control over the most basic characteristics of this information medium. They are more free to determine the order within which they read individual passages than are readers of books: further, the reader's choices also define the boundaries of the text and even the identity of the author (if one can properly speak of such a unitary figure in this kind of dispersed medium).

Hypertext systems provide different levels of access and control over text. One begins with access to the technology for reading hypertext (now becoming widely available, in the industrialised countries at least). The next issue is the right and power to use such technology once it becomes widespread enough to serve as a major form of publication. Some readers might well have only partial permission to access a hypertext structure, so that portions of it remain forbidden, out of sight, and perhaps entirely unknown. In print technology, we normally have access to the published version of books but not to the full reports by referees, author's contract, manuscript before it has undergone copyediting, and so on. Conventionally, we do not consider such materials to be *part of* the book. Electronic linking has the potential, however, radically to redefine the nature of the text, by connecting the so-called "main text" to a host of ancillary ones (that then lose the status of ancillary-ness). Who, then, will control access to such materials: the author, the publisher, or the reader?

A second level of access to hypertext involves the links themselves that define the essence of this information technology. In the future one can expect that all forms of hypertext will have the capacities of the Intermedia system to create links to texts over which others have editorial control. This ability to make links to blocks for which one does not possess the right to make verbal or other changes has no analogy in the world of print technology. One effect of this kind of linking is that it permits an author to freeze or preserve her text—or that portion or aspect of it that we today term text. It also creates an intermediate realm between the writer and reader, thus further blurring the distinction between these roles. In addition to having the rights to read and link blocks, one can also have the right to create them. If one also has the power to create electronic links between one's text and those already on a hypertext system, then one enters the world of hypertext in a way that has no analogy in the world of book technology.

In the educational uses of hypertext, reshaping the roles of reader and author also reshapes those of student and teacher, for this information medium enforces several kinds of collaborative learning. Granting the student far more control over her reading path obviously empowers her in a range of ways, of which one is to encourage active explorations by the reader and another is to enable the student to contextualize what she reads. However, such empowerment leads directly to questions about the politics of hypertext.

By so emphasizing connectivity, hypertext demands the presence of many blocks of text that can link to one another. At one level, the individual book is the basic unit of print text. But in an important sense, there is no exactly similar basic unit in hypertext. Hypertext, instead, has mini- and macro-units—that is, the individual blocks and the entire system that comprises all texts, or at least all texts making up a particular discipline or subject area. Decisions about relevance obviously bear heavy ideological freight, and hypertext's very emphasis upon connectivity makes the absence or exclusion of texts far more significant than it would be in print technology. Since books already have a physically fixed, separate existence, they exist in an isolation that only individual acts of intellection and memory violate, though to be sure culture consists precisely in sharing such acts among its constituent members. Hypertext, in contrast, records these connections and thus makes them capable of being shared, but one consequence is that excluding any particular bit of text from the metatext makes it drop relatively much farther out of sight. When every connection requires a particular level of effort, particularly when physical effort is required to procure a copy of an individual work, availability and accessibility become essentially equal, as they are for the skilled reader in a modern library. When, however, some connections require no more effort than does continuing to read the same text, unconnected texts are experienced as lying much farther off, and availability and accessibility become very different matters. In such a situation, publication means gaining access to the metatext and being merged with it.

### Current hypermedia applications

It is intriguing to note that the theoretical essays in this collection are closely engaged with the Continental theories of textuality of the past twenty years, whereas the actual hypertext applications described have a strongly historical or cross-cultural bias. The most intense work in applying hypertext to literature has been found in biblical (**De Rose**) and classical studies (**Crane and Mylonas**), and in *Context32*, which centers on the Victorian period.[24] What these fields have in common is a unified, interdisciplinary perspective, and a certain remoteness from the everyday background of undergraduates. Additionally, all the fields had a large pre-existing body of scholarship which had been pressing against the limits of traditional methods of organizing knowledge in usable form. Hypertext and hypermedia offered to scholars in these areas a mode of presentation with obvious practical advantages.[25] There was a relatively limited body of primary texts, but with a corpus of

---

commentary that could be handled efficiently by building a complex structure of internal and external links. These first hypertext projects assumed that the object of study in these three fields involved not just a group of texts but a civilization, a context; this assumption translated into eagerness to exploit hypermedia's capacity to integrate text, graphics, animation, and sound. Finally, the unfamiliarity of these civilizations required making explicit a mass of everyday detail. A modern text has no need for links to an explanatory file or image for an automobile or TV set; a classical one, in contrast, needs materials on a chariot, a scroll or the Lydian mode, and hypermedia is ideally suited to showing them.

Within these historical projects, however, we can already distinguish between two different aims. Hypermedia units on the Bible or the classics are to a large extent electronic reference works; they use modern technology to deliver, in a more unified and efficient way, the kinds of resources available in annotated editions, encyclopedias, and cultural histories. *Context32* has a rather different aim: starting from the premise that any distinctive culture is made up of a complex and "overdetermined" structure of relations, the unit encourages its student users to explore the multiple links between elements—political, religious, literary, etc.—of Victorian society, and thus come to appreciate the interrelatedness of the whole. The implicit underlying model is that the most representative Victorian texts—say, *In Memoriam*—are those that have the greatest number of relevant links to other nodes. These links operate, also, in two directions. Outwards, there is much in *In Memoriam* that needs to be explained by citing major tenets of Victorian culture. Inwards, many central intellectual issues of the time, such as skepticism or the nature of nature, can be effectively instantiated from passages in the poem. If the governing metaphor of *Perseus* or the Dallas Bible Project is the annotated edition, the metaphor of *Context32* is closer to an expanded citation index. Those authors or works that are most frequently cited—in hypermedia terms, have the most links to other nodes—are the ones that are most culturally central. There is, of course, a circularity here: are works important because they are cited, or are they cited because they are important? But in the relativist world of modern thought, we take such mutual determinations more and more for granted. Any large intellectual structure will generate its own centers and priorities through the cumulative choices of its adherents—evolving intelligibly, but without a single founding intentionality, like Saussure's model of language development.[26]

One can distinguish therefore between a hypermedia unit as a *resource* or as an *environment* (corresponding roughly to our earlier division between passive and interactive systems). In the former case, experts in a particular field make an initial investment of time and equipment to make the resource available to colleagues and students. Once the investment has been made, users interact with the system as individuals, extracting information in a more unified and efficient way than was previously possible. The *Joseph Andrews* corpus of materials, for example, might be a convenient accessory to someone wanting to write a term-paper on the novel, or revise it for an exam. (**Delany & Gilbert**) The limitation of these materials, however, could be that the organization of its materials is a fixed one: once the student has extracted what she needs, she might not want to have anything more to do with the unit. In the case of a much larger corpus like *Perseus*, interest might not drop off so sharply; but to a large extent it remains a one-way delivery system for packaged information.

In interactive hypermedia systems, however, readers and writers share the same environments; users can contribute links and new blocks to the metatext, which thus becomes an open-ended structure of knowledge that readers continuously extend and re-organize. During the past several decades teachers of English at Brown, Yale, and other universities have experimented with hypertext as a means of creating a community of students' critical discourse. In the 1970s, Robert Scholes, James Catano, and Nancy Comely had students at Brown University create commentary on poetry using Andries van Dam's FRESS system.[27] At Yale University Stuart Moulthrop developed an experimental hypertext unit, on Thomas Pynchon's *Gravity's Rainbow,* that has as its main purpose the sharing of responses to the novel by a group of readers. Passages are displayed in a window and readers are encouraged to add "Comments" or "Links" (i.e. citation of relevant other passages in the novel). The unit is thus an electronic resource for representing, organizing and preserving the intertextuality of a live seminar.[28] At Brown, students in undergraduate and graduate courses have created various kinds of communal metatexts since 1987. Creating hundreds of individual blocks that range from full length essays to brief paragraphs, graduate students have contributed heavily to a hypermedia presentation of *In Memoriam,* which has been made available as a self-contained web, and undergraduates have produced bodies of material on almost all the major works read in an introductory survey and seminar on Victorian poetry. A recent final assignment for the survey course, for example, produced a body of materials on Wole Soyinka and Nigeria, including discussions of individual poems from *A Shuttle in the Crypt,* Nigeria under colonialism, the Biafran War, and Yoruba myth, religion, kingship, and art.[29]

The hypermedia *environment* may also present fundamental difficulties at the level of structure that derive from the nature of computer-supported collaborative work. The structure of a hypermedia *resource* is likely to be fairly simple, often based on a "hub and spoke" or "tree diagram" design. (**Delany & Gilbert**) A sentence in Joyce's *Ulysses,* for example, might be linked to three or four notes on different points of explication, to a parallel passage elsewhere in the novel, to a visual image, and to a few bars of a song.[30] The implicit structure here is a series of spokes radiating out from each word or passage in the novel that requires explication. If each passage thus becomes a node in a hypermedia structure, then the overall form would be a linear series of nodes, proceeding sequentially through the novel, with each node having its own one-directional links to a cluster of supplementary files. Such hypermedia materials have little more complexity, structurally at least, than Weldon Thornton's *Allusions in "Ulysses"* (1968), which provides explanatory notes for each page of the novel. A hypermedia *environment,* on the other hand, would in principle allow for anything defined as a node to be linked bi-directionally to any other node—which, of course, corresponds much more closely to the actual mental activities involved in reading and teaching *Ulysses,* where consideration of a particular phrase typically sets off a chain of connections through a space made up of both the text of the novel and a large body of commentary.

This work of reading involves, first, a linear progression through the "main" text; but two other kinds of mental process are also involved, which we may call *association* and *instantiation.* Association is a centrifugal movement, whereby an individual block radiates out into the textual field. For example, the phrase "new womanly man," used to describe Bloom, will call up all kinds of parallels, from the myth of Tiresias to the priest in *Portrait* who speaks to Stephen of the "jupes" (skirts) worn by certain orders. A hypermedia environment would not just list these parallels; it would also allow for links between them—and, more importantly, for structuring those links into a pattern that goes beyond simple annotation into the realm of interpretation. Instantiation reverses this movement of the mind: we begin with the general, such as Joyce's theory of the bisexuality of the artist, then develop a structure of evidentiary support for the theory in the text.

Hypertext designers face the challenge of representing, in the form of nodes and links, the actual complexity of building interpretations through reading, association and instantiation. In the mind of the critic, a link is not just a line between two blocks; it is a particular *kind* of connection, related to a whole family of kindred modes of explanation (such as, for example, Catholicism, Irish nationalism or Freudianism). Although computer-based visualization is now an important means of interpreting complex data in the sciences, its value in literary criticism has yet to be established.[31] The ability of hypertext to re-organize the traditional form of the book is surely useful on the level of information-handling, but more questionable when used to present interpretations in spatial or diagrammatic form. Progress in this area would require critics to become more self-conscious about spatial metaphors they currently use—for, say, the structure of narrative, or for levels of the mind in Freudian criticism—and also to take advantage of new opportunities to build models of interpretation on the computer screen. At the same time, any attempt to formalize mental activity will have its own pitfalls. A "designed" structure for intellectual work may provide only a somewhat shallow and barren environment, like a modern suburb or shopping mall; whereas the print media has developed organically with features added according to need in different eras, like an old-established city.

Another area needing work in hypermedia environments is the control of multiple contributions. Simple annotation can be handled quite straightforwardly, as we have seen, but anything that affects structure is more problematic. **De Rose** points out that even a basic hypertext Bible could easily have a million links. What kind of coherence can a complex hypermedia environment preserve if all users have the power to create new links and delete existing ones? Yet it is a fundamental premise of environments like *Context32* that making links is the primary means of mapping interpretations onto what would otherwise be just a miscellaneous heap of literary information.[32] At the very least, workable hypermedia requires some central editorial control over the manipulation of nodes and links, and to have some provision for re-setting the environment to the structure first presented by its designer. Beyond this, we need to recognize a kind of systole and diastole in collaborative work. In one phase, people try to fuse their joint efforts into a single, fixed and authoritative form: classic examples would be the production of the King James Bible and the drafting of the U.S. Constitution. Yet the achievement of such a marmoreal text immediately provokes, reactively, a centrifugal movement of interpretation, as new pluralisms irresistibly assert themselves, and new texts swarm around the fixed center.

Large bodies of hypertext materials demand something akin to a "cat's cradle" facility, that would present information in different configurations—corresponding to different modes of interpretation—while preserving the integrity of the whole. This particular problem has several dimensions (or solutions). First, every hypertext corpus, even those composed of a fairly small number of blocks, possesses the capacity of multiple organization. Any such corpus allows readers to choose different reading paths, but it also allows different author-readers to create alternate assemblages of links, or webs as they are termed in Intermedia.[33] Such capacities have already been exploited in Intermedia: different webs, including those for Cell Biology (*Biology*), the literature survey (*Context32*), *In Memoriam*, Renaissance cultural history (*Weissman*), and Nuclear Arms and Arms Control (*Nuclear*), share documents. Opening any web provides an almost entirely different context for the shared documents. For example, Peter Heywood, Professor of Biology, has created various documents on Darwin and natural selection that in his web relate to materials on the cell, whereas in the *Context32* and *In Memoriam* webs they relate to Tennyson and Victorian cultural history and science.[34]

A second resource for multiple configurations of the same documents involves the use of several, potentially rival, overview documents. Readers following a text-centered approach can choose to work from the *Great Expectations* Overview (OV), whereas those interested in author-centered ones choose the Dickens OV. Furthermore, those interested in Victorianism, Feminism, Darwinism can also draw on many of the same documents from these Overviews. As hypertext corpora increase dramatically in size and scale, part of that increase will inevitably involve multiple means of organizing documents.

One can also imagine yet another form of multiple configuration, one that involves not the organization of metatexts but they way they appear to each reader. In future environments, readers will be able to configure the way information comes to them. Contemporary combinations of hardware and software already permit one to manipulate existing hypertext systems in various ways, including typing commands from the keyboard, using a mouse to choose items from pulldown menus, and using a mouse or similar device, such as a roller ball or touch screen, to perform the same operation by a sequence of actions. One can, for example, open a document in Intermedia by double-clicking a mouse or ball device, by pulling down a menu and choosing "open" from the command list, or by simultaneously pressing the control key and "f" (for "follow link"). In the future one should be able to choose color, font size, icons, or even if the computer speaks to one rather than provides material for reading. Similarly, one can already use hypertext on small screens that force layering of documents or large ones that permit an entirely different graphic organization of materials, and we expect that those who read or use hypermedia will in future have a choice of working with screens, projected images, or total environments.[35] At present, computer screens offer far less pleasant reading experiences than does the high-quality printed page, but screens will change, and someday scholars examining texts originally derived from manuscripts may well choose among views of the original manuscript hand, a screen version of high resolution printed text, and an enlarged projected image.

The ease of contributing to the educational metatext in an environment like Intermedia can produce so much material that one requires some means of preventing readers from becoming swamped by information. Several possible solutions exist. First, a body of materials can have a gatekeeper, someone analogous to an editor, who permits certain contributions to enter the corpus permanently, or who decides how long they remain available—during the course of an exercise, throughout an entire course, during later iterations of the same course, or in a version of the materials exported to other courses or other institutions.

Second, the hypermedia system can employ hierarchies of permissions that permit users to read, link to, or modify texts. In most instances, we expect that authors will fix their blocks by limiting to themselves so-called write permission but that they will permit others to annotate their words or images by creating links. Such a system of hierarchical permissions can also control the growth of a body of materials. Other means of preventing abundant information from swamping the reader include filtering and full text searches. Student users faced with several hundred blocks comparing novels of Dickens and Austen could filter by author or author-group and thereby keep out of sight all materials except those created by a particular faculty member, course, or class (this would require "tagging" the block, when created, with appropriate classifications). Full text searching, which can be used as a means of filtering if one includes authors in the search field, can produce any document that seems relevant. One can, for example, request "Austen," "Dickens," and "theme," if one wishes to find documents comparing the themes of both novelists, and one can limit the search even more by indicating titles of individual novels. With *metatexts*, which will form when systems join together, eventually on a national and international basis, other resources, including those of Artificial Intelligence (AI) will become necessary. Some therefore have proposed that hypermedia systems will eventually serve as guides to the reader, and researchers have already created systems that observe an individual reader's choices and use them to create a profile that places favored materials first.

## Hypertext as a resource for literary criticism and theory

By a hypermedia resource for literary criticism and theory we mean an assembly of hypertext features that would assist the conceptual and procedural activities of experienced literary scholars and theorists. Hypertext obviously has broad implications for literary practice and education, but how will it change our work in literary criticism, theory, and scholarship? When a literary worker can read and write in an information medium that allows her to create electronic links between passages of text, the experience of that text and what she does with it change radically.

At the moment, scholars typically begin by encountering a primary text that they analyze for intrinsic structure, then combine with other texts—which may be themselves primary or secondary (i.e. scholarly literature commenting on primary texts). They also consult works in other media—sound, graphic, video—and they may also communicate, formally or informally, with others in their field. Finally, work on the primary text leads to the production of another text, either delivered in the classroom or distributed as a formal addition to secondary literature in the field. In practice, scholars experience a complex interweaving of these various functions as they pursue a number of teaching and research projects at the same time.

The texts with which the scholar, critic, and teacher work exist, as we have seen, physically isolated from each other, and literary workers rely on a range of mechanisms that propose, indicate, or demonstrate relations. Such mechanisms include alluding to other texts, explicitly naming them, and quoting selections from them, either in the main text or in notes, or listing them in bibliographies. The scholar who creates a text indicates these contextual relations, which the reader takes as cues for certain kinds of behavior. Foot- and endnotes, like other forms of scholarly reference, frequently direct the reader to leave the so-called main text and work with another physically discrete text; such consultation may require substantial effort and cause considerable delay.

How would hypermedia change the way we work? First of all, our experience of texts, as we have seen, would change radically. Instead of encountering physically discrete texts reproduced on a largely opaque surface, we would read the virtual image of a text on a surface (the screen) behind which there always exists an unbounded field of other texts. The textual universe would, moreover, include a far larger visual component, as graphics, images, and animation become as easy to link as is another text.[36] Hypermedia scholarship and criticism will permit creating webs of primary texts out of unusual materials or of those difficult to obtain. Most important perhaps from the vantage point of one comparing present-day scholarly and critical work to those carried out in hypermedia, we will always be conscious of texts as existing within a network of other texts. Scholarly readers will experience texts as Barthean networks in part because future hypermedia systems, like Intermedia today, will provide dynamic graphic maps or web views that reveal all documents linked to that being read. Larger screens or projection of the image will also present several documents open at the same time.

In a fully developed hypermedia environment, such intrinsic connectivity will change the way scholars and critics produce texts. Most obviously, quoting and citing will change. If we can link directly to the full text of *Ulysses*, Ellman's biography of Joyce, or other secondary works, the text we produce exists in some sense closer to those source texts than a printed one ever can, since the reader can easily obtain either the passage to which we link or the entire text surrounding it. This new kind of scholarly writing both gains and loses power by its instantiation in hypermedia. It gains power because it can easily gain entrance to an enormous number of other texts and therefore has the potential of generating greater support or conviction for its arguments. It loses power because this text can no longer as easily restrict access to other texts. Literary critics have traditionally built up their arguments by removing a block from one context and incorporating it into their own, now dominant, textual structure. But hypertext prevents one from moving a block so far from its immediate textual context. Furthermore, hypertext removes much of the printed book's splendid isolation. Considered as a publication medium, hypertext makes publication more equivalent to joining a network. A published book quickly shucks its reviews, gaining a scholarly and critical life of its own as the hostile or qualifying reviews gradually fall out of sight. The hypertext equivalent to the book will travel on trailing, not clouds of glory but its entire critical heritage. Readers will of course have the power of hiding such materials until needed, but they will always be there, waiting for the occasion when some reader needs them.

Electronic linking will change scholarly production in yet other ways as well. Adding links to our basic conception of text introduces a new conception of literary work: one can produce a text in which the entity created consists largely or entirely of links. In a sense such contributions to scholarship and criticism are hardly new, for we can all think of scholarly and critical works, some of which achieve considerable reputation, that do little more than gather points previously made by others. Only half in jest, the great critic Walter Benjamin proposed to write a book consisting entirely of quotations!

A comprehensive hypermedia environment for literary study would be based on scholars' workstations with appropriate communications and peripherals. The textual foundation (or "textbase") of this environment would be a large corpus of literary texts in machine-readable form.[37] Access to the corpus would be controlled by a customized hypermedia program that would both operate on the corpus directly, and control a variety of other resources.[38] These resources could include text analysis programs,[39] hypermedia units such as *Context32* and *Perseus*, HUMANIST (an international e-mail forum with over 400 participating scholars), the institution's on-line library catalogue, and the Modern Language Association bibliography on CD. A literature department, working collaboratively, could steadily enrich the information base of the environment, and develop complex links between its elements. For example, it should become possible to take a concept like "the marriage market" and elicit relevant textual units and links between several Victorian novels; to multiply commentaries on complex texts like *Moby Dick, Finnegans Wake* or *Gravity's Rainbow;* and in general to accumulate information at a central server and deliver it to the individual workstation in a customised form, instead of making researchers seek it on foot at the library.

To begin with, such a hypermedia resource for literary analysis would simply assist scholars to use a large and complex information base. Later, however, its designers would profit from iterative or dialogic processes, which trace the user's path through the corpus and develop better models of high-level mental activities. Like the "knowledge engineering" already in common use elsewhere, designers could thus elicit from literary scholars how they define and link conceptual units when they generate new interpretations from an extensive and "fuzzy" knowledge base. It should also be possible to develop individual profiles that would note a user's special interests, load them into a query engine, and extract from the literary textbase evidence likely to be relevant to the user's projects.[40]

## Developing hypertext: who pays?

Finally, some thoughts on the practical constraints on developing literary hypermedia applications. For traditional literary scholarship and critical theory, individual scholars usually initiate projects and publish the results as a journal article or book. Such work is typically subsidized: scholars receive released time to do research, and organs of distribution also benefit largely from institutional subsidies. Hypermedia projects, unfortunately, do not fit comfortably into this established pattern. Faculty developers cannot work without fairly advanced computer equipment and often need research assistants to do programming and data entry. Users need access to similar equipment to run hypermedia applications. Although the equipment is becoming more generally available, a literary scholar interested in hypermedia must operate more like a scientist, with substantial research funding for equipment and salaries. To develop a hypermedia unit for a course is far more demanding and time-consuming than just preparing lecture-notes; on the other hand, such a unit can then be used at many other institutions. Unfortunately, software development is often not recognized as equivalent to conventional publication, with its known rewards of tenure and promotion. Indeed, "publication" is a problem for literary software, because there is no well-established system either of peer review or of retail distribution.

As a result of these barriers, the most significant literary hypermedia projects have been funded on an experimental basis by foundations and corporate sponsors, such as the Annenberg/CPB Project, Apple Computers, and IBM for Intermedia and *Context32* and the Annenberg/CPB Project for *Perseus*. Much of this support has gone into developing basic hypermedia programs: Intermedia required about 45 person/years of programming to bring to its current stage of development.[41] In order to find wider application, hypermedia needs to move into the mainstream of scholarly work in the humanities—which will require regular funding on a similar basis to programs already defined as core activities of universities and colleges. This climb to a plateau of centrality and legitimacy should be achieved over the next five years, provided that improvements are made in a number of strategic areas. These improvements include:

1. Standardized hypertext and hypermedia formats to allow easy exchange of materials; such standardization includes multiple active windows and

sophisticated text-handling, widely available on powerful networked workstations.

2. Recognition of hypermedia development as a scholarly activity equivalent to conventional publication.

3. Recognition by universities that in order to work effectively humanities scholars now need regular and substantial funding for computer equipment and research assistance.

4. Effective distribution of hypermedia materials, through some combination of traditional publishing, commercial software outlets and university consortiums.

5. Changes to copyright laws to enable major literary textbases to be made accessible and modifiable in electronic form.

## The future

*Technology and the intellectual environment*

The development of literary hypertext will take place in an emerging global information environment of the archive, the computer, and telecommunications. Unlike the hub-and-spoke pattern of time-sharing mainframes with terminals, the new environment will be one in which information access and processing will be not just distributed, but also de-centered: any individual workstation will be able to achieve virtual presence at any other node on the global network. Storage and processing power at the workstation level will increase by several orders of magnitude during the next decade; fibre optic links will provide near-instant access to massive textbases; literary workgroups will be largely able to disregard geographical constraints.[42]

The computer network itself can be seen as a powerful metaphor, corresponding to a kind of animate hypermedia structure. The elements of the network include electronic mail, file transfer, computer conferencing, remote access to textbases and manipulation of them. These facilities enable each individual scholar to be linked to a constantly shifting structure of information sources, and of relevant other users. As we all know, the most effective way to conduct a search for information is often to find out who has already done it and ask them directly. Electronic conferences like HUMANIST already handle many queries. These are seen by hundreds of scholars;

several are likely to reply, and the inquirer can then consolidate their answers. For many purposes, this kind of personal mediation between a user and the electronic archive will continue, just as today we often consult a librarian rather than making our own search of the stacks. Moulthrop has suggested that a new profession may emerge, of expert navigators through the electronic information environment who will offer their services to end-users.[43] However, we can already see that individual scholars on the network play many different roles, according to their varying fields of expertise or ignorance, and according to whether they are acquiring or transmitting information. Though much remains to be done, technological development is working rapidly, and on many fronts, to make the entire cultural archive of text and images accessible, and to allow users of the archive to associate freely and effectively to communicate their results. Instead of having to rely on a few dictionaries of quotations that index memorable phrases, scholars will be able to search the textbase for any sequence of words relevant to their current projects. As in Claude Lévi-Strauss's metaphor of *bricolage,* units of knowledge will be extracted from one hypertext structure, with the aid of the computer, and re-assembled into another.

*The New Alexandria and Xanadu*

The French textual archive, *Frantext,* already has in machine-readable form about 200 million words of text, eighty percent of them literary. The Association for Computational Linguistics is assembling a textbase of 50-100 million words, and the National Endowmen for the Humanities has awarded a planning grant for a "Center for Machine-readable Texts in the Humanities," to be based at Princeton and Rutgers. In Britain there are plans for a "British National Corpus," associated with the Oxford English Dictionary. By the middle of the nineties, then, it is reasonable to assume that most of the major English literary texts will be on-line; the main obstacle to building such an archive will be the copyright laws, which need radical adaptation to the era of electronic storage and reproduction.[44] For more than two thousand years, literary scholars have engaged in the three-fold work of gathering selected texts from the archive, re-ordering and supplementing them, then re-inserting these new textual entities into the archive through some form of publication. All of these three stages have now been revolutionized by the computer: the first by the development of machine-readable text archives, the second by the word-processor, the third by desk-top publishing, network file transfer, and electronic mail. Still in its early stages, however, is the application of hypertext to integrate these scholarly activities, by providing a controlling metaphor for text-handling. A useful prototype exists in the *Arts and Humanities Citation Index,* now available on-line. The AHCI provides a schematic map of scholarly intertextuality; but it is only a schema, because, like an on-line library catalogue, the AHCI gives access to locations but not the underlying full-texts. Furthermore, AHCI has no thematic or subject ordering, so that its main use is in tracing links between authors (though, within the author category, there is a break-down to the level of individual texts).

A true "New Alexandria" or "Xanadu" or "Seamless Information Environment" for literary scholars would have some of the following features.[45] It would include a substantial proportion of all current scholarly and creative writing, in machine-readable form and accessible to a large body of users and contributors. Users could search the archive with "trawler" programs adapted to their personal interests; they would also be able to load up their own texts. An accounting mechanism would charge users for access, and credit them for access to their own texts by others. The archive would probably evolve into "formal" and "informal" sectors: the former would only accept new texts by peer review, the latter would have universal access. "Publication" would be on demand, whenever users chose to download a text to a printer.[46] The effect on existing channels of publication is hard to estimate, though it seems likely that a large share of scholarly and scientific writing might be disseminated solely through the New Alexandria.

The role of hypertext in the New Alexandria would be to provide a flexible and efficient means of defining nodes and links—that is, to impose structures on what would otherwise be a shapeless mass of "words, words, words." It goes without saying that the implementation of such a hypertext facility would be a highly difficult intellectual task. Nonetheless, the first stage could be based on established methods of textual mapping, ones that work with such relatively objective markers as books, articles, authors, subject descriptors and page numbers. Conceptually, the problem here would be simply one of re-classification: to take the navigational markers that help users find their way around a traditional library, and adapt them to a textbase stored electronically rather than as marks on paper. In the second stage, the aim would be to support nodes and links as defined by the individual user, so that the scholar could do electronically what she now does manually in, for example, assembling the relevant texts to be cited in a scholarly article.

It is already clear that there are no major technical or financial obstacles to the establishment of very large electronic bases of text, sound, graphics and video in the near future (although materials with some commercial value and published since about 1910 are likely to be sequestered by copyright, unless the law is changed). To make this mass usable, however, will require many different kinds of programs— so different that the umbrella term of "hypermedia" for such programs may become dangerously vague. To speak only of texts: some programs will be straightforward adaptations of traditional library classification systems, with similar advantages (uniformity and objectivity) and disadvantages (lack of responsiveness to individual interests). Others will be used to build specialized textual subsets, analogous to, say, an annotated anthology in book form—but with additional features made possible by computerized text-handling. More advanced programs will try to provide some of the flexibility and intuitiveness used by an expert critic when combing through texts and developing a thesis. This is an iterative or dialogical process, in which the germ of an idea is reinforced with evidence, but thereby also modified and the relevant evidentiary field redefined; and so on, through various articulations and drafts.

We can expect a "toolbox" of hypertext programs to be developed to support this kind of critical work. Some tools will be "trawlers" that go into the textbase in search of relevant blocks. In the first generation these will be conventional search engines, working algorithmically to precisely defined specifications. Later, artificial intelligence faculties will be added: these will make the search process reciprocal, by identifying a user's established interests and constantly searching the textbase for matching blocks. In turn, the user will be able to "train" her trawler by giving feedback on whether hits are relevant or not.[47] Other tools will combine blocks by rules of association to produce, not interpretation itself, but the kind of clustering of evidence around a thesis that forms the elements from which interpretations are made. Others will make it possible to present alternative structurings of literary works, perhaps with a visualization facility to bring out patterns in complex sets of thematic or syntactic data.[48] In all this work, the first challenge will be to formalize, in whatever degree is feasible, the kinds of mental operations that a literary critic performs when analyzing a text.[49] Once these operations have been modelled in a hypertext program, however crudely, it should be possible to sharpen the tool by the kind of iterative movement—from textbase to structure and back—already described. We emphasize the term "tool" because a large body of modern literary theory warns us against the presumption that interpretations might be generated mechanically from a textbase by any computer program whatsoever.[50] The work presented in this anthology suggests a less ambitious, yet still revolutionary agenda for literary scholars: that we have new and powerful methods for organizing texts, on all levels from a single lyric to a massive textbase; and that scholars have much to gain from exploiting these methods over the whole field of literary studies.

## Notes

1. Throughout this collection, essays included in it are referred to by the author's name in **bold**.

2. The term *Hypertext* was coined by Theodor H. Nelson in the 1960s.

3. Roland Barthes, *S/Z*, trans. Richard Miller (New York: Hill & Wang, 1974). We have generally used the term "blocks" here, though its connotations are unfortunate, given the actual fluidity and readiness to bond of electronic texts. See also the discussion of "nodes" in **Slatin**.

4. Vannevar Bush, "As We May Think," *Atlantic Monthly* 176 (July 1945): 101-08. James M. Nyce and Paul Kahn have shown that Bush had written a longer version of this essay by 1937: "Innovation, Pragmatism, and Technological Continuity: Vannevar Bush's Memex," *Journal of the American Association for Information Science*, 40 (1989): 214-220.

5. In oral cultures, of course, the text had quite a different status in the mind, one that was closer in some respects to the hypertextual model. See Walter J. Ong, *Orality and Literacy: The Technologizing of the Word* (London: Methuen, 1982).

6. Lyrical poems are a special case: they are independent works, but have a close intertextual relationship with others in the same tradition, or by the same author.

7. We may here distinguish between hypertext and a related concept, Standard Generalized Mark-up Language (SGML). SGML concerns the marking out of units in an electronic text and then attaching to them a "tag" or descriptive category (such as "noun phrase" or "animal image"). A program can then sort the tags to support grammatical or stylistic analysis. SGML thus sorts textual units by categories; hypertext links the units into larger structures.

8. **Yankelovich, Meyrowitz**, and **van Dam**, in this volume p. 59.

9. Gibson, *Neuromancer* (New York: Ace Books, 1984); see also his *Burning Chrome* (1986) and *Mona Lisa Overdrive* (1988). In his survey of hypertext, Jeff Conklin recommends *Neuromancer*, perhaps the most famous exemplar of cyperpunk science-fiction, as the best illustration of what living in a hypertext environment will be like: "Hypertext: an Introduction and Survey," *IEEE Computer* 20:9 (1987):17-41.

10. G. Pascal Zachary, "Artificial Reality: Computer Simulations One Day May Provide Surreal Experiences," *Wall Street Journal* (23 January 1990): A1, A9.

11. For some speculations on these textual megastructures or "docuverses," see the discussion of the "New Alexandria" below, and **Yankelovich** "From Electronic Books to Electronic Libraries" in this volume.

12. A notable proto-hypertextual work is Humphrey Jennings' *Pandemonium: the Coming of the Machine as Seen by Contemporary Observers, 1660-1886* (New York: The Free Press, 1985). This is a chronological series of short passages and images on the Industrial Revolution; Jennings' posthumous editor, Charles Madge, listed sixteen "Theme Sequences," each of them an alternate ordering of groups of passages. Jennings' remarkable work could very easily and usefully be adapted for hypertext presentation.

13. Examples of educational hypertext include Ben Schneiderman's Hyperties Holocaust materials, the many sets of HyperCard materials, including the Harvard Perseus Project (**Crane and Mylonas**), and the Intermedia materials developed at Brown. Among the applications of hypertext to poetry and fiction one can number Michael Joyce's "Afternoon," Stuart **Moulthrop**'s adaptation of Borges's "Forking Paths" to both HyperCard and StorySpace, and William **Dickey**'s mixed media poetry in HyperCard.

14. For the general issues involving Milton's use of biblical types, see Barbara Kiefer Lewalski, "Typological Symbolism and the 'Progress of the Soul' in Seventeenth-Century Literature," *Literary Uses of Typology from the Late Middle Ages to the Present*, ed. Earl Miner (Princeton: Princeton University Press, 1977), 79-114; and William Madsen, *From Shadowy Types to Truth: Studies in Milton's Symbolism* (New Haven: Yale University Press, 1968).

15. Kenneth Morrell, "Teaching with *HyperCard*. An Evaluation of the Computer-based Section in Literature and Arts C-14: The Concept of the Hero in Hellenic Civilization." Perseus Project Working Paper 3. Cambridge, MA: Department of Classics, Harvard University, 1988.

16. Marshall McLuhan, *The Gutenberg Galaxy: The Making of Typographic Man* (Toronto: University of Toronto Press, 1962); Elizabeth L. Eisenstein, *The Printing Press as an Agent of Change: Communications and Cultural Transformations in Early-Modern Europe*, 2 vols. (Cambridge: Cambridge University Press, 1979); and J. David Bolter, *Writing Space: The Computer, Hypertext and the History of Writing* (Hillsdale, N.J.: Lawrence Erlbaum, 1990). We would like to thank Professor Bolter for sharing a

draft of his work with us before publication.

17. McLuhan, *Gutenberg Galaxy*, 229-233.

18. Thaïs E. Morgan, "Is There an Intertext in This Text?: Literary and Interdisciplinary Approaches to Intertextuality," *American Journal of Semiotics* 3 (1985): 1-2.

19. Jacques Derrida, "Structure, Sign and Play in the Discourse of the Human Sciences," in J. Macksey & E. Donato, eds., *The Structuralist Controversy: The Languages of Criticism and the Sciences of Man* (Baltimore: Johns Hopkins University Press, 1972), 251.

20. Derrida, "Structure, Sign and Play," 271; see also Louis Althusser, *For Marx*, trans. Ben Brewster (London: Verso, 1979), 131-151.

21. Alan Howard, "Hypermedia and the Future of Ethnography," *Cultural Anthropology* 3 (1988), 304-305, observes how these factors also shape—and constrain—the nature of research in a non-literary field.

22. Toril Moi, *Sexual/Textual Politics: Feminist Literary Theory* (London and New York: Methuen, 1985). Against critics like Elaine Showalter who aim to create a "separate canon of women's writing, not to abolish all canons," Moi points out that "a new canon would not be intrinsically less oppressive than the old" (78).

23. See McCluhan, *Gutenberg Galaxy*, and Eisenstein, *The Printing Press*.

24. Though it is not described here, the Dartmouth *Dante* project has similar parameters.

25. **Graham's** project is historical, but is in addition a natural application for hypermedia because its subject, the seventeenth-century emblem book, was originally composed in a mixed-media (text and graphic) mode.

26. A recent study of the *Arts and Humanities Citation Index* for 1976-83 found the five most frequently cited works to be, in order: R. Kuhn, *The Structure of Scientific Revolutions*; J. Joyce, *Ulysses*; N. Frye, *Anatomy of Criticism*; L. Wittgenstein, *Philosophical Investigations*; N. Chomsky, *Aspects of the Theory of Syntax*. E. C. Garfield, "A Different Sort of Great-Books List: the 50 20th Century Works Most Cited in the *AHCI*, 1976-83," *Current Contents* 16 (20 April 1987): 3-7.

27. See James Catano, "Poetry and Computers: Experimenting with Communal

---

Text," *Computers and the Humanities* 13 (1979): 269-275.

28. A weakness of the *Gravity's Rainbow* unit, in its present form, is that it does not include a complete electronic text of the novel, or any program for searching it.

29. The two most ambitious student contributions to *Context32* have been Barry J. Fishman's one-hunded page honors thesis on Graham Swift and Thomas G. Bowie's hypermedia unit on World War I, the technology of war, and contemporary Anglo-American literature, which he created as part of his pre-doctoral examinations.

30. Delany & Gilbert are considering design issues for a hypermedia unit on *Ulysses*, tentatively called "Penelope's Web."

31. Some of the stylistic analysis of Jane Austen in J. F. Burrows, *Computation into Criticism: A Study of Jane Austen's Novels and an Experiment in Method* (Oxford: Clarendon Press, 1987) is presented in graphic form. See also the diagrams of Freudian response theory in Norman Holland, *The Dynamics of Literary Response* (New York: Oxford University Press, 1968).

32. Landow has pointed out that if one simply printed out all the files in *Context32* the resulting dossier would not make much sense; it is the hypertext structure of nodes and links that gives it coherence.

33. One relatively efficient means of creating sets of such links for the same materials involves full text searching and corollary automatic linking, both developed for Intermedia 4.0 by James H. Coombs.

34. IRIS developers are currently developing means of opening and closing several webs simultaneously.

35. For fictional speculations about such a writing environment, see George P. Landow, "Ms. Austen's Submission," *IF*, 1 (1989), a short story examining the political realities of the author's existence in a world when all publishing involves gaining entrance to electronic networks. *IF*, an electronic periodical edited by Gordon Howell, is available from Edinburgh on BITNET, the international computer network linking universities and research facilities.

36. The most advanced current example of combining media is described in **Friedlander.**

37. A reasonable starting size for such a corpus, using current resources, might be

500MB—equivalent to about 600 novels.

38. Current work on this concept, by P. Delany & J. Gilbert, uses HyperCard in a networked Macintosh laboratory.

39. For a survey of available programs see S. Stigleman, "Text Management Software," *Public Access Computer Systems Review* 1:1 (1990).

40. In Chapter 5 of Dorothy L. Sayers' *Whose Body?* Bunter performs a similar service for Lord Peter Wimsey, scanning the morning newspapers and marking passages relevant to Wimsey's current case.

41. Since April 1989 Apple Computing has distributed *Intermedia* as a commercial research product.

42. Senator Albert Gore, Jr. has introduced legislation to establish a national fibre optic research network in the U.S. A precursor of this network, NSFNET, expects to transmit at 45 megabits in 1990, the equivalent of 3,000 double-spaced pages per second. See Albert Gore, "Remarks on the NREN," *EDUCOM Review* 25 (Summer 1990): 12-16.

43. S. Moulthrop, "The Politics of Hypertext," (unpublished).

44. What is required is some kind of monitoring or sampling system that will automatically give credit to originators for the use of their texts. A crude but functional example of such a system is Canada's "Public Lending Right" program: this searches the holdings of ten major libraries with computerized catalogues, and makes an annual payment (currently $40) for each "hit" of a book by a registered author (who must be a Canadian resident). The maximum annual payment is $4,000 a year. Funds to support the scheme are provided by the federal government, about $5 million in 1989-90. Norway collects about $7 million (U.S.) a year in fees for xerox copying; the money is then distributed to authors through writers' unions. Each non-fiction writer currently receives about $2,000 a year from this scheme.

45. The first term has been used by Andries van Dam, "Address," *Hypertext '87* the last by Nicole Yankelovich, Norman Meyrowitz, and Stephen Drucker, "Intermedia: The Concept and the Construction of a Seamless Information Environment," *IEEE Computer* 21 (1988): 81-96. See also Ted Nelson, *Literary Machines* (Self-published: P.O. Box 128, Swarthmore, PA. 1981), for the proposed implementation now called the Xanadu project; and **Yankelovich** "From Electronic Books to Electronic Libraries" in this volume.

46. It would be reasonable to make a separate charge for such "publication," but it would probably not be technically possible to monitor the movement of texts from memory files to printers. The French telephone information utility, *Minitel*, credits information providers each time their files are called up on a user's screen.

47. Not unlike the "runner" in the antique trade, who earns commissions by making the rounds; at each dealer he looks for pieces likely to appeal to the specialized interests of all the other dealers with whom he is familiar.

48. See Bolter, *Writing Space,* for the use of the "StorySpace" program to bring out the spatial form of texts.

49. See, for example, Landow's discussion of how a sophisticated critic constructs a much more complex structure of links and determinations than a novice: "Hypertext in Literary Education, Criticism and Scholarship," *Computers and the Humanities* 3 (1989): 173-198.

50. See, for example, Stanley Fish, "What is Stylistics and Why Are They Saying Such Terrible Things about it?" in S. Chatman, ed., *Approaches to Poetics* (New York: Columbia University Press, 1973); and Hubert L. Dreyfus, *What Computers Can't Do: A Critique of Artificial Intelligence* (New York: Harper & Row, 1972).

# Part II

Theory

# Reading and Writing the Electronic Book

Nicole Yankelovich and Norman Meyrowitz
Institute for Research in Information and Scholarship, Brown University

Andries van Dam
Department of Computer Science, Brown University

*Editor's Note: This article was written in 1985. It is printed here without change, as an account of how hypertext evolved before it came into wide use in the late 1980's. For current perspective on these issues see Yankelovich's "From Electronic Books to Electronic Libraries: Revisiting 'Reading and Writing the Electronic Book.'"*

Juxtaposing "electronic books" and hard-copy books creates a useful framework for critically examining the computer's role in document preparation and presentation. Although electronic document systems are not directly comparable to paper books, the two nevertheless serve a number of common purposes. Both are used as sources of information, as learning devices, and as mechanisms for communication between people who are distant in time or place.

By considering the strengths and weaknesses of paper and electronic documents, it is possible to formulate a set of capabilities that electronic document systems should possess to maximize the advantages of the electronic medium and overcome some of the disadvantages inherent in the print medium. After outlining these general capabilities, the article describes four document systems developed or under development at Brown University that illustrate many of the different necessary functions.

### Print medium

Scholars, or "knowledge workers," rely heavily on print media, even though electronic creation and dissemination of information is possible with today's technology. In some cases, this reliance on print is part of a long, ingrained tradition, but in other cases, print is still simply the most appropriate vehicle, either because electronic document systems are impractical to use or because they do not meet a particular objective as well as does paper.

The most important fundamental property of books is that they are static. Once printed, a book cannot be altered except by reprinting, and at no time do readers have the opportunity to change or manipulate its contents. The static nature of books is both their biggest asset and their most serious shortcoming.

A review of the assets and shortcomings of books is helpful in establishing a list of capabilities essential for high-quality electronic document systems (Table 1).

| CHARACTERISTIC | ADVANTAGES | DISADVANTAGES |
|---|---|---|
| Integrity of information | Historical value<br>Never inaccessible because of unreliable hardware | Readers can never alter content<br>Readers cannot customize information<br>Cannot conform to user preferences<br>(e.g. type size, margin width) |
| Physical entities | Portable<br>Allows browsing and exploring<br>Allows annotation and underlining<br>Aesthetically appealing | Limited to 2-D information<br>Limited to static text and graphics<br>Costly to reproduce for quickly outdated information<br>Often hard to locate specific information |
| Static | | Cannot handle sound or motion<br>Difficult to create multiple indices |
| Advanced technology | Well-defined and accepted standards<br>Typography, graphic design, and photo reproduction refined fields<br>High-resolution print and graphics<br>Easy to read | Joint authorship difficult<br>Re-keying text is error-prone |

Table 1. Print medium: advantages and disadvantages

**Electronic medium**

Electronic document systems have their own advantages and limitations. In some cases they are more powerful or appropriate than paper books for meeting the range of information needs of scholars within the university community. In other cases, books are more useful.

*Advantages*

Theodore Nelson and Douglas Engelbart were among the first to articulate the benefits of electronic document systems.[1] In the early 1960's, they recognized that computers were well suited to helping scholars and others create *connectivity*—webs of related information. In the print medium scholars often mark up books, articles, and papers. When a phrase or illustration sparks a connection to an idea in another book in a scholar's mind, he or she writes that connection, or "link, " down *next to* the phrase or picture that sparked the thought. Providing footnotes, references, and word glosses in books is an author's way of making annotations or explicitly indicating connections between his or her writing and other documents, schools of thought, and definitions. These standard devices provide readers with pointers to additional reading and information sources that will enrich the understanding of the subject matter of books so annotated. Creating webs of information and adding to them are integral to all scholarly work, and in the domain of scholarship these webs are commonly called *literatures*. Nelson defines "a literature" (as in "the scientific literature" or a field of discourse) "as a system of interconnected writings." [2]

George Landow of Brown's English Department sees connections and the act of following links as crucial to education. In his teaching, he is particularly interested in helping students see links between the literature they read and such things as art, politics, philosophical thought, and religious doctrine.

Nelson and Landow both stress the importance of *observing existing connections,* which can be done by studying "the literature," and *making new connections.* Electronic document systems help scholars both create connections and follow those made by others. Because electronic books allow flexible organization of material, they provide authors and readers with a greater degree of freedom than printed books. Explicit connections—"links"—allowing readers to travel from document to document (as one does with an encyclopedia) or from one place in a document to another in the same document can be made effortlessly by authors, thus fostering the creation of *information webs.* With the electronic medium, readers are not obliged to search through library stacks to look up referenced books and articles; they can quickly follow trails of footnotes without losing their original context.

Linking scholars together—intercommunicability—is an essential aspect of connectivity. Electronic document systems running either on a multiuser, time-shared system or on a series of networked workstations allow authors and readers to communicate with one another in a number of ways. Colleagues can easily view one another's documents (if given permission), send and receive personal electronic messages, and jointly edit the same document without leaving their own workplace. These types of communication capabilities may foster "on-line communities"[3] of researchers or students and enhance the ability of scholars to make meaningful connections.

Perhaps the greatest advantage of electronic documents over paper ones is their ability to handle many more graphic elements. By combining a variety of media, electronic books can provide not only static images, but also dynamics (e.g., computer animations and computer-controlled video sequences), interactivity (e.g., ability to move objects, change and edit objects, and change states), and sound (e.g., computer-generated or audio disk recordings). These features all help in creating better *audiovisualization*. For example, a biology student might be able to rotate and slice a three-dimensional model of a plant cell while reading related material, or a theater arts professor might have students examine video recordings of theatrical productions in parallel with blocking diagrams.

Electronic document systems can be useful tools for visualizing the structure of the information web as well as visualizing the individual concepts or processes contained in that structure. Not only can they allow scholars to make and follow links, but they can also provide a diagrammatic overview of the web of connections. Different "maps" of information webs can be generated to illustrate the connections that exist in a body of material. Some types of maps, however, are easier to generate than others. For example, it is possible to create a map of a reader's path through a document corpus or a diagram of all possible links from the reader's current position, but as the number of connections and quantity of information increases, so does the difficulty of generating maps of the entire information web. Since most readers cannot readily understand a diagram with hundreds of crisscrossing interconnections, the problem of distilling or summarizing the information must be addressed. In addition, authors may often make circular references, causing even more complexities in graphically representing the web of connections.

The paper medium does not allow a reader to alter the contents of a book. Electronic documents, however, are dynamic in the sense that both authors and readers can customize the material contained within a corpus of documents. For example, in a military setting, an author may want to provide complete access to certain information to those with the appropriate security clearance and only partial access to all others. If working with paper, this author would be forced to publish separate books for each constituency. Readers also may want to "filter" —limit access to—the information. A literature student, for example, might want to look at only critical commentaries on Shakespeare's plays, while an acting student might be interested in solely the original texts. Filtering permits readers to select only information they consider pertinent. A set of selection criteria or *attributes,* somewhat similar to index terms in the back of a book, can define relationships between information blocks or can identify structural components. For instance, a lawyer might want to apply a filter that would display all cases mentioning the name "J. Smith," to examine all cases that "support" a particular decision, or to view the first sentence of every major decision in a given area.

Nicholas Negroponte's idea of "idiosyncratic systems"[4] goes a step beyond filtering. He suggests that electronic documents adaptively display not only *what* material readers wish to see, but also *how* they would like it presented. For example, one reader might indicate a preference for as much graphic information as possible, while another might like the same information but with a more even mix of graphics and text. Negroponte's notion of an idiosyncratic document system can be generalized by creating a knowledge base containing profiles of both the readers and the information within the system. Rather than being powerful multimedia repositories for information, such systems would become "assistants" by not just presenting information, but also by carrying on a dialog with the reader. Although research on "automated authoring" is underway at Brown, MIT, and elsewhere, future knowledge-based electronic document systems are beyond the scope of this article, which focuses on present and near-term issues.

As with hard copy manuscripts, it is possible to preserve multiple versions of a single electronic document. Authors can save a document at any point in the creation process and can produce hard copy renderings of the same information (at least all text and static graphics).

Finally, the electronic medium can aid dramatically in the updating and dissemination of information. In many cases, editing an electronic document (using interactive editors for text, graphics, music, etc.) is far more efficient than making changes to a printed book. In addition, the cost of dissemination (in terms of both money and of natural resources) one day may be greatly reduced by the advent of national networks and high-density storage devices (e.g., diskettes, video disks, CD ROMs, etc).

*Disadvantages*

A major shortcoming in most electronic document systems developed using current technology is their failure to provide adequate information about where readers are in a document. Readers of paper books can always tell if they are "at the end of the book" or "three-quarters through it." If electronic books were merely linear sequences on a computer screen, then a two-dimensional gauge or a simple numbering scheme would suffice. However, because they are nonsequentially organized and the "middle" for one reader might be the "end" for another, a reader can follow link after link and feel disoriented.

Although it is possible to store documents in various stages of revision, the electronic medium does not encourage one to do so. With current text-editing systems, authors must have a sense of history to consciously save "old" versions of documents created with interactive editors. Even when the versions have been saved, it is difficult to see where changes have been made in a document that always looks "clean" no matter how drastically it has been revised. Authors working in teams also find it difficult to notice changes made by co-authors when edited versions contain no "markup" symbols and none of the visual cues offered by color pens and handwriting styles in the print medium.

For those who must rely on hard copy of an electronic document for some purposes, a linking structure can be seen as a disadvantage, as printing a branching document in a linear fashion poses both technical and conceptual problems.

Aside from the issues mentioned so far, there are some disadvantages to electronic document systems that arise from the limitations of hardware. Many people complain about eyestrain from working at a computer, even with high-resolution graphic display screens; others are attached to the "feel" and aesthetic appeal of bound volumes. Cost is still a major limiting factor to the widespread use of electronic document systems. High resolution displays and computer systems powerful enough to run the document software are still expensive and not at all portable, especially systems that run on hardware capable of displaying both color graphics and video on the same screen.

In short, electronic document systems using today's hardware and software offer substantial advantages over paper books in providing aids for connectivity, audiovisualization, dynamics, customizability, interactivity, and rapid information retrieval, but also have a number of drawbacks in providing spatial orientation, historical tracing, joint editing, visual clarity, portability, and cost. While these limitations are not intrinsic to the electronic medium, they are problems that must be considered in the development of current and next-generation electronic document systems.

## Desirable features for multimedia electronic document systems

An analysis of the aforementioned pros and cons suggests a number of design features that will maximize the advantages and minimize the current disadvantages of using the electronic medium for document preparation and presentation. To meet the needs of scholars and other knowledge workers, the minimal set of capabilities incorporated into an electronic document system should include tools for

(1) promoting connectivity,

(2) promoting audiovisualization,

(3) creating and revising documents,

(4) browsing, searching, customizing, and retrieving information, and

(5) preserving the historical integrity of information.

These capabilities are explained in detail below and represent capabilities and functions for the current or next-generation electronic document systems. These systems, in effect, are databases composed of text, graphics, dynamics, interactivity, and multimedia components, in contrast to future electronic document systems that will surely be founded on knowledge bases. Stephen Weyer and Alan Borning's Electronic Encyclopedia project represents one interesting example of a prototype knowledge-based system. [5]

*Tools to promote connectivity.*

The first essential capability of a good electronic document system is to provide a means for promoting the connection of ideas and the communication between individual scholars. These capabilities can be conceived of as a set of tools for creating a hypertext structure, the underlying framework of all electronic document systems developed or under development at Brown University.

The term *hypertext*, coined by Nelson,[6] denotes nonsequential writing and reading. Both an author's tool and a reader's medium, a hypertext document system allows authors or groups of authors to *link* information together, create *paths* through a corpus of related material, *annotate* existing texts, and create notes that point readers to either bibliographic data or the body of the referenced text. Hypertext can allow the creation of an automated encyclopedia of sorts: readers can browse through linked, cross-referenced, annotated texts in an orderly but nonsequential manner. For example, to learn about Greece from an ordinary encyclopedia, students must look up "Greece" and then retrieve volume after volume to find the host of other articles cross-referenced there (Acropolis, Plato, Crete, etc.). In a hypertext-based encyclopedia, however, students would browse through connected articles simply by touching the computer-equivalents of an encyclopedia's "See also . . ." references.

As early as 1945, a non-computer-based hypertext system was envisioned by Vannevar Bush, who pictured a "memex" device in which individuals would store all their books, records, and communications, form trails through them, and rapidly retrieve specific information contained within them.[7] In 1967 and 1968, Nelson and researchers at Brown University developed an early hypertext-based text editing system[8] inspired in part by Bush's vision and in parallel with Douglas Engelbart's pioneering editing system, NLS (oNLine System). NLS, now called Augment, allows text and line graphics to be organized in a hierarchical outline structure upon which one can superimpose a network of links that point to discrete blocks of information in the document.[9] More recently, Donald Thursh at the University of Illinois College of Medicine used the hypertext concept to create a "Living Textbook of Pathology"[10] in the PLATO environment.

Researchers at Xerox's Palo Alto Research Center (PARC) are currently developing a sophisticated hypertext system called "Notecards" that runs in the Interlisp environment on a powerful graphics-based workstation.[11] Although the system is still under development, it already provides a large number of linking facilities, maps of the information web, and integration with graphics.

By extension, we use the word *hypermedia* to denote the functionality of hypertext but with additional components such as two- and three-dimensional structured graphics, paint graphics, spreadsheets, video, sound, and animation. With hypermedia, an author can create links to complex diagrams, texts, photographs, video disks, audio recordings, and the like.

MIT's Spatial Data-Management System (SDMS)[12] and the interactive automobile repair manual[13] are also examples of existing systems with hypermedia components. Digital Equipment Corporation's Interactive Video Information System (IVIS) is one of the first systems commercially available that allows full integration of text, graphics, computer animation, and video on the same display screen, using a specialized programming language for authoring.

To summarize, the basic capabilities implied by the terms *hypertext* and *hypermedia* include linking together discrete *blocks* (e.g., word, paragraph, text document, graphical object, spreadsheet cell, and video frame) to form *webs* of information, following different paths through the information webs, and attaching annotations (special types of links) to any block of information. Typically, different information blocks are created using separate *applications* or *editors*. A hypertext document system allows authors to link together only information blocks created with a single application, a text editor, while a hypermedia document system provides linking capabilities between heterogeneous blocks created with different applications such as a painting program, a chart package, or a music editor. Early systems force the links to be essentially programmed, while newer systems provide interactive link creation as a fundamental component.

Multiuser access to information is another fundamental capability that must be present to promote connectivity. A group of scholars working together should be able to annotate each other's documents. This means that the system must provide multiple users with access to the same *corpus* of documents. At the least, multiple users must have "read access" to a colleague's documents; at best, they should be allowed to create new links within a colleague's document (either to annotations or to other documents) and to edit the document in a controlled fashion.

The multiuser access problem brings with it extremely complicated issues pertaining to access rights and update consistency. For instance, if user A edits a document and adds a link, do these changes show up immediately in other users' views of this document? Should all users have the ability to add links? Should all users be able to delete links? Can user C delete a document to which other users have linked? Few of the electronic book implementations have tackled this problem on a large scale (Englebart's NLS goes the furthest in providing support over national networks), and it stands as an important research question if electronic books are to be accepted.

To facilitate distribution of documents to a broader audience than a scholar's immediate community, multimedia document systems should provide tools for electronic dissemination. Currently, this would include automatic transfer of finished documents to typesetting equipment or the incorporation of powerful electronic mail or conferencing systems that make use of national and international networks. In the future, it would be desirable to subsume separate electronic mail or conferencing systems under a powerful hypertext/hypermedia system that allows the linking of documents across long-haul networks and that encourages the creation and exchange of references as opposed to files.[14]

---

*Tools to aid in creating audiovisualization.*

While a text-editing system with hypertext capabilities is useful, it can be argued that the advantages of a paper book still equal or outweigh the advantages of such computer-based text systems. However, when an author can add visuals and sound—not possible in paper books—the scale clearly begins to tip in favor of the electronic format; tools for creating visual and audio components are equally as important as those for promoting connectivity. The music faculty at Brown, for example, believe that multimedia systems could revolutionize the teaching of music. With present teaching techniques it is hard for music students to make the connection between the written notes and the musical sounds without one-on-one instruction. Integrating a music editor, a piano keyboard, and a synthesizer would allow students to *hear* every note they *see* as they write or play the notes. A text only document system—which might include many of the essential ingredients for connectivity—does not provide adequate tools for producing visual and aural aids. There is, however, a large continuum between text only and full multimedia systems. A two-dimensional structured graphics editor (such as MacDraw for the Apple Macintosh) might be adequate for creating simple static illustrations, and a low-level graphics package might be all that is necessary for generating maps of the information web; however, more extensive multimedia capabilities are required to produce dynamic electronic documents.

There is a spectrum of media that can be included in an electronic book. Static text, structured graphics, bitmap images, charts, and graphs fall at the low end of the spectrum. The inclusion of animation, computer-generated sound, and audio and video recordings adds a richness to electronic document systems that is impossible to recreate with paper media. Moreover, each medium in such a system is subject to some level of *interactive control*—methods for readers to move, change, and manipulate the material rather than just view it. For instance, readers may want to manipulate graphical objects, as in the biological cell rotation example, or they may want to alter or experiment with animation sequences, seeking answers to "what if" questions. Readers can even become characters in a dynamic story by influencing the progress of the plot.

As mentioned earlier, it is easy to become disoriented in a complex electronic information web. Authors and readers alike need visual cues that will help them determine where they are in the web of information, and also need graphical means for organizing and reorganizing their material. Tools that promote spatial orientation can include schematics of the information web, maps indicating all possible path options at a given time, and diagrams of specific paths a reader has already taken. For example, MIT's Spatial Database-Management System displays a "world view," an overview of Dataland with a "you-are-here" marker.

For maps to be extremely useful and readable, they must be able to represent varying levels of detail. To get a general idea of how a body of information is structured, it is best not to display a detailed "road map" when a "globe" is all that is needed. To create global views, document systems must have facilities for summarizing, compacting, and extracting the essence of the stored material. However, once readers are in the midst of the web or already familiar with its overall structure, they will require more detailed road maps that show all the links in a given subsection.

For each reader, the system should always save an encoding of the current position, viewing parameters, and past travelling information—*the document state*—so that each reader of a document may pick up where he or she left off and not be forced to re-create the exact links selected and searches made to return to the current position in the information web.

The effectiveness of visuals, whether in conjuring up concrete images of complex concepts or providing a map of the information web, depends largely on the quality of the final images. Several system features have an impact on the quality of the graphics: tools that promote good graphic design, high-resolution display screens, and color. People who are not professional graphic artists may not be able to produce professional-looking images; however, with features like rulers, gravity grids, automatic justification, alignment, and some simple design rules, they should be able to create reasonable visuals.

*Tools for creating and revising documents*

Since electronic documents are mutable entities that can be interacted with and modified, they must contain tools not only for presenting information, but also for *creating* it. These tools can take many forms, from batch text processors to interactive paint programs, chart packages, or music editors. Most desirable, of course, is a system that provides *direct manipulation:* such systems allow authors to interactively create, edit, and format documents directly in the view in which they will be presented on the screen. This provides the ability to make well-designed documents interactively and is very close to what-you-see-is-what-you-get (WYSIWYG) editing, which refers to on-screen views that appear as close as possible (given the limitations of screen size and resolution) to the way the document would appear if printed. In these direct manipulation systems, users can be presented with one of two interface paradigms: *procedural* or *declarative.* In the procedural interface, the reader specifies exactly *how* formatting should take place, putting in typeface, margin, line length, and leading information explicitly to arrive at a desired presentation image. In the declarative interface, the user specifies exactly *what* document entities and logical structures are desired (numbered points, chapter headings, indented quotations), and the system automatically formats those entities based upon a separately supplied style sheet specifying formatting rules to be applied interactively. The declarative system removes the responsibility for formatting from the author; all that the author needs to do is specify the document entities. For text and two dimensional graphics (free-hand structured graphics, charts, diagrams, etc.), direct manipulation editors of both types are commercially available for small computer systems; however, user-level editors for three-dimensional image creation exist only on expensive computer-aided design stations, and those for real-time animation exist only in experimental laboratories.

The creation of data can be handled in substantially different ways. Some systems have separate tools for authoring the document and for presenting it to readers. Many frame-oriented CAI programs fall into this category. Instructors (authors) are given the freedom to create frames of information and link them together sequentially or nonsequentially (by indicating branch points). Students (readers) may have the ability to interact with the lesson and sometimes to browse through the frames, but they are not permitted to alter the links or add their own connections. Futhermore, the systems almost never allow student readers to collaborate, share ideas with other students, or comment on each other's work. In some cases, the authoring tools are resident on large time-shared computers, while the final document is presented on small stand-alone microcomputers. Ideally, authors and readers should have the same set of integrated tools that allow them to browse through other material during the document preparation process and to add annotations and original links as they progress through an information web. In effect, the boundary between author and reader should largely disappear.

It is important to consider not only the quality of the authoring tools, but also how these tools relate to one another. On one end of the *integration* continuum, documents containing different types of information (e.g., text, music, spreadsheet) are created with separate application programs, and the "electronic document" is comprised of many linked documents, each of a single medium. A little farther along on the continuum is the "cut, copy, paste" paradigm. Here, it is possible to copy bits between heterogeneous applications (e.g., paste a spreadsheet into a text document). This paradigm thus provides some integration, but loses important semantic information (all numbers in the spreadsheet are now treated as text strings). The next logical step in the continuum may be called "reference copy, paste." At this level of integration, a spreadsheet that is copied and pasted into a text document retains its "spreadsheetness." If the original spreadsheet document is updated, all copies, or *instances*, of the spreadsheet are automatically updated (typically today, only data from certain applications can be used in a reference copy action).

At the highest end, a fully-integrated multimedia document system would allow reference copying and pasting of all data types and would include a context-sensitive cursor. As the author moved the cursor over the spreadsheet, all spreadsheet editing functions would be made available; as the cursor moved over some musical notation, all music editing functions would automatically be activated; and so forth. The Macintosh desktop environment[15] is one example of "cut, copy, paste" integration, while office systems such as Lotus Jazz offer several special cases of "reference copy, paste" integration.

It is nearly impossible to retrofit independently written applications into an integrated environment. Achieving the highest degree of integration requires either (1) monolithic applications that understand every type of data structure that one might want to use, (2) a universal data structure (UDS) such that any application can convert between the UDS and its own data structure (an extremely difficult problem that is prone to losing semantic information in the conversion), or (3) attaching functionality not to an application, but to the particular entities that are the focus of attention. In such an object-oriented system, "objects" are self-contained entities encapsulating information about all possible operations that can be performed on them, thus allowing reference copying between all applications that share the same object library and object memory. The third alternative shows the most promise but is still an open issue, given the difficulty of creating a memory that allows efficient multiuser, concurrent access to very large numbers of objects, not to mention the cultural, sociological, and economic problem of getting the programming profession to switch from conventional programming to object-oriented programming.

*Tools for browsing, searching, personalizing, and retrieving information*

Database functions underlie all electronic document systems. Thus a useful document system should take advantage of this underlying structure and provide authors with a set of searching and filtering features, including the ability to search using a single criterion *(simple searching)*, to search using multiple criteria *(Boolean searching)*, or to customize the presentation in other ways.

The same criteria used for searching can also allow authors to restrict access to documents to specific readers and to groups of readers. Similarly, readers can selectively view the contents of a corpus so as to eliminate material that is not currently relevant. By providing methods for authors to associate *keywords* with any discrete block of information, a document system can filter the information for readers using these terms. Newspeek, a system developed at MIT for creating personalized newspapers, is a good example of information filtering. Readers submit lists of keywords that describe their interests. As stories come over the AP and UPI wires, the system filters stories according to each reader's list and prepares a custom newspaper for each individual.[16]

Keywords can also be associated with links to facilitate searching and browsing. A link always represents a relationship between two items. Attaching a keyword (or multiple keywords) to a link allows authors to explicitly name or define the existing relationship. Keywords associated with links might include such terms as "example" (meaning A is an example of B), "supports" (meaning A is an argument that supports B), or "child" (meaning A is the child of B).

Filtering can also be accomplished by associating attributes other than keywords to blocks and links. Different structures within documents can be named so that information can be filtered according to level of detail. An outline illustrates the point best. In NLS and Brown's FRESS system, for example, each level of an outline is identified as a separate structure, allowing readers to expand and contract the outline to see more or less detail. In text documents, sentences, paragraphs, and subject headings can all be identified as separate structures; however, it is considerably more difficult to make such distinctions in other media.

Using keywords and filters for finding specific information, hiding unnecessary detail, or tailoring the format of the material illustrate how the electronic medium allows readers to personalize the presentation of information in ways that are not possible with paper books.

The maps mentioned earlier not only provide a visual summary of the information space, but in fact are critical for browsing and information retrieval. The maps show the connectivity between documents rather than the content of the documents themselves. If these maps are supplemented with capabilities allowing users to travel by pointing to specific sections of the map, the map becomes a convenient way to move quickly through the web via the connections. This traveling can be done with the goal of discovering, for example, an appropriate detailed document or even the pattern of connections between information in the web.

*Tools for preserving historical integrity of information*

An electronic document system should allow authors to preserve a historical record of the creation of a document. Periodically saving versions of the document is one possible option; saving a keystroke/ button push record of all updates is another. Finding viable methods for saving each draft version of a document has been one of the major research tasks of the Xanadu project initiated by Nelson.[17] Clearly, allowing authors to print their material at any time is an essential feature, particularly if the author prefers editing on paper.

One method of encouraging electronic editing of documents, particularly if several authors or editors are working together, is to provide *markup* tools. Annoland,[18] a hypertext-based system developed by Richard Burton, John Seely Brown, and others at Xerox PARC, includes an option that causes the delete operation to overstrike the target text with x marks rather than removing them from the screen. Authors can temporarily "turn off" the editing symbols and see a clean copy of the document, perhaps with insertions by other individuals appearing in a different font. Editing symbols and edit marks identified by users are two more examples of attributes that can be used for filtering information. Markup features allow an author to immediately pick out the places where changes to a document have been made; these are particularly useful when combined with filtering so that an author can see only one editor's changes at a time (just as one would be able to distinguish different editors' marks by pen color or handwriting). As multimedia document systems become more widely used, markup techniques will have to be developed for editing nontextual information.

## Survey of existing systems at Brown University

Researchers at Brown University have been experimenting with electronic document systems since the late 1960's. We have chosen to describe several systems developed or under development at Brown to illustrate concrete implementations of many of the features described earlier, and we encourage the reader to extend these illustrations by examining other important work such as NLS, Xanadu, the systems of MIT's Architecture Machine Group,[19] Xerox's Notecards and Annoland,[20] the Living Text,[21] and the Electronic Encyclopedia.[22]

Although each of Brown's four systems described below have markedly different user interfaces, they all have an underlying hypertext or hypermedia structure. The first and oldest of the four systems, FRESS, handles primarily text, while the current development project, Intermedia, should provide a high level of integration for a host of multimedia documents. The descriptions below highlight important or unique features of each system.

### Fress

FRESS (File Retrieval and Editing System), solely a hypertext document system, allowed authors to create links within any text document or among any number of text documents. FRESS was essentially a text only system (links could be made to some graphics when using an IMLAC PDS-ID display) and was developed under the VM/CMS time-sharing system in the late 1960's as a successor to the Hypertext Editing System.[23] The system contained important "navigational," or linking, facilities. It also was designed for multiple users, although it did not support concurrent updating of a single file.

Authors created FRESS documents using a full, interactive text editor with batch formatting. They could insert a marker at any point in a text document, which became the source, and "link" that selection to any other *destination* point in the same document or a different one. FRESS had two types of links: *tags* and *jumps*. A tag— a one-way link—indicated a connection to a single element such as an annotation, definition, or footnote. When the reader pointed to a tag with a light pen, the associated text appeared in another window on the screen for reference while the reader remained in the main document. Unlike a tag, a jump—a bidirectional link— indicated a path to another document. By following a jump, the reader was transferred from one document to another, and up to seven windows could be used to display documents simultaneously. By inserting links, authors could create paths through a large number of documents for themselves or others to explore. Since cross-reference markers (destinations of links) were displayed in the text, readers could backtrack through a sequence of links, retracing their steps through a path.

FRESS allowed authors to attach "keywords" to links, thus providing a facility for readers to filter the information through which they wished to browse, and allowed users to name blocks of text for subsequent referencing and searching. With these facilities, a student reader could choose to see only annotations left by the professor, examine only those links that led to literary criticism of a poem, ignore for the moment all the comments written by classmates, or select all poems written by a certain poet or on a certain subject.

FRESS was used in production for more than a decade at Brown for both on-line documents and hard-copy manuscript production. Two educational experiments— one in a course on energy and one in a course on poetry— were conducted using hypertext "corpuses" created in the FRESS system. [24]

For the functions FRESS provided, it had two major drawbacks. First, students in the experimental courses often did not create many of their own links because the commands necessary to establish links were somewhat complex. Second, the system provided no spatial cues, and readers found it difficult to remember where they were in the information web.

To summarize, FRESS provided a set of essential tools for promoting connectivity, and also provided facilities for customizing an individual's view of a hypertext corpus. Audiovisualization, dynamics, and integration of applications as described above are not relevant to this early system.

*The Electronic Document System.*

Far more modern than FRESS, the Electronic Document System, completed in 1982,[25] represents Brown's first hypermedia system. The system, which is made up of three subsystems (the Picture Layout System, the Document Layout System, and the Document Presentation System), was developed on a DEC VAX 11/780 and uses a Ramtek 9400 color display screen (1024 by 1280 resolution) plus a data tablet. The Electronic Document System's high-resolution color graphics capability, its graphic representation of the information web, and its ability to incorporate animation sequences set it apart from the earlier text-oriented FRESS system.

Briefly, graphic designers or artists use the Picture Layout System, a structured graphics editor, to "draw" images that may include text. Before, during, or after graphics for individual pages are produced, the author uses the Document Layout System (DLS) to construct the web structure of the document. Making use of multiple windows, authors can create blank pages and chapters and fill the pages with pictures created with the graphics editor. As necessary, authors link pages together by creating sensitive areas on the pages called *buttons.* Authors will often reserve one window in DLS to display the overall structure of the document— chapters nested as deeply as desired within chapters, pages nested within chapters, and keyworded links connecting the pages. Special keyworded windows can also be created so authors may see only links labeled with a particular keyword.

In the Document Presentation System (DPS) readers select buttons with a pointing device to traverse links created in the Document Layout System. Actions other than "get new page" can be associated with buttons. Most notably, buttons can activate dynamic actions such as triggering animation sequences (animation scripts are created outside the system using DIAL[26]), exiting from the system, turning on graphic overlays, or activating the annotation facility.

To date, two prototype maintenance-and-repair manuals have been created using the Electronic Document System: one for a computerized numerical control system and one for naval sonar equipment. A reader traversing through the sonar manual, for example, either selects choices from a menu or picks the "NEXT" button located at the bottom of every page to follow a path through the document.

An author uses the Document Layout System to predefine a number of different paths for different classes of readers. In this particular document, the author has created "novice," "intermediate," and "expert" paths, and by using keyworded links has been able to further customize each reader's experience depending on the choices each reader makes and actions that have occurred during the current session. Specifically, if a novice wishes to see an explanation of power supply failures, he or she is automatically given a step-by-step procedure to follow, while an expert requesting the same information is given a much briefer checklist of trouble-shooting procedures.

The most interesting aspects of the Electronic Document System include the graphical representation of the underlying information web provided for authors and the two forms of "maps" provided for readers. The first type of map provides readers with a history of their path through the document in the form of a "timeline" with miniatures of the pages visited and allows them to select any page's icon and return to it. The second type of map helps to orient the reader spatially. In the center of the "neighbors" screen, the system displays a miniature of the reader's current page. On the left side, it shows miniature pictures of all the pages that the reader could possibly have come from, on the right side, all the pages to which the reader can currently go. Again, all icons may be selected as the "next" page. While this feature is useful, it falls short of helping the reader to visualize the entire system of connections in the document, as can be done in the Document Layout System.

Another interesting feature included in the graphics editor is a "reference copy, paste" capability. If the need arises to use any drawing more than once, it is possible to create "instances" of the drawing (which can be scaled) in any number of other Picture Layout documents. Editing the original drawing will cause the changes to appear in all instances of it.

The separate drawing, authoring, and viewing facilities, and the absence of multiuser capabilities, three-dimensional modeling capabilities, and a text editor in the suite of applications that make up this system are severe disadvantages, as is the considerable computing power necessary to allow the system to run at a reasonable speed. On the positive side, the Electronic Document System permits both readers and authors to perform all operations graphically without requiring a text editor or a special command language for specifying links.

*BALSA: An Introduction to Nuclear Arms Issues:*

BALSA (Brown Algorithm Simulator and Animator) is not in fact a general-purpose electronic document system in our sense; rather, it is an environment designed to facilitate the creation of computer science educational software. It has a number of powerful features for animating complex algorithms such as sorting, searching, binary tree creation, etc.[27] BALSA is included here because an educational program created within the BALSA environment for a course on arms control has many of the features of an electronic book.

The program, "An Introduction to Nuclear Arms Issues," organizes a body of information around a *timeline*.[28] Each event on the timeline is linked to an expanded textual explanation of the topic, one or more graphic images that are sometimes animated or interactive, and lists containing suggestions for further reading, possible essay topics, footnotes, and definitions of technical terms. Students are able to browse through the topics on the timeline in any order, or choose from five information filters to customize the information presented to them. A student wishing to review only technical information about weapon systems would select the "TECH" filter from the pop-up menu. Hitting the return key would then cause the student to travel sequentially through all blocks of information related to weapons systems. As the student progresses through the material, the current topic is highlighted on the timeline to provide spatial and historical orientation.

Several events on the timeline are linked to interactive material. A student who selects "National Survey" from the 1984 position on the timeline, for example, is presented with a series of survey questions to answer. After answering each question, the student is provided with (linked to) a graph indicating how his or her answer compares to the national sample and a block of text discussing the particular statistic.

The major difference between the nuclear arms program and the two systems described previously is that this program provides no user-level authoring tools. A programmer is required to add the text, create the graphics, program the interaction, and edit the timeline. The timeline structure, however, has provided one useful model for structuring a body of related information. Unlike the history and neighbors diagrams in the Document Presentation System, the timeline provides readers with an overview of the entire information web.


*Intermedia*

Intermedia, currently under development at Brown's Institute for Research in Information and Scholarship, is a multimedia system that will ideally provide most of the major capabilities desirable for a good electronic document system. An assumption underlying the design of Intermedia is that users will be most likely to take advantage of the system's capabilities if they can create links as part of their regular work with spreadsheets, word processors, graphics editors, or other media. Therefore, Intermedia is not a separate application, but rather a framework for a collection of tools that allow authors to make links between standard types of documents created with heterogeneous applications.[29]

The structure of the Intermedia user environment facilitates connectivity, audiovisualization, creation of material, and complex filtering of information. Its architecture is similar to the window-based desktop environment provided on the Apple Lisa, in which multiple applications run simultaneously. Each application allows the user to create material of different types: a text-editing application is used to create text documents, a music editor is used to create musical scores, and a spreadsheet application is used to create financial models. An application can either be "off" (not being used) or "running," meaning it has opened one or more windows and provided an interface to create or modify material. Multiple applications of the same type (e.g., multiple music editors) can run simultaneously.

The material an application creates is the *document*, a part of which is viewed in the application's window. While the application is running, the document can be updated interactively, and is edited and viewed in the application window, a facility adhering to the principle of direct manipulation. When the application terminates, the document can be stored on disk for later retrieval by the application. The *desktop manager* (also known as the display manager, the graphical shell, the window manager, or the finder in various systems) provides the ability to name, open, close, move, and organize applications, windows, and documents.

This standard type of user environment supports an integrated application domain at the user level by providing the basic ability to cut or copy text (and some graphics) from one application to another. In copying and pasting, one picks a source selection, chooses the copy command, picks a destination selection, and chooses the paste command to paste the source selection at the destination selection. When the operation is finished, there is a duplicate of the source at the destination, and no semantic tie between the two. The process of creating links mirrors the copy, paste operation—the most familiar command in the standard desktop. One simply picks a source selection, called a *block,* chooses the "start link" command (Figure 1a), picks a destination block, and chooses the "complete link" command (Figure 1b). When the operation is finished, there is a bidirectional tie between the source and destination blocks (Figure 1c) such that whenever a user selects the source block and issues the "follow" command, the document containing the destination is activated, with the destination block highlighted in another window on the screen and the destination document retrieved from storage if necessary.

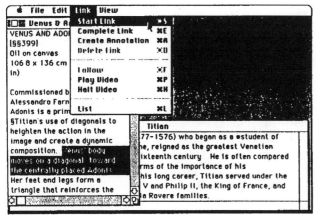

Figure 1a.

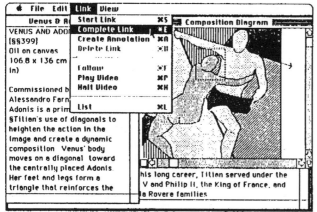

Figure 1b.

Figure 1c.

Figure 1: Intermedia prototype. (a) In a corpus of art history materials, the user has already created a link from a biography of Titian to a detailed article describing one of his works. The User now highlights a portion of the text within the article and then selects the "Start Link" command. (b)The user opens the Composition Diagram and selects a portion of the bit map. This selection will become the link after the "Complete Link" command is issued. (c) A link is established between a selection of text in the article on Venus and Adonis and the Composition Diagram. The program places bullet markers at both the source and destination points to indicate the existence of a link.

*Nicole Yankelovich, Norman Meyrowitz, Andries van Dam*

The applications now under development and the documents they generate include a text processor, presentation-graphics editor, paint-graphics editor, constraint-based animation application, timeline editor, geographic map editor, videodisc access building block, and subject-specific building blocks.

In addition to the linking capability, many other features are included to aid in navigation and information retrieval. A user can create *paths,* named trails, through a particular set of links. After issuing the command "start me on the Novice path," a user can issue a "next link" command that will automatically jump to the next item in the path, or the "previous link" command to go to the previous block. A special *system path* keeps track of users' entire Intermedia sessions (like the history facility in the Document Presentation System) so that they can take side trails serendipitously and go back, step-by-step, the way they came.

Keyworded blocks and links are also integral to the Intermedia environment. Keywords applied to links allow the user to attach one or more attributes to a link; later users can apply filters to the document so that only link symbols meeting their filtering criteria are shown on the screen. Similarly, users can filter blocks within a document according to simple or Boolean search arguments. The result of a search can be stored in a *search list* for later perusal.

Intermedia blocks, links, keywords, and paths associated with a set of documents are stored in a *web.* The web is essentially a way of defining a context or database in which a typically large set of related block, link, keyword, and path information is stored. The web allows individual users, groups of users, or, in the extreme, an entire campus to create a shared web of materials from different applications. Two webs might exist that reference the same documents but have an entirely different set of links. For example, the English Department might have a web referencing all of the Shakespearean tragedies along with links pertaining to color imagery in those plays, while the Religious Studies Department might have a web referencing those same plays with links pertaining to religious symbolism.

The system also provides ways to generate diagrams of the information web at different levels of detail. A *global map* gives a high-level view of the web, showing links at a document-to-document level. A *tracking map* provides a continually updated graphical view of the currently active document and its links, and can be viewed at the following four levels of detail: (1) document-to-document; (2) document-to-block; (3) block-to-document; or (4) block-to-block. With each document, one can store filtering and viewing attributes so that a document's map, rather than its contents, can be viewed by the user; the map is generated on the fly. By providing easy-to-use facilities for linking, saving paths, retracing paths, and viewing the information web at several levels of detail, Intermedia promotes connectivity by combining the most significant features of FRESS and the Electronic Document System.

While facilities for visualizing the web structures are provided by the Intermedia framework itself, other audiovisualization tools such as graphics editing, three-dimensional modeling, sound generation, and animation must be provided by individual applications within the framework. For example, a "timeline" application could be included as an additional aid to viewing the organization of the information visually, and an audiodisc control application could be added to allow blocks to be linked to audio segments. Any multimedia component can be included in the Intermedia environment if its design adheres to the standard user interface conventions of the system and if it includes the standard methods for users to identify discrete blocks of information that can serve as source and destination points for links and allows users to create and travel through the links themselves.

The Intermedia user environment, although still at the prototype stage, already provides most of the necessary linking facilities included in Brown's early electronic document systems, including text, line graphics, and videodisc applications. An early version of the final system is scheduled for testing in an English literature course beginning in January 1986.

## Conclusion

Multimedia electronic documents can be enormously useful adjuncts to the existing teaching, research, and learning tools of scholars, but to do this they must provide facilities that are different from and more powerful than those of paper books. These facilities, which include tools to promote connectivity, enhance audiovisualization, aid in the creation and revision of information, facilitate the search for and retrieval of data, and maintain historical integrity of materials, represent the set of features that the electronic document systems developed at Brown aim to encompass. Not all, however, can be accomplished fully with existing technology.

Five areas, in particular, point to the need for further research. The first, concurrent distributed file access over a network, is a problem that must be tackled before sophisticated tools for joint authoring can be included in electronic document systems. The concurrent distributed file access problem is particularly acute in cases when a group of scholars would like the freedom to edit documents in the information web while others are editing, reading, or creating links to and from the same documents. Distributed database techniques will have to be developed and incorporated into multimedia document systems intended for multiple users.

Related to this challenge is the goal of high-level integration of applications. Methods must be found for software developers working separately to create multimedia applications that work together in a consistent user environment. The most promising current technology is that of object-oriented programming.

Third, the art of graphic design for electronic multimedia presentation of information is still young. Today's graphic design specialists concern themselves only with the linear presentation of material, while graphic design for electronic media introduces the elements of change and time. How should a document be presented on the screen if each reader sees a uniq:1e sequence of information blocks, and how should multimedia components be combined to present the reader with the pleasing, crisp appearance commonly expected by readers of books?

Fourth, the graphic design issue raises questions of standardization. User interface standards are needed in order to give users a sense of familiarity with the electronic tools, but these standards must, at the same time, be flexible enough to accommodate the full range of applications any one scholar requires.

Last is the problem of interoperability. If the proliferation of hardware and software systems continues, incompatibility may mean that electronic books run the risk of being usable on only a small number of systems. Currently, different readers have available machines with substantially different software, memory, and input and output capabilities. Over the five centuries since the print medium was introduced, a high degree of standardization has been developed that allows books to be used universally. Although it may not take quite so many years to develop a universally accepted format for electronic books, interoperability still looms as a major obstacle to electronic book publishing and dissemination on a wide scale. Until hardware and software become standardized, research and standards in the area of document exchange formats and systems that tailor the electronic document presentation to the type of hardware currently in use are of primary importance.

The pursuit of these goals will be a challenging one. At Brown, by separating application-specific components from an application-independent linking structure in Intermedia, we hope to take a first step toward providing a framework for multimedia systems for the knowledge worker. With the current upsurge of high quality work in this area at other institutions, we expect the remainder of this decade to be a fruitful one for this important field.

## Acknowledgments

We wish to thank the many researchers at Brown University involved in the development of the four systems described in this article. In particular we would like to single out all of the researchers responsible for developing and enriching the FRESS hypertext system; Steve Feiner, David Salesin, Sandor Nagy, Randy Pausch, Gerry Weil, Imre Kovacs, Charles Tompkins, and Steve Hanson for their work in creating the Electronic Document System and the Sonar Maintenance and Repair Manual; Bob Sedgewick and Marc Brown for creating BALSA and many algorithm animations; Liz Waymire for the development of "An Introduction to Nuclear Arms Issues" within the BALSA environment; and Steve Drucker, Page Elmore, Charlie Evett, Matt Evett, Nan Garrett, Ed Grossman, Bern Haan, and Karen Smith for their contributions to the design of the Intermedia environment. We owe thanks to Helen DeAndrade for creating an art history corpus for the Intermedia prototype system. Lynne O'Brien and Trina Avery deserve special thanks for their insightful comments and careful editing of this article. We are also indebted to our reviewers for raising important technical issues and providing constructive suggestions for revisions.

We would like to thank IBM, the Annenberg/CPB Project, the Office of Naval Research, the Exxon Education Foundation, and the National Endowment for the Humanities for their generous financial support of the various projects described in this article.

## Notes

1. T. H. Nelson, *Literary Machines,* Swarthmore, Penn., 1981. Available from author. D. C. Engelbart and W. K. English, "A Research Center for Augmenting Human Intellect," *Proc. FJCC* 33, (Fall 1968): 395-410.

2. T. H. Nelson, "Replacing the Printed Word: A Complete Literary System," *InformationProcessing80,* S. H. Lavington, North-Holland Publishing Co., IF10 1980: 1013-1023.

3. A. van Dam and D. E. Rice, "Computers and Publishing: Writing, Editing and Printing," in *Advances in Computers* (New York, Academic Press: 1970).

4. N. Negroponte, "An Idiosyncratic Systems Approach to Interactive Graphics," paper presented at ACM/SIGGRAPH Workshop on User-Oriented Design of Interactive Graphics Systems, Pittsburgh, Penn., Oct. 14-15, 1976.

5. S. Weyer and A. Borning, "A Prototype Electronic Encyclopedia," *ACM Trans. Office Information Systems* (Jan. 1985): 63-88.

6. See note 1.

7. V. Bush, "As We May Think," *Atlantic Monthly,* July 1945: 101.

8. S. Carmody et al., "A Hypertext Editing System for the /360," *Pertinent Concepts in Computer Graphics,* M. Faiman and J. Nievergelt (eds.) (Urbana: Univ. of Illinois Press, 1969), 291-330.

9. D.C. Englebart and W.K. English, "A Research Center"; N. Meyrowitz and A. van Dam, "Interactive Text Editing Systems: Part 1," *Computing Surveys* (Sept. 1982): 321-352.

10. D. R. Thursh and F. Mabry, "A Knowledge-Based System for Pathology Education," *Bull. Pathology Education* (Fall 1980): 36-45.

11. F. Halasz and R. Trigg, personal communication.

12. R. Bolt, *Spatial Data-Management,* Architecture Machine Group, M.I.T., Cambridge, Mass., 1979.

13. D. Backer and S. Gano, "Dynamically Alterable Videodisk Displays," *Proc. Graphics Interface 82,* Toronto, May 17-21,1982: 365-37.

14. Nelson *Literary Machines,* and Englebart, "A Research Center" above; also **Yankelovich** in this volume.

15. *Inside Macintosh,* Apple Computer, Inc., Cupertino, Calif., 1985.

16. W. Bender, "Imaging and Interactivity," *Fifteenth Joint Conf. Image Technology,* Tokyo, Nov. 26, 1984.

17. Nelson, *Literary Machines.*

18. J. S. Brown, "Process versus Product: a Perspective on Tools for Communal and Informal Electronic Learning," in *Education in the Electronic Age: A Report From the Learning Lab,* WNET/Thirteen Learning Lab, New York, 1983: 41-58.

19. Bolt, *Spatial Data-Management.*

20. Brown, "Process versus Product".

21. Thursh and Mabry, "A Knowledge-Based System".

22. Weyer and Borning, "A Prototype".

23. Carmody et al., "A Hypertext Editing System".

24. J. Catano, "Poetry and Computers: Experimenting with Communal Text," *Computers and the Humanities* (1979): 269-275.

25. S. Feiner, S. Nagy, and A. van Dam, "An Experimental System for Creating and Presenting Interactive Graphical Documents," *Trans. Graphics* (1982): 59-77.

26. S. Feiner, D. Salesin, and T. Banchoff, "DIAL: A Diagrammatic Animation Language," *IEEE Computer Graphics and Applications,* Sept. 1982: 43-54.

27. M. H. Brown and R. Sedgewick, "A System for Algorithm Animation," *SIGGRAPH'84 Conference Proc.— Computer Graphics* (1984): 177-186.

28. N. Yankelovich et al., "The Sampler Companion," IRIS Technical Report 85-1, Inst. Research in Information and Scholarship, Brown Univ., March 1985.

29. N. Meyrowitz, "Networks of Scholar's Workstations: End-User Computing in a University Community," IRIS Technical Report 85-3, Inst. Research in Information and Scholarship, Brown Univ., June 1985.

# The Rhetoric of Hypermedia: Some Rules for Authors

George P. Landow
Department of English, Brown University

## Introduction

Hypermedia, which changes the way texts exist and the way we read them, requires a new rhetoric and a new stylistics. The defining characteristics of this new information medium derive from its use of blocks of text joined by electronic links, for this combination emphasizes multiple connections rather than linear reading or linear organization. The hypermedia author cannot realize the enormous potential of the medium to change our relation to language and text simply by linking one passage or image to others. In other words, linking, by itself, is not enough. Simply linking one text to another fails to achieve the expected benefits of hypermedia and can even alienate the user. The author of a story, article, or book does not expect to make much sense by stringing together sentences and paragraphs without various stylistic devices and rhetorical conventions. To communicate effectively, hypermedia authors must make use of a range of techniques, suited to their medium, that will enable the reader to process the information presented by this new technology.

Intermedia, which has features not available in other hypermedia systems, has been described elsewhere.[1] In the following pages I refer frequently to experience gained working with it, for two reasons. First, any really workable hypermedia system, one that can realize the potential of this new form of information technology, must have *at least* the features of Intermedia. Second, despite possessing features that orient readers, Intermedia still requires authors to employ a rhetoric of linking. Since this advanced hypertext system still requires additional author-created stylistic devices, it provides a good point of departure for discussing general issues of hypermedia rhetoric and stylistics.

Although hypermedia redefines some of the basic characteristics of page-bound text, such as the rigidly hierarchical distinction between a main text and its annotation in scholarly works, it still depends upon many of the same organizing principles that make page-bound discourse coherent and even pleasurable to read.

In other words, hypermedia requires stylistic and rhetorical devices just as does book-text, though, as one might expect, a new technology of information creates demands for novel devices.

One begins any discussion of the new rhetoric needed for hypermedia with the recognition that authors of hypertext and hypermedia materials confront three related problems: First, what must they do to orient readers and help them read efficiently and with pleasure? Second, how can they inform those reading a document where the links in that document lead? Third, how can they assist readers who have just entered a new document to feel at home there? Drawing upon the analogy of travel, we can say that the first problem concerns *navigation* information necessary for making one's way through the materials.[2] The second concerns *exit* or *departure* information and the third *arrival* or *entrance* information. In each case, creators of hypermedia materials must decide what readers need to know at either end of a hypermedia link in order to make use of what they find there. The general issue here is one of interpretation. To enable readers to function efficiently, how much interpretation must the designer-author attach to the system as a whole, to link pathways, and to documents at the end of links?

The following discussion of the rhetoric of hypermedia proceds by first looking at problems intrinsic to this information technology, after which it examines some system-generated solutions to them. Finally, after pointing to problems not solved by these means, it suggests rhetorical devices hypermedia authors can use in composing documents and in linking them to one other.

## General observations

Images bare of text or images with only titles confuse readers, who cannot quickly and easily determine why links to such material have been included. Once confused, readers resent the presence of the link. Before observing several solutions to this fundamental problem, let us note the basic assumptions underlying these annoyed reactions, the most important of which is the assumption by readers that links represent useful, interesting—in a word, significant—relationships. Such assumptions, we must realize, do not derive from overestimations of hypermedia but are intrinsic to such systems. In fact, because links play such a primary role in hypertext and hypermedia, they influence the content they convey and thus exemplify the McLuhanesque principle that the medium is the message—or at least that every medium of communication itself communicates an identifiable bias or message.[3]

Hypermedia as a medium conveys the strong impression that its links signify coherent, purposeful, and above all *useful* relationships. From which follows:

**Rule 1. The very existence of links in hypermedia conditions the reader to expect purposeful, important relationships between linked materials.**

**Rule 2. The emphasis upon linking materials in hypermedia stimulates and encourages habits of relational thinking in the reader.** Such intrinsic hypermedia emphasis upon interconnectedness (or connectivity) provides a powerful means of teaching sophisticated critical thinking, particularly that which builds upon multi-causal analyses and relating different kinds of data. But one must note a third, cautionary principle:

**Rule 3. Since Hypermedia systems predispose users to expect such significant relationships among documents, those documents that disappoint these expectations appear particularly incoherent and nonsignificant.** When users follow links and encounter materials that do not appear to possess a significant relation to the document from which the link pathway originated, they feel confused and resentful.

Brief texts in the form of titles do not always provide enough information about images to the reader, because titles do not sufficiently establish a relationship between two linked documents. Inadequately presented visual information characterizes many illustrated textbooks, particularly literary anthologies, that include portraits of authors, works of art, and other supposedly relevant visual materials. Students generally ignore such materials. Books permit the student reader to avoid apparently nonsignificant or insignificant materials—one simply glances at them and turns the page or, in many cases, simply never glances at them at all—but hypermedia systems, whose linkages suggest that the user will encounter significant relationships between materials, make ignoring such materials more difficult. They force the reader to confront relationality—or its absence.

## System-generated means of orienting the reader

Hypermedia linking is a double-edged sword that offers readers information in new, more efficient ways but, taken by itself, simple linking also has the capacity to confuse them and leave them in that condition E. Jeffrey Conklin has described as "lost in hyperspace."[4] Although some authors on the subject of hypermedia navigation and orientation write as if hypermedia systems are composed only of links and the materials they connect, in fact any workable system requires more support from both the system itself and the author who uses it. My experience with Intermedia suggests that navigation and orientation are no longer serious and unresolved problems. Using system features, the reader can locate something or travel to it by means of (1) full text searches, (2) folders, (3) links, (4) web views, and (5) menus of link choices from a particular marker. One always knows what documents "surround" the document one is reading, and one can always travel to an overview document, which in most cases gets one off in the direction one wishes to head.

The most important of these features is a dynamic system-generated tracking map, the conception of which has evolved considerably since developers at the Institute for Research in Information and Scholarship (IRIS) first proposed providing readers with a visual image of the links that join visual and text documents on Intermedia. This basic idea evolved through three stages. The first, the Global Tracking Map, provided graphic information about all links and documents in a particular body of linked documents. Activating the icon for a particular hypertext corpus, such as *Context32, Nuclear Arms,* or *Biology,* simultaneously activated that hypertext web and generated a document in which icons representing each document in the web were joined by lines representing links between pairs of documents. This Global Tracking Map, which functioned only during early stages of Intermedia's development, immediately demonstrated that such a device was virtually useless for all but the smallest documents sets or webs. Although pictures of it have appeared in articles on hypertext, the Global Tracking Map was never used educationally and was never part of any released version of Intermedia.[5]

Instead, IRIS developed the Local Tracking Map, which presented icons for all documents linked to that one currently activated. As before, the reader chooses a particular web and opens it by double clicking upon its icon or by first activating it and then choosing "open" from the Intermedia menu. The reader then moves the Local Tracking Map to one side of the screen, which permits her to work with an individual document and the tracking map it generates open side by side. Each time the reader opens a new document or activates a previously opened one, the Local Tracking Map transforms itself, thus informing the reader about where she can go. This information alone serves to remove much potential disorientation from the reader's experience.

In its third instantiation, the Local Tracking Map, which now bears the name "Web View," adds two chief features. First, double-clicking on any icon in the Web View opens the document represented by that icon, thereby adding another way of making one's way through materials on Intermedia. Second, the Web View presents a history of the reader's path by means of a vertical array of icons that indicate the titles of documents previously opened; additional smaller icons show that the document was opened from a folder, by following a link, or by reactivating a document previously opened on the desktop.[6]

## Overviews and other author-generated means of orienting the reader

Although this dynamic tracking map (or web view) succeeds well in orienting the reader, it works even better when combined with author-generated overview files or other forms of intellectual mapping. A *Context32* overview surrounds one concept (Victorianism, Darwinism) or entity (Joyce, Lawrence) by a series of others (literary relations, cultural context, economic background) to each of which many documents may link. Whereas the Web View presents all documents attached to the entire overview, the overview has a hierarchical organization, but does not reveal the nature or number of documents linked to each block (whose presence is indicated by a link marker). Intermedia provides two ways of obtaining this information—a menu is activated by following links from a particular link marker, and the Web View. Clicking upon a particular link and thus activating it darkens all the links attached to that block in the Web View. Thus, working together, individual documents and the Web View continually inform the reader what information lies one jump away from the current text. This combination of materials generated by authors and Intermedia well exemplifies the way hypertext authors employ what are essentially stylistic and rhetorical devices to supplement system design and work synergistically with it.[7]

These features of the Intermedia system solve the basic problem of orienting readers. In hypermedia documents implemented on systems like HyperCard™ that permit readers to see only a single document at a time, one becomes easily disoriented, and designers have made use of homecards that return one to the first screen and various other devices.[8] These systems, however, are essentially disorienting because they provide no overall view of materials and neither do they give readers enough information about where links will take them. Disorientation, then, arises when readers find themselves within a hypermedia system and feel that they do not know "where" they are and also when they are within a particular document and do not know how to return to a document read earlier or how to find one they expect exists or would like to exist.

The problem of reader orientation is hardly new to information technology. Listeners and readers have always had difficulty orienting themselves within a stream of language. Writing provided a means of recording spoken language, and recording it allowed its audience to re-examine something that would otherwise vanish. Although writing preserves important parts of spoken language, it neither records all of it nor does it, by itself, offer any means of finding something thus recorded. For thousands of years ancient documents appeared in the form of a manuscript scroll or codex that was extraordinarily difficult to use because it provided no means of locating individual passages. Even after the invention of bound volumes of manuscripts, readers did not have the numbered pages, indices, and tables of contents that characterize modern book technology (**Bolter**). The printed book's combination of a fixed text and multiple identical copies for the first time permitted the development of sophisticated devices of information retrieval, and led directly to major changes in the intellectual cosmos of the West.[9]

These examples from older information technology remind us that such technologies consist of more than means of recording language and other data. To be usable, technologies of recording data also require corollary ones that provide readers with access to it. Such corollary technologies for accessing, navigating, and retrieving information range from pagination and indexing to rhetorical devices that permit readers to follow complex reasoning. Some of the devices or techniques of book technology, such as pagination and the linear arrangement of argument, obviously derive from its defining characteristics as an economical, fixed, indefinitely repeatable text that readers can examine in physical isolation from other readers and other texts.

Hypermedia, which changes the nature of text, requires new means of orienting the reader and new means of retrieving information. At least in the earlier stages of hypertext and hypermedia, authors must take pains to ensure that readers perceive some of the differences between this new form of text and earlier ones.

**Rule 4. The author of hypermedia materials must provide devices that stimulate the reader to think and explore.**

**Rule 5. The author of hypermedia must employ stylistic devices that permit readers to navigate materials easily and enjoyably.** These devices serve both as navigational aids for readers and as means of reassuring them.

**Rule 6. Devices of orientation permit readers (a) to determine their present location, (b) to have some idea of that location's relation to other materials, (c) to return to their starting point, and (d) to explore materials not directly linked to those in which they presently find themselves.**

The designers of Intermedia have provided solutions to many of these problems that face hypermedia readers and authors. Although other systems do not have to use precisely these solutions, they should have some analogous means of assisting readers. The Intermedia folder system permits readers to begin their search for information by viewing a hierarchical organization. Although readers use links as their primary means of moving throughout the system, they begin each session by confronting a desktop on which appear subject folders ranging from Anthropology and Biology to Visual Arts. After opening a web that generates a selection of links, readers wanting (to retrieve) information about Dickens's novel *Great Expectations* begin by opening the English folder, after which they open that labeled "Dickens." Once inside the Dickens folder, they chose either the Dickens overview (Figure 1) or the *Great Expectations* overview. At this point, readers use links to navigate through the materials. The folder system, which provides a clear point of departure, also serves as an alternate, if not always efficient, means of browsing. Equally important, the desktop and folder system efficiently serve to orient the reader by making movement back to documents opened previously a quick and easy matter.

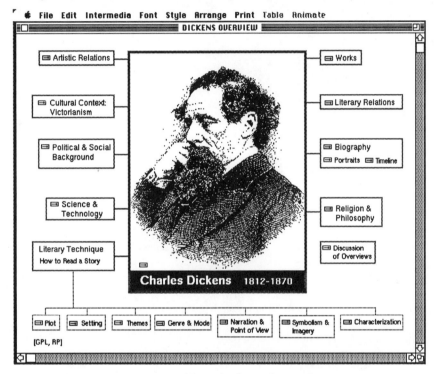

Figure 1: Dickens OV, an overview file in the form of a graphic concept map.

The web view generated by Intermedia (Figure 2) similarly provides readers another efficient means of moving through the materials. By simultaneously offering a record of the documents at which one has looked and a means of returning to them, the web view allows readers to benefit from their most recent experiences and retrieve information they need. Furthermore, by conveying information about the documents linked to the document one has activated, the web view also shows readers their present position in relation to other materials and also furnishes an efficient means of traveling to them. Both the web view and folder system thus permit readers to orient themselves comfortably in a welter of information.

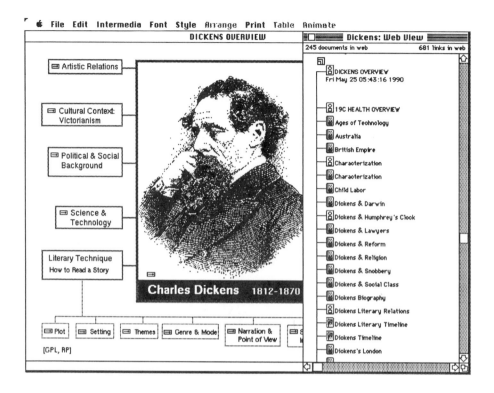

Figure 2: a web view. The web view, which here appears overlaying the right of the Dickens OV, contains an icon for each document linked to this overview. Clicking upon an icon brings readers to the document it represents. In contrast to the hierarchically organized concept map created by an author, the web view is system generated and shows all documents that are linked to the document as a whole (in this case the overview).

Link markers and block descriptors (Figure 3), the labels Intermedia authors attach to linked blocks, emphasize the presence of individual points of departure and multiple points of arrival rather than navigation of the entire system. Link markers and block descriptors, in other words, assist readers in orienting themselves in relation to individual links and groups of links, whereas the web view and folder system assist them in orienting themselves in relation to larger portions of the materials. Although these various Intermedia features remove many sources of reader disorientation, the hypermedia author must take advantage of them. In particular, authors should label folders and descriptions of linked blocks with an eye to clarity and efficiency.

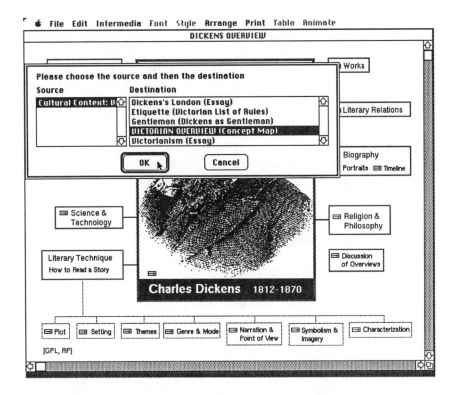

Figure 3: a menu for block descriptors.  This menu, which Intermedia produces when a link marker leads to one or more documents, provides titles of documents and, within parentheses, descriptions of individual linked blocks.

Some hypertext systems like Intermedia provide several means of helping orient the reader; others provide little built-in assistance to solving basic problems of orientation. But whatever system authors use, they  should use overview and gateway documents, which are devices entirely under their own control. Overview documents, which can take many forms, are author-created (as opposed to system-generated) documents that serve as directories to aid in navigating the materials. Overviews assist readers to gain convenient access to all the materials in many documents or to a broad topic that cuts across several disciplines, such as Victorianism, a term that provides a nexus for  investigating the arts and literature, religion and philosophy, political, military, and social history, and the history of science and technology.

Furthermore, one should consider using some form of overview when too many links attach to a single block for the reader to evaluate them conveniently. Unlike some other hypermedia systems that permit only one link per block or screen, Intermedia permits an indefinite number of links to attach to each link marker. Overusing this feature, which supports the capacity of hypermedia to model complex relationships, can create too many linked documents. A variety of factors makes defining "too many" difficult to do. In some unusual cases more than 100 documents can conveniently link to a single block and be conveniently accessed from a single link marker. The *In Memoriam* overview has the text "individual sections" to which all 133 sections of the poem link, and since the menu that appears when readers follow the link simply lists the sections in numerical order, this large number of linked documents creates no problems. Similarly, another part of this same document links to several dozen uses of several words or phrases found throughout the poem. Because, like the linking of individual sections, this linking of terms takes the form of a list, a menu containing many items works well.

Most of the time, however, authors link different kinds of documents on different subjects, and long lists here confuse. When planning to link more than five or six documents on the same subject, particularly when these appear in a list with documents on different subjects, one should consider organizing materials in one subject by an overview and linking that overview instead. For example, rather than link several dozen documents about a range of subjects to a label "Social and Political History" in the Victorian overview, one does better to organize them with secondary overviews for public health, the British Empire, and political history and then link these overviews. Since a body of hypermedia materials has the capacity to grow and change, adding both links and documents, one can expect that the nature and number of such secondary overviews will change as the other materials do.

Here are six ways of presenting secondary overviews:

i. Graphic concept map. One of the most important forms is the graphic concept map (Dickens OV; Figure 1).[10] This kind of graphic concept map, which informs the reader what information is available about a particular topic, contains links to that information. These graphic representations of information organize a body of complex ideas so that readers can better comprehend them.[11] At the same time, the overview suggests that all these various ideas relate to some central phenomenon or impinge upon it. This center may take the form of an author (Tennyson, Darwin), chronological or period term (Eighteenth Century, Victorian), idea or movement (Realism, Feminism), or other concept (Biblical Typology, Religion in England). The implied and often reinforced message of such arrangements is simply that any idea that the reader makes the center of his or her investigations exists situated within a field of other phenomena, which may or may not relate to it causally. Such graphic presentation of materials depicts the informing idea or hidden agenda of hypermedia materials, namely, that one proceeds in understanding any particular phenomenon by relating it to other contexts.

ii. Flow chart suggesting vector forces. Another kind of graphic concept overview, the flow chart suggesting vector forces, uses arrows to show lines of influence or causal connection. "Dickens's Literary Relations" (Figure 4), for example, uses arrows to show his relation to authors who influenced him, those he influenced, and those with whom he existed in terms of mutual influence. This form of graphic overview proves particularly useful when presenting clear historical relationships.

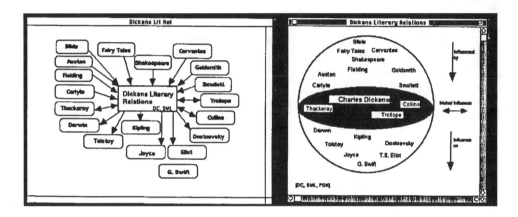

Figure 4: flow chart suggesting Vector forces: two versions of "Dicken's Literary Relations."

iii. Timeline. The "Nuclear Arms Timeline" (Figure 5) shows another kind of graphic overview document. At Brown we have created this document using InterVal, the Intermedia timeline editor, but one can easily create similar documents using any text editor. Timelines are a means of clearly organizing materials or even entire courses that have a strong chronological orientation. Any timeline with links in fact serves as an overview for the materials it joins. Although timelines provide a means of organization particularly convenient to authors, remember that they may simplify complex relationships and have little to compel the interest of a reader unacquainted with their subject.

iv. Natural object. Images of natural objects, like the photograph of the moon (Figure 6), or maps provide a kind of naturally occurring concept map that authors can easily apply. Attaching links to labels in technical diagrams similarly provides an obvious way of enriching conventional information technology.

v. Outline. As "Race and Class OV" (Figure 7), a text document, shows, outlines add a graphic component to text by breaking up the flow that characterizes discursive prose. By abandoning the table-of-contents or list mode that character-

---

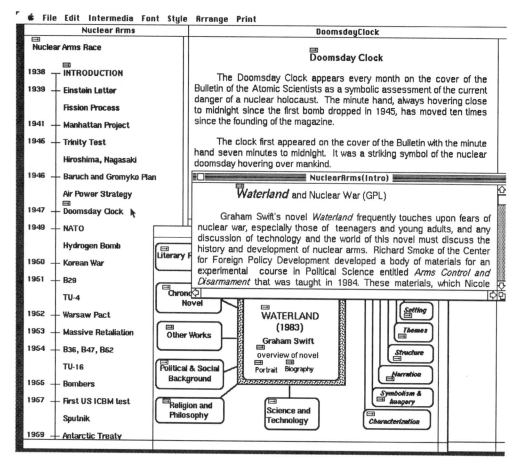

Figure 5: timeline and gateway file that leads to it from the literature materials. The timeline, which appears on the left, serves as the overview for these chronologically arranged materials. A brief essay on the Doomsday Clock is to the right of the timeline, and immediately below appears "*Waterland* and Nuclear Disarmament," the gateway document that serves as a bridge between materials on a contemporary British novel and the timeline.

izes page-bound, printed text, one liberates hypermedia from the restrictions of print and enables it to do what it does best: present networks of relationships while also enabling the reader easily to traverse those relationships, establishing connections between paired sets of data among larger groupings of material. If hypermedia is characterized by connectivity, to realize its potential one must employ devices that emphasize that quality. Lists, tables of contents, and indices, though still of use, do not work in this manner.

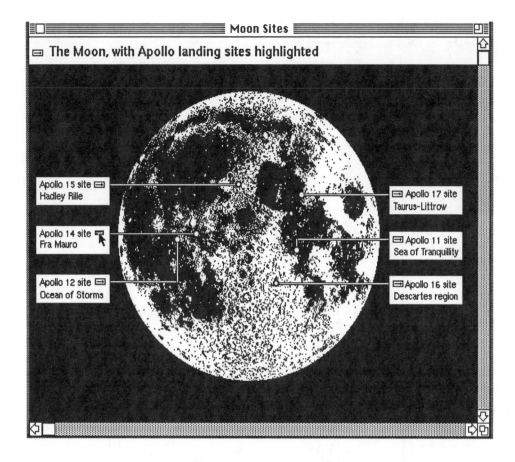

Figure 6: diagram of a natural object used as an overview: "Moon Sites [The Moon, with Apollo landing sites highlighted]."

vi. Text as its own overview.  When converting text documents originally created for book technology to presentation on hypermedia, one may occasionally use the document itself as its own overview. As we have already observed, any single document in a hypermedia system can serve as a directory since, once opened, it provides the immediate center and reference point for the reader's next act of exploration. The combination of link markers within the document and a web view that shows readers a general picture of where those links connect make the text serve as a directory. The author of educational materials, particularly those involving literary texts or those which place primary emphasis on the details of a text,  may therefore wish to take advantage of this quality of hypermedia. Section 7 of *In Memoriam* (Figure 8) exemplifies a brief text document that functions as its own overview. Other examples include the full text of Kipling's short story "Mary Postgate" as well as shorter works.

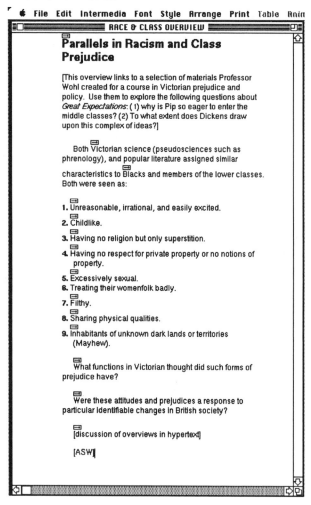

Figure 7: overviews in the form of an outline: "Class and Race OV."

Hypermedia is reader oriented because readers continually recenter and reorganize the materials they encounter according to their own interests. In creating hypermedia documents, therefore, authors should take advantage of multiple linking to offer directories in various forms for the same general materials.

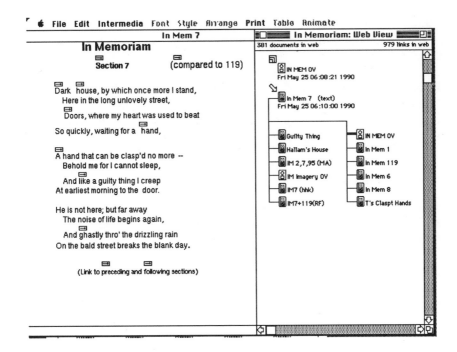

Figure 8: text document as its own overviews: "*In Memoriam*, Section 7." The web view, which appears at the right, shows the documents linked to this section of Tennson's poem. The thick line distinguishing "IN MEM OV," the abbreviated title of "*In Memoriam* OV," shows that the reader traveled to the present document by following a link from there.

**Rule 7. Authors should consider employing several overviews to organize the same body of material and to assist readers to gain easy access to it.**

Readers should, for example, have overviews for both an author and a work by that author.

Closely related to overviews and directories are those documents that serve as gateways between courses or bodies of materials in separate disciplines. One such gateway document joins the materials that support several English courses and those that support *Nuclear Arms and Arms Control* offered by Richard Smoke of Brown University's Center for Foreign Policy Development. The literary materials discuss Victorian technology, canals, and railroads but contain no parallel documents about nuclear technology and the anti-nuclear movement, two subjects that  play a significant part in Graham Swift's *Waterland* (1983), a novel read in one of  the literature courses. Therefore, a brief document that announces the connections between *Waterland* and the subject of nuclear disarmament links to the science and technology section in the *Waterland* OV and also to the timeline that the nuclear-arms-course materials employ as a directory (Figure 5). This brief document enables students in the introductory survey of English literature to explore the materials created for a course in another discipline. Similarly, students from that other discipline can now encounter materials showing the effects on contemporary fiction of the concerns covered in their political science course.

### The rhetoric of departure

Readers of hypermedia need some indication of where they can find links and then, after they have found these indications, where those links will lead them and why they are led there. Intermedia provides a link marker in the form of a small horizontal rectangle within which appears an arrow. Although Intermedia provides readers with this clear means of ascertaining the presence of links, they still require additional information about where following the links will lead. The system provides two means of informing the reader, one general and the other specific. The web view, with which the reader can navigate through the system of linked documents, shows all documents connected to the active document—that which the reader has activated either by opening it or by clicking upon it if it was previously opened. The web view, however, does not indicate to which link a document connects. The second, more specific information furnished by Intermedia takes the form of block descriptors that appear in menus when the reader follows a link marker that leads to two or more documents.

As useful as is system-provided information, authors of graphic and textual documents still have to assist readers by following several rules.

**Rule 8. Never place link markers independent of accompanying text or image.**

In text documents Intermedia automatically places link markers adjacent to text since it only allows one to create links after highlighting a letter, word, or phrase. But Intermedia does permit placement of links anywhere in graphic documents, and they can appear to float free. Similarly HyperCard permits placing buttons independent of text or graphics, and such free floating buttons and linker markers confuse and disorient.

**Rule 9. When creating a link or positioning a link marker that indicates the presence of a link, remember that all links are bidirectional.**

Some systems, like HyperCard, only permit uni-directional linking, which removes much of the power and freedom of hypermedia. The author should manually create bidirectional links. When creating such links that permit the reader to travel in both directions, the author should realize that readers may approach them with more than one purpose in mind. Therefore,

**Rule 10. Avoid linking to words or phrases that only provide appropriate points of arrival but give the reader no suggestion of where the link might lead on departure.**

When two or more documents link to a particular marker, such emphasis on bidirectionality of the link is not so crucial since the system will indicate these multiple destinations. In Intermedia one solution to the need for providing information lies in appending multiple documents to a single marker, but such a procedure still requires the reader to activate the link marker before being able to obtain information and is hence not entirely satisfactory. A better approach requires finding some way to append information to the link marker.

**Rule 11. Place the link marker in close proximity to a text that indicates the probable nature of the link destination.**

Both text and graphic documents require following this last rule. Looking at the Dickens OV (Figure 1), a graphic overview document that surrounds the poet with a range of subjects necessary to understand his works, one sees that each of the separate boxes contains texts that specify in varying degrees what the reader can expect to find on arrival at the link destination. The boxes labeled "Biography" and "[biographical] Timeline" clearly indicate their destinations. That labeled "Literary Relations" leads to another graphic directory file, which takes a standard form, and after exploring the materials on a few authors or subjects, readers learn to expect this kind of graphic representation of literary relationships. Since more variety exists in relation to other materials organized by the overview, readers do not know in advance exactly what to expect from each label.

Authors need to use specifying texts in text documents as well. When an essay on a modern author contains a link marker near "Freudianism," "World War I," or some aspect of literary technique, such as "Theme" or "Imagery," readers can expect to encounter an essay on these subjects or a diagrammatic analysis of them. The point is that readers need a general idea of what to expect before they set out on their explorations. Thus,

**Rule 12. When creating documents, assist readers by phrasing statements or posing questions that provide obvious occasions for following links.**

**Rule 13. When possible provide specific information about a link destination by directly drawing attention to it.**

The most precise use of text to specify a link destination takes the form of specific directions that invite readers to make their way there. For example, the document entitled "Point of View in 'The Prussian Officer'" begins, "Point of View [link to definition]," and in the document entitled "Neoclassical Couplet" the following sentence appears next to a sample of Pope's satire on women: "Follow to see a woman's view;" which leads to Lady Mary Wortley Montague's couplets. This device, which must be used sparingly, is particularly useful when indicating bibliographical information, definitions of key terms, and the presence of opposing points of view.

### The rhetoric of arrival (graphic documents)

Conventional titles do not adequately direct the reader how to relate a graphic image to other materials. In contrast, "Victorian Design: Medieval Revival" (Figure 9), an illustration of an item exhibited at the 1851 Crystal Palace exhibition, the first world's fair, exemplifies the kind of encoding or rhetoric required to enable the user to make sense of graphic documents—that is, to discern one or more conceptual relationships among them and the documents to which they link. The appended text reads: "This curiosity from the Crystal Palace exhibition of 1851 is a not a suit of armor but a stove built in the shape of one. What do such bizarre glances back at the past tell us about the Victorian age, which invented the idea of Progress as we know it? In the poems you have read can you find any examples of thus clothing modern purposes in ancient forms?" Readers who highlight the link marker and issue a command to follow receive a menu of various Victorian literary works, including Tennyson's "Morte d'Arthur," a poem set in medieval England, and "Tithonus," one set in the Greece of ancient myth. Experience with these materials has taught that to be educationally effective they must follow these general principles of hypermedia rhetoric:

> **Rule 14. Linked graphic materials must appear with appended texts that enable the user to establish a relation between a point of departure and that of arrival.** The solution we have adopted at IRIS appears in Figure 9, whose text (a) provided factual information, (b) encourages readers to relate that information to a problem on which they are working, and (c) contains links that allow them to pursue various investigations. From this rule follow two more:

---

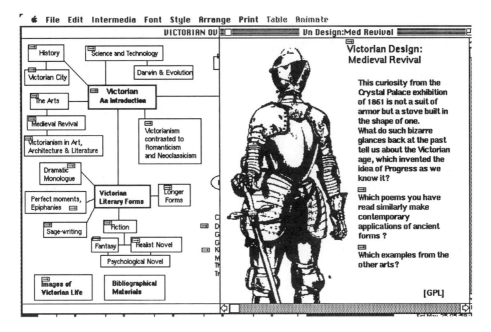

Figure 9: use of text to orient the reader upon arrival in a graphics file: "Victorian Design: Medieval Revival." Note the use of queries to direct the reader to additional links.

> **Rule 15.** The entire text accompanying visual material and not just the opening sentence or two serves as an introduction. And
>
> **Rule 16.** The text accompanying an image does not have to specify all relevant information the author wishes the reader to have; rather, emphasizing that a relationship exists at all may be enough. From which follows:
>
> **Rule 17.** Texts serve not only to provide information but also to reassure the reader that the link embodies a significant relationship and to provide some hint, however, incomplete, of how that relationship can be formulated by the reader.

The visual information, which provides interesting data of an unexpected sort, also enforces the principle that relevance is in the mind of the beholder and that the investigator's function in whatever field is to inquire what connections might exist among various kinds of data and how their relative value might be determined.

## The rhetoric of arrival (text documents)

In general, text documents create far fewer problems for readers who have entered them by links than do graphic ones. The principles that apply to providing information in largely visual documents also apply to text documents, but few problems occur when linking text to text, because two system features, link markers and block extents, help direct the reader. For example, when one follows a link from Benjamin Disraeli's biography to an essay entitled "British Empire," one enters that essay at the point where the destination of the link appears. The link marker, which is activated when one arrives in a new document, appears darkened and therefore attracts the reader's attention. The system also surrounds the entire block of linked text with a dotted line. Most such links are self-explanatory because the linked blocks and document titles together contain two sets of similar or identical terms. In this case the name "Disraeli" appears in the title of the first document and "British Empire" within the linked block, and "Disraeli" appears in the linked block of the second document and "British Empire" in the title.

## Document length in hypermedia

What rules of style or document preparation follow from the fact that hypermedia is made up of blocks of text joined by links? Whereas print technology emphasizes the capacity of language to form a linear stream of text that moves unrelentingly forward, hypermedia encourages branching and creating multiple routes to the same point. Each information medium has its obvious strengths, but those of hypermedia depend upon its being composed of individual segments that can join to other segments in multiple ways and by multiple routes. Hypermedia naturally leads to conceiving documents in terms of separate brief reading units. Whereas organizing one's data and interpretation for presentation in a print medium necessarily leads to fitting them into a linear arrangement, hypermedia, which permits linear linking, nonetheless encourages parallel, rather than linear, arguments. Such structures necessarily require a more active reader. Since a major source of all these characteristics of hypermedia derive from these linked reading units, one has to create hypermedia with that fact in mind. Therefore,

> **Rule 18. When creating documents for hypermedia, conceive the text units as brief passages in order to take maximum advantage of the linking capacities of hypermedia.**

Whatever its ultimate effect on scholarly and creative writing, hypermedia today frequently contains text transferred from printed books. Such materials combine the two technologies of writing by attaching linked documents, which may contain images, to a fixed stream of text. Anyone preparing such materials confronts the problem of how best to preserve the integrity of the older text, which may be a literary, philosophical, or other work whose overall structure plays an important role in its effect. The basic question when adapting text created for print technology to hypermedia is: can one divide the original into reading units shorter than those in which it appeared in a book, or does such presentation violate its integrity? Some literary works, such as sonnet sequences or Pascal's *Pensées*, seem easily adapted to hypermedia since they originally have the form of brief sections, but other works do not seem adaptable without violence to the original.

> **Rule 19. When adapting for hypermedia presentation documents created according to book technology, do not violate the original organization. However, when the text naturally divides into sections, these provide the basis of text blocks. The hypermedia version must contain linkages between previous and following sections to retain a sense of the original organization.**

## Rules for dynamic data in hypermedia

The preceding discussion has focused upon ways of linking together documents composed of words, images, diagrams, and combinations of these forms of data, all of which are essentially static. Kinetic or dynamic information, which includes animation and sound (animal cries, human speech, or music), adds an element of linearity to hypermedia. This presents no fundamental difficulty, or even novelty, since individual blocks of text, particularly those with few links, offer a linear reading path. Nonetheless, data like speech or visual movement are different in that they involve a process. When one follows a link from a text discussing, say, mitosis to digitized animation of a cell dividing, one cues the beginning of a sequential action. Such dynamic data can place the reader in a relatively passive role and turn hypermedia into a broadcast, rather than an interactive, medium. Systems designers and hypermedia authors therefore have to empower readers in at least two ways. First, they must permit readers to stop the process and exit the environment easily. Second, they must indicate that particular links lead to dynamic data. One may use labels or icons for this purpose, and one may also connect the link-marker to an additional document, such as a menu or command box, that informs users precisely the kind of process-information they can activate.[12]

## Conclusion

Information technology that employs electronically linked blocks of words and images requires rhetorical and stylistic rules different from those for one employing physically isolated pages set in a fixed sequence. Within text blocks, the same transitional and organizing devices apply to hypermedia and book text. When blocks of text link electronically to one another, however, a new range of problems and possibilities appear. As our notions of the nature of text change, so must our means of composing it.

---

### Notes

1. See **Kahn** in this volume and Nicole Yankelovich, Norman Meyrowitz, and Stephen Drucker, "Intermedia: The Concept and the Construction of a Seamless Information Environment," *IEEE Computer* 21 (1988): 81-96.

2. Unfortunately, no analogy maps reality with complete accuracy. Navigation, the art of controlling the course of a plane or ship, presupposes a spatial world, but one does not entirely experience hypertext as a spatial world. In navigation one must determine one's spatial position in relation to landmarks or astral locations and then decide upon a means of moving toward one's goal, which lies out of sight at some spatial distance. Because it takes time to move across the separating distance, one also experiences that distance as time: one's ship lies so many nautical miles and therefore so many days and hours from one's goal. The reader, however, does not experience hypertext in this way. The reader of *Paradise Lost*, for example, experiences as equally close the linked parts of Homer and Vergil to which the poem's opening section allude and linked lines on the next page or in the next book. Because hypertext linking takes relatively the same amount of time to traverse, all linked texts are experienced as lying at the same "distance" from the point of departure. Thus, whereas navigation presupposes that one finds oneself at the center of a spatial world in which desired items lie at varying distances from one's own location, hypertext presupposes an experiential world in which the goal is always potentially but one jump or link away.

3. Marshall McLuhan, *The Gutenberg Galaxy: The Making of Typographic Man* (Toronto: University of Toronto Press, 1962).

4. E. Jeffrey Conklin, "Hypertext: An Introduction and Survey," *IEEE Computer* 20:9 (1987), 38, mentions "Getting 'lost in space,'" but I believe he used the phrase I quote in the text during sessions at Hypertext '87.

---

5. Conklin, "Hypertext: An Introduction and Survey," 39, includes an illustration of the global tracking map to exemplify a "tangled web of links."

6. Kenneth Utting and Nicole Yankelovich, "Context and Orientation in Hypermedia Networks," *ACM Transactions on Information Systems* 7 (1989): 58-84, which surveys various attempted solutions to the problems of hypertext orientation, provides illustrations of the three stages of the Intermedia dynamic hypergraph.

7. Intermedia 4.0, which saw completion in time for Hypertext '89 in November 1989, includes full-text searching, a feature that promises to change readers' habits of working with materials on Intermedia. Since it has not yet been used in the Intermedia classroom at Brown, I concentrate above on features in use for several iterations of my survey course.

8. For one solution in a HyperCard structure see **Delany and Gilbert** in this volume.

9. Elizabeth L. Eisenstein, *The Printing Press as an Agent of Change: Communications and Cultural Transformations in Early-Modern Europe*, 2 vols. (Cambridge: Cambridge University Press, 1979).

10. Paul Kahn, Julie Launhardt, Krzystof Lenk, and Ronnie Peters, "Design of Hypermedia Publications: Issues and Solutions," *Electronic Publishing '90*, forthcoming, contains a statement of design principles by the team that produced many of the overview and other documents that illustrate this discussion.

11. Alexander J. Romiszowski, "The Hypertext/Hypermedia Solution—But What Exactly Is the Problem?" in *Designing Hypertext/Hypermedia for Learning*, ed. David H. Jonassen and Heinz Mandl (Heildelberg: Springer-Verlag, 1990), contains a bibliography listing sources on information mapping. Paul Kahn, Julie Launhardt, Krzysztof Lenk, and Ronnie Peters, "Design Issues of Hypermedia Publications: Issues and Solutions," *Electronic Publishing '90*, applies the principles of graphic design to overviews and other forms of concept maps.

12. Such documents in the form of a control panel, which permits the reader to manipulate the process to the extent of replaying all or part of a sequence, make the reader more active. See also Murugappan Palaniappan, Nicole Yankelovich, and Mark Sawtelle, "Linking Active Anchors: A Stage in the Evolution of Hypermedia," *IRIS Technical Report 89-5* (Providence, R. I.: Institute for Research in Information and Scholarship, 1989).

# Topographic Writing: Hypertext and the Electronic Writing Space[1]

Jay David Bolter
Department of Classics, University of North Carolina, Chapel Hill

Ted Nelson, who coined the term, has defined "hypertext" as "non-sequential writing with reader-controlled links."[2] Good as this succinct definition is, it omits an aspect of hypertext that I wish to emphasize: hypertext as a method for exploring the visual and conceptual writing space presented to us by computer technology. Writing is always spatial, and each technology in the history of writing (e.g. the clay tablet, the papyrus roll, the codex, the printed book) has presented writers and readers with a different space to exploit. The computer is our newest technology of writing, and we are still learning how to use its space. Different computer programs have given us different geometries with which to structure this new writing space. We began with word processing, which is almost strictly linear, and then moved to outline processing, which allows us to create two-dimensional hierarchies of text. Now we are facing the ultimate freedom offered by the hypertextual network. Hypertext forces us to redefine text both as a structure of visible elements on the screen and as a structure of signs in the minds of writers and their readers. The *computer as hypertext* invites us to write with signs that have both an intrinsic and extrinsic signficance. That is, the signs have a meaning that may be explained in words, but they also have meaning as elements in a larger structure of verbal and visual gestures. Both words and structures are visible and manipulable in the electronic space.

## Writing places

With or without the computer, whenever we write, we write topically. We conceive of our text as a set of verbal gestures, large and small. To write is to do things with topics—to add, delete, and arrange them. The computer changes the nature of writing simply by giving visual expression to our acts of conceiving and manipulating topics. A writer working with a word processor spends much of the time entering words letter by letter, just as he or she does at a typewriter. Revising is a different matter. With most word processors, writers can delete or replace an entire word; they can highlight phrases, sentences, or paragraphs. They can erase a sentence with a single keystroke; they can select a paragraph, cut it from its current location, and insert it elsewhere, even into another document. In using these facilities, the writer is thinking and writing in terms of verbal units or topics, whose meaning transcends their constituent words. The Greek word *topos* meant literally a place, and ancient rhetoric used the word to refer to commonplaces, conventional units or methods of thought. In the Renaissance, topics became headings that could be used to organize any field of knowledge, and these headings were often set out in elaborate diagrams.[3] Our English word *topic* is appropriate for the computer because its etymology suggests the spatial character of electronic writing: topics exist in a writing space that is not only a visual surface but also a data structure in the computer. The programmers who designed word processors recognized the importance of topical writing, when they gave us operations for adding or deleting sentences and paragraphs as units. They did not, however, take the further step of allowing a writer to associate a name or a visual symbol with such topical units. This important step lends the unit a conceptual identity. The unit symbol becomes an abiding element in the writer's thinking and expression, because its constituent words or phrases can be put out of sight.

On a printed or typed page, we indent and separate paragraphs to indicate the topical structure. Within each paragraph, however, we have only punctuation, occurring in the stream of words, to mark finer structure. A better representation of topical writing is the conventional outline, in which major topics are designated by Roman numerals, subtopics by capital letters, sub-subtopics by Arabic numerals, and so on. Each point of an outline serves to organize and situate the topics subordinate to it, and the outline as a whole is a static representation, a snapshot, of the textual organization. The conventions of outlining turn the writing surface into a tiered space in which the numbering and indentation of lines represent the hierarchy of the author's ideas. A paragraphed text is the flattening or linearization of an outline.

The word processor, which imitates the layout of the typed page, also flattens the text. It offers the writer little help in conceiving the evolving structure of the text. Although the word processor allows the writer to define a verbal unit in order to move or delete it, the definition lasts only until the operation is complete. Whereas the word processor offers the writer only temporary access to his or her structure, another class of programs called *outline processors* makes structure a permanent feature of the text. An outline processor sets the traditional written outline in motion. A writer can add points to an electronic outline in any order while the computer continually renumbers to reflect additions or deletions. The writer can promote minor points to major ones, and the computer will again renumber. The writer can collapse the outline in order to see only those points above a certain level, an action that gives an overview of the evolving text. In short the writer can think globally about the text: one can treat topics as unitary symbols and write with those symbols, just as in a word processor one writes with words.

Writing in topics is not a replacement for writing with words; the writer must eventually attend to the details of his or her prose. The outline processor contains within it a conventional word processor, so that the writer can attach text to each of the points in the outline. But in using an outline processor, writers are not aware of a rigid distinction between outlining and prose writing: they move easily back and forth between structure and prose. What is new is that the points of the outline become functional elements in the text, because when the points move the words move with them. In this way the computer makes visible and almost palpable what writers have always known: that the identifying and arranging of topics is itself an act of writing. Outline processing is writing at a different granularity, a replication on a higher level of the conventional act of writing by choosing and arranging words. The symbols of this higher writing are simply longer and more complicated "words," verbal gestures that may be whole sentences or paragraphs.

In an outline processor, then, the prose remains, but it is encased in a formally operative structure. With a pen or typewriter, writing meant literally to form letters on a page, figuratively to create verbal structures. In an electronic writing system, the figurative process becomes a literal act. By defining topical symbols, the writer can, like the programmer or the mathematician, abstract himself or herself temporarily from the details of the prose, and the value of this abstraction lies in seeing more clearly the structural skeleton of the text. It is not possible or desirable that the prose writer should become a mathematician or that human language should be reduced to a system of logical symbols. The result of giving language wholeheartedly over to formalism would simply be the impoverishment of language. On the other hand, the electronic medium can permit us to play creatively with formal structures in our writing without abandoning the richness of natural language.

## Electronic trees

It is no accident that the computer can serve as an outline processor. The machine is designed to create and track such formal structures, which are important for all its various uses. The computer's memory and central processing unit are intricate hierarchies of electronic components. Layers of software in turn transform the machine's physical space of electronic circuits into a space of symbolic information, and it is in this space that a new kind of writing can be located. Like the space of the modern physicist, the space of the computer is shaped by the objects that occupy it.

The computer programmer forms his or her space by filling it with symbolic elements and then by connecting these elements as the program requires. Any symbol in the space can refer to another symbol by using its numerical address. Pointers hold together the structure of computer programs, and programming itself may be defined as the art of building symbolic structures in the space that the computer provides—a definition that makes programming a species of writing.

One such programming structure, which represents hierarchy, is called a *tree*. Trees (and their relatives such as *lists, stacks,* and *networks)* are ubiquitous in programs that must record and track large bodies of information or of information subject to frequent change. Tree diagrams, in which elements are connected by branches as in a genealogical tree, have a long history in writing as well. They date back at least to the early Middle Ages and are not uncommon in medieval and Renaissance books, where they were used for the spatial arrangement of topics.[4] The traditional outline is a strict hierarchy that can just as easily be represented by a tree diagram.

Both the tree and the outline give us a better reading of structure than does ordinary paragraphing, because they mold the visual space of the text in a way that reflects its structure. A printed page of paragraphs is by comparison a flat and uninteresting space, as is the window of a word processor. A writer can use a word processor to type an outline, and, if the word processor permits graphics, the writer can insert a tree diagram into the text. But the outline or diagram will then be stored as a picture, a sequence of bits to be shown on the screen; the picture will not be treated as a data stucture and will not inform the space in which the writer is working. The writer will not be able to change the structure by manipulating the outline, as he or she can in an outline processor, and that ability is necessary for true electronic writing. In using an outline processor, the writer can intervene at any level of the evolving structure. And if the writer gives the reader a diskette rather than a printed version, then the reader too gains immediate access to that structure. All this is possible, because the writing space itself has become a tree, a hierarchy of topical elements.

The electronic writing space is extremely malleable. It can be fashioned into one tree or into a forest of hierarchical trees. In any printed or written text, one hierarchical order always precludes others. The static medium of print demands that the writer settle on one order of topics, although the writer may find that the topics could be arranged equally well in, say, three orders corresponding to three electronic outlines. Unlike the space of the printed book, the computer's writing space can represent any relationships that can be defined as the interplay of pointers and elements. Multiple relationships pose no special problem. A writer could therefore maintain three outlines, each of which deployed the same topics in a different order. These outlines may all reside in the computer's memory at the same time, each activated at the writer's request. The writer may choose to examine topics from any of the three vantage points and then switch to another; he or she may alter one outline while leaving the others intact; he or she may alter any of the outlines themselves without revising the text in any one of the topics. The structure of an electronic text is in this sense abstracted from its verbal expression.

This multiplicity and abstraction already render the electronic writing space more flexible than its predecessors. And if all writing were only hierarchical, then the outline processor itself would be revolutionary in its freeing of writing from the frozen structure of the printed page. But there is one further step to be taken in liberating the text.

## Hypertext

The goal of conventional writing is to create a perfect hierarchy, but it is not always easy to maintain the discipline of such a structure. All writers have had the experience of being overwhelmed with ideas as they write. The act of writing itself releases a flood of thoughts—one idea suggesting another and then another, as the writer struggles to get them down in some form before they slip from his conscious grasp. "I only wish I could write with both hands," noted Saint Teresa, "so as not to forget one thing while I am saying another."[5] Romantics like Carlyle founded their psychology of literature upon this experience. The experience is not limited to saints and sages: many, perhaps most, writers begin their work with a jumble of verbal ideas and only a vague sense of how these ideas will fit together. The writer may start by laying out topics in an arrangement less formal than an outline: he or she may organize by association rather than strict subordination. Teachers of writing often encourage their students to begin by sketching out topics and connecting them through lines of association, and they call this activity "prewriting." What students create in prewriting is a network of elements—exactly what computer programmers mean by the data structure they call a network. The computer can maintain such a network of topics, which reflects the writer's progress as he or she trims the network by removing connections and establishing subordination until there is a strict hierarchy. In the world of print, at least in nonfiction, associative writing is considered only a preliminary stage.

Association is not really prior to writing, as the term "prewriting" suggests. Association is always present in any text: one word echoes another; one sentence or paragraph recalls others earlier in the text and looks forward to still others. A writer cannot help but write associatively: even if he or she begins with an outline and remains faithful to it, the result is always a network of verbal elements. The hierarchy (in the form of paragraphs, sections, and chapters) is an attempt to impose order on verbal ideas that are always prone to subvert that order. The associative relationships define alternative organizations that lie beneath the order of pages and chapters that a printed text presents to the world. These alternatives constitute subversive texts-behind-the-text.

Previous technologies of writing, which could not easily accomodate such alternatives, tended to ignore them. The ancient papyrus roll was strongly linear in its presentation of text. The codex, especially in the later Middle Ages, and then the printed book have made better efforts to accommodate association as well as hierarchy. In a modern book the table of contents (listing chapters and sometimes sections) defines the hierarchy, while the indices record associative lines of thought that permeate the text. An index permits the reader to locate passages that share the same word, phrase, or subject and so associates passages that may be widely separated in the pagination of the book. In one sense the index defines other books that could be constructed from the materials at hand, other themes that the author could have formed into an analytical narrative, and so invites the reader to read the book in alternative ways. An index transforms a book from a tree into a network, offering multiplicity in place of a single order of paragraphs and pages.

There need not be any privileged element in a network, as there always is in a tree, no single topic that dominates all others. Instead of strict subordination, we have paths that weave their way through the textual space. A full-fledged hypertext can only be represented by the network, as in Figure. 1. If all texts are ultimately networks of verbal elements, the computer is the first medium that can record and present these networks to writers and readers. Just as the outline processor treats text as a hierarchy, other computer programs can fashion the text into a general network or hypertext.

**Writing Space**

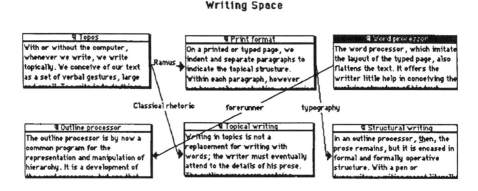

Figure 1: a hypertext is a network of textual elements and connections.

A hypertext consists of topics and their connections, where again the topics may be paragraphs, sentences, individual words, or indeed digitized graphics. A hypertext is like a printed book that the author has attacked with a pair of scissors and cut into convenient verbal sizes. Electronic hypertext does not simply dissolve into a disordered bundle of slips, as the printed book must, for the author also defines a scheme of electronic connections to indicate relationships among the slips. In fashioning a hypertext, a writer might begin with a passage of continuous prose and then add notes or glosses on important words in the passage. The glosses themselves could contain glosses, leading the reader to further texts. A hypertextual network can extend indefinitely, as a printed text cannot.

A computer hypertext might serve, for example, to collect scholars' notes on complex texts such as Joyce's *Ulysses* and *Finnegans Wake*. The computer can record and update the collective work of many scholars who continue today adding to, refining, and revising the glosses; it can connect notes to other notes as appropriate. Such exegesis, currently recorded in books and journals, would be both easier to use and more appropriate as a hypertext, because *Ulysses* and particularly *Finnegans Wake* are themselves hypertexts that have been flattened out to fit on the printed page. But an author does not have to be as experimental as Joyce to profit from hypertext. A historian might choose to write an essay in which each paragraph or section is a topic in a hypertextual network. The connections would indicate possible orders in which topics could be assembled and read, and each order of reading might produce a different literary and analytic result. A mathematician might choose to write a hypertextbook that could tailor itself to different students with differing degrees of mathematical proficiency. Hypertext can serve for all sorts of more popular materials as well: directories, catalogues, how-to manuals—wherever the reader wishes to move through the text in a variety of orders. In fact thousands of such hypertexts are already available, written for display by HyperCard, a program for the Apple Macintosh computer.

In general, the connections of a hypertext are organized into paths that make operational sense to author and reader. Each topic may participate in several paths, and its significance will depend upon which paths the reader has traveled in order to arrive at that topic. In print, only a few paths can be suggested or followed. In an electronic version the texture of the text becomes thicker, and its paths can serve many functions. Paths can, as in a tree structure, indicate subordination. They can also remind the writer of relationships among topics that had to be sacrificed for the sake of an eventual hierarchy. They can express cyclic relationships among topics that can never be hierarchical. They can categorize topics for later revision: the writer might wish to join two paths together or intersect two paths and preserve only those elements common to both. In the electronic medium, hierarchical and associative thinking may coexist in the structure of a text, since the computer can take care of the mechanics of maintaining and presenting both networks and trees. In the medium of print, the writer may use an index to show alternatives, but these alternatives must always contend with the fixed order of the pages of the book. The canonical order is defined by the book's pagination, and all other suggested orders remain subordinate. A hypertext has no canonical order. Every path defines an equally convincing and appropriate reading, and in that simple fact the reader's relationship to the text changes radically. A text as a network has no univocal sense; it is a multiplicity without the imposition of a principle of domination.

In place of hierarchy, we have a writing that is not only topical: we might also call it "topographic." The word "topography" originally meant a written description of a place, such as an ancient geographer might give. Only later did the word come to refer to mapping or charting—that is, to a visual and mathematical rather than verbal description. Electronic writing is both a visual and verbal description. It is not the writing of a place, but rather a writing *with* places, with spatially realized topics. Topographic writing challenges the idea that writing should be merely the servant of spoken language. The writer and reader can create and examine signs and structures on the computer screen that have no easy equivalent in speech. The point is obvious when the text is a collection of images stored on a video disk, but it is equally true for a purely verbal text that has been fashioned as a tree or a network of topics and connections.

Topographic writing as a mode is not even limited to the computer medium. It is possible to write topographically for print or even in manuscript. Whenever we divide our text into unitary topics and organize those units into a connected structure and whenever we conceive of this textual structure spatially as well as verbally, we are writing topographically. As we shall see in a later chapter, many literary artists in the twentieth century have adopted this mode of writing. Although the computer is not necessary for topographic writing, it is only in the computer that the mode becomes a natural, and therefore also a conventional, way to write.

### Hypermedia

Some word processors already permit the writer to insert diagrams and pictures directly into his text. But in word processing the graphic image is not really part of the text; it is merely allowed to coexist with the verbal text. We have seen in Fig. 1 above that the computer has the capacity to integrate word and image more subtly, to make text itself graphic by representing its structure graphically to the writer and the reader. The computer can even dissolve the distinction between the standard-ized letter forms and symbols of the writer's own making. True electronic writing is not limited to verbal text: the writeable elements may be words, images, sounds, or even actions that the computer is directed to perform. The writer could use his or her network to organize pictures on videodisk or music and voices on an audio playback device. Instead of moving from paragraph to paragraph in a verbal text, the reader might be shown videotaped scenes of a play in a variety of orders.[6] The reader might move through an aural landscape created by various recorded sounds or walk through a city by viewing photographs of various buildings.[7] Any combi-nation of these elements is possible. The same computer screen might display verbal text below or beside a video image; it might combine sound and verbal writing. These combinations have come to be called *hypermedia* and are already quite so-phisticated. Hypermedia shows even more clearly than verbal hypertext how the computer can expand the traditional writing space of the written or printed page.

The introduction of video images might seem to turn electronic writing into mere television. Television itself often displays words on the screen, but it robs the displayed words of their cognitive value. Text on television is mere ornamentation; words appear most often to reinforce the spoken message or to decorate the packages of products being advertised. In fact, hypermedia is the revenge of text upon television.[8]   In television, text is absorbed into the video image, but in hypermedia the televised image becomes part of the text. This incorporation is literally true in MIT's Project Athena, in which the reader can run a videotape in a window on his computer screen. The video image therefore sits among the other textual elements for the reader to examine.[9] The Intermedia system developed at Brown University is another instance of texts and images read and written in the same computer environment.[10]

Once video images and sound are taken into the computer in this fashion, they too become topical elements. Writers can fashion these elements into a structure. They can write with images, because they can direct one topical image to refer to another and join visual and verbal topics in the same network. A journalist might select examples from a library of digitized still pictures and form them into a pictorial essay. An art historian might take images of Renaissance painting and attach explanatory comments. In fact, one can link the comments not only to the whole painting, but also to given areas of the image. The eyes of one portrait may refer to a comment, which may in turn link to eyes of other portrait examples. Other parts of the painting would lead to other comments and other examples. The reader would begin with the first picture and then choose to read the network of examples and explanations in a variety of orders, based on an interest in hands, eyes, or other elements of Renaissance technique. In each case the elements of the pictures have themselves become signs that refer to verbal topics and to other pictures.[11] The image is functioning symbolically within the writer's text.

Such multimedia texts are by no means the death of writing. A hypermedia display is still a text, a weaving together of elements treated symbolically. Hypermedia simply extends the principles of electronic writing into the domain of sound and image. The computer's control of structure promises to create a synaesthesia in which anything that can be seen or heard may contribute to the texture of the text. These synaesthetic texts will have the same qualities as electronic verbal texts. They too will be flexible, dynamic, and interactive; they too will blur the distinction between writer and reader.


### The first collaborative hypertext

Although experiments have been conducted since the 1960s, workable hypertext systems such as Intermedia are relatively recent. It was not until the advent of personal computers and workstations that hypertext could be made available to a large audience of writers and readers. On the other hand, the principle of hypertext has been implicit in computer programming for much longer. Hypertext is the interactive interconnection of a set of symbolic elements, and many kinds of computer programs (databases, simulation programs, even programs for artificial intelligence) are special cases of that principle. Hypertext shows how programming and conventional prose writing can combine in the space provided by the computer. It puts at the disposal of writers data structures (trees and networks) that have been used for decades by programmers. Conversely, it makes us realize that the programmer's data structures are formalized versions of the textual strategies that writers have exploited for centuries.

Important anticipations of hypertext can be found in the computerized communications networks, such as ARPANET or BITNET, put in place in the 1960s and 1970s. Such a network constitutes the physical embodiment of hypertext. Each element or *node* in the network is a computer installation, while the connections among these elements are cables and microwave and satellite links. Each computer node serves dozens or hundreds of individual subscribers, and these subscribers both produce and read messages created by others within their computing facility, around the nation, or around the world. Some messages travel a single path through the communications links until they reach their marked destination, while general messages spread out to all the elements in the net. At any one moment the network holds a vast text of interrelated writings—the intersection of thousands of messages on hundreds of topics. It is a hypertext that no one reader can hope to encompass, one that changes moment by moment as messages are added and deleted.

Subscribers use these networks both for personal mail and to conduct ongoing discussions in so-called "newsgroups." When one subscriber in a newsgroup "publishes" a message, it travels to all the dozens or hundreds of others who belong to that group. The message may elicit responses, which in turn travel back and forth and spawn further responses. The prose of these messages is almost as casual as conversation, precisely because publication in this medium is both easy and almost unrestricted. The transition from reader to writer is completely natural. Readers of one message can with a few keystrokes send off a reply. They may even incorporate part of the original message in the reply, blurring the distinction between their own text and the text to which they are responding. There is also little respect for the conventions of the prior medium of print. Subscribers often type newspaper articles or excerpts from books into their replies without concern for copyright. The notion of copyright seems faintly absurd, since their messages are copied and relayed automatically hundreds of times in a matter of hours.

Writing for such a network is by nature topographical: relatively small units of prose are sent and received. The medium itself encourages brevity, since two correspondents can send and receive several messages in one day. And the addresses of the messages provide a primitive system of links. To reply to a given message is to link your text to the earlier one, and both message and reply may then circulate for days around the network provoking other reponses. No user is bound to read or reply to anything; instead, any message can refer to any other or ignore all previous messages and strike out in a new direction. A communications network is therefore a hypertext in which no one writer or reader has substantial control, and because no one has control, no one has substantial responsibility. The situation is different for hypertext systems for microcomputers, where there is one author and one reader. There the twin issues of control and responsibility are paramount.

## Writers and readers of hypertext

When we receive a written or typed letter, we hold in our own hands the paper that the sender also has handled. We see and touch the inkmarks that he or she has made. With electronic mail we receive bits of information that correspond to the tapping of keys on the writer's keyboard. We read this information as patches of light on our computer screen, and we touch nothing that the writer has touched. Like all other kinds of writing, electronic writing is an act of postponement or deferral. As writers, we defer our words by setting them down on a writing surface for later reading by ourselves or by others. The reader's task is to reactivate the words on the page and to devise for them a new context, which may be close to or far removed from the author's original context. There is always a gulf between author and reader, a gap that the technique of writing first creates and then mediates. In one sense the computer opens a particularly wide gap because of the abstract nature of electronic technology. On the other hand, the author has a unique opportunity to control the procedure of reading, because he or she can program restrictions into the text itself.

Computer-assisted instruction, for example, is nothing other than a hypertext in which the author has restricted the ways in which the student/reader can proceed. In typical computer-assisted instruction the program poses a question and awaits an answer from the student. If the student gives the correct answer, the program may present another question. If the student gives an incorrect answer, the program may explain the student's error. If the student makes the same error repeatedly, the program may present a review of the point that the student has failed to grasp. In most cases, these questions and explanations are texts that the teacher/programmer has composed and stored in advance. However, good programming can make these simple programs seem uncannily clever in replying to student. In fact such a program takes on a persona created for it by the teacher/programmer, as it transfers the teacher's words into the new context of the student's learning session. In general, the reader of an electronic text is made aware of the author's simultaneous presence in and absence from the text, because the reader constantly confronts structural choices defined by the author. If the program allows the reader to make changes in the text or to add his own connections (as some hypertext systems do), then the game becomes still more complex. As readers we become our own authors, determining the structure of the text for the next reader, or perhaps for ourselves in our next reading.

Electronic text is the first text in which the elements of meaning, of structure, and of visual display are fundamentally unstable. Unlike the printing press or the medieval codex, the computer does not require that any aspect of writing be determined in advance for the whole life of a text. This restlessness is inherent in a technology that records information by collecting for fractions of a second evanescent electrons at tiny junctions of silicon and metal. All information, all data, in the computer world is a kind of controlled movement, and so the natural inclination of computer writing is to change, to grow, and finally to disappear. Nor is it surprising that these constant motions place electronic writing in a kaleidoscope of relationships with the earlier technologies of typewriting, printing, and handwriting.

Eventually, the new dialectic structure of hypertext will compel us, as Derrida put it, to "reread past writing according to a different organization of space."[12] Texts that were originally written for print or manuscript can not only be transferred to machine-readable form, but also translated into hypertextual structures. In some cases the translation would restore to these texts their original, conversational tone. Many of the texts of Aristotle, for example, are notes and excerpts from lectures that the philosopher delivered over many years; they were put together either by

Aristotle himself or by ancient editors. For decades modern scholars have been trying to sort out the pieces. Printed editions make each text into a single, monumental treatise, but an electronic edition of Aristotle could record and present all the various chronological and thematic orders that scholars have proposed. This might be the best way for readers to approach the carefully interwoven philosophy of Aristotle: following the electronic links would allow readers to sample from various texts and move progressively deeper into the problems that each text poses. This moving back and forth is the way that scholars reread and study Aristotle even now. The computer simply makes explicit the implicit act of deeply informed reading, which unlike casual reading is truly a dialogue with the text.

Rather than eliminating works of the past or making them irrelevant, the electronic writing space gives them a new "typography." For hypertext is the typography of the electronic medium. A text always undergoes typographical changes as it moves from one writing space to another. The Greek classics, for example, have moved from the papyrus roll, to codex, and finally the printed book. When we read a paperback edition in English of Plato's dialogues or Sophocles' tragedy, we are aware of the translation from ancient Greek to a modern language. But we should also remember that the original text had no book or scene divisions, no paragraphing, no indices, no punctuation, and even no word division. All these conventions of modern printing make significant organizational intrusions into the original work. They make reading Sophocles easier, but they change the Sophocles that we read. We would find it very difficult to read an English manuscript of the fourteenth century, or even an early printed book, because of the visual conventions. Electronic versions of old texts will not violate their sanctity for the first time: these texts have always been subject to typographic change; they have already been violated.

When it comes to texts written in and for the electronic medium—and a few such texts have already been written—no translation is needed. The new works do not have a single linear order, corresponding to the page of the book or the columns of the papyrus roll, and so there is no order to violate. Precisely this lack of a fixed order and commitment to a linear argument will frustrate those used to working with and writing for the medium of print, just as it will liberate those willing to experiment with a new form of dialogue. For writers of the new dialogue, the task will be to build, in place of a single argument, a structure of possibilities. The new dialogue will be, as Plato demanded, interactive: it will provide different answers to each reader and may also in Plato's words from the *Phaedrus* know "before whom to be silent."

## Notes

1. True to the spirit of hypertext, portions of this paper have appeared in other places: principally *Writing Space: The Computer, Hypertext and the History of Writing* (Hillsdale, N.J.: Lawrence Erlbaum, 1990). Reprinted with permission. Portions appeared earlier in (and are reprinted with permission from) "Beyond Word Processing: The Computer as a New Writing Space," *Language and Communication* 9 (1989): 129-142.

2. This definition was offered in the course of his talk "Hyperworld: One for All and A.ll for One," delivered on November 14, 1987 at HyperText'87, a conference held at the University of North Carolina at Chapel Hill.

3. See Walter J. Ong, *Ramus, Method, and the Decay of Dialogue: From the Art of Discourse to the Art of Reason* (Cambridge, MA: Harvard University Press, 1958), 104-130.

4. Ong, *Ramus*, 74-83, 199-202, and 314-318.

5. See *Complete Works of St. Teresa of Jesus*, trans. E. Allison Peers (London: Sheed and Ward, 1972), vol. 2, 88.

6. See **Friedlander** in this volume.

7. Such was the Aspen project. See Stewart Brand, *The media lab: Inventing the future at M.I.T.* (New York: Penguin Books, 1987), 141-142.

8. Michael Joyce, "Siren shapes: Exploratory and constructive hypertexts," *Academic Computing* 3:4 (1988): 14.

9. For a description of Project Athena, see E. Balkovich, S. Lerman, and R. P. Parmelee, "Computing in Higher Education: The Athena Project," *Computer* 18 (1985): 112-125.

10. See Nicole Yankelovich, Bernard J. Haan, Norman K. Meyrowitz, and Steven M. Drucker, "Intermedia: The Concept and the Construction of a Seamless Information Environment," *Computer* 21 (1988): 81-96.

11. See **Graham** in this volume.

12. Jacques Derrida, *Of Grammatology*, trans. Gayatri Spivak (Baltimore: Johns Hopkins University Press, 1976), 86.

# Reading from the Map: Metonymy and Metaphor in the Fiction of Forking Paths

Stuart Moulthrop

Department of English, University of Texas at Austin

The literary affiliations of hypertextual fiction can be traced in several directions: to contemporary experimentalists like Alain Robbe-Grillet, Marc Saporta, Milorad Pavic and Julio Cortazar; to theorists of reading like Roland Barthes and Wolfgang Iser; to modernists like Joyce, Woolf, and Faulkner; or to an older tradition of narrative eccentricity epitomized by Rabelais, Cervantes, and Sterne. All of these links are significant, but none goes as far toward defining the issues at stake in narrative hypertext as does a sequence of short stories that appeared in the early forties: Jorge Luis Borges' "Garden of Forking Paths." Though they come from a time long before the advent of electronic textuality, Borges' stories frame fundamental questions about the limits of narrative as a representation of time, questions that inform hypertextual fiction. Like that earlier passage from innocence to experience, our fall into hypertext involves our departure from a Garden. I have tried to explore some implications of this departure, both theoretical and practical, and have found signs that the world that lies before us may be significantly different from the paradise of the printed book.

Borges' Garden is composed of eight stories ("Tlön, Uqbar, Orbis Tertius," "The Approach to Al-Mu'tasim," "Pierre Menard, Author of Don Quixote," "The Circular Ruins," "The Babylon Lottery," "An Examination of the Work of Herbert Quain," "The Library of Babel," and "The Garden of Forking Paths"). These fictions concern themselves largely with labyrinthine structures of language: with games, fictions, and encyclopedias that attempt to encompass or evoke entire worlds, a theme that receives its most salient treatment in the title story. In that story Yu Tsun, an expatriate Chinese scholar, learns from Stephen Albert, a British sinologist, of a philosophic theory postulated by Yu Tsun's great-grandfather, Ts'ui Pên. His ancestor, Yu learns, embraced a radical alternative to the concept of time accepted by Europeans:

In contrast to Newton and Schopenhauer, your ancestor did not believe in a uniform, absolute time. He believed in an infinite series of times, in a growing, dizzying net of divergent, convergent, and parallel times. This network of times which approached one another, forked, broke off, or were unaware of one another for centuries, embraces all possibilities of time.[1]

Ts'ui Pên's theory of time as plenum rather than linear continuum evokes the Borgesian master trope of the labyrinth, and indeed Yu Tsun's illustrious ancestor is known to have committed his life's work to two great projects: the writing of a masterpiece of fiction and the creation of a "strictly infinite" labyrinth. For years the great man's descendants have believed that he achieved neither of these projects, since he left behind him no trace of the labyrinth and only a fragment of the novel, "an indeterminate heap of contradictory drafts." Stephen Albert corrects this misconception by demonstrating that the book and the labyrinth are one. Ts'ui Pên's inconsistent narrative, in which the hero dies in the third chapter but reappears in the fourth, comprises a "labyrinth of symbols . . . an invisible labyrinth of time" in which the reader's imagination may wander endlessly.

As is evident from the title, Ts'ui Pên's fantastic novel is more than a radical revision of temporal theory. The phrase, "Garden of Forking Paths," is itself a symbolic labyrinth, a dense network of convergent and divergent associations. It is the name of Ts'ui Pên's masterwork, but the nature of this undertaking is by no means clear — is it a narrative, a ludic maze, or a philosophic treatise? At the same time, "The Garden of Forking Paths" names both the fiction that contains Ts'ui Pên's history and the sequence of stories which it completes. The title phrase thus cannot be constrained to a simple denotation. It does not exhaust itself in the identification of a single writing, but instead refers with deliberate ambiguity to a multiplicity of discourses.

This system of "Forking Paths" is larger than any single fiction, and with good reason. Borges' network of real and imagined writings constitutes a metafiction, a self-conscious critique of the representation of time in conventional narrative. While the stories deal repeatedly with universal fictions, they are at the same time informed by a deep skepticism about univocality and reductive interpretation. In the terms later defined by Roland Barthes, Borges' labyrinth of symbols is not "work" but "text:"

The work does not upset monistic philosophies, for which plurality is evil. Thus, when it is compared with the work, the text might well take as its motto the words of the man possessed by devils: "My name is legion, for we are many."[2]

As a pluralistic system, the fiction of forking paths answers to no requirement of closure or definitive performance. We can no more specify its meaning than the descendants of Ts'ui Pên could reduce his omnichronic novel to a single reading. The garden of forking paths is capable of containing multitudes, and to impose any single tendency on it would be to bind the proliferation of meaning within absurdly narrow constraints.

Yet on one of its levels, Borges' labyrinthine text is intimately concerned with such a restriction. If we read "The Garden of Forking Paths" not as the novel of Ts'ui Pên or the labyrinth of Jorge Luis Borges, but as the story of Yu Tsun and Stephen Albert, we must confront a dire reductiveness. The title story contains not one plot element but two. The plot of enlightenment in which Yu Tsun learns of his ancestor's theory of time intersects disastrously with a plot of espionage. The year is 1916 and Yu Tsun is an agent of German intelligence working undercover in England. He has learned the location of a strategic British artillery park in France, but he has also breached his cover and is about to be intercepted by a British counterspy, Richard Madden. He must convey the name of the French town to Berlin before Madden catches up to him, but the only instrument of communication he possesses is a revolver ("Vaguely I thought that a pistol report can be heard at a great distance"). Yu must commit a murder sufficiently shocking to generate coverage in the major newspapers, and the name of the victim must be the name of the town in France: Albert. Thus after Stephen Albert delivers to Yu the lost secret of his ancestor, Yu must kill him in order to convey his own secret. But the two secrets have utterly opposite values — the message of the Garden (to the extent that we speak of its having one, general message) concerns plenitude and inexhaustible continuity — while the message of the bullet is a sordid cryptographic reduction. It replaces the living, human significance of "Stephen Albert" (host, mentor, new-found friend) with a murderous military imperative (bomb the town of Albert). The real abomination of Yu's crime lies not in the fact that he has shot an innocent man, but in that he has shot him in the name of denotative expediency.

The trenchant irony of this situation ultimately recoils upon the fictional structure that contains it. Albert lays before Yu (and the pun here seems too powerful to ignore, even if it is an artifact of translation) an understanding of human affairs unconstrained by fatality or determinism; but of course that vision is chimerical, an hallucination much like the one Yu Tsun experiences shortly before firing the fatal bullet:

> It seemed to me that the humid garden that surrounded the house was
> infinitely saturated with invisible persons. Those persons were Albert and
> I, secret, busy and multiform in other dimensions of time. I raised my eyes

and the tenuous nightmare dissolved. In the yellow and black garden there was only one man; but this man was as strong as a statue... this man was approaching along the path and he was Captain Richard Madden.[3]

The vision of "multiform" human potential must yield to a more drastically determined vision: the advance of the detective who will commit Yu Tsun to his dishonorable fate. The unreal "nightmare" of "invisible persons" is replaced by the actual appearance of the pursuer, inexorable and substantial ("strong as a statue"). This transformation is dictated by the form of the narrative itself, described by Borges in his prologue to the eight stories as "a detective story [whose] readers will assist at the execution... of a crime, a crime whose purpose will not be unknown to them, but which they will not understand... until the last paragraph."[4] The story called "The Garden of Forking Paths" is designed around a specific effect of revelation, as are all detective stories. It must reach a single, preordained conclusion, the endgame in which Yu Tsun's only option is to murder Stephen Albert.

Yet the story is not so mechanical as Borges' disingenuous synopsis suggests. An ordinary detective narrative will offer its reader a certain satisfaction in the tying up of loose ends, but the reader of "The Garden of Forking Paths" is much more likely to feel betrayed by the operations of plot that force Yu Tsun into treachery, and is more likely to share Yu's "weariness" with that process on the final page. "The Garden of Forking Paths" is a labyrinth of symbols. It is not simply a detective fiction, but a detective fiction whose conclusion initiates a critique of narrative closure. Yu's hallucination of multiform, invisible persons has a double valence. It discards as unreal the alternative outcomes that the present narrative cannot provide, but at the same time it gestures toward a realm of experience greater than that contained in any specific history, toward the universe of non-Newtonian time (or narrative) envisioned by Ts'ui Pên.

Peter Brooks, invoking the Russian Formalist distinction between *sjuzet* or narrative possibility and *fabula* or actual discourse, contends that Yu's murderous reduction is counterbalanced by the labyrinth itself: ". . . this dastardly future of treachery and murder . . . is 'merely' an escape from the labyrinth, which remains unaffected, which indeed deconstructs this outcome as simply one contingency, a possible fabula produced by a truly infinite sjuzet."[5] In Brooks' view, "The Garden of Forking Paths" subverts its own closure, raising crucial questions about the way narrative structures and represents the experience of time. Must the relationship between singular *fabula* and infinite *sjuzet* always be one of reduction and betrayal? If other outcomes are imaginable, for what reason are they excluded from the telling? Barthes has observed that "the Text's metaphor is that of the network: if the Text expands, it is under the effect of a combinatorial, a systematics (an image that comes close to modern biology's views on the living being)."[6] Surely it is just this "organic," brachiating structure that Borges' labyrinthine fictions approximate — and just as surely, the reader is meant to set this structure in sharp contrast against the spareness of "singular fabula" to which ordinary narrative restricts us.

Before the advent of electronic textuality, Brooks' "deconstruction" of fictional necessity was as far as one could take the critique of fictional closure developed in "The Garden of Forking Paths." For all their allusiveness and formal instability, Borges' stories are at root not "texts" but "works": definitive, material productions restricted both by the immutability of their medium (the printed page) and by social practices (authoritative texts, the law of copyright) to a single set of discursive possibilities. Critics may point to the radical indeterminacy of the text, but their discourses are at best accretions, secondary interpretive layers. From a Barthesian standpoint these layers might be considered combinatorial branches of the "text," but nonetheless they remain formally distinct from the original discourse. Even under deconstruction, the last word of the primary narrative still belongs to Borges, and any overtures to alternative outcomes are checked by the ironic tension of formal closure.

Yet as Brooks points out, fiction always contains a countertendency that militates against this law of absolute singularity: "Any narrative . . . wants at its end to refer us back to its middle, to the web of the text: to recapture us in its doomed energies."[7] In the medium of electronic hypertext, this narrative "desire" can be satisfied in ways that are impossible in conventional fiction.[8] Ts'ui Pên's Garden of Forking Paths is a remarkably prescient approximation of hypertextual narrative, which does indeed take the form of a matrix of inconsistent "drafts" (or more accurately, narrative units). Depending upon reader response, these units may be assembled into any one of a large number of alternative linear discourses. In a hypertextual version of the "Garden of Forking Paths," Yu Tsun's vision of alternate selves would be no illusion, at least from a readerly point of view. The "future" (or ending) in which Yu sacrifices friendship to duty could be avoided; the reader could select a different way through the garden of forking paths. Indeed, Borges' text already contains pathmarks for some of these divergent routes. Having explained Ts'ui Pên's conception of time, Stephen Albert avers that:

> We do not exist in the majority of those times; in some you exist, and not I; in others I, and not you; in others, both of us. In the present one, which a favorable fate has granted me, you have arrived at my house; in another, while crossing the garden, you found me dead; in still another, I utter these same words, but I am a mistake, a ghost.[9]

Dispensing with the elegant detachment of a purely theoretical deconstruction, a hypertextual fiction would take it upon itself to explore these and other excluded possibilities, along with various networks of narrative that might pertain to them.

Following this line of reasoning, I produced an electronic "forking paths," a hypertextual treatment of Borges' story originally intended as a demonstration for an advanced undergraduate course in narrative theory. Strictly speaking, my text is a fictional pastiche or collage. The skeletal structure is a series of text files comprising nearly all of Borges' narrative in its original sequence. Each unit or "node" in this structure also contains numerous links that lead away from the sequence, branching out to nodes containing added material, which themselves contain a variety of links that proceed toward, away from, or parallel to the main narrative. Some of these additions are digressive — there is an account of Yu Tsun's earlier dealings with Viktor Runeberg and the German intelligence chief, for instance. Others contain glosses or parodies, such as a narrative leap that transports action-hungry readers to the British front lines, where they encounter scenes of carnage and death. Still others pursue alternatives to choices made in the original narrative — advised to turn always to the left on his way to Stephen Albert's, Yu turns right instead and finds himself at the house of Stephen Albert's jilted lover, who has her own plot to hatch. These links are sufficiently numerous and convoluted to ensure that the reader must at some point leave the Borgesian text and encounter some strain of alternative discourse. In a rather limited and tentative way, the electronic "forking paths" represents a hypertextual realization of Borges' textual theorizing.

This practice by me of literary appropriation is thoroughly anticipated in Borges' fictions themselves — in "Pierre Menard, Author of the Quixote," where a contemporary writer "modernizes" Cervantes by rediscovering his text verbatim; or in "The Circular Ruins," which Borges solemnly confesses to have stolen from the imaginary author Herbert Quain. Thus the "forking paths" pastiche can hardly be called an original conception — though it may represent the first use of electronic hypertext for such a purpose. But if unoriginal, the "forking paths" hypertext does present a set of questions about narrative which are quite distinct from those raised by its print precursor. Borges' deconstruction of ending instigates a critique of narrative authority; it calls into question the chain of authorial decisions that ordain one outcome at the expense of others. Electronic hypertext treats this critique as axiomatic and embraces a multitude of variations, among which (in principle at least) none is privileged. This approach by no means resolves the problem of authorial intention — even the most densely ramified hypertext will never be "strictly infinite," and so must manifest some form of intentional limitation.[10] Arguably, however, the true innovation of hypertext lies not in its effect upon authorship, but in its transformation of reading. The electronic "forking paths" empowers its readers in ways that Borges can invoke only by hypothesis. It gives readers an actual choice of procedures and outcomes.

In Borges' conventional narrative, readers are asked to imagine a world of multiplicity from within an overwhelmingly linear and exclusive medium. For hypertextual readers the situation is reversed—given a text that may contain almost any permutation of a given narrative situation, their task is to elicit a rational reduction of this field of possibilities that answers to their own engagement with the text. At face value this activity does not seem dramatically different from the act of reading required by the conventional text — it seems entirely consonant, for instance, with Wolfgang Iser's definition of reading as a dynamic process: "As the reader passes through the various perspectives offered by the text and relates the different views and patterns to one another he sets the work in motion, and so sets himself in motion, too."[11] If reading has always been dynamic, then hypertext represents merely the technical application of a standard interpretive practice. To a large extent this is clearly the case — like the codex it supercedes, hypertext is an incremental development in the technology of writing. But incremental developments (again as in the case of the codex) can sometimes have implications for our understanding of literary forms which are incommensurate with their novelty. Though hypertextual reading seems theoretically very similar to conventional reading, there are in fact substantial practical differences in the way readers of hypertext interpret fictional discourse, and these differences suggest that the fiction of forking paths may represent a significant departure from the fiction of the printed page.

We owe this discovery to yet another episode of textual appropriation. I wrote a first version of "forking paths" in the spring of 1986, using a rudimentary text-linking program of my own design. Around that time I received a beta test copy of Storyspace, a full-fledged hypertext system, and decided to transfer "forking paths" to Storyspace.[12] In the fall of 1987, Jane Yellowlees Douglas, an instructor in the writing program at New York University and another beta tester for Storyspace, assigned her students in an introductory writing course to read and respond to the "forking paths" hypertext. I did not learn about this use of "forking paths" for some months. I had absolutely no objection to Douglas' use of the text, but had I known about it I would have pointed out a crucial problem: in translating "forking paths" to Storyspace, I had left out the original instructions to the reader, intending to write a better set once I knew more about Storyspace. The copy of "forking paths" that Douglas' students received gave them no clue about how they might find their way through the textual labyrinth. It left them, as some have described the phenomenon, "lost in hyperspace."

All of Douglas' students expressed frustration with "forking paths," complaining that it did not provide a coherent narrative line, that its temporal and thematic focus shifted unpredictably, and that a character could die in one node and reappear in the next. This is of course much the same response that Ts'ui Pên's novel draws from its unenlightened readers in Borges' story. The students' perplexity — entirely understandable in the absence of instructions – was aggravated by the fact that the choice of branches in the "forking paths" hypertext is controlled by word association. Here for instance is the opening passage of Borges' narrative:

> On page 22 of Liddell Hart's History of World War I you will read that an attack against the Serre-Montauban line by thirteen British divisions (supported by 1,400 artillery pieces), planned for the 24th of July, 1916, had to be postponed until the morning of the 29th. The torrential rains, Captain Liddell Hart comments, caused this delay, an insignificant one, to be sure.[13]

On encountering this passage in the hypertext, a reader must choose a word or phrase that contains some possibility for further development. Thus "page 22" might bring up a reproduction of that page in Liddell Hart, "delay" could open into the next node of Borges' story, which purports to be the true explanation for this delay, and "insignificant" could lead to some kind of ironic reflection on the project of the narrative itself.

In its original, pre-Storyspace form, "forking paths" did not allow any other means of transition between nodes, and indeed even readers who had been fully acquainted with the idea of verbal links were severely frustrated when an obviously fertile word (such as "attack" in the first node) failed to produce a transition. This vexation was at least partly intentional. I wanted to produce a hypertext that would invite its readers (as "forking paths" explicitly does at one point) to assume the mantle of authorship and expand the existing structure. Restricting the linking convention to the phrase or word level seemed a sensible course. I assumed that readers — even when they began to behave as co-authors — would engage the text first at the level of local syntax. This assumption seemed to follow from a fundamental precept of narrative theory, that stories are constituted as a dialectic of continuity and closure, each fragmentary unit of the text (word, sentence, page, scene) yielding to the next in a chain of substitutions or metonymies that builds toward a final realization of the narrative as a whole, or a metaphor. Peter Brooks, drawing on Roman Jakobson, Tsvetan Todorov, and Jean Paul Sartre, concludes that "[w]e read the incidents of narration as 'promises and annunciations' of final coherence, that metaphor may be reached through the chain of metonymies: across the bulk of the as yet unread middle pages, the end calls to the beginning, transforms and enhances it."[14] According to this idealist view, readers move from the confusion and multitude of narrative syntax to the shining wholeness of ending, where all parts achieve a satisfying integration. We negotiate the perplexities of the middle in order to reach the promised revelation of the end; metonymy precedes and enables metaphor. This theory is admirably suited to the interpretation of conventional narratives (not surprisingly, since it evolved mainly from readings of nineteenth century fiction); but it probably does not hold for hypertext.

Some time after her students turned in their responses to "forking paths," Jane Douglas called me with a series of questions about the structure of the text that had been raised by her experience in class. Among other things, she wanted to know why the narrative did not follow a coherent line of development when its constituent nodes were read in left-to-right sequence. This seemed an odd question, since I had never envisioned anyone trying to read "forking paths" in that way. One of the most powerful features of Storyspace is a mapping function that represents the structure of the hypertext as a series of boxes and lines (nodes and links) lying in a plane:[15]

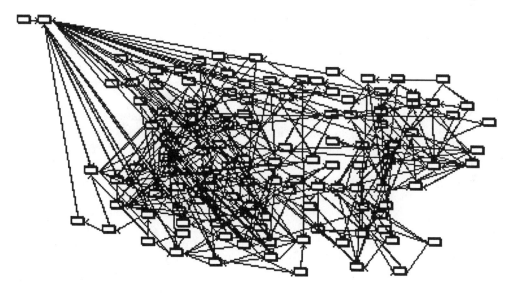

Figure 1: reduced Storyspace map of "forking paths"

Referring to this map, one could speak of left-right or east-west (as well as north-south) sequences; but as I understood it the map would not have been accessible to Douglas' students, who were using ReadingSpace, a subset of the main system that does not allow readers to modify or manipulate text.

Indeed the student readers could not see the actual map, but I had forgotten that ReadingSpace as it was then configured included a set of functions (Right, Left, Up, Down) that permitted "blind navigation" of the hypertext. In fact, Jane Douglas informed me, virtually all of her students had given up trying to find verbal cues after a few nodes, and had opted instead to browse the text with these spatial operators. They were intuitively reconstructing the map they could not actually see. The student readers did not think of "forking paths" as a continuous stream of language but as a labyrinthine structure existing in two-dimensional space. As one student explained in his response:

> It seemed as though, with very few exceptions, "right" was the only choice one could make in terms of movement within the story. The "up" option always took you back to the beginning, which was frustrating.... It was an interesting experience, and if there were more travel options (other than just "right"), I would have enjoyed it more.

These informal observations involved only a small number of students and were based on a text which made engagement with local verbal structure deliberately problematic. They certainly do not imply any general theory of interpretation for hypertextual fiction. However, the experience of Jane Douglas' students with "forking paths" does indicate that hypertexts may not obey the same principles that govern traditional narratives. In particular, these observations suggest that hypertext drastically alters — perhaps even inverts — the relationship between metonymy and metaphor in conventional narrative. Douglas' students were not "reading for the plot"; they had given up hope that the metonymic flow of language in any given node would take them coherently to a conclusion. Instead they were plotting their own readings through a cartographic space, hoping to discover a design which, though it was in no way "promised," might prove to be buried or scattered in the text. The map, which represents the text as totality or metaphor, was not something to be reached through the devious paths of discursive metonymy, rather it was a primary conceptual framework, providing the essential categories of "right," "left," "up," and "down" by which these readers oriented themselves. Metaphor here was not identified with finality or revelation, but with the initial incitement to hypertextual reading, the sense of being precipitated into an unexplored space.

It is certainly true that this metaphoric priority has analogues in conventional fiction. Brooks points out that traditional narrative discourse ordinarily begins at a time after the events it relates, so that we turn the pages with "an anticipation of retrospection."[16] One's first physical encounter with a novel, in which one gauges its length and density, produces a sense of the work as a whole. The physical presence of the book itself is an implicit annunciation of closure and design. But in conventional fiction, singular linearity demands that this anticipation of order remain unfulfilled until the last moment if the story is to sustain the reader's interest. One could read the final chapter of *Tom Jones* or *Bleak House* or *A Farewell to Arms* first, but doing so would ruin the mechanics of sequential revelation on which these novels depend.

The status of the initial metaphor in hypertextual fiction is considerably different. To conceive of a text as a navigable space is not the same as seeing it in terms of a single, predetermined course of reading. The early intimations of wholeness provided by conventional fiction necessitate and authorize the chain of particulars out of which the telling is constituted; but in hypertext the metaphor of the map does not prefer any one metonymic system. Rather it enables the reader to construct a large number of such systems, even when (as in the case of the "forking paths" pastiche) these constructions have not been foreseen by the text's designer. The initial metaphor in hypertext is not an imperfect annunciation destined for fulfillment. Instead it is a system which is already present as a totality, but which invites the reader not to ratify its wholeness, but to deconstruct it. Metonymy does not simply serve metaphor in hypertextual fiction, rather it coexists with metaphor in a complex dialectical relationship. The reader discovers pathways through the textual labyrinth, and these pathways may constitute coherent and closural narrative lines. But each of these traversals from metonymy to metaphor is itself contained within the larger structure of the hypertext, and cannot of itself exhaust that structure's possibilities.

As we have noticed, however, no hypertextual product can realize the "strictly infinite labyrinth" of Borges' fantasy. From this it would seem to follow that the unconventional dialectic of metonymy and metaphor in hypertextual fiction is essentially an illusion. No matter how numerous the branches, some reader (probably with the aid of a computer program) could work out all the permutations of a given structure and reduce the hypertext to a finite series of linear narratives, the whole of which could be treated as an eccentric but still quite conventional fiction. In spite of the wild proliferation of metonymic possibilities, the stable reign of metaphoric coherence can be restored. Even a fiction of forking paths may be reduced and confined to a single metaphoric identity.

These conclusions are valid so long as we consider hypertext an electronic cognate of what Barthes referred to as the literary "work" — a discrete and identifiable hierarchy of language, a "bound volume" in the sense of a volume with boundaries, even if those boundaries now delimit magnetic storage space rather than shelf space. But to restrict the idea of hypertextual literature to this model seems immensely shortsighted. The clear tendency of hypertext is not to remain "work" but to become "text" — a polymorphous and protean network of language which makes the concept of "binding" highly problematic. The message of the hypertextual medium, like that of "The Garden of Forking Paths," concerns the possibility of infinite difference. But unlike Borges' story, which must collapse back into singularity, there is a way in which hypertextual fiction could in fact achieve infinity — not an oxymoronic "strict" infinity, but the unrestricted infinity of read/write textuality. Readers of hypertext are already empowered to read interactively, making choices among a set of predetermined pathways and in the process becoming acutely aware of possibilities which the present network does not support. Since electronic writing relies not on indelible printing but on easily permutable magnetic records and display images, it is always both a medium of reception and a means of production. It follows that readers could very easily learn to approach hypertexts not interactively but proactively, not as players but as masters of the game.

Once one understands this potential in hypertextual fiction, it becomes possible to see its transformation of metaphor and metonymy in a new light. The textual map is not a static representation of limited potentiality, but what Jay David Bolter has called a "writing space," a field whose boundaries can always be expanded by the introduction of new material.[17] Therefore the map is only a provisional metaphor for the text — or more precisely, any given mapping of the text may itself become a metonymy, an approximation of total meaning which will eventually be superceded by a later expansion of the text.

That closure may relapse into continuity, metaphor into metonymy, is hardly a startling discovery: it is an observation that post-structuralist critics have been making about conventional fiction for more than two decades.[18] Our literary culture has tended to minimize the practical consequences of this realization. Indeed, in the broadest view there are no practical consequences: though a deconstructive interpretation may affect an author's canonical valuation, it has no effect upon the integrity of his work. Our understanding of a Dickens novel may change after we learn to appreciate its commitment to indeterminacy, and this new understanding may alter the virtual text we construct in our minds. But the actual structure of Dickens' discourse remains untouched, protected by its mantle of authority, and the inviolate stability of this primary text colors our interpretive departures with an inevitable irony.

However, if hypertextual narrative is allowed to carry out fully its transformation of metaphor and metonymy, a new fiction could develop without such guarantees of integrity. Such a form of writing might come close to realizing Roland Barthes' vision of "the Text" as "that social space that leaves no language safe or untouched, that allows no enunciative subject to hold the position of judge, teacher, analyst, confessor, or decoder."[19] At this point it is impossible to say what literary life would be like in such an environment — the prospects are both enchanting and dismaying. The "fall" into hypertext may prove fortunate or it may turn out otherwise. It does seem clear, however, that any venture out of the Garden and into the fiction of forking paths launches us into a new and discontinuous space of writing.

---

## Notes

1. Jorge Luis Borges, "The Garden of Forking Paths," trans. Donald A. Yates, in *Labyrinths* (New York: New Directions, 1962), 28.

2. Roland Barthes, "From Work to Text." trans. Josue Harari, in *Textual Strategies*, ed. Josue Harari (Ithaca: Cornell UP, 1979), 77.

3. Borges, "Forking Paths," 28.

4. Jorge Luis Borges, "Prologue," trans. Anthony Kerrigan, in *Ficciones*, ed. Anthony Kerrigan (New York: Grove Press, 1962), 15.

5. Peter Brooks, *Reading for the Plot: Design and Intention in Narrative* (New York: Vintage Books, 1984), 319.

6. Barthes, "Work to Text," 78.

7. Brooks, *Reading for the Plot*, 109-10.

8. Hypertextual fictions can be produced in print (e.g. Cortazar's *Hopscotch*, Pavic's *Dictionary of the Khazars*), but such efforts are less interesting than their electronic counterparts for two reasons: first, they entail an arduous process of page-flipping, reinforcing the sense that alternative narrative sequences violate the primary order of the work; second, any printed narrative is materially and formally closed in ways that electronic texts are not.

9. Borges, "Forking Paths," 28.

10. My colleague Jane Y. Douglas holds that hypertext actually makes authorial intention a great deal more central and problematic than it is in conventional

writing. I am indebted here to her "Beyond Orality and Literacy: Toward Articulating a Paradigm for the Electronic Age," *Computers and Composition* (August, 1989).

11. Wolfgang Iser. *The Act of Reading: A Theory of Aesthetic Response* (Baltimore: Johns Hopkins University Press, 1978), 21.

12. Storyspace was created by Jay David Bolter, Michael Joyce, and John B. Smith and is available from Eastgate Systems, P.O. Box 1307, Cambridge, MA 02238.

13. Borges, "Forking Paths," 19.

14. Brooks, *Reading for the Plot*, 93-94.

15. Similar mapping functions can be found in other programs, such as NoteCards and Intermedia, and could arguably be considered a basic requirement of all true hypertext systems.

16. Brooks, *Reading for the Plot*, 23.

17. This is literally true of the map environment in Bolter's Storyspace program, which can be expanded in three dimensions, constrained only by the memory available in one's computer. I am indebted to Bolter's discussion of these issues in a draft of his book, *Writing Space* (Hillsdale, NJ: Lawrence Erlbaum Associates, 1990).

18. See for instance J. Hillis Miller's introduction to *Bleak House* (Harmondsworth: Penguin, 1971), where he argues that the novel's elaborate interpretive games demonstrate the falseness of metaphoric structures, which inevitably collapse into further chains of metonymy.

19. Barthes, "Work to Text," 81.

# From Electronic Books to Electronic Libraries: Revisiting "Reading and Writing the Electronic Book"

Nicole Yankelovich

Institute for Research in Information and Scholarship, Brown University

In our 1985 article, we analyzed the pros and cons of "electronic books" and described a set of features that would maximize the advantages of using the electronic medium for "document preparation and presentation." Now, five years later, scholars who make heavy use of computers for tasks other than word processing, particularly in the humanities, are still in the minority. There are, however, an increasing number of examples of projects which use electronic resources both to prepare and present scholarly works. The articles included in this volume, for instance, demonstrate how electronic book technology has fundamentally changed and improved the way a number of literary scholars create, organize, and present their ideas.

As electronic book technology is folded into reasonably priced commercial products, we shall begin to see more and more scholars following the lead of the editors and authors of this volume. As they do so, the amount of material in electronic form will increase steadily. People will want to share their linked collections of documents with colleagues around the country. They will want to publish these electronic collections for a broader audience. They will want to keep abreast of new work in their field as it is completed, cutting across the lengthy cycles of book and journal publication. And they will eventually expect to have their library's holdings in electronic form.

So, although today's electronic materials exist primarily on a small scale—book size—tomorrow's collections will be much larger—library size. One fundamental challenge for the next five years, therefore, is to ensure that the electronic book technology can scale up.

In "Reading and Writing the Electronic Book" we identified five types of tools essential for a successful electronic document system. Those ingredients are still as important today as they were in 1985, but now I would like to add to the list another set of five capabilities that will be crucial for electronic *library* systems.

### Wide-area hypermedia

The first major step toward electronic libraries involves transforming hypermedia from a local- to a wide-area technology. As scholars establish an increasing number of national and international collaborations with colleagues, technology must allow geographically-dispersed work groups to make links between shared information.

Hypermedia-based electronic document systems today either run on personal computers or on workstations connected to a local area network. In order to make sharing linked collections of multimedia documents with colleagues across the country and around the world as easy as sending electronic mail, substantial technological advances must be made. Take, for example, co-authors of a book at different universities. They can use electronic mail for some communication, but they currently have no easy way of sharing electronic versions of fully formatted text with illustrations. There are also no annotation tools available that would allow one co-author to link comments to the other's sections across the long-distance network. And although they can use electronic mail to pass a manuscript back and forth, collaborators cannot actually share a view of the same manuscript at the same time.

With wide-area hypermedia technology, the co-authors could share the same document, create links to it, and annotate each other's sections as if the document were local to both their workstations. To make hypermedia a wide-area technology, computer manufacturers must include a linking protocol as part of the standard computer operating environment. Documents must be uniquely identifiable across the wide area network, and links must be represented in a way that supports their distribution across many sites.[1]

Once links can be shared across national networks, electronic mail applications must be modified to support linking functionality. Imagine the convenience of being able to mail a message to a co-author saying "I've just rewritten part of Chapter II. Follow this link (—>) to see the parts I've modified." The recipient of the mail message could then follow the link to the appropriate location in Chapter II and see the changes within the context of surrounding passages.

Wide-area hypermedia also opens up new possibilities for national electronic publications and electronic archives. As large-scale, collaborative research projects become more prevalent, results can be made immediately available to others around the country, complete with linked cross-references and other more subjective connections. Take for example, the Brown University Women Writers Project.[2] A team of researchers from Brown, the University of Pennsylvania, the University of New Hampshire, and Texas A&M are collecting all literature written in English by women writers between 1330 and 1830. The project leaders estimate that it will take ten years to collect a majority of the works and put them into electronic form. As the project is currently conceived, the team will periodically publish the works both in printed volumes and in electronic form on CD ROM. Wide-area hypermedia capabilities could substantially augment a project of this magnitude, allowing researchers and students around the country to have much more immediate access to up-to-date information than is now possible.

Members of the project team might become "web editors," entering and linking materials as they were discovered. As soon as a new work was linked into the collection, researchers and students around the country studying women writers could have remote access to the Women Writers collection in its most up-to-date form as if it were stored on their local file server. Not only could they see the materials, but they could create links from their own writing to the original source materials. When their own writing is then published electronically, readers could follow the links back into the Women Writers collection, see quotations in their original context, and review the underpinnings of a critical argument.

### Full-text search

As collections the size of the Women Writers Project and larger develop, users will encounter increasing difficulty locating specific information by following links. The integration of full-text retrieval with hypermedia is another major component that is crucial to scaling up electronic book technology to library-size collections of materials. No matter how well organized a large collection of linked documents may be, browsers still have difficulty finding specific information solely by inspecting folders and following links.

In our current Intermedia system, we have introduced a Document Search tool that allows users to find text in any type of document. Each time a new document is created and saved, the text of the document becomes automatically indexed without any user intervention. For example, in our hypermedia publication called *The Dickens Web*, users can retrieve all documents that mention Jane Austen, be they text, graphics, timeline, animation or video documents, as long as the text "Jane Austen" appears somewhere in their content, document name, or folder name. When the documents are retrieved, they can be sorted based on their probable relevance to the user's query (see Figure 1).[3]

---

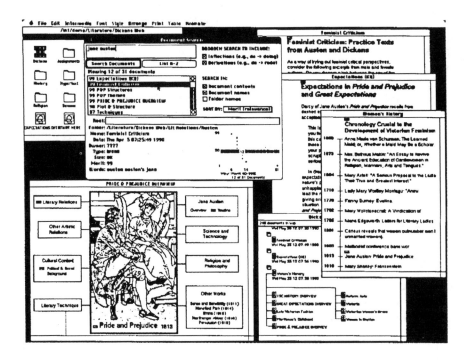

Figure 1: while browsing through The Dickens Web, Intermedia users can search for text throughout the database of linked documents using the Document Search tool (upper left). When retrieved, documents are displayed in a list, ranked according to their probably relevance to the user's query. In this example, the user has opened a graphics document, two text documents, and a timeline document from the list of documents retrieved which contain the text "Jane Austen."

Document Search becomes most useful as the size of a linked collection increases. Browsers can use full-text searches to find documents of interest and then follow links to locate related material.

### Information agents

Full-text searching is crucial, but in a large, ever-changing information environment, full-text retrieval alone is not enough. People need some mechanism for keeping abreast of new and modified information. For example, a graduate student investigating motifs of wandering in works by American or British women writers should not have to issue a query every day to discover if any new writings have been added to the Women Writers collection. Instead, it would be much more time-efficient for the student to ask an information assistant or agent to run the query once a day and report back whenever relevant additions appeared in the collection. Likewise, an information agent might keep collaborators aware of each other's activities. For example, researchers who collectively work on the Women Writers Project need to know what documents or links have been created or updated since their last session and by whom.

A number of researchers have done interesting work in the area of agents.[4] Most of this work, however, requires that users specify a set of rules governing the behavior of agents. Another approach, which we find preferable, involves designing agents that operate in conjunction with interactive applications with which users are already familiar. In the case of the graduate student looking for wandering motifs, he or she could use an application such as our Document Search tool to search for occurrences of "wander, ramble, stray, excursion, recluse, vagrant." As usual, the application would provide a list of documents ranked according to their probable relevance to the search request. If the result list proves interesting, the student would then *register* the query with the information agent, specifying how often it should be run and how the results should be communicated. When new results became available, the agent would generate electronic mail indicating that new material has been located, or the agent might generate a FAX with the actual list of documents. To review the new material most effectively, the student will probably want to interact with the results in their "native" environment, in this case the Document Search application.

In "Reading and Writing the Electronic Book" we argued that, to be most effective, hypermedia capabilities had to work across the whole range of applications a person might have in his or her electronic environment. The same argument holds true for agents. Users should be able to have their agents invoke any number of familiar applications to work for them behind the scenes. Of course, not all applications lend themselves to working on background tasks. Text and graphics editors, for example, are best used interactively, but any type of information retrieval application acting on collections such as bibliographic databases, medical databases, electronic journals, or electronic bulletin boards appears ideally suited for information-gathering missions on behalf of the user.

## Integration of reference works

Keeping abreast of information created or modified by other people is part of the information retrieval problem. Another is the need to look up information in both published and personal reference works without leaving the context of the current document. Our work in Intermedia has shown the power of providing immediate access to the contents of a dictionary and thesaurus. These reference works are among the most heavily used Intermedia facilities.

In Intermedia, users can look up words in Houghton Mifflin's *American Heritage Dictionary, College Edition* and *Roget's II: The New Thesaurus* from within any application. If users wish to conduct more sophisticated searches, they have the option of opening the InterLex application window which provides an interface to the reference works themselves. From this window, users can search the various fields of the reference work. For example, a user can look for the word "wandering" in the definition parts of each dictionary entry, thereby finding all entries related to the concept of wandering.[5]

Part of the power of these tools derives from Intermedia's morphological analysis service, which Document Search also employs. Whenever a user selects a word to look up in the dictionary or enters a word to search for in the document collection, the word is analyzed so that inflections (plurals, verb tenses, etc.) and derivations (words with the same root) will also be retrieved. For example, looking up the word "wandering" will open the definition for "wander," and searching for the word "eat" will retrieve documents containing the words "eat," "ate," "eating," "eats," "eater," and "eaten." Users find morphological analysis techniques far easier to understand than truncation operators (the use of special characters to match multiple word forms, as in "eat*"). The automatic expansion of words to include all members of their inflectional and derivational sets substantially improves the yield of a search while freeing the user to think about searching for concepts rather than for word forms.

The dictionary and thesaurus are extremely useful resources, but they represent only two of many possible reference works a reader might want to consult. In the future, we envision that readers will have an electronic bookshelf filled with both published and unpublished reference works. Helped by techniques of morphological analysis, readers will browse through reference works by interacting with them directly as they now do in Intermedia with the dictionary and thesaurus. In addition, they should be able to specify a reference path, so that when they select a word in a document to look up, the word will be looked up in some or all of the works stored in their bookshelf. For example, a student reading an on-line essay about World War II might select a location name in the essay and be able to look up that name in a map from *The Chronological Atlas of World War Two*, in passages found in *The Dictionary of War Quotations*, and in a glossary created for the course the student is taking—all sources stored in his or her personal bookshelf. Another user might create a bookshelf containing an encyclopedia, a foreign language dictionary, a dictionary of musical terms, and a Who's Who of women writers put together by the Women Writers Project. For users in a networked environment, these bookshelves would not contain copies of the reference works, but only pointers to these works. The reference works would actually only be stored once on a network-based server.

## Filtering

Scaling up also implies paring down. Information filtering, one means of "paring down," offers a solution to the problem of becoming completely overwhelmed by an enormous influx of new information. A professor teaching a course on women writers, for example, might feel that students faced with the entire Women Writers collection would feel intimidated by the quantity of material. He or she might therefore employ a filter that limited the scope of the collection for students, effectively creating a tailored anthology for them.

In "Reading and Writing the Electronic Book" we described a scheme whereby users would assign keywords to "blocks" and "links" and then filter information based on these user-defined attributes. After observing early Intermedia users, we concluded that the majority of users were unlikely to expend the time and mental effort required to keyword blocks and links, even if the user interface was fast and easy to use. In addition, as the literature on information retrieval shows, even those readers willing to expend the necessary effort to provide keywords have difficulty assigning them consistently.[6]

Our initial concept of filtering data by user-specified keywords may have been naive, but as the quantity of information increases, filtering itself becomes more and more imperative. There are a number of possible alternative approaches to the problem of limiting the scope of information an individual views at one time. One simple scheme bases filters solely on system-assigned attributes of data such as author or creation date. The sorts of filters a user could then apply would include "Show me all documents and links created since yesterday," "Show me only documents created by members of my immediate work group," or "Show me only links to animation documents created in the past year." A more complex scheme bases filters on both system-assigned attributes and full text retrieval. Now the user could apply a filter such as "Show me only documents that contain the text 'Jane Austen.' In that set of documents, display only links to illustrations."

Filtering information, which presents us with a major challenge, suffers from the traditional information retrieval problem of balancing the opposing needs of precision and recall. On the one hand, users must not feel overwhelmed by floods of new information; on the other hand, they must not miss relevant information the system has decided to filter out. Our goal, therefore, must be to adjust the flow of information towards some ideal happy medium, perhaps allowing users to indicate interactively when they find erring on the side of too much information appropriate and when on the side of too little.

### Conclusion: the role of users

For literary scholars and others, specific technical challenges are not as important as the issues and opportunities raised by technological advances. Software designers create mechanisms, but the community of readers and writers must establish policies. For instance, each discipline must decide what it means to "publish" a document or a collection, and each must establish a convention for differentiating between refereed works and those placed on a network at the initiative of an individual author.

Wide-area hypermedia coupled with information agents will inevitably raise readers' expectations about the degree of connectivity between new material and old, changing the way writers will think about composing books, articles, and teaching materials. No longer will books be stand-alone items or will articles exist solely in the context of a single journal. With electronic library technology, each publication will exist situated in a much larger context. In scaling up electronic book technology to include wide-area hypermedia, full-text retrieval, information agents, easy access to reference works, and information filtering, writers using this new technology must reconsider how best to present ideas in such a richly interconnected environment and how to organize materials so as to enhance the reader's experience.

---

### Notes

1. Norman K. Meyrowitz, "The Missing Link: Why We're All Doing Hypertext Wrong," in *The Society of Text: Hypertext, Hypermedia, and the Social Construction of Information*, ed. Edward Barrett (Cambridge, MA: MIT Press, 1989), 107-114.

2. Anne Diffily, "Bringing Women's Voices to Life," *Brown Alumni Monthly* 90 (April 1990): 39-47.

3. For Intermedia see Nicole Yankelovich, Bernard J. Haan, Norman Meyrowitz, and Steven M. Drucker, "Intermedia: The Concept and the Construction of a

---

Seamless Information Environment," *IEEE Computer* 21 (January 1988): 81-96; Mark Walter, "IRIS Intermedia: Pushing the Boundaries of Hypertext," *The Seybold Report on Publishing Systems* 18 (August 7, 1989): 21-32; and Norman K. Meyrowitz, "The Link to Tomorrow," *UNIX Review* 8 (February 1990): 58-67. For the Intermedia Document Search tool, see James H. Coombs, "Hypertext, Full Text, and Automatic Linking," *Proceedings of the 13th International Conference on Research and Development in Information Retrieval* (SIGIR'90), Brussels, Belgium, September 5-7, 1990.

4. C. Kamila Robertson, Donald L. McCracken, and Alan Newell, "The ZOG Approach to Man-Machine Communication," *International Journal of Man-Machine Studies* 14 (1981): 461-488; Donald L. McCracken and Robert M. Akscyn, "Experience with the ZOG Human-Computer Interface System," *International Journal of Man-Machine Studies* 21 (1984): 293-310; W. Bruce Croft and L. S. Lefkowitz, "Task Support in an Office System," *Transactions on Office Information Systems* 2 (1984): 197-212; A. R. Kaye and G. M. Karam, "Cooperating Knowledge-based Assistants for the Office," *Transactions on Office Information Systems* 5 (1987): 297-326; K. Crowston and T. W. Malone, "Computational Agents to Support Cooperative Work," *Technical Report* WP 2008-88, Sloan School of Management, MIT, Cambridge, MA, 1988; R. E. Kahn and V. G. Cerf, "The World of Knowbots," Draft report, Corporation for National Research Initiatives, 1988; and K. Lai, T. W. Malone and K. Yu, "Object Lens: A 'Spreadsheet' for Cooperative Work," *Transactions on Office Information Systems* 6 (1988): 332-353.

5. James H. Coombs, "Cognitive Tools: From Dictionary to IRIS InterLex," Submitted to Communications of the ACM (in review), and Walter, "IRIS Intermedia."

6. G.W. Furnas, T.K. Landauer, L.M. Gomez and S.T. Dumais, "The Vocabulary Problem in Human-System Communication," *Communications of the ACM* 30 (1987): 964-971.

# Poem Descending a Staircase: Hypertext and the Simultaneity of Experience

William Dickey
Department of English and Creative Writing, San Francisco State University

> For if there are (at a venture) seventy-six different times all ticking in the mind at once, how many people are there not—Heaven help us—all having lodgment at one time or another in the human spirit? Some say two thousand and fifty-two. So that it is the most usual thing in the world for a person to say, directly they are alone, Orlando? (if that is one's name) meaning by that, Come, come! I'm sick to death of this particular self. I want another.[1]

For Virginia Woolf's hero-heroine, Orlando, possessed of two or more sexes, at least 76 different times, perhaps 2052 selves, and a life extending from the Elizabethan period to 1928 and beyond, to call impatiently for another identity presents no formidable problem. Orlando is, as his/her fiction/biography closes, the representative of concepts of relative self and relative fictional authority which can be found in the English novel at least as early as *The Expedition of Humphry Clinker*, and which greatly accelerate in the period following World War I. Woolf's distrust of the authority of a single narrating voice, a single composed rhetorical language—"I begin to long for some little language such as lovers use, broken words, inarticulate words, like the shuffling of feet on the pavement," Bernard says in *The Waves*[2]—can be paralleled in the work of many other writers, in Hemingway's minimalist language, in the repetition and variation of simple linguistic structures in Gertrude Stein, in the fragmentation of tone and perspective in *The Waste Land*, in the tissue of multilingual puns which make even of one word a lexicon in *Finnegans Wake*. Orlando's assumption that we live not consecutively in one of our times and then in another, but in all of our times simultaneously, Bernard's sense of the inadequacy of a linear word-order language, with its elaborate hierarchical structures of subordination, to convey our experience truthfully, are echoed in twentieth century concerns with aleatory elements in the work of art, concerns that devalue the linear structures of causative plot, of cause-and-effect as a meaningful ordering of events and responses in our contemporary world. Karl Shapiro, commenting on his own

*The Bourgeois Poet*, suggests the seductiveness of the idea of chance organization:

> Mr. Dickey wonders about the order of the poems in the final work. So does my publisher. So do I. Most books of poems, curiously, do have an order. At one point I literally did the Jackson Pollock or *I Ching* trick: I dropped the pages from the top of a ladder and picked them up at random. There is no order, thematic or chronological.[3]

Jacob Bronowski, in a passage which is to me of extraordinary importance, speaks of the human concerns involved in the making of tools:

> I have described the hand when it uses a tool as an instrument of discovery; it is the theme of this essay. We see this every time a child learns to couple hand and tool together—to lace its shoes, to thread a needle, to fly a kite or to play a penny whistle. With the practical action there goes another, namely finding pleasure in the action for its own sake—in the skill that one perfects, and perfects by being pleased with it. This at bottom is responsible for every work of art, and science too: our poetic delight in what human beings do because they can do it. The most exciting thing about that is that the poetic use in the end has the truly profound results. Even in prehistory man already made tools that have an edge finer than they need have. The finer edge in its turn gave the tool a finer use, a practical refinement and extension to processes for which the tool had not been designed.[4]

My purpose in this paper is to suggest that in the computer, and especially in such computer applications, or environments, as hypertext, the late twentieth century has been provided with a tool for artistic composition which not only admits, but encourages, several of the concerns of contemporary art that I have mentioned. These concerns include multiplicity of perspective, variability of the structures and vocabulary of language, including the extension of the idea of language to non-linguistic elements ("the shuffling of feet on the pavement"), rejection of a single rhetorical authority and of linear causative organizations as providing the appropriate pattern for a work of literary art, admission of aleatory organizations and relationships as more accurate representations of experience, and at least an effective illusion of the simultaneity of experience. As in Duchamp's *Nude Descending a Staircase,* we understand our experience as process rather than product, and in that process are at all steps and all stances of the staircase's descent at the same time. I want further to suggest that the conceptual possibilities of computer composition and of hypertext are essentially opposed to the restrictive definition of artistic genres, like those of writing and painting, and to the discrimination of different modes of literary transmission, as in oral and written traditions. Finally,

I want to call attention to the accessibility of the tool which, following Bronowski's description of the tool-making process, has been placed in our hands so that we can create with it something it was not intended for.

"At any rate, when a subject is highly controversial," Virginia Woolf says in *A Room of One's Own*, "one cannot hope to tell the truth. One can only show how one came to hold whatever opinion one does hold."[5] The use of the computer as a tool for artistic composition is new enough to have no formal history, and my discussion of it is necessarily autobiographical, an account of how I came to hold the opinions I do hold.

These opinions began to form when I first used the computer as a tool for the composition of poems, replacing such previous tools as a pencil, a broad-nibbed calligraphic pen, an IBM Selectric typewriter. And my first discoveries as to the new potentials of the tool were concerned with ideas of space and with the authority of the page. Composition on a computer screen is tentative, fluid, changeable in a way that no previous method of composition I can think of approximates. Rob Swigart has said of writing on a computer that "it allows text to go through a phase-shift from solid to fluid. Words and phrases, sentences and paragraphs flow and find their own level. Paper is solid, hard, intractable. Once finished, text may be frozen onto paper, but until then it is dynamic and alive on screen."[6] No one who has worked with students composing poems on sheets of paper, within the boundaries of the persistently defining rectangle, can be unaware of the extent to which the order in which lines are placed on the page becomes an authority, even a tyranny, and how difficult it is to shift them once their first relationship has been established. The freedom with which one moves from place to place in a poem on the computer screen is an inducement to regard the poem as a set of potential relationships rather than as a train of completed statements successively welded into place. This freedom further encourages a new pattern of visual perception of the poem. To shape a poem into Easter wings, as George Herbert does,[7] or to make a poem accompanying the gift of a bottle of Burgundy look like a bottle of Burgundy,[8] a task undertaken by John Hollander, may seem like a trick—Addison dismissed it as such in his essay on false wit[9]—but it does require that the poem exist in more than its textual dimension, that it possess a contributing visual identity as well. Guillaume Apollinaire's *Calligrammes*, typeset and page-bounded, have a look of amateur discomfort, as if their page presentation could only roughly approximate the poet's visual intention;[10] that a poem might be a picture, as the Horatian epigraph to Addison's essay suggests, is a concept computer composition readily facilitates.

A related conceptual element of computer composition involves the interplay of text and space, and the question of whether, by making it easier for the poem to occupy a less bounded, less determined spatial frame, the meaning of the poem can come to depend more on its silences, can take place in the mind of the viewer who is offered deliberate room in which to form his own associations, to become a more active participant in the process of the poem.

The possibilities I have described thus far are those available to anyone using a computer and any word-processing program; they involve, essentially, elements of text and space, and the ease with which these elements can be manipulated in the process of composition. With the introduction of hypertext environments into the accessible computer world, much more complex interactions become possible.

In speaking of hypertext, I am confined by my own experience to one application or environment, HyperCard; but I believe that HyperCard possesses enough of the central elements of hypertext programs to permit me to generalize from it.

HyperCard provides an initial pattern of expectation which, following the example of Bronowski's tool-users, it is possible for the learner of the program almost immediately to extend, or perhaps subvert. As HyperCard is delivered, it includes a number of useful businesslike capabilities: telephone directories, address books, calendars, the periodical table of the elements—all of those functions without which the operations of a modern corporate office would be seriously impaired. Much of the literature that has swelled to accompany HyperCard is based on similar expectations: instructions are provided for budgets, inventories, invoices. This presumption of business applications has been extended, in the academic world, toward impressive combinations of text and graphic elements, catalogs of flora or fauna, or programs that relate the poetry of a period to its art and architecture. These possibilities, and others more closely integral to the process of artistic composition, are principally dependent upon two attributes of the HyperCard program: its central metaphor, and its tools.

The central metaphor of HyperCard is that of a stack of cards, each the size of the Macintosh SE computer screen, only one of which can be viewed at any given time. The cards possess great flexibility of arrangement. A stack of them can be seen as a continuous circle, which can be viewed equally well forward or backward. Links between cards may be easily established by the installation of buttons: when a mouse is clicked on a particular button the viewer is directed along that button's link, and any card can have multiple buttons, providing for a number of alternative routes through the HyperCard poem. It is also possible, by installing a script on the initial card of a HyperCard stack, to insert a randomizing command for that stack, so that the order in which the cards are encountered by the viewer will be different on each successive experience of the poem.

---

The effect of this central metaphor of HyperCard is to abolish the concept of the poem as having a single linear authority, the authority of consecutive plot-governed narrative, the authority of succession on a fixed immutable page. The poem may begin with any one of its parts, stanzas, images, to which any other part of the poem may succeed. This system of organization requires that that part of the poem represented on any one card must be a sufficiently independent statement to be able to generate a sense of poetic meaning as it follows or is followed by any other statement the poem contains. As in the relationship between text and space that I discussed previously, the viewer of the poem becomes involved in the process of connection and relationship; more of the meaning of the poem begins to exist in its silences.

The freedom from linearity afforded the HyperCard poem has the advantage of permitting other structures, geometries of organization, to become a part of the viewer's experience of the poem. The poem may be designed in a pattern of nested squares, as a group of chained circles, as a braid of different visual and graphic themes, as a double helix. The poem may present a single main sequence from which word or image associations lead into sub-sequences and then return. The experience of the poem may be the experience of a maze, in which choices are made, to turn left or right, choices which either force a new experience of a sequence of cards in reverse order, or lead into fresh areas of exploration. Whatever underlying pattern or geometry is built into the poem will not be immediately apparent to the viewer, who can encounter only one card of the poem at a time; the recognition of such structure can come only gradually, so that the viewer's apprehension of the visual and conceptual shape of the poem is generated in the process of viewing it, rather than appearing as an initial given. The sense of chance, of an aleatory element affecting the viewer's understanding of the work, has been incorporated as a fundamental element of the poem.

The processes I am describing sound as if they could be difficult to employ; I think it is important to stress the fact that they are easily accessible, that they can be used without a knowledge of programming or of HyperCard's programming language, HyperTalk. And even that language is, at least on first encounter, anything but recondite. If we follow the simple directions on the package, it should be considerably easier to construct a HyperCard poem than to assemble a desk-file imported from Brazil, with instructions that have only partially emerged from the Portuguese.

The central metaphor of HyperCard, then, permits us any number of different departures from the poem's usual expectations of linear order, and from the expectations a word-order language like English generates of hierarchical relation-

---

ships of greater and lesser importance, of dominance and dependence; it is not easily possible to diagram a structure all of whose parts are interchangeable, so that what is the equivalent of the subject of a sentence on a first viewing becomes an object the next time it is encountered.

If the metaphor permits the poet this freedom of variable organization of his work, the tools provided with HyperCard are an invitation to undermine our customary distinction between modes of representation of experience, our sense, for instance, of the radical difference between alphanumeric text and graphic illustration. This is not a distinction that has always prevailed in the history of Western art: in a work like the *Book of Kells*, for example, text and illustration are understood as one continuous language of representation; the lettering is itself a visual element of the work, rather than serving as an anonymous medium through which information is to be conveyed.

HyperCard provides to its user the tools customary to computer painting programs: a variety of typographic fonts, freehand line drawing, manipulable circles and squares and irregular polygons, simulations of brush strokes of different widths and different densities, the ability to fill backgrounds or selected areas of the card with a variety of replicative patterns. It also permits the importation of graphic images from disk albums of clip art, or, given a scanner, from any other sources of graphics. And it allows images, either those designed with its own tools or those imported, to be rotated, copied into multiples, cut, rejoined in new visual arrangements, suddenly reversed from black on white to white on black. With some limitations, it encourages the interpenetration of textual and graphic elements, the design of a poem in which a dinosaur lumbers into our consciousness, wearing designer sunglasses and complaining, in 18-point Palatino with 12-point subtexts, about the many vicissitudes of life in the Mesozoic. The environment also permits other visual effects more usually associated with film than with poetry: one screen can shrink into an iris to permit the appearance of the next screen, or gradually wipe away from right to left, or disappear with an apparent closing of Venetian blinds.

Beyond these visual capabilities are others which I have myself only begun to explore: the inclusion in the HyperCard poem of musical or unmusical sound, of spoken words or phrases; Bernard's search for a little language like the shuffling of feet on the pavement could without undue difficulty be accompanied, in a Hyper-Card poem, by the sound of actual feet shuffling, or, if that should seem too mundane, by a simple sequence of harpsichord notes, the harpsichord, together with beeps, boings and the sound of breaking glass, being one of the voices native to HyperCard. Whole disks of sounds are available for importation to the poem; voices can be spoken into a microphone and digitized by a program like MacRecorder, to which a tape deck can also be attached. And if the combination of textual, graphic and aural elements is insufficient to represent the creative energy of the poet, it is further possible to proceed to at least the simpler forms of animation. Such complex multi-sensory and multi-media experiences are a commonplace part of our lives: we encounter them, designed by expert technicians and produced on costly and sophisticated computer equipment, daily in television commercials. But that art form, like the art form of the *Book of Kells*, is an enterprise for specialists; the importance of HyperCard as a tool for poets lies in the fact that one does not need to be a specialist to use it, that the capability of breaking down accepted distinctions between genres of representation is available to anyone with access to a particular, and reasonably inexpensive, computer.

At this point we confront an aesthetic question that has been much in evidence in twentieth-century poetry: whether the reality of the poem lies in its fixed printed form, a continuous and unchanging authority, or whether the poem becomes real each time it is performed, recited from memory, on a stage, by its author, or experienced in the simulated performance in which we hear the spoken language behind the text we are scanning on the printed page. As soon as we move away from textual and graphics elements in the poem, as soon as we introduce such elements as randomization, or sound, or animation, we have arrived at a work of art for which the page is no longer an adequate representation; at best the page can provide a kind of vocal or orchestral score for the poem, and even there its nature will be limiting and misleading, as it enforces its own qualities of linearity and singleness on works that are no longer governed by those qualities.

We are accustomed, in studying the work of poets, both of our own age and of other periods, to see the process of composition as a gradual arrival at the poem's perfected form: when Pope changes the line "The fourfold Walls in breathing Statues grace" to "The Walls in venerable Order grace" we assume, perhaps unfortunately in this case, that we have come closer to the poem's ultimate reality.[11] We look to variorum editions, of Shakespeare, of Yeats, to follow the development of the poem to the exact form that finally defines it. This is the mode of written transmission of a literature, and in it the page representation is our source for and our understanding of authority. The mode of oral transmission is different, and to assume that any one of the variant forms of the ballad *Mary Hamilton*, with its conflation of events at the courts of Mary, Queen of Scots, and Czar Peter of Russia,[12] is in itself definitive and final, is to impose an artificial authority on a variable and changing work, a work whose reality eventually consists in all of its performances.

Composition on a computer, with its rapidity, and the ease with which changes of text can be made, made more easily by overwriting than by saving each variant of a poem as it is produced, is closer in some respects to oral literature than to the definitions of authority of written transmission. If, given such possibilities as those HyperCard affords us, no experience of a poem will be the same as the previous experience, though all experiences will have elements in common, we can see further similarities to the ballad tradition, to the reality of the poem existing as a complex of variants, in which each viewing is the equivalent of a performance. This view will be markedly enhanced if, as seems likely enough, HyperCard poems are published not in reductive book form, but by being transmitted, on disk or through computer bulletin boards, from one viewer to another, and if one viewer should then be tempted to extend and vary, to continue and enlarge the poetic experience of the work he has received, as Wallace Stevens, given a four line poem by William Carlos Williams, enlarged and extended it into a different poetic experience which vibrates between two sensibilities, two poetic consciousnesses, two worlds.[13]

I have been speaking primarily of poetry, because it is in this area that my own experiments with hypertext lie. I see no reason, however, why the properties of hypertext ought not to be as applicable to fiction as to poetry. Robert Pinsky, writing of interactive computer fiction, though not specifically of hypertext, arrives at other similarities to oral literature: "But in fact, behind this seeming freedom—and interaction, with its distortions and oddities, does in a way heighten the plot's freely wandering, dreamy quality of romance—stands some of the autocracy of the riddle."[14] Pinsky's observation reinforces my own feeling that as computer composition opens new possibilities of interplay between modes of representation, as it departs from linearity and the authority of text into association and performance, it may generate conceptions of form which have elements in common with those upon which oral transmission of literature has been dependent: the riddle, the circular epic journey.

"Now to sum up," Bernard says, opening the final section of *The Waves*.[15] Like Bernard, I do not find summing up an easy task, because whatever is happening, whatever is going to happen, with the computer composition of poetry and fiction, and with the use of hypertext environments in that composition, is only at its beginning. But that beginning, in ways I have tried to suggest, appears to me to have provided, for a number of concerns, about time, about linearity, about the limitations of written language and rhetorical authority, that have been characteristic of twentieth century literature in English, a more appropriate, flexible and experimental vehicle than has heretofore been available. The artistic need anticipated the tool; the tool, in its rapid and successive refinements, is already involved with the realization of works of art for which it was not intended.

---

## Notes

1. Virginia Woolf, *Orlando: A Biography* (New York: Harcourt Brace Jovanovich, n.d., first published 1928), 308.

2. Virginia Woolf, *The Waves* (New York: Harcourt Brace, 1931), 238.

3. Karl Shapiro, "The Bourgois Poet," in *The Contemporary Poet as Artist and Critic,* ed. Anthony Ostroff (Boston: Little Brown, 1964), 214.

4. J. Bronowski, *The Ascent of Man* (Boston: Little Brown, 1973), 116.

5. Virginia Woolf, *A Room of One's Own* (London: Hogarth Press, 1929), 7.

6. Rob Swigart, "A Note on Using the Computer to Write," *New England Review and Bread Loaf Quarterly* 10 (Autumn 1987): 54.

7. George Herbert, "Easter Wings," in *English Seventeenth Century Verse,* ed. Louis L. Martz (New York, Norton, 1973), I, 148.

8. John Hollander, "For a Thirtieth Birthday, with a Bottle of Burgundy," in *Movie-Going and Other Poems* (New York: Atheneum, 1962), 37.

9. Joseph Addison, Richard Steele and others, *The Spectator* (New York: E.P. Dutton, 1958), No. 58, I, 176.

10. Guillaume Apollinaire, *Calligrammes,* trans. Anne Hyde Greet (Berkeley: University of California Press, 1980). The approximation is sometimes typographically happier in the translations than in the original printings of the poems, but some sense of constraint remains.

11. Alexander Pope, "The Temple of Fame," in *The Rape of the Lock and Other Poems,* ed. Geoffrey Tillotson, second ed. (London: Methuen, and New Haven: Yale University Press, 1954), 249.

12. *The English and Scottish Popular Ballads,* ed. Francis James Child (New York: Folklore Press, 1957), III, 379-399.

13. Wallace Stevens, "Nuances of a Theme by Williams," in *The Collected Poems of Wallace Stevens* (New York, Alfred A. Knopf, 1955), 18.

14. Robert Pinsky, "A Brief Description of *Mindwheel*," *New England Review and Bread Loaf Quarterly* 10 (Autumn 1987): 65.

15. Woolf, *The Waves*, 238.

# Reading Hypertext: Order and Coherence in a New Medium

John Slatin
Department of English, University of Texas at Austin

The basic point I have to make is almost embarrassingly simple: hypertext is very different from more traditional forms of text. The differences are a function of technology, and are so various, at once so minute and so vast, as to make hypertext a new medium for thought and expression—the first verbal medium, after programming languages, to emerge from the computer revolution. (The computer has spawned new media in the visual arts and music as well.) As a new medium, hypertext is also very different from both word processing and desktop publishing, two other computer technologies which have had an enormous impact on the production of texts. Both word processing and desktop publishing have as their goal the production of conventional printed documents, whereas hypertext exists and can exist only online, only in the computer. A new medium involves both a new practice and a new rhetoric, a new body of theory. I hope this paper will serve as a step in that direction.

The first requirement for a rhetoric of hypertext is that it must take the computer actively into account as a medium for composition and thought—not just as a presentational device and not simply as an extension of the typewriter. This means different things, depending on the level of abstraction at which one stands. At some levels, for example, one has to deal not only with knowledge as constructed by humans for humans, but also with data structures, with the representation—or, more accurately, the re-construction—of knowledge (if the term still applies) in hardware and software. It means, also, that the rhetoric itself must be abstract, like Wallace Stevens's Supreme Fiction, in order to permit movement up and down the ladder of abstraction and to permit the articulation of principles that will enable practice. By the same token, the rhetoric of hypertext will have to be capable of change: for it is tied to a still immature (perhaps perpetually immature) technology which is itself changing at an exponential rate.

On the assumption, then, that description is the first step toward theory,[1] I will contrast hypertext with more traditional text. I will focus on the assumptions each makes about what readers do and the ways in which those assumptions about reading affect the author's understanding of composition. For the purposes of this discussion, taking the computer into account means that we have to find ways of talking about "documents" that have multiple points of entry, multiple exit points, and multiple pathways between points of entry and exit points. Moreover, we must find ways to talk about the still more exciting kinds of activity fostered by this proliferation of possibilities: I mean interactive reading and its more or less inevitable concomitant, interactive writing, or co-authorship.

Widespread literacy is a comparatively recent phenomenon—that is to say that in Western societies such as those of Europe, and North America, general literacy is at best a couple of hundred years old. But Western culture was a print culture long before the coming of general literacy, and the text environment we are all familiar with is the product of fully mature, highly stable manuscript and print technologies which have been in place for many centuries. Our principles and strategies for effective written communication are therefore based on long-established assumptions about readers and reading. It will be helpful to consider these assumptions briefly before going on to discuss the different assumptions embedded in the design of hypertext and hypermedia systems.

The assumption that reading is a sequential and continuous process is the foundation on which everything else rests.[2] The reader is expected to begin at a clearly marked point whose appropriateness has been determined by the author—usually with considerable effort: one of the hardest moments in any writing project is to figure out where to start—and to proceed from that beginning to an ending which is just as clearly marked and which has also been determined by the author in accordance with his or her understanding of the subject matter and the reader. The reader's progress from the beginning to the end of the text follows a route which has been carefully laid out for the sole purpose of ensuring that the reader does indeed get from the beginning to the end in the way writer wants him or her to get there.

All but the most naive and inexperienced writers recognize that all but the most naive and inexperienced readers inevitably and rightly make inferences about what's going to happen next, on the basis of what they have already read—not only in the current text, but in other texts resembling it. The reader's perception of the predictability of a given text is an important factor in his or her qualitative evaluation of the text.

Prediction operates on a number of different levels and is determined by different things at different levels of abstraction. The predictability of a given text is a function of the relationships among phenomena at microscopic, macroscopic, and meta-textual levels of abstraction. At the microscopic levels, the reader's ability to predict the course of the text from moment to moment is a function of such factors as paragraphing, sentence length, complexity of phrasing, vocabulary, and so on— that is, the factors that are evaluated in producing a so-called "readability index." Indeed, one might descend even further down the ladder of abstraction and argue that prediction takes place at the graphemic or phonemic levels as well.[3] At the macroscopic levels, the reader is aware of such things as general subject matter, topics and subtopics, and the structural devices organizing the text as a whole— sections, chapters, and subchapters, and so forth. At this level the reader is also at least subliminally aware of such things as how much more material there is to read. On what we might call the metatextual level, the reader makes inferences about the text as a whole, based on his or her understanding of the larger context to which s/he regards the text as belonging. These inferences are often implicit, or else they may take the form of mental or marginal annotations; in any case, they are outside the text and separate from it. But, as I shall explain later on, they are *integral* to hypertext.

The end product of the writing process is a text written or printed on paper, and then, often, sewn or glued or otherwise bound between covers. This is obvious, I know, and yet it needs to be said. Every writer has had the awful experience of opening a book or article hot off the press, only to stare in horror at a glaring error in a crucial passage that somehow escaped the most agonizing scrutiny. The fixity of the printed text as an object in physical space makes the text as an object in mental space seem equally stable and fixed. Or at least that's how we tend to want it. As Richard Lanham has said, "It was establishing the original text that the Renaissance scholars thought their main task, and generations of textual editors since have renewed their labors. The aim of all this was to fix the text forever."[4] The continuing controversy over Hans-Walter Gabler's edition of Joyce's *Ulysses* makes abundantly clear just how intense the desire "to fix the text forever" can be.[5] Gabler's re-conception of the editing process may have occurred "independently of his decision to use the computer,"[6] but the controversy over his "synoptic" version of *Ulysses* offers a clear illustration of the way computers will revolutionize our understanding of text. Every word in Gabler's synoptic text was written by Joyce himself—and yet the final "reading text" is a text no one ever wrote—it had never existed prior to its publication. (In this sense, Gabler's *Ulysses* resembles Benoit Mandelbrot's fractals, in which recursive mathematical formulae are graphically plotted to produce visual structures that, while in some cases resembling phenomena in the day-to-day world, have no counterpart in that world.) Gabler's is a simulated *Ulysses*, like the *Don Quixote* that would be produced by Borges' Pierre Menard if Menard were real and if he had a computer. This is what becomes of the work of art in an age of electronic reproduction. Text is always mutable, always subject to inadvertent error and deliberate change, and it has to be coerced into standing still—that's why publishers charge you money if you make too many changes in a text after it's been typeset.

For all these reasons—because a text looks like a permanent thing, because readers expect to begin at the beginning and end at the end and to know which is which (that's why students so often begin the last paragraph with *In conclusion*), because readers expect to get from beginning to end *via* a clearly-marked route—sequence is of paramount concern to a writer. Much of his or her effort goes into figuring out the correct sequence for the material that's going to be presented. The writer's job in this context is to contrive a sequence that will not only determine the reader's experience and understanding of the material but will also seem to the reader to have been the only possible sequence for that material; you want it to seem to have been somehow inevitable.

Of course this inevitability has a good deal to do with the issue of predictability I raised earlier. Readers have to be able to predict what will come next, at least up to a point, or they start to feel lost, which makes them start to feel nervous, which makes them want to put down what they're reading and go watch a football game or something—at which point the writer has failed miserably. But the flip side is just as bad, and the end result is going to be the same.

Writing that's too predictable is governed by a presupposition succinctly expressed by a certain hotel chain's ad campaigns. The presupposition that there should be "no surprises" may be fine for hotels. But it becomes a fundamental conceptual error where writing is concerned.

The informational value of a given document is not simply a function of the quantity of data it presents or the facts it contains. At one level of abstraction, what we call information may indeed consist in numbers, dates, and other data, other facts. But as Gregory Bateson says, "All receipt of information is necessarily receipt of the news of *difference*."[7] At a somewhat higher level of abstraction, therefore, none of these data can be considered information until they have been contextualized, arranged in such a way that both the significant differences and the significant relationships among them may become apparent to the intended reader. In Christopher Dede's terms, this is when information becomes knowledge.[8] In other words, as literary artists and their readers have always known, there can be no information without surprise.

Rhetoric typically has little to say about the physical processes by which a text is brought into being. Or I could put it even more strongly and say that rhetoric has traditionally been indifferent to the technology of communication. One reason for this indifference is that the technology is so mature that it's simply taken for granted, so that it is essentially invisible *as* technology. There was a point in history, of course, when writing itself was a radically innovative technology and was regarded as such, as Eric A. Havelock, Father Walter J. Ong, and Richard Lanham have shown us.[9] The computerization of writing has similarly made the technology itself highly visible, especially in the cases of desktop publishing and hypertext/ hypermedia. By contrast with traditional text, hypertext and hypermedia depend upon an emergent technology which is still immature and still subject to radical transformation; indeed, all indications are that accelerating change is an inherent characteristic of this technology. It may *never* stabilize. Thus rhetoric for hypertext cannot afford to disregard the technological substrate upon which composition and reading depend.

There are many continuities between conventional text and hypertext. Anyone involved in creating a hyperdocument will still have to worry about the problems I've outlined so far. But hypertext is a very different kind of beast than a conventional text, and creating a hyperdocument poses some very different problems as well. The remainder of this paper will concentrate on those differences and their implications.

First of all, the hyperdocument may well contain material from several different media such as text, graphics, video, and sound. While this is an important factor, I don't think it's decisive. After all, printed books often contain text, line drawings, tables of data, reproductions of visual images, and so forth—though of course they cannot manage full motion video or sound. Besides containing different types of materials than those to be found in printed text, the hyperdocument is likely to contain considerably more material than a printed book. Again, this is not a decisive difference in itself: encyclopedias also contain an enormous quantity of material. The quantity of material in a hyperdocument does pose problems, and it does make for complexity. But the greatest difference between text and hypertext is not in the relative quantity of material each form handles: it's in the technology that handles the material.

What makes all the difference in the world is the fact that hypertext exists and can exist only in an online environment. This is crucial, not just because it substitutes monitors, keyboards, and mice for the customary physical apparatus associated with text—paper, books, pencils, and so forth. The fact that hypertext exists only in the online environment is crucial because, as Douglas Hofstadter says, "It is the organization of memory that defines what concepts are."[10] Hypertext uses machine memory in a way that has no analogue in the traditional text environment, where composition relies on the organization of human memory. It is the organization of memory in the computer and in the mind that defines hypertext and makes it fundamentally different from conventional text.

In such an environment, the problem is not simply to develop effective strategies for implementing well known and long established principles of effective communication. On the contrary, one of the chief functions of rhetoric in the hypertext environment is to discover the principles of effective communication and then develop ways of implementing those principles through the available technology.

The rapidly evolving technological environment makes hypertext possible by permitting the embodiment of a very different set of assumptions about readers and reading—and about thinking. These assumptions in turn form the basis for decisions made in the process of creating a hyperdocument.

Reading, in hypertext, is understood as a discontinuous or non-linear process which, like thinking, is associative in nature, as opposed to the sequential process envisioned by conventional text. Associative thinking is more difficult to follow than linear thinking. Linear thinking specifies the steps it has taken; associative thinking is discontinuous—a series of jumps like the movement of electrons or the movements of the mind in creating metaphor. This discontinuity is not fortuitous; rather, as Stewart Brand points out, it is a basic aspect of the digital encoding of information. Brand offers the illuminating contrast between the surface of a traditional phonograph album, with its continuous grooves, and the surface of a compact disc, with its distinct, discontinuous pits.[11]

Reading in this sense has little to do with traditional notions of beginning at the beginning and going through to the end. Instead, the reader begins at a point of his or her own choosing—a point chosen from a potentially very large number of possible starting points. The reader proceeds from there by following a series of links connecting documents to one another, exiting not at a point defined by the author as "The End" but rather when s/he has had enough. Accordingly, the most common metaphors in discussions of hypertext equate reading with the navigation or traversal of large, open (and usually poorly-charted) spaces. As Jeff Conklin has pointed out, because the hyperdocument contains so much material, and because relations between the components of the hyperdocument are not always spelled out, there is a significant danger that the reader will get lost or become badly disoriented.[12]

The difficulty is compounded because hypertext systems tend to envision three different types of readers: the reader as browser, as user, or as co-author. The relationship between these three classes can be fuzzy and therefore difficult to manage. One function a rhetoric for hypertext will have to serve will be to provide ways of negotiating it.

The browser is someone who wanders rather aimlessly (but not carelessly) through an area, picking things up and putting them down as curiosity or momentary interest dictates. In this respect the browser is someone who reads for pleasure, with this important difference: there is no expectation that the browser will go through all of the available material; often the expectation is just the reverse. It is difficult to predict the browser's pathway through the material—and in fact it is less important to predict the pathway the browser will take than it is to provide a backtracking mechanism, what Mark Bernstein calls a Hansel-&-Gretel trail of breadcrumbs to allow the browser to re-trace his or her steps at will.[13] (Of course this same mechanism is essential for readers in the two remaining categories as well.)

By contrast with the browser, the user is a reader with a clear—and often clearly limited—purpose. He or she enters the hyperdocument in search, usually, of specific information and leaves it again after locating that information. The user's path is relatively predictable, provided those who have created the hyperdocument have a sufficient understanding of the task domain. In these respects, then, the user resembles a typical student doing the assigned reading for a course. But there is also an important difference between the user and the student, which is most clearly recognized from the vantage-point of the author rather than the reader. The author(s) of a hypertext documentation system (for, e.g., a software product like Microsoft QuickBASIC 4.5™) will have met their goal when the user finds the information s/he needs and returns to the work in progress. The instructor designing a set of hypertext course materials may well not be satisfied with such an outcome, however: the instructor aims at a dynamic process, in which the student moves among three different states: from a user the student becomes a browser (and may then become a user once again). Ultimately, the student becomes fully involved as *co-author*. Thus what looks like a hierarchy of readers collapses.

One of the most important differences between conventional text and hypertext is that most hypertext systems, though not all, allow readers to interact with the system to such an extent that some readers may become actively involved in the creation of an evolving hyperdocument. Co-authorship may take a number of different forms—from relatively simple, brief annotations of or comments on existing material, to the creation of new links connecting material not previously linked, to the modification of existing material or the creation of new materials, or both. Both literary theorists (e.g., Wolfgang Iser, Paul Ricoeur, Stanley Fish) and cognitive scientists like Jerome Bruner have talked for years about the reader's involvement in the construction of textual meaning. But hypertext's capacity for literally interactive reading and co-authorship represents a radical departure from traditional relationships between readers and texts. The implications of this departure from traditional relationships between readers and texts are enormous, both for the creative arts[14] and for education: as many theorists now agree, understanding comes about when the mind acts upon the material. Marshall McLuhan's distinction between hot and cool media is relevant here—a cool medium being one that invites active participation, a hot one being one before which one sits passively. McLuhan was thinking, of course, about the difference between print and television, but one might argue that hypertext combines the heat and visual excitement of film, video, and television with text's cool invitation to participate.[15]

"Writing," in the hypertext environment, becomes the more comprehensive activity called "authoring." Authoring may involve not only the composition of text, but also screen layout and other things that fall under the general rubric of interface design; it may also involve a certain amount of programming (as in Apple's HyperCard, where complex navigational and other processes are scripted by the stack's author). Perhaps most importantly, authoring involves the creation and management of links between nodes.

Ted Nelson, who coined the term "hypertext," defines hypertext as "non-sequential writing."[16] This means writing in which the logical connections between elements are primarily associative rather than syllogistic, as in conventional text. One implication of this is that the hyperdocument "grows" by a process of accretion, whereas the conventional document tends to have been winnowed out of a larger mass of material. That is, in preparing to write a conventional document, you almost inevitably assemble more material than you can possibly use; the closer you come to final copy, the more you find yourself excluding material that "doesn't fit" the subject as you've finally defined it. Hypertext, by contrast, is an inclusive medium. Thanks to the capability of creating nodes and links, material not linearly related to the point being discussed at the moment but still associated with that point may be placed in a node of its own and linked to other nodes as appropriate; the material need not be thrown away. In much the same way, no individual point of view need be excluded.

This inclusiveness makes it unlikely that any one individual will see all the elements making up the system. It also means that the hyperdocument is in fact a collection of possible documents, any one of which may be actualized by readers pursuing or creating links between elements of the system.[17]

The end product of the authoring process, the hyperdocument, is not a closed system, like a book; it is rather an open and dynamic system. The hyperdocument is an online system or network whose constituents are of two basic types: nodes and links. Nodes may consist of documents, images, or other materials electronically connected—linked—to one or more other documents or images. Very likely, the different nodes will represent the work of quite a few individuals, who may have been working at different times and in different locations. Indeed, one impetus for the development of hypertext systems has been in the need to address exactly this issue among members of development teams. The development of protocols and procedures for co-authorship thus becomes an important issue.[18] So does the development of procedures for moving through the system.

The reader's progress through a conventional text is governed by the arrangement of the material; the burden of prediction falls more heavily upon the reader than on the writer. This situation becomes considerably more complicated in hypertext. Given a system of discrete and interconnected nodes, the reader/user must decide which links to follow; in order to make that decision intelligently, s/he must be able to make reliable predictions about the consequences of particular choices. But the freedom of movement and action available to the reader—a freedom including the possibility of co-authorship—means that the hypertext author has to make predictions as well: for the author, the difficulty at any given moment is to provide freedom of movement and interaction, while at the same time remaining able to predict where the reader/user will go next . The most effective solution here, I think, will be to treat each node as if it were certain to be the reader's next destination. This is time-consuming in the short run, but in the long run probably saves time by creating a more readily usable system.

This brings us to the issue of linkage, the mechanism that creates the hyperdocument and allows the reader to move through it. Douglas Hofstadter has suggested that the perception of relatedness is a defining characteristic—perhaps *the* defining characteristic—of intelligent behavior. Hypertext embodies this idea, for everything in hypertext depends upon linkage, upon connectivity between and among the various elements in the system. Linkage, in hypertext, plays a role corresponding to that of sequence in conventional text. A hypertext link is the electronic representation of a perceived relationship between two pieces of material, which become nodes once the relationship has been instantiated electronically. That is, the link *simulates* the connections in the mind of the author or reader; and it is precisely because the electronic link is only a simulation that problems will arise.

The interdependency of links and nodes is such that it is impossible to talk about one without talking about the other. Thus the question of how to define a node (*block* is an alternative term in the literature on hypertext) leads to additional questions about linkage. These lead in turn to questions about structure and coherence, and so back again to the issue of prediction.

A node is any object which is linked to another object. It may be as large as an entire book or as small as a single character (theoretically, it could be as small as a single pixel [picture element] on a display), though such extremes seem hardly practical; it may consist of a document or a block of text within a larger document; it may be a drawing, a digitized photograph, a (digitized) detail of a painting, a sound recording, a motion picture, or a scene—even a frame—from a motion picture.

There is no set answer to the question, how big should a node be? just as there is no set answer to the question, how long is a paragraph? Like the paragraph, the hypertext node is a way of structuring attention, and its boundaries, like those of the paragraph, are somewhat arbitrary. A node may contain a single paragraph; it may contain many; it may contain something else entirely. Jeff Conklin offers criteria for guidance in determining node size. To what extent, he asks, is the information in question so tightly bound together that (a) you always want to view it together; (b) you never want to take it apart; and (c) you rarely even want to reference parts of it outside of the context of the rest.[19] In other words, a node is an integrated and self-sufficient unit; its size will be a function of the complexity of the integration. This in turn is contingent upon the author's perception of the nature of the material it contains and the relation of that material to other things in the hyperdocument.

The individual node, then, behaves in certain respects like a more conventional text. But the node is not just a self-contained unit. A node cannot, by definition, be entirely free of links—a node is a knot, is always embedded in a system—and that connectedness in turn gives the node its definition. "A node is something through which other things pass, and which is created by their passage."[20]

A text becomes a node when it is electronically placed in relation to other materials (documentary or otherwise), which may (or may not) already contain links to other elements within the system. The difficulty here, of course, is that what are to me self-evident associations may not be even faintly apparent to you, and vice versa. This imposes an obligation on the author(s) of a hyperdocument which has no exact parallel for the writer of conventional text: the nodes must seem complete in themselves, yet at the same time their relations to other nodes must be intelligible. The problem of relationality here is analogous to the problems of intertextuality confronting readers of, say 20th-century poetry.[21] This problem becomes increasingly challenging as the hyperdocument expands. Links exist for many different reasons—that is, to represent many different kinds of relationships between objects; the more links there are between the current node and other elements of the hyperdocument, then, the greater the necessity of identifying the attached material clearly—especially when the reader is allowed considerable freedom in choosing among the available links.[22]

These identifiers carry an enormous burden. Indeed they are often asked to do the kind of explanatory work that ordinarily takes several sentences or paragraphs. Not surprisingly, there are several different methods of identifying link or node types. Some hypertext systems, such as MCC's gIBIS, use "typed nodes" (Conklin), while others—Xerox PARC's NoteCards, for example—employ "link types."[23] These systems allow the co-author creating a new node to choose from a list of pre-defined relationship categories, whose names then become part of the node or link.

HyperTIES, developed by Ben Shneiderman at the University of Maryland and distributed by Cognetics Corporation, offers a variation on this approach, by encouraging the author to compose a brief (two-line) description of the linked node. In HyperTIES, where reading is defined primarily as browsing and where browsing is completely separate from authoring, activating a link is a two-step process. The first step, clicking on a highlighted word or phrase, brings up the description of the attached node; the second step either brings up the attached node or returns the browser to the current screen.

The developers of Intermedia at Brown University have chosen a third alternative. Links belong to "webs" rather than to documents; webs are displayed onscreen as visual maps. An Intermedia document is first displayed as if it were freestanding; then, when the user opens a web, the links belonging to that web are displayed.[24] This approach allows an individual node to be placed within multiple frames of reference, or "webs," while avoiding both the screen clutter and the mental clutter that can accrue so easily when multiple links radiate to and from a node. Which links the user sees will depend upon which web s/he has elected to open.

As the Intermedia approach suggests, one way to address the question of how many links a node should have is by turning it into the question of how many links should be displayed at any moment. Research on memory suggests that we can hang on to between five and seven "chunks" of information at a time, and that creating links between these chunks is a way to increase the effective size of the chunk. However, the number of chunks that can be retained decreases in inverse proportion to their size.[25]

Probably no single method of identifying nodes and their relationships to other nodes is adequate to all needs; some combination will be needed. Choosing from a list of predefined relationships has certain advantages, since there is a strong likelihood that a newly created node will fall within an existing classification. However, the list must offer real choices without becoming so big as to make choice impossible. And co-authors will still want to be able to define and use new categories. Co-authors may also wish to give a fuller description of the attached node than the list approach permits; something like the HyperTIES strategy becomes appropriate here. And when a given node has multiple links to and from other nodes, it may be advisable to use an Intermedia-style mapping strategy.

The approach you choose to the problem of identifying links and nodes will depend on several factors: your understanding of the ways in which the material is related; your sense of who your readers are (are they primarily browsers? users? co-authors?). Your sense of what you want those readers to do is especially important.

You don't have to worry about interactive readers when you write a conventional text—the only thing you want the reader to do is to go on to the next sentence. But in hypertext, where there are a number of possible "next sentences" or nodes for the reader to go on to, you do have to make some decisions about what ought to happen next. That is, do you care whether the reader (a) opens a specific node or sequence of nodes; (b) chooses more or less randomly from the available links; (c) creates a new node, linking it not only to the current node but also to such other nodes as the reader—now a co-author—deems appropriate?

If you want the reader to open a specific node or sequence of nodes, you can either try to influence the reader's course of action, for example by highlighting a "preferred pathway" through the material, or you can simply pre-empt the reader's choice by automating the sequence or hiding links you don't want the reader to pursue. (Though if you take that route you give up many of the advantages of hypertext, it seems to me.) Or if you don't have a preference about the sequence the reader follows, you may opt not to give directions, leaving the choice of which links to activate—or whether to activate any link at all—entirely up to the reader. If you want to encourage response—that is, if you want the reader actually to get involved as a co-author—you should say so somewhere on the screen and make it as easy as possible for the reader to change roles. In HyperCard, for instance, you can script a button to open up a text field with a date/time stamp and the name of the new co-author; you can even let the co-author enter keywords to make later searches faster.

I've already said that the author of a hyperdocument has a hard time trying to predict where the reader will go from any given point. The reader who activates a link often has a hard time, too, because it can be so difficult to predict what the result will be. The more cryptic the link or node identifiers are, the harder it is for the reader to predict the results of activating a particular link. The harder it is to make such predictions, the greater the likelihood that the reader will simply opt out of the process in frustration. And even if the reader does go ahead there is no guarantee that s/he will know the place when s/he gets there.

The reader has to make several different kinds of predictions. First, s/he has to predict the kind of material s/he will encounter upon activating a link. It would be quite distressing, for example, to activate a link in the expectation of moving to a narrative explanation of some issue, if in fact the associated node contains only raw data in tabular form. Second, s/he makes some predictions about the content of the node: at the most general level, the reader makes some kind of assumption about the closeness of the relationship between the current node and the material linked to it.

The questions of link and node labeling which are obviously of such central importance here impinge on the issue of predictability at what I have been calling the macroscopic level. At the microscopic level, predictability revolves around such things as screen-design: typography, visual effects, layout of information on the screen, and so forth, all have an impact on the reader's ability to organize the material in his or her own mind, and thus on his or her ability to operate effectively within the hypertext environment.

Typographical conventions are such that the reader of a conventional text has a pretty good idea what kind of object will appear next. The period at the end of a sentence leads one to expect a capital letter and the beginning of a new object belonging to the same class—a new sentence; the blank space at the end of a paragraph signals the beginning of a new paragraph; and so on. The signals in hypertext systems aren't nearly so clear.

Because the technology isn't mature enough yet to support a single set of conventions, each hypertext system has to develop its own conventions. For that reason, it is probably necessary to incorporate procedural discussions about these conventions into the hyperdocument itself; thus one element of the hyperdocument will be an ongoing critique of its own procedures. Participants might consider, for example, whether to assign specific fonts to individual co-authors so that their contributions can be readily identified; text styles might be assigned to specific node or link types; a question might always be italicized, for instance, while an explanation might be underlined; and so on. Color can be used for similar purposes in systems where color is available. So can visual effects such as wipes, dissolves, and zooms, which are available in HyperCard. These and other special effects can easily become distracting or even annoying, but if particular devices are consistently and intelligently used in association with particular node types, they can also function as more or less subliminal aids to prediction, helping the reader to perceive the hyperdocument as coherent.

We regard a conventional text as coherent to the extent that all the material it contains strikes us being (a) related in an appropriately direct way to the subject and to the author's thesis; and (b) arranged in the appropriate sequence. The perception of coherence in hypertext seems to me much more problematic, however, though I don't have time to do more than suggest what might be involved. Nor do I know enough to do more than that.

I think of hypertext coherence as appearing at the metatextual level—that is, at the level where the reader perceives what Gregory Bateson calls "the pattern which connects."[26] The "pattern which connects" is the organizing notion around which all the disparate elements of the hyperdocument revolve. (An author's feel for "the pattern which connects" plays a significant part in decisions about node size and linkage as well.) This can be a relatively straightforward thing—a given hyperdocument might contain all the materials generated during a particular design project, for instance. This metatextual level is perhaps best represented by a visual map of some kind, whose nodes would open up to map subordinate patterns. This map ought to be readily accessible from any point in the hyperdocument, which suggests that it might be "iconized" and placed at a consistent screen location. This sounds simple enough, perhaps; but it becomes problematic again when we remember that we're dealing with a fluid system and multiple participants, and we start to ask whose understanding such maps represent. Maybe there needs to be a facility to allow any user to create such a map, whether for private consideration only or for public use might be up to the reader/co-author.

Conceptually, hypertext has a place, I think, in any environment where it's necessary or desirable to bring together large, complex, highly diversified bodies of information in such a way as to emphasize their interconnectedness—especially if physical space is at a premium, as of course it is on board a space station or an orbital device, or in a control room—or, for that matter, in a classroom.[27]

Perhaps the greatest value of hypertext is in its ability to link enormous quantities of material that, in a conventional text environment, would be kept separate, perhaps even in different buildings, so that things which someone perceives as being related do in fact become related. Hypertext is weakest when it comes to spelling out what these relationships entail; it is important to say this, because the techniques for explanation are quite highly developed within traditional rhetoric, and it would be a mistake to abandon them as outmoded.

Hypertext places different demands on both readers and authors than those facing readers and authors of conventional text. The principal reason for this, in my view, is that hypertext is truly a new medium. Employing the full resources of technology to represent and correlate information, hypertext grants both readers and authors an unprecedented degree of freedom to arrange materials as they deem best, and it permits interaction between readers and authors to an unprecedented degree. In so transforming the methods of organization which have served traditional text for millennia, hypertext requires authors and system designers to find new methods of indicating relationships, representing and constructing knowledge, and achieving coherence.

## Notes

1. See Gregory Bateson, *Mind and Nature: A Necessary Unity* (New York: Bantam Books, 1980).

2. See, for instance, Stanley Fish, *Self-Consuming Artifacts: The Experience of Seventeenth-Century Literature* (Berkeley: University of California Press, 1972).

3. Dennis Fry, *Homo Loquens: Man as a Talking Animal* (Cambridge: Cambridge University Press, 1977).

4. "Convergent Pressures: Social, Technological, Theoretical," Conference on the Future of Doctoral Studies in English (Panel on Proposals for Change). Wayzata, Minnesota, April 1987.

5. Charles Rossman, "The New *Ulysses:* The Hidden Controversy," *New York Review of Books* 25:19 (1988): 53-58.

6. Michael Groden, "Editing Joyce's *Ulysses:* An International Effort," *Scholarly Publishing in an Era of Change: Proceedings of the Second Annual Meeting, Society for Scholarly Publishing, Minneapolis, Minnesota June 2-4, 1980.* Ed. Ethel C. Langlois (Washington, D.C.: Society for Scholarly Publishing, 1981), 29.

7. *Mind and Nature,* 32.

8. "The Role of Hypertext in Transforming Information into Knowledge," Proceedings NECC'88. Dallas, Texas: 15-17 June 1988.

9. Havelock, *The Literate Revolution in Greece and Its Cultural Consequences* (Princeton: Princeton University Press, 1982); Ong, *Orality and Literacy: The Technologizing of the Word* (London: Methuen, 1982). Lanham, "The Electronic Word: Literary Study and the Digital Revolution," *New Literary History* 20:2 (1989): 265-90.

10. *Metamagical Themas: Questing for the Essence of Mind and Pattern* (New York: Bantam Books, 1986), 528.

11. *The Media Lab: Inventing the Future at MIT* (New York: Viking, 1987), 18.

12. *A Survey of Hypertext.* MCC Technical Report Number STP-356-86 (Austin, TX: MCC, 1986).

13. "The Bookmark and the Compass: Orientation Tools for Hypertext Users," *ACM SIGOIS Bulletin* 9 (October 1988): 34- 45.

14. See, for instance, Stuart Moulthrop, "Containing Multitudes: The Problem of Closure in Interactive Fiction," *ACH Newsletter* 10 (1988): 1-7; and Richard Ziegfeld, "Interactive Fiction: A New Literary Genre?" *New Literary History* 20:2 (1989): 340-72.

15. McLuhan, *Understanding Media: The Extensions of Man* (New York: New American Library, 1964), and Lanham, "The Electronic Word."

16. *Literary Machines* (San Antonio, TX: Theodor Holm Nelson, 1987), 1, 17.

17. John M. Slatin, "Hypertext and the Teaching of Writing," In Edward Barrett, ed., *Text, Context, and Hypertext* (Cambridge, MA.: The MIT Press, 1988), 113.

18. See Conklin, *A Survey*; Randall H. Trigg, Lucy A. Suchman and Frank G. Halasz, "Supporting Collaboration in NoteCards," Proceedings of the Conference on Computer-Supported Cooperative Work. Austin, TX. 3-5 December 1986; Lucy A. Suchman and Randall H. Trigg, "A Framework for Studying Research Collaboration," Proceedings of the Conference on Computer-Supported Cooperative Work. Austin, TX. 3-5 December 1986.

19. Conklin, *A Survey*, 38-40.

20. Slatin, "Hypertext and the Teaching of Writing," 126. See also **Harpold** in this volume.

21. See Slatin, "Hypertext and the Teaching of Writing," for a fuller discussion.

22. For several pertinent rules of thumb see **Landow** in this volume; also his "Hypertext in Literary Education, Criticism, and Scholarship," *Computers and the Humanities* 23:3 (1989): 173-198.

23. See Trigg, et al., "Supporting Collaboration."

24. L. Nancy Garrett, Karen Smith, and Norman Meyrowitz, "Intermedia: Issues, Strategies, and Tactics in the Design of a Hypermedia Document System," Proceedings of the Conference on Computer-Supported Cooperative Work. Austin, Texas. 3-5 December 1986. See also **Yankelovich, Meyrowitz & van Dam** in this volume.

25. Robert Kozma, "Designing Cognitive Tools for Computers." Presentation at Hypertext Workshop. Intelligent Systems Branch, Air Force Human Resources Laboratory, Brooks AFB, Texas. 23 February 1988.

26. *Mind and Nature*, 12.

27. Slatin, "Text and Context"; Conrade C. Jaffe and Patrick J. Lynch, "Hypermedia for Education in the Life Sciences," *Academic Computing* 4:1 (1989): 10-13, 52-57; John R. Bourne, Jeff Cantwell, Arthur J. Brodersen, Brian Antao, Antonis Koussis and Yen-Chun Huang, "Intelligent Hypertutoring in Engineering," *Academic Computing* 4:1 (September 1989): 18-20, 36-48.

# Threnody: Psychoanalytic Digressions on the Subject of Hypertexts

Terence Harpold
Department of Comparative Literature, University of Pennsylvania

## In lieu of an introduction

Briefly, an itinerary. This essay will propose the framework of a psychoanalytic theory of narrative digression in hypertexts. Digression, detour, swerve, split, cut—I'm going to apply several names to the narrative turns of hypertexts. The idea that is common to all of these names is that turning is a circular process that is also divisive: a turn *toward* a destination is also a turn *away from* an origin; turning encircles a place that is neither origin nor destination, and the shape of the turn divides you from its center. The different names for that turn describe not only a trajectory but also the contour of a place that you never get to.

I have in mind an etiology of that place and the turn around it. If, as I will contend, hypertexts make explicit on the level of narrative divisive effects enacted on the speaking subject at the most elementary levels of language, then those effects are not only characteristic of the docuverse as a discursive artefact, but they are also symptomatic of the speaking subject's relation to its structure. That relation is, I will argue, characterized by conditions and effects analogous to those shaping the discourse of obsessional neurosis. The subject rehearsing the ritual circuit of obsessional discourse and the subject navigating the gap-ridden fabric of a hypertext do so at a cost, that of an erasure of subjectivity.

To represent this structure of erasure, I will propose, in place of the customary metaphor of a docuverse constituted by a set of linked threads, another metaphor: the docuverse as a weave of *knotted* threads. The figure of the knot is preferable to that of the link in that it figures both the interlaced relations of discrete narratives and the gaps between them. The gaps are what interests me most.[1]

### The shape of the turn: the effects of narrative excess

A survey of the literature on hypertext design quickly demonstrates that principal among difficulties in the implementation of complex hypertexts are the problems posed by navigation. How will the user move between points in the web without straying so far from the origin that she no longer has a sense of the shape or direction of the path that she is following—without, that is, becoming "lost in hyperspace?"[2] The more data that is distributed in the hypertext, and the more numerous the links between segments of that data, the greater the problems associated with finding one's way through the structure of the hypertext. As the docuverse grows complex beyond the limits supported by the method of navigation, the user will not only forfeit a workable vision of the density and direction of threads, but she will also (and this, I believe, is the most significant aspect of this phenomenon) lose her place as participant (reader, author) in the hypertextual narratives. As the turns become more frequent and the digressions more vigorous, the user risks becoming *lost* in the docuverse.

This phenomenon of loss is grounded, paradoxically, in the narrative *excesses* of hypertexts. They are sustained by a paratextual apparatus that in conventional, "linear" literature is assigned a decidedly secondary role—the footnote at the bottom of the page, the interchapter heading, the marginal scribble of a reader who got to this page before us.[3] In hypertexts, however, the relations of priority and subordination that would otherwise define the limits of paratextuality are greatly complicated by the ambiguous relations of the linked texts. Divisions of text that have grown out of the traditions of movable type and paper media (pages, chapters, books), though frequently retained in some form by designers of hypertexts, are inadequate to represent the insistent and dynamic "linkedness" of hypertexts.[4] Detours are in a real sense what hypertexts are *about*; the multiplicity and effects of these detours are what distinguishes hypertexts from other kinds of textuality. I'm not claiming that we don't encounter relations of logical subordination between primary and ancillary texts in a docuverse, but only that these relations—and the topography of the textual corpus that they describe on another level—are not a priori characteristics of the link that joins two threads in a hypertext. Once you see that the link functions as a more radical sign of intertextuality than does, for example, a footnote marker in a paper text, the textual corpus has a very different shape from that to which you've grown accustomed.[5]

### Holes in the web: detour as gap

I said before that a hypertextual detour is a turn toward, away from, and, most important for my purposes, a turn around a place. It's a turn around a place you never get to, where something drops away between the multiple paths you might follow. The consequence of this falling away is that the fabric of a hypertext is riddled with holes, and navigation among them has a subversive effect on the navigating subject. By "subversive," I don't mean that hypertextual digressions have a political value (they do, but that's not my point here),[6] but rather that they are rooted in disruptive structures at the most elementary level of language. And by "subject," I mean something more precise than reader or author: the speaking, writing, reading subject, the speaking being whose position in a Symbolic order is marked by the effects of language.

Now, I'm assuming here a wider set of notions about language and those who inhabit it than can be addressed in this limited forum.[7] The version of semiology I'm applying has a frankly Lacanian flavor, because I'm taking the argument to a frankly Lacanian destination. To summarize Lacan's theory of the sign would require a considerable digression that would distract my reader from the relatively limited goals of this essay. The essential aspects of that theory for my purpose lie in its emphasis on the relations between signifiers, their dynamics, and their priority over the signifieds to which they correspond. For Lacan, language is structured as a system of pure differences on the level of its signifiers, in which the signified, rather than grounding the signifier to a thing represented, is a function of the difference and the slippage between signifiers. The signifying chain is profoundly and irretrievably marked with a cut that divides signifier from signifier, and from the signified that it ostensibly represents. That cut also informs the discourse of the speaking subject on all levels, dividing her from that about which she speaks, and, more importantly, from herself, who is a signifier for another subject whom she takes herself to be.

These spirals of misprision and division are deployed across the highest and lowest levels of hypertextual discourse. This is what takes place at the hypertextual detour: a diachronic characteristic of narrative digression—the turn at the link—replays the turn at the synchronic level of the link as a signifier *of pure difference*. On each level, meaning is a function of difference: the slippage in the signifying chain at the level of the sign is articulated at the higher level of narrative, in the slippage between linked threads in the weave of a docuverse. The gap-ridden structure of the hypertext makes explicit the underlying gaps in the fabric of language from which it is constructed, and in which the consumer of the hypertext is constituted as a subject of language.

The analogy is simple, but it has profound consequences for how you view the speaking subject who would navigate the slippage between the threads. The distribution of threads in a hypertext is a direct consequence of the detours that open up at the places where the threads are joined. Writing or reading the threads, moving along the weave of the hypertextual fabric, subjects the writer and the reader to the individual and cumulative effects of the dislocations at each detour in the tapestry.

### Detour as cut: narrative dismemberment and the fading of the subject

Detour. Cut. If we think of the hypertext as a textual corpus fragmented by the divisive effects of shifting threads, the image of a textual dismemberment comes to mind. Other forms of cutting will soon follow.

Consider a hypertext as though it were the discourse of an analysand, signifying in its gaps, its stumbling, its fragmentation. Seen in this light, the vigorous digression that distinguishes a hypertext from a linear text, and its consequences for the speaking subject, begin to look really interesting on the level of *symptom*. The detours in a hypertext correspond on the level of narrative to the gaps in the analysand's discourse that Lacan calls the "inter-dit": that which cannot be said, in the place of the spoken- or written-between. It's another place you can never get to, where the transparency and monumentality of the classical Cartesian subject is divided and passes through what Lacan calls the effects of "fading".[8]

"Fading" is Lacan's spin on Ernest Jones' "aphanisis".[9] Jones coined the term to describe a basis for castration anxiety in both sexes, in an underlying fear of the disappearance of sexual desire. For Lacan, the erasure of sexual difference that aphanisis implies doesn't make any sense, but the elementary structure of disappearance it describes fits nicely with his phenomenology of subjectivity. Lacan calls this effect the subject's fading: the subject assumes a position in the Symbolic order marked by the signifier that takes her place, in which assumption she is paradoxically made manifest in her disappearance. Eclipsed by the signifier that takes a place for her and from her, she obtains meaning in the fabric of language.[10]

Think of docuverses as elaborate tissues, and their narrative swerves as ruptures in the weave that mark the places where threads fall away from one another. In each point of rupture, the link functions as a signifier of pure difference, and the narrative is therein divided on the highest and lowest levels, in the scene of the subject's fading. If you consider for a moment what it is meant literally when a reader says that she has become lost in a narrative, you'll see that the digression that "causes" the loss subverts the subject at the most elementary level—and that the break of the digression is coextensive with the place of the subject in the narrative. In the detour around the link, the position of the hypertextual subject is sustained and disabled by the gap that opens up in the detour. The gap in the narrative corresponds to a gap in subjectivity that cannot be assimilated to the correlation or intersection of the texts

---

linked by the detour. Seen in this light, hypertextual navigation is a recursive process that parses the subject as it parses the text, uncovering a gap at the center of the experience of moving from "here" to "there", and the from/to fold marks the division of subjectivity. Within the narrative structure of the hypertext, navigation follows a looping path returning to the gap, supported by anticipation and a corresponding retrograde movement that encircles the subject's pursuit of meaning.[11] The center of the gap—and the focus of the pursuit—is the subject's fading.

## Dismemberment and death

Early in Sterne's novel, Tristram Shandy remarks that "digressions are the sunshine;—they are the life, the soul of reading." Even a cursory reading of the novel will reveal that the Shandyean digression conceals a darker, more mortal secret. The importance of castration motifs in the novel is well-documented, the hobbyhorsical melodrama of Uncle Toby's wound, Tristram's encounters with the nose-squashing forceps of Dr. Slop and the circumcising edge of the window-sash being the best-known of these motifs. The novel's narrative excesses reveal a loss on the level of subjectivity, and its digressive structures encircle a wound for which castration is the symbol.

Tristram's breathless journey to the continent in book 7 is a mad rush away from Death, who has come knocking at his door—as he must, given the impossibility of Tristram's endeavor to arrest the effects of time by writing to the moment. Tristram's flight looks a lot like the detour around the fading of the subject that is played out in hypertextual digression, in that place where the effects of language come to bear in the moment of the detour. It also looks a lot like the flight from an erasure of the subject that frays the multiple threads of obsessional discourse.

Freud observed in his analysis of the Rat-Man that the obsessional's thoughts are characterized by a severance of connections between parallel, opposing and related ideas.[12] The elementary structure of obsessional logic is an ellipsis punctuating a gap between connected ideas, where something fell away from consciousness. The obsessional's discourse hinges on these ellipses, shifting around them in changing alignments, but continually retracing the contour of the thing that is excluded from conscious thought. In other words, the obsessional's behavior makes "the fullest possible use of displacement" (241) to get around the place it can't get to.

The place it can't get to is the place of the obsessional's mortality. As the Rat-Man's case demonstrates, the circuit of obsessional thought is a circuit around the impossibility of reimbursing a debt—a lack, a gap—that divides the subject with its imperative. That imperative is, psychoanalysis tells us, shaped by the obsessional's repeated refusal of the possibility of her own death.[13] Obsessionals rehearse in every turn of their ritual behavior the moment of a mortality they are unable to accept. "Their thoughts," says Freud, "are unceasingly occupied with other people's length of life and possibility of death; their superstitious propensities have had no other content to begin with, and have perhaps no other source whatever."[14]

Lacan takes a slightly different turn on this definition, and the point I want to make may be clearer in light of it. For Lacan, the different neuroses rehearse the same event—the splitting and consequent erasure of the subject in the cut between signifiers—in different ways, according to how the cut is dramatized. In the insufferable pleasure of her symptom, the hysteric repeats the alienation that is the effect of the cut; the obsessional's pleasure, on the other hand, is what he finds in continually repeating the cut's trauma.[15] The repetition of this trauma in the fabric of discourse is the clue to the status of a hypertext as an obsessional narrative of the scene of the cut.

Hypertexts appear to be stitched together out of nothing but connections, but the real status of these connections depends on how you regard the movement of the narrative across the links. Remember that the nature of the relation between the linked texts is not an attribute that needs to be defined in order to establish the link. Entering the web requires a confidence in a myth that presumes connections can be made between dismembered portions of a corpus that are, on an elementary level, disjoint. Like the turns of the obsessional's thoughts, the detour of the link encircles a gap in the narrative that marks a falling away which corresponds, I have argued, to the fading of the subject on the level of the turn as signifier of detour. The turn rehearses that fading within the moment of the detour and across the structure of the docuverse. The hypertext looks like an obsessional's discourse because it is grounded in mortality on the level of narrative structure, by a slipping away of thread from thread at points of division and erasure that look like points of intersection.[16]

## Filling in the gaps; or, tying the knot

The subject's fading has a kind of flip side, a turn, that Jacques-Alain Miller has named "suture".[17] Suture describes a closing of the gap in language by the subject's assumption of the place of the gap. It maintains, if you will, what you can see of the subject as she fades. By assuming a proper name that represents and obscures the gap between signifiers, the subject maintains an illusory bridge across the gap; she gains a position in the Symbolic at the expense of her being. Suture, in other words, binds the subject to the signifying chain and closes the wound of subjectivity. Keep in mind, however, that this closure, although necessary for the subject's functioning in the Symbolic as signifier, is only provisional. The wound can be bandaged but not healed. We're still turning around a place that we can't get to.

I want to move back now, with the idea of suture in mind, from the synchronic level of gaps in the signifying chain to the diachronic level of narrative dismemberment. I would like to suggest that Miller's "suture" describes the effect on the hypertextual subject of the global binding of the docuverse across its disjoint threads. At each point of detour there is a simultaneous closure of the break in the narrative and a falling away from each other of the joined threads. This results in a provisional resolution of the effect of fading that the structure of dismemberment plays out on the level of the narrative. Narrative suture is what shores up the gaps in hypertextual discourse; it's what makes credible the link's function as a marker of connection and integration, rather than one of division and fragmentation.

Sutures are held together with knots, and knots are, I believe, better suited than are links to the description of these structures of detour, division and gap. Whereas metaphors of linking suggest an intersection of two or more threads at a common point, metaphors of knotting suggest a more dynamic interlacing of the threads, each looping around the other at a central point of detour.[18] A knot can be thought of as an extension of suture: suture describes the effect of the knot; the knot describes the site of the suture, where multiple threads enclose a gap. The point in all this is very simple—and it is, I think, as summary a description of the structure of narrative digression as "getting lost" is of the effects of narrative excess: *if you take apart a knot, there is nothing inside it.*[19]

## Tying knots: the social fabric of digression

When knots are drawn tightly, they obscure the gaps they enclose. Many knots drawn across a frayed fabric can shore up gaps all over the place. I've been describing the effects of hypertextual digression as though they were limited to an individual subject, when they are, I would add, equally descriptive of effects produced on a broader, social register. The collaborative efforts of authors and readers in hypertext systems that enable users to add to the tissue of the docuverse compound many times over the effects of narrative dismemberment. The involutions that these extensions of the weave produce are too complex for me to go into here, though I will state simply that I consider them to be extensions of the same structures of detour, fading, and knotting that shape the individual narrative detour. I've not, after all, made any distinction between the readers and authors in my discussion of the hypertextual subject, and I don't see any: the structure of detour

---

that hypertexts exemplify operates across such distinctions, and the subject who navigates the docuverse inhabits its gaps and slippages without regard for the origin of the individual instance of digression.

I would, moreover, suggest that the collaborative effects of narrative detour introduced by multiple hypertext authors reinforce communal concerns prompted by the drama of the cut of subjectivity. These loopings and the knots that bind them are the traces of collective structures enclosing and obscuring the gap of subjectivity. What distinguishes hypertexts as collaborative efforts from other forms of textuality-as-detour is that they concretize in a social form the significance of the structures of gap and erasure in narrative digression. Each contributor to the hypertext plays out her own drama in a social ritual of suture across the dismemberment of the collective corpus. The paths that are laid out by successive readers in the docuverse are much like Tristram's frenetic but equivocal flight from mortality. Even as they bind the body of the text, they reveal its erasures and its wounds.

The paradoxical function of death in obsessional discourse comes back here on the level of myth. Freud observes that obsessionals "need the help of the possibility of death chiefly in order that it may act as a solution of conflicts they have left unresolved".[20] The social space of the hypertext requires the death of the subject that inhabits its detours in order to resolve the desire to flee death that its structure reveals. The weave is sustained by the subject's fading, and that fading moves the users to cover it with the threads that are, further, sustained by the fading. Our urge to add to the web is the flip side of its dizzying disorientation: both are shaped by a collective fantasy that seeks to obscure that which the web subtracts from us.

In his "Jerome, or Death in the Life of the Obsessional," Serge Leclaire recounts his patient's dream of a mummy, borne aloft in an open sarcophagus: "Suddenly, as the procession advances, the mummy liquefies. All that is left in the sarcophagus is a red juice whose horrifying aspect is veiled by the certainty that these are but the unguents that had served to embalm the body" (101). What's left after the dissolution of the textual corpus is the stuff that holds it together, even as that stuff dissolves in the moment the subject represents her own mortality. We can turn around and around that moment and never close the wound it covers. The fabric of a docuverse will grow increasingly complex, increasingly knotted, the monumental figure of the body progressively ritualized into a totemic object, only to collapse into dissolution when you look at it closely. Knots hold together the bandages of the dismembered body, but they do not heal its wounds.

# Notes

1. I will be referring throughout this essay to the effects of digression in hyper*texts*. My descriptions of these effects can be applied equally well to the narrative structures of hyper*media* docuverses, that is, docuverses including visual and audio material in addition to textual material. I'm favoring the term "hypertext" because it suggests better than "hypermedia" a complex of metaphors having to do with textuality as fabric, weave, web, etc.

2. Jeff Conklin, "Hypertext: An Introduction and Survey," *IEEE Computer* 20:9 (1987): 17-41; Kenneth Utting and Nicole Yankelovich, "Context and Orientation in Hypermedia Networks," Institute for Research in Information and Scholarship Technical Report 88-2, 1988; Deborah M. Edwards and Lynda Hardman, "'Lost in Hyperspace': Cognitive Mapping and Navigation in a Hypertext Environment," in *Hypertext: Theory into Practice*, ed. Ray McAleese (Oxford: Intellect,1989). 104-125. Ray McAleese observes that these navigation problems are increased many times over by the higher density of visual and audio information in hypermedia docuverses: "Navigation and Browsing in Hypertext," in *Hypertext: Theory into Practice*, 6-44.

3. Gérard Genette, *Seuils* (Paris: Editions du Seuil, 1987).

4. Why these structures are retained in hypertext applications is a question worthy of close consideration. Some probable explanations: 1) there are advantages to maintaining familiar metaphors for the user who is likely to spend most of her time consuming texts in a paper-bound linear format; 2) most current hypertexts are assembled from existing texts that were structured in these formats; 3) electronic text simply has not been around long enough, and in sufficient quantity and complexity to generate a widely recognizable set of distinct metaphors for content segmentation and sequence.

5. A thorough study of paratextual relations in hypertexts would require an exhaustive inventory of hypertextual digressions. Before this can be undertaken, the existing hypertextual corpus will have to be greatly expanded to order to obtain a sufficient set of examples from which to develop the inventory. Recent works that have begun to address this issue include: on hypertextual content, Rainer Hammwöhner and Ulrich Thiel, "Content Oriented Relations Between Text Units: A Structural Model for Hypertexts," in *Proceedings Hypertext '87*. (Chapel Hill, NC: Association for Computing Machinery, 1987), 155-174; on paths, Utting, "Context and Orientation"; on links, Steven J. DeRose, "Expanding the Notion of Links," in

*Proceedings Hypertext '89* (Pittsburgh, PA: Association for Computing Machinery, 1989), 249-257; on browsing mechanisms, McAleese, "Navigation and Browsing"; on navigational strategies, Jakob Nielsen, "The Art of Navigating Through Hypertext," *Communications of the ACM* 33 (1990): 296-310, and H. Van Dyke Parunak, "Hypermedia Topologies and User Navigation," *Proceedings Hypertext '89*, 43-50; on "rules" for hypertext implementation, George Landow, "Relationally Encoded Links and the Rhetoric of Hypertext," in *Proceedings Hypertext '87*, 331-343, and "The Rhetoric of Hypermedia: Some Rules for Authors," in the present volume.

6. For an analysis of the political character of hypertext as a discursive form see Stuart Moulthrop, "In the Zones: Hypertext and the Politics of Interpretation," *Writing on the Edge* 1 (1989): 18-27; and "Hypertext and 'the Hyperreal'," *Proceedings Hypertext '89* (Pittsburgh, PA: Association for Computing Machinery, 1989), 259-267.

7. This is perhaps the place to note that this essay is extracted from a much longer work in progress on the subject of narrative digression.

8. Lacan, Jacques, "The Subversion of the Subject and the Dialectic of Desire in the Freudian Unconscious," in Lacan, *Ecrits: A Selection*, ed. and trans. Alan Sheridan (New York: W.W. Norton, 1977), 299.

9. Ernest Jones, "Early Development of Female Sexuality," in *Papers on Psychoanalysis* (London: Baillière, 1950), 438-51.

10. For a brief but suggestive application of *aphanisis* to narrative theory see Régis Durand, "On *Aphanisis*: A Note on the Dramaturgy of the Subject in Narrative Analysis," in *Lacan and Narration: The Psychoanalytic Difference in Narrative Theory*, ed. Robert Con Davis (Baltimore: Johns Hopkins University Press, 1983), 860-870.

11. Cf. Lacan's extended discussion of the graphs of the subject's subversion in, "The Subversion of the Subject."

12. Sigmund Freud, "Notes Upon a Case of Obsessional Neurosis," in *The Standard Edition of the Complete Psychological Works of Sigmund Freud*, ed. James Strachey. 24 vols. (London: Hogarth Press, 1953-74). 10:231.

13. Serge Leclaire, "Jerome, or Death in the Life of the Obsessional," in *Returning to Freud: Clinical Psychoanalysis in the School of Lacan*, ed. and trans. Stuart Schneiderman (New Haven: Yale University Press, 1980), 107.

14. Freud, "Notes Upon a Case," 236.

15. Jacques Lacan, "Desire and the Interpretation of Desire in *Hamlet*,"*Yale French Studies* 55/56 (1980): 11-52.

16. According to Lacan, the pervert's relation to the cut is analogous to that of the neurotic, except that the pervert, rather than pursuing the cut in a fantasy replaying the torn fabric of discourse, pursues it in a fantasmatic object that subtends that discourse: "Desire and the Interpretation of Desire," 16. How the elements of narrative dismemberment display a pathology depends on how you consider the elements of the dismemberment. If you think of a hypertext as purely a constellation of link-points, rather than as a weave crossed over, sewn out of and around gaps at the points of the links, what you get is a kind of collection of perverse objects that take the place of the tear in the weave.

17. Jacques-Alain Miller, "La Suture (Eléments de la logique du signifiant)," *Cahiers Pour l'Analyse* 1 (1966): 39-51.

18. See Tuve's discussion of *entrelacement* as a model of the radically digressive structures of Medieval and Renaissance allegory, *Allegorical Imagery: Some Medieval Books and Their Posterity* (Princeton: Princeton University Press, 1966). The figure of the knot that I'm proposing here is related to the *braid* that Roland Barthes uses to describe the relation of codes in the classical text; see *S/Z*, trans. Richard Miller (New York: Hill and Wang, 1974), 160. The advantage of k*not* over *braid* is that the former maintains the suggestion of conjunction that I think is the main feature of *link*.

19. The figure of the knot doesn't replace other names for the shape and effect of this narrative turn: cut, fading, dismemberment, tear, suture, etc. All these terms taken together—there are no doubt others better suited to other ways of interpreting narrative digression—form a kind of anatomy of the effects of narrative detour enacted at the moment a text becomes a hypertext. My intention here is not to be exhaustive, but rather to address the specific effects of this turn in relation to a splitting of the subject enacted by the breaks in language that inform digression at the lowest and highest levels.

20. Freud, "Notes Upon a Case," 236.

# Part III

Applications

# Biblical Studies and Hypertext

Steven J. DeRose
Electronic Book Technologies, Providence, Rhode Island

## Introduction

The field of biblical studies involves the careful, systematic investigation of a very complex set of documents whose primary sources, the Jewish and Christian Scriptures, have been studied for many centuries. Consequently, there exists a vast corpus of secondary sources relevant to researchers in this field that includes translations, commentaries, and various language references. These sources form an intricate and highly interconnected network, for the representation of which hypertext is an appropriate tool.

The number of documents involved and the closeness of their connections pose particular problems for the design, implementation, and use of hypertext and hypermedia systems. In particular, the immense number of links that must be created and maintained constrains the way in which designers structure the data, and it also imposes difficult requirements on display and navigation tools. If the time users must wait for certain operations is related too closely to the number of links to or from their text, a system may become unacceptably slow. Likewise, if users cannot quickly hide links that are not relevant to their current purposes, they may give up rather than drown in a sea of options.

In this paper I shall discuss some of the problems that the materials of biblical studies pose for hypertext systems, particularly in regard to the range of linking facilities needed. I will draw a number of examples from the CD Word project at Dallas Theological Seminary, which has gathered a range of primary and secondary documents for biblical studies into a highly linked electronic database that is intended to facilitate the work of students, researchers, and clergy by making these tools accessible and navigable.[1] Later in the paper I will describe CD Word itself in more detail.

The complexities I describe are not unique; but the biblical corpus quickly raises key issues of hypertext design in a way that other bodies of text do not.

## Characteristics of biblical documents

*Structure*

All documents have structure; texts composed in natural languages have linguistic structure. For my purposes here it is sufficient to note that this structure extends far above sentence level, all the way up to units we might call "discourses" or (in concession to written language) "documents," and to note that this structure is largely hierarchical.[2]

In biblical texts, some of these discourse-level units are approximated by a standard reference scheme that divides the texts into books, chapters, and verses. A verse often corresponds to a sentence; a chapter to a group of paragraphs on a given topic. This structure is *canonical*; that is, it applies not only to the primary texts, but also to translations and even to some commentaries. Agreement on the names for these units allows scholars to refer (read, "link") to them conveniently. By "conveniently," I mean that the references are brief, unambiguous, mnemonic, and standard or portable.

Other discourse units such as paragraphs are normally marked by typographic conventions, which were also introduced by scholars, and are sometimes themselves the topic of scholarly debate.[3] Many kinds of linguistic units are left implicit (noun phrase, pericope, etc).

Scholars frequently wish to explicate the implicit structures. Therefore, scholarly hypertext systems must support multiple partially-related structures applied to the same text, and such systems must provide means for examining and modifying these structures.

Documents in printed form have an additional hierarchical structure. Pages are divided into one or more columns and other areas, such as figure blocks, footnote areas, and marginalia. Some of these units are further divided, for example, into printed lines. Normally these units have no significance for the biblical scholar; they are merely artifacts of printing that depend on such matters as the size of the animals or trees from which writing materials came, or perhaps on the height of the shelves in a particular monastic library. Later, the amount of cold type a printer owned or the size of printing plates had a similar effect; and now perhaps the size of affordable computer displays does, too. My point here is that some aspects of the appearance of the text are usually an artifact of technology, not an inherent property of the text itself. If one reprints a document in a way that happens to change every line and page break in it, it is still in a significant sense the same document.

Nevertheless, there are exceptions. When working with literary texts, minutely examining the form of certain manuscripts is necessary at crucial points, since matters of form affect decisions about content. In the First Folio of Shakespeare, a page's position within a signature affects the spelling of some words. The printer apparently had insufficient type to set an entire group of pages at once. Thus (say) pages one and eight would be set and printed (since they go on the same sheet), followed by two and seven, then three and six, and finally four and five. Barring hand counting of character widths, the printer could only estimate what word should begin page eight. Depending on the estimates, the last pages set could be over- or under-full and would be adjusted to fit, often by changing spellings. In such cases the layout of a particular edition must be represented; but for most documents it can safely be ignored so long as an appropriate display can be generated on any medium at need.[4]

Secondary sources for biblical study have different structures. Many, such as lexica, Bible dictionaries, and the like, are essentially databases with a simple indexing method (i.e., alphabetical order of key words). The fact that they are printed in a particular way is a property of paper, print technology, and our need to find entries quickly by hand. Even in these cases, the internal structure of each entry is complex, with hierarchical layers of definitions, citations, and cross-references.

Since an adequate hypertext system must retain all of these structures, most of which are hierarchical, the card metaphor that characterizes some hypertext systems is obviously inadequate. Few literary documents are atomized into card-sized thoughts. Indeed one could only painfully read a book published on 3x5 cards!

*Versions*

A second important characteristic of the biblical text is that we do not have it. We do not have *the* text of the Bible. Instead, we have thousands of manuscripts that are descendants of a presumed original text, and we have families of textual witnesses that point toward primitive variant rescensions. Although most classical texts similarly exist in varying manuscripts, they present less complex problems of textual variants because fewer have come down to us.

The manuscripts that bear witness to an ancient text are not all copies of an original. Rather, parent manuscripts were copied some number of times, and then some or all of the copies were copied, and so on. Thus we have a tree, not a list, of document versions, with many intermediate versions missing. Storing this kind of version structure is difficult, as is making it available to the user in a comprehensible fashion. Although the Xanadu™ system[5] permits tree-structured versioning, it does not provide a convenient mechanism for naming and accessing versions. Few other hypertext systems even address the question of versions.

One might also ask whether translations of the text should be treated as versions. The line is hard to draw; what of a translation that consists merely of substituting modernized spellings of the original language's words? And what of a text that substitutes for each word, the root word-form from which it is derived (such a text is useful for certain philological pursuits)? And are various English translations properly treated as versions of each other?

My inclination is to say that these things are not in fact versions but texts that have the property of sharing the same document structure. More accurately, they share one structure, namely that of book/chapter/verse. They share not only the Document Type Definition — that of books divided into chapters that are divided into verses — but at an abstract level they also share the particular divisions and particular formal names of the instances of books, chapters, and verses . Many documents share the structure of the Bible, and users often wish to relate documents in terms of that structure.

The versioning problem for ancient texts is actually even more complicated. First, we do not know the genetic relationships among manuscript versions with certainty, and so they are subject to interpretation, or, if you will, to "versioning." Second, since any copyist might have referred to more than one earlier version, the dependencies between manuscript versions become not the usual tree, in which every branch has but one source, but a more complex structure known as a "directed acyclic graph" or "DAG." So far as I know, no hypertext system yet supports this degree of complexity in the version structure of its documents. However, this complexity has been found useful in handling successive revisions to computer programs and documentation, and some products in that field begin to address these problems.[6]

*Annotation*

A hypertext system adequate for biblical studies has to support the various kinds of annotation that have been developed in this field. For example, at least six projects have provided grammatical category annotations for the New Testament.[7] Word-roots and word-by-word English glosses are available, as are special codings that provide access to other lexical tools. These often are published in an inter-linear form that aligns annotation(s) underneath the words to which they apply. Again, few programs supply this display feature available in book technology.

Printed Bibles frequently include extensive marginalia, including cross-references to related passages, notations of significant alternate readings (whether arising from manuscript variations or from ambiguities of translation), and discussions of interpretation. Portions of the Hebrew Bible may include musical notations. Greek poetry can be usefully annotated for its meter, though there is little Greek poetry in the biblical text.

Annotations generally mirror the structure of the text being annotated. However, because the structural relationships in the Bible are more fine-grained than in most other texts, applying to words or even parts of words, annotations only apply to a particular document (or perhaps set of documents): for example, English glosses for the successive words of the Hebrew text cannot be applied straightforwardly to a Greek or English translation of that text. In addition, since annotations, unlike versions, usually have little interest apart from the text they annotate, a display system must be able to show annotations simultaneously with the text and in appropriate relation to it.

*Frequent quotation*

A fourth distinguishing characteristic of the biblical text is the degree to which it has been annotated and referred to. Commentaries of many types confront the researcher, ranging from one-volume general works to entire articles and books devoted to a single difficult verse or phrase. In this situation, the use of page numbers for cross-reference is simply not adequate for the degree of precise reference required. Because page and line numbers change with every new edition, scholars adopted a standard system of numbering verses in the Bible similar to that used by classical philologists. Many modern editions of classical authors, including the complete works of Plato and Aristotle, refer to a particular edition whose page and line numbers are used. Editions that do not follow the same page and line breaking supply the standard numbering, usually in the margin.

Standard naming and numbering conventions provide effective single-directional links from a commentary *to* biblical texts. Before hypertext, however, scholars starting at the biblical text had no means to discover the links from a passage in scripture to another text. Manuscript and book technology, in other words, make impossible fully answering questions such as "What commentaries refer to this Psalm?"

With the advent of hypertext we have become accustomed to asking such questions. But with this capability comes the danger that we may get the answers. When the docuverse arrives and provides the typical student an online library of a few thousand biblical reference sources, the incautious questioner will be answered with thousands of links. Since many of the passages a student wishes to investigate are those that others have found interesting, the worst case is the most likely one.

I shall discuss the difficulties of bidirectional linking in more detail below. Now it suffices to note that to support bidirectional linking at all, one must (1) modify the biblical text every time it is linked to (i.e., add some indicator by which the computer can find the other end of the link); (2) maintain a connection from the biblical passage to a database which *is* so modified; or (3) perform prohibitive searches every time a link is to be followed in reverse. Whichever solution one chooses must be carefully protected against problems of scale.

*Frequent and complex searching*

A final problem designers of biblical hypertext must confront is that scholars often wish to find instances of particular structural, lexical, and other patterns in the Bible. These patterns often cannot be characterized by simple strings of characters, such as may be searched for with typical "find" commands. Since links will never exist to everything one might wish to reach, sophisticated retrieval is therefore an essential component of a hypertext system used for biblical studies.

Beyond the commonplace text-editor "find" functions, the researcher will often wish to specify logical, positional, and sequential relationships between items. For example, one might request all chapters containing two particular words that are no more than three verses apart and that do not contain either of two other words. Searches may also refer to various annotations, such as word-root, grammatical form, or thematic ones.

Flexible means are necessary for specifying where to search. It is often useful to restrict investigation to particular subsets of the biblical corpus. For example, the four Gospels, the first three (Synoptic) Gospels, the Epistles of Paul, and the books of Moses (the Pentateuch) are such meaningful groups of books.

The most computationally challenging needs with respect to searching are due to particular characteristics of the biblical languages. English, fortunately for computer designers, has one of the simplest writing systems known; but searching tools designed for English therefore frequently fall short when applied to other languages. For example, English uses essentially no accents or other diacritical marks. In Greek, on the other hand, there are two "breathing" marks, three accents, and at least two other diacritics commonly in use. When searching for a particular word, the user usually wants to ignore these marks entirely. Even when searching with regard to accents, the acute accent should usually be considered synonymous with the grave.

Hebrew is even more complex than Greek, since it represents vowels by diacritical marks rather than by full-fledged characters. Most ancient manuscripts, moreover, do not use these diacritical marks, so although some modern editions of the Hebrew text may include these vowel points, the user would frequently like to ignore them in searching. Furthermore, in Hebrew various linguistic processes alter roots internally, rather than merely at the ends as is generally true in English and Greek. In many non-Semitic languages one can find most inflected forms of a word by searching for a string of central characters. For example, in Greek one can search for the verb "λεγω" by searching for "λεγ" and capture the forms for different persons and numbers (though not, in this case, all different tenses). This method works less well for Hebrew.

Since biblical and literary scholars often concern themselves more with themes than with particular words, they require a system that also allows searching for groups of related words. Standard lists of Greek synonyms are available, similar to an English thesaurus, and can be used to obtain much of the desired effect.

Various writing conventions themselves also complicate searching. In searching documents entered from paper, for example, one must to be able to combine the parts of words hyphenated across lines. In English, a search for "will" should find instances of "won't," because it is a contracted or short form of "will not." A similar process in Greek called "crasis" creates parallel problems for the designer of scholarly hypertext systems.

*Similar phenomena in other fields*

None of these problems is entirely unique to the biblical corpus. All natural language documents, for example, share the property of having structure. The biblical texts may be exceptional in the extent to which alternative structures are proposed and discussed, but all printed documents exhibit at least two structures, logical and physical, and information retrieval systems need to account for them. Problems discovered in a particular field later reveal themselves in a much broader context. I suggest that this is the case with the challenges posed for hypertext and hypermedia systems by the complexities of biblical studies. Though some fields may not exhibit the same complexity of interconnection and retrieval needs, many of the same problems arise in another form or on a smaller scale.

## A taxonomy of links

The biblical studies corpus shows that links involve much more complicated theoretical and design issues than may at first appear. This section will describe several sorts of links that differ not only in purpose but in structure, function, and preferred means of implementation. These link types fit together to form a taxonomy of functions.[8]

### Associative links

Associative links are the usual stock in trade of hypertext systems. They attach arbitrary pieces of documents to each other, like strings tied from one place to another. In general, they can represent any concept their creator desires. Because of this, they cannot be replaced by retrieval algorithms, or even by unilateral creation on the part of a system "author." Rather, every user must be able to create them on the fly and to organize them in whatever way seems appropriate.

Because these links serve many purposes, they are usually labelled according to type. Trigg has proposed a taxonomy that insightfully covers a large range of needs.[9] But no taxonomy is adequate. Consider the following example: over the course of many years one may have been collecting blocks of literary and other nonbiblical text that appear to allude to a particular Bible passage. An allusion may or may not be evident from the particular words used; when it is not, larger thematic and stylistic factors are often involved. Because of this complexity, one cannot expect to find all desired text blocks with a retrieval request, however sophisticated it may be. So each time the user comes across a passage of interest, a link is made to it. From time to time the user might examine all of the fragments found so far and look for patterns of style, distribution, and so on.

In order to find all of these links, either they must all originate from a common place, or there must be a means of separating them out from all other links. One can create a document for this purpose and modify it by adding each link as found; then examining all links out of that document accomplishes the desired end. However, a few problems remain. First, since the example is a collection gathered over many years on an occasional basis, the file's name or location might easily be forgotten, leaving no way to recover the work. Second and more significant, if the system supports bi-directional links then there are links attached to the literary fragments, which will be utterly mysterious except in a particular context. Not only will other users have no clue where the links lead but even their creator may eventually forget their purpose or destination.

---

Filtering links based on attributes other than type, such as date and creator, mitigates this problem to some extent, but even this solution merely approximates what is essentially an issue of type. The Brown/IRIS Intermedia system provides another alternative via "webs," which are independent sets of links, that may be activated or inactivated as desired. One can think of a web as a meta-type of link; webs do provide many of the benefits of flexible link-typing.

Associative links, then, should permit an unbounded number of types, and they should be sensitive to those types. The display should be able to indicate a link's type, so a user pursuing several types can tell at a glance which displayed links serve which purposes. Of course one display option is "none," so links not of interest need not distract the reader at all.

There is a major problem with an unbounded set of types, however: the problem of standardization. If users can create their own type-names at will, they will certainly produce eventual confusion. In a worldwide community of users there is the problem of language: are links whose types are named by "synonymous" German and English words actually of the same type? Even in a single language users may find many names for the same thing, and the same name for distinct things. How, then, can one resolve the semantics of link types?

The same problem has often been observed in electronic mail forums, bulletin boards, and other online media. Bulletin board systems that do not enforce a list of topics quickly bog down in inconsistency. Users who wish to view all postings relevant to "Macintosh" must also check under "Mac," "Apple Macintosh," "Mac Software Development," "Mac II," and countless other topics and misspelled topics. On the other hand, if the system allows only one topic it will bog down when a discussion splits, with groups, say, of users and developers who share few common interests forced into the same category.

Similarly, in the design of document markup systems there is no easy way to enforce the semantics of element names. If one user chooses to label all paragraphs as <block_quote> and all block quotes as <paragraph>, there is no way for the computer to detect the semantic change in order to respond in a way other users would likely consider appropriate. Moreover, it seems clear that the tagset consisting of <book>, <chapter>, <verse>, <poetry_line>, etc. is better than an identically used tagset consisting of <tag1>, <tag2>, <tag3>, <tag4>, etc. But the reason it is better can be apparent only to sentient or very sophisticated systems.

Even if a standard list of element names is available (such as the Association of American Publishers SGML-conforming set), new or forgotten uses will constantly arise. An example pointed out to me by James H. Coombs is that the AAP tagset provides no tags for poetry. A common (and unfortunate) response of users is to choose an existing tag that gets the desired typographic effect, despite any opacity of the tag's name. For example, a user may choose to tag "theorems," "lemmas," and "formulas" as "examples" because the appearance is correct in their particular word-processor. This choice of an inappropriate tag may pose no problem until the appearance must change; at that time someone must intuit the author's intent and re-tag each element unambiguously.

In the same way, no closed taxonomy of types can be defined for associative links, yet total lack of standardization has its own dangers. I advocate allowing any user to add to the taxonomy, but only by choosing to make each new tag a sub-type of an already existing type. This solution has many of the same advantages (and limitations) as object-type inheritance systems in object oriented programming systems. Interested readers may wish to consult the object oriented programming literature for discussion of these issues.

Another important characteristic of associative links is that they often point to standardized locations. Frequently one wishes to refer to a particular discourse unit such as a paragraph or chapter, or to a unit such as a single animation frame or a bar or phrase of music. Some systems allow links only to and from points; others allow arbitrary ranges of text; a few even allow discontiguous ranges. Nevertheless, the most frequent references will be to units that users find conceptually salient. Particularly important are links to those units for which users have names. These links should be especially convenient to create and access.

*Structure-representing links*

Documents have particular structures that reflect their linguistic, thematic, and other significances. For most documents there is only one relevant structure, though for biblical and other literary texts there may be many, either reflecting competing theories about the "true" structure or reflecting different but compatible view-points.

Perhaps the easiest way to identify structure-representing ("s-r") links is that they form the basis for linearizing the text, i.e., for presenting it as a sequence of elements. This solution does not contradict my claim that the primary document structure is a hierarchy, because a hierarchy can be unambiguously traversed to produce a sequence of its elements, and if element boundaries are represented, it can be unambiguously reconstructed from that sequence. Despite the fact that any particular viewing session is *a* linearization, some documents probably exist that need never be formally linearized. However, we have millions of texts that have come to us only in linearized form, whose authors thought carefully about that constraint when composing them. Since these documents will not go away we ought to provide for them. Our linguistic communication is also linear; we can only utter a stream of phonemes.

Most hypertext systems, if they consider s-r links at all, treat them as merely a special case of associative links. But they are distinct in several ways, and they deserve distinct treatment. First, the fact that these links reflect linguistic structure (in however rudimentary a fashion) imposes special requirements on display. For example, these links should normally be traversed automatically in a particular order as the user scrolls through a document, rather than being followed only on request.

Second, the hierarchical structure should be protected. This need precludes anomalous documents, such as those in which paragraphs contain chapters, though the user who has need for non-hierarchical documents is not constrained, since there are many other kinds of links available. Since non-hierarchical documents may have no clear linearization at all, they make search and retrieval difficult, for they provide no single sequence for reference in putting bounds on context and proximity.

Third, s-r links characteristically point to sequences of other s-r links and not to spans of text. For example, a section may be a sequence of paragraphs; it is not a sequence of ranges of characters. If we were to represent a section in the latter fashion, we would miss the insight that certain portions of the section are the targets of paragraph-links, and that this is not mere chance.

Fourth, unlike associative links, the set of s-r link types is fairly constrained. New types are needed from time to time, but a small set such as the AAP tag set is much more adequate than a similar set of associative link types could be.

The types above all must be stored individually, and so are collectively called "extensional links." Those which follow, however, could be generated by rule, and so are collectively called "intensional links."

*Isomorphic links*

Isomorphic links represent the correspondences between structural elements in separate documents. I have discussed above the many documents that share the element structure of the Bible; a similar problem arises with documents that exist in several versions but that share most of their structure. Any hypertext system that can relate such documents must provide for connecting the corresponding elements.

The distinguishing characteristic of isomorphic links is that they tie together like-named elements of documents. "Like-positioned elements" would not be adequate; one can imagine a non-biblical book that happens to have the same distribution of chapters and verses as a book of the Bible. Similarly, there are important biblical manuscripts that lack certain structural elements or that have them in a slightly different order. Yet despite these differences there exists an abstract (meta-) document we call the "Bible," which is recognizable though represented by thousands of concrete manuscripts, editions, and translations. By providing the ability to name document elements similarly despite their existing in diverse documents, the needed level of abstraction can be achieved.

In reading meta-documents, the most common need involves viewing simultaneously several concrete instances of a particular text phenomenon. Parallel, synchronized windows or panes are the usual solutionas, for example, in CD Word. For documents with commensurable element names this solution is relatively easy, but even the canonical reference system for the Bible is not quite consistent. Six problems arise in relation to meta-documents:

(1) Missing elements: Certain elements may be entirely missing, for example the last several verses of the Gospel of Mark in many manuscripts, or passages not discussed in a generally verse-by-verse commentary.

(2) Re-ordered elements: Two versions of a document may differ only in the order of elements common to both. For example, an editor may convince an author that the presentation would be clearer with chapters and sections in another order. When comparing versions, the system should be able to determine for the user that the text has in fact been reordered rather than changed, and the system should be able to provide a high-level view that shows the structural changes themselves.

(3) Separate vs. merged elements: There are cases where adjacent verses, or even adjacent psalms, are counted as a single verse or psalm in some traditions, thus making numbering in different versions diverge.

(4) Uncounted elements: In Hebrew, superscriptions at the start of each psalm count as verses, while in Greek they do not; this different treatment

of superscriptions throws off verse numbering much as does the previous problem.

(5) Element granularity: In the case of a Bible text and a commentary, the commentary may proceed chapter by chapter, or even pericope by pericope, rather than match the entire element-structure down to the verses. The notion of isomorphy is then inadequate, and it must either be simulated by grouping smaller elements in new ways, or an additional structure must be predicated of all relevant documents. In the case of annotations, correspondences may apply at a level more fine-grained than usual; for this case see the following section. In the case of translations, there is often little useful structural correspondence at the word level, although there is usually semantic correspondence. Rather, structural isomorphy only extends down to the sentence, clause, or perhaps verse level, or in some cases not even that far. The standard biblical verse divisions work well for most purposes, but for translations into some non-Indo-European languages the discourse structure is different enough to affect even the verse structure.

(6) Element size: A commentary may spend several pages on a single difficult verse. In such cases it is important to scroll intuitively. A partial solution is to continue scrolling both texts until the end of the shortest element becomes visible, and then to prevent scrolling that text on to its next element until the end of the longest version of the current element appears. This solution does not solve the case where even the shortest version is larger than the available space. Individual scroll control for each version's window or pane guarantees complete access, but it leads to a sometimes disconcerting conflict of control, because scrolling is automatic and manual at the same time.[10]

In all of these cases the user can become confused while examining two or more versions in parallel. The system must make clear where portions of the versions correspond and where elements are simply missing. When standard reference schemes do not quite agree, the system must make clear which version's scheme takes priority and what the differences between them are.

### Annotation links

Annotation links are similar to isomorphic links, but are used to represent connections from portions of a text to information about the text. The most common cases are (1) grammatical category annotations, which connect word instances to members of a list of possible categories, and (2) glosses, which connect word instances to words of another language.[11]  However, annotations may be applied at any level of document structure.

Often an annotation is selected from a fixed set of items, perhaps a list such as {noun, verb, adjective, adverb, particle}. It is useful if a system can enforce such user-defined constraints, but I have seen no hypermedia system that can do so.[12]

One difficulty with annotation links is that they are likely to be attached to every word of a lengthy text. The user probably does not want to see them in the same way as associative links.  Instead, they should either be available to pop up on request, or (in the case of word-level annotations) be followed automatically and displayed interlinearly.  The sheer number of annotation links requires that they receive careful consideration during system design.

*Implicit links*

Implicit links can be inferred algorithmically from elements of the source document. Therefore they need not be stored one by one anywhere.  For example, each word of a natural language text should be implicitly linked to the corresponding entry in each dictionary that is available for the language in use. This linking is useful in texts with specialized vocabulary, in multi-lingual settings, in linguistic research, and in any situation where readers might not be as expert as the text's author.  Similarly, any pieces of text that are cross-references to other texts (such as bibliography entries) should function as such.

In the simplest case the system need only extract the selected word or text and use it as a key (or perhaps an element name) leading into the dictionary document. However, complexities arise. First, there may be many dictionaries for a language, and new ones may be added at any time.  Therefore one must support meta-documents such as are discussed above under isomorphic links. Furthermore, such links should lead only to those dictionaries relevant to the language in use.  This requirement implies that the system should always know in what language its data are expressed.  Even this simple requirement is not addressed by most interface platforms, which recognize only fonts, not languages.

Second, the word form found in the text may not be the same as the name of the dictionary or other main entry. In English all the inflected forms (e.g. "run," "runs," "running," and "ran") could be listed as keys that lead to the same dictionary entry.[13] But in Greek there are several hundred potential inflected forms for every verb, making this method unworkable. Dictionary implicit links can be supported by programs that try to reduce word forms to roots (getting to the right entry most of the time), or by creating a word root annotation for every word and using it as the basis for implicit links. The former solution can apply to any text in a language; the latter requires that annotations be assigned in advance. With the latter method the user should not be compelled to follow the annotation link and then to follow another (implicit) link to the dictionary; the process must be streamlined to be effective.

The same method used for dictionary links may be applied to encyclopedias, libraries of images, and so on. For example, one may have online maps of all the world's countries, and it is reasonable to expect access to them from any instance of a country name in any text. Yet one should not have to mark every country name in the text as such.

The difficulty still remains, that most reference works depend upon the reader's ingenuity and prior knowledge. For example, for a scholar using book technology, a thorough study of "atonement" requires looking up articles on "blood sacrifice," among other topics. A particular Bible dictionary might discuss the desired topic under either or both of these headings. Such links can only be made implicit if a method can be given for finding them. CD Word uses a table of topic name equivalents, but this solution runs into problems in the general case, because two topic names may be equivalent only for certain purposes. These are well-known problems in information retrieval; as with finding word roots, useful but not perfect solutions exist.

Standardized reference methods constitute a second type of implicit link. Appearing in print, "Matt 1:10" is a link to chapter one, verse ten of Matthew's Gospel. It is an abstract link, leading to a structural element that transcends the particular manuscripts, versions, translations, and other documents that instantiate the notion "Bible." The reader reasonably expects that every such reference in any online text links to the correct verse, even if the author of the text containing the reference has not been kind enough to create an associative link, or even to mark up the reference as such. These links may be handled in much the same manner as dictionary look-ups; in the same way, some special processing may be required to reduce them to a standard form.[14]

Implicit links to meta-documents cannot, by definition, be followed except to some particular instance(s) of the document. One cannot, in other words, display "Matthew 1:10," but only a particular version or translation of it. Thus a hypertext system that supports abstract documents must allow the user to specify concrete instances. The user could choose a favorite instance in advance, or the system could supply menus of available documents from which the user would choose when following a link.[15]

Bibliographic references are similar but even more varied. Internal references may be as brief as "cf chapter 10." References to other works, which may be very complex, appear in many different forms as dictated by the kind of document referenced and by personal and editorial tastes. In the foreseeable future only some of these references will be available online, but in fields of wide interest the percentage will increase quickly.

It is worth noting that implicit links are used all the time in print technology, and so they will be an important part of what users desire for some time to come. Bibliographical references pose the particular problem that they commonly point to page numbers. This manner of citation is most frequently a consequence of the limitations of print technology; there has in the past been no convenient way to refer to particular paragraphs or other units (except, as already noted, named units such as numbered chapters or sections). I think it safe to presume that if authors had been able to refer conveniently to conceptually salient units, then they would often have done so. However, we have millions of books that refer to pages of other books. Furthermore, there will be many occasions for making references from the docuverse out to paper documents, or to documents that may be temporarily or partially in paper form, and so our online document systems must provide convenient support for page references.[16]

This difficulty requires that we mark up at least some documents for their page structure as well as for their logical structure. A few references also specify smaller units such as "column 2" or "paragraph 3." In any case, here again we see the need for multiple independent structures overlaid on single documents.

Implicit links may also come directly to the user's mind; a user should be able to request a particular verse by name. It should not be necessary for him or her to create a new document, type in the reference, save the document, and then invoke an implicit link.

*Retrieval links*

The last kind of link I will discuss is a subtype of the implicit link. Whereas the implicit link is defined globally (for example, it can be a system universal that words are linked to dictionary entries), the retrieval link is defined for a particular document or location. In both cases the links are unidirectional. For example, an author may wish to refer to a contemporary scholar's discussions or uses of a particular term. The author may wish to provide readers with a link (or links) to all of the scholar's relevant texts. An exhaustive list is possible but only remains valid so long as the scholar publishes no new material on the subject. If the desired passages can be characterized by content (say, by the presence of certain words), then the author may instead provide a retrieval link, which supplies the characterization in some formal notation. Readers may then follow the link and retrieve the full set of relevant texts, even if the set changes by publication of new documents, by movement of old documents into the online docuverse, or in other ways.

This kind of link is useful in lexicographic studies. In biblical studies it is often important to know how often particular words are used by a particular writer; if one's analysis of manuscripts changes, the totals may change. In less closed corpora such as classical literature, from time to time new works may be discovered by known authors, with similar consequences for our understanding of their style.

The retrieval link provides a flexibility not otherwise available. In formal terms, it provides for defining an individual link intensionally (as a function that finds the desired ends) rather than extensionally (as a list of desired ends). So long as the universe of potential link ends does not change, and so long as the list is known to be complete, these definitions produce the same result. But the retrieval link survives changes much more effectively.

*How many links did you say you want?*

Given this range of link kinds, how many links does a biblical hypertext corpus require? Let us consider the Hebrew Bible as an example. In the 39 books (excluding the Apocrypha) there are about 930 chapters, 23,000 verses, and 417,000 words.

The total number of associative links is unbounded, but let us consider just those that one finds in the average study Bible. Attached to each verse one can expect cross references to perhaps two or three other verses. This yields a total of at least 46,000 associative links.[17] I am not including the links that connect passages to related commentary entries, Bible dictionaries, and so on; if these are not (where possible) handled as implicit links, the figure of 46,000 would greatly increase.

Structure-representing links exist for each book, chapter, and verse. I will ignore those that represent smaller units, such as emphatic phrases and poetry lines, and still count a total of 23,969.

Isomorphic links must exist between all versions, for each structural element. If they do not, then for completeness one must repeat the associative links for each version. I will take the more efficient course and count the number of s-r links per version, times the number of versions. For the Jewish Scriptures the minimum configuration would include the Hebrew text, the Greek Septuagint, and one English translation. Half a dozen English translations are more likely, so let us assume 8*23,969 or 191,752 isomorphic links. Paper Bibles exist with up to eight translations displayed in parallel. Note that I have still made no mention of the structures that relate variant manuscripts.

Annotations merely of grammatical category and word root, attached to each word of the Hebrew text, add 834,000 more links. I will omit the many footnotes and other idiosyncratic annotations found in study Bibles.

Implicit links certainly need not be stored. If they were, there would be 417,000 (one per word instance) dictionary links, and many times that number if multiple dictionaries could not be treated as instances of a meta-document.

I will not count any retrieval links in this example, because no equivalent exists in the usual paper study Bibles. Some Bibles include an abridged concordance that approximates this function, but I will ignore that here.

Thus just to support the features of typical paper media we must include over one million explicit links. Of course any class of link can be implemented in some other fashion, so as not to count as a "link" in terms of a particular implementation; but this will merely shift the load, and it will probably compromise the structural integrity of the design. For example, annotations could be interspersed between words of text, and (usually) suppressed during display; but this increases the amount of "text" to be read from disks, and imposes a time cost for filtering the display. However they are construed, this many links can severely tax the storage, retrieval, display, and navigational capabilities of a hypertext system.

# Notes

1. CD Word has been developed by Dallas Seminary through private financial sponsorship, with the assistance of Owl International (Office Workstations Ltd., maker of GUIDE™) and Fulcrum Technologies Inc. (maker of OEM full-text retrieval software). The Project Steering Committee included Mark Bailey, Darrell Bock, Jon Boring, Robin Cover, and Burge Troxel. I would like to thank Robin Cover for numerous helpful comments on this paper, and the Brown University Computing in the Humanities Users' Group for many enlightening discussions of hypertext. I served as a consultant to the CD Word project, but the opinions expressed here are my own and do not necessarily reflect the views of the project or other staff.

2. Not all linguistic structures are hierarchical; those which are not are among the most theoretically interesting. Pronouns, for example, refer to other units in ways which are not hierarchical. One might draw an analogy from pronouns to associative links in hypertext, but I will not pursue it here.

3. For a discussion of the expressions of markup structure, see James H. Coombs, Allen H. Renear, and Steven J. DeRose, "Markup Systems and the Future of Scholarly Text Processing," *Communications of the Association for Computing Machinery* (November 1987): 933-947. Early biblical manuscripts were written with no markup at all—no inter-word spaces, punctuation, capitalization, etc.

4. I learned of the significance of page location in the First Folio from Michael Sperberg-McQueen, "Structuring text for Research," presented at the Graphics Communications Association conference, November 16-18, 1988, Boston, Massachusetts.

5. Theodor H. Nelson, *Literary Machines*. Edition 87.1. South Bend, IN: The Distributors, 1987.

6. See, for example, William Aegerter, "Change Control: A Structured Form of Hypertext," in *Proceedings of Hypertext '87* (Chapel Hill: University of North Carolina, 1987).

7. The best known are probably the GramCord project and the *Analytical Greek New Testament*.

8. Link types are discussed individually in what follows; their taxonomic relationships are discussed in S. DeRose, "Expanding the Notion of Links," *Proceedings of Hypertext 89* (Baltimore: ACM Press, 1989), 249-258.

9. Randall H. Trigg, "A Network-based Approach to Text Handling for the On-Line Community." Ph.D. thesis, University of Maryland, 1983.

10. This problem can be seen with Microsoft Word™'s synchronized main text and footnote panes on the Macintosh; when either pane is scrolled far enough, the other pane jumps to match.

11. Word *instances,* not word *forms,* because different instances often require different annotations. For example, a large percentage of word forms can represent more than one grammatical category, even in highly inflected languages such as Greek; similarly a given word in one language does not in general have only one best equivalent in another language.

12. The "Interlinear Text Processor" program developed by several of my colleagues at the Summer Institute of Linguistics addresses the problems of text annotation, and supports such constraints, but is not a general hypertext system.

13. Even this solution is imperfect.

14. CD Word reduces biblical references to standard form during data preparation rather than on the fly. This procedure is necessary because the abbreviatory conventions, which are complex, differ slightly from document to document. For example, "First Timothy 4:12" might be abbreviated as "1T4.12," "1 Tim 4:12," "1Tm412," or in several other ways. There are also bewildering abbreviations for sets of verses, such as "Romans 1:1,2-3;2;3:1-4,6,9,11-20;10-12." In this case, the hyphen has lowest priority, followed by the comma, and finally the semicolon.

15. A prototype I prepared of the Computing Environment for Literary, Linguistic, and Anthropological Research ("CELLAR") under development at the Summer Institute of Linguistics, supports menus of target documents for implicit links.

16. Perhaps even more difficult is the problem of referring to elements of a hypertext from paper, since pages are not meaningful, and element identifiers do not seem intuitive.

17. If my word processor supported particularly sophisticated links, I might have been able to define this number in terms of the earlier specification of the number of verses, and been guaranteed consistency in the face of changes.

# Ancient Materials, Modern Media: Shaping the Study of Classics with Hypermedia

Gregory Crane
Elli Mylonas
Department of the Classics, Harvard University

Over the long term, external forces will compel all of us in every discipline to store more and more of our primary information in electronic form. One recent event at Harvard University may serve as a symbol of this trend. In the past, our colleagues felt confident that virtually all relevant information could be found somewhere in the stacks of Widener Library. Although any one book might be out on loan, in theory everything was under a single roof. This proud ideal, though never quite realized, was not very far from reality, and it shaped the expectations of many scholars. An expert must have control over all the secondary literature—or at least know that all the necessary material is within reach.

For most subjects within the humanities, Widener covers the entire range of modern scholarship—all the major works from the time of Humboldt up until the present. A Homerist can find original copies of Wolff's 1795 *Prolegomena ad Homerum*. which defined the "Homeric Question." All the important editions and commentaries have their place on the shelf. Yet in the 1980s a change took place—remarkable because it was inevitable and because its effect was stunning. Widener Library, the pride of Harvard's Faculty of Arts and Sciences, and one of the finest University libraries in the world, was full. For every book that entered, another book was shipped out to storage miles away.

At first, the exhaustion of space excited little attention among faculty or students: few noticed any diminution in the holdings and scholarship marched on. This small change is a single instance and, like the closing the American frontier, primarily symbolic; but it is a powerful symbol. The physical limits of Widener Library did not affect the faculty until the university administration demonstrated concretely how hopeless the situation was: the university purchased a prime piece of real estate not one hundred meters from Widener and promptly made plans to build, not a new library, but a hotel. Even had they elected to build a new library building, it would only have been able to hold five years worth of acquisitions. The new Alexandria, spared the torch, disperses itself for lack of space at a single and central location.

Fifty years from now, when our present undergraduates turn seventy, not a single book presently in Widener Library will remain on the shelf—and this figure assumes no increase in the yearly production of printed matter. Of course, all of the books are still in some sense available. It is possible to recall a book from its warehouse or to locate the proper sheet of microfiche, but such access is not equivalent to retrieving the book from the shelf. Now we can still browse the stacks and instantly put our hands on two centuries of work; but this era is passing, and future scholars will have to become accustomed to new methods of research and information retrieval.

Information stored in electronic form is a growing reality that can not only replace many of the conventional library capabilities that are being lost, but provide new tools as well. Most important, it may be stored in a single place and consulted from virtually anywhere. An online archive under a mountain in the Rockies or in a Maine forest can serve an almost limitless number of researchers hundreds and thousands of miles away. The scholar can consult works rapidly on the screen, capture the most relevant parts of the information to disk locally, or print out the most important sections. Such an ethereal research library is not yet fully realised, but the barriers that separate us from such a resource have progressively less to do with technology and more to do with politics and tradition. Economic factors alone will impel us towards a electronic and ubiquitous Alexandria, and this transition will generate one of the great scholarly revolutions of the coming century.

Furthermore, the greater ease and speed with which new and old scholarship may be reached will have effects on the amount of information scholars will come to expect, and the way that they use it in their research. Traditional research methods are enhanced when the texts are stored and manipulated electronically. Whereas thirty years ago, compiling a concordance or making a lexical analysis of a text was a lengthy, painstaking scholarly task, now, this same work can be done with much greater ease by a computer. When a whole corpus is available online, even a graduate student can, using search programs, discover results that in the past required years spent reading extensively in diverse texts. That is not to say that the computerization of traditional research obviates the need for critical and analytical reasoning about results that have been generated, but it does eliminate a large amount of the intellectual legwork previously required. The greater temporal and geographical access to information also has political effects on a scholar. A younger scholar, or one who is at an institution which does not own all the necessary scholarly texts and commentaries, can still get access to the same sources as her more experienced or fortunately-placed colleagues.

However, beyond the enhancement of traditional scholarly work, the transformation of texts into electronic databases is opening the doors to innovative ways of conducting teaching and scholarship. Hypertext[1] and other computer-supported methods of reading and displaying information are not yet in widespread use among the scholarly community. As more and more information makes the leap from traditional to electronic form, and as more software appears with which to manipulate it more scholars become eager to take advantage of such modes of expression. By integrating their own research into a hypertext, scholars can map their associative and analytical trails through a docuverse, and thus make their mental processes explicit. Students can then use a network of links and trails laid by their professor as a foundation for their own work. On the expert level, scholars can more easily integrate work that does not fall under their particular area of expertise.

## The computer and classical studies

The closing of the traditional bibliographic frontier and the consequent move towards electronic databases apply to all disciplines, not just to classics. Why, then, have classicists in particular applied so much energy and attention to electronic databases? Their enthusiastic participation in the electronic age can be ascribed to the early work of several members of the discipline in classical computing, and to the scholarly methodology that the discipline imposes on its practitioners, because of nature of the information which they have available. Already in the mid-sixties David Packard was writing programs in IBM/360 assembler for morphology, concording and metrical analysis. Computer assisted Greek and Latin language instruction have existed since the time of the *Plato* system, in the late 1960s. The *Thesaurus Linguae Graecae (TLG)*, a four hundred megabyte database of all of Greek literature from Homer to the sixth century AD, was begun in 1973, and is nearing completion. Also underway are databases of Greek inscriptions, papyrus fragments, prosopographical information and the transformation into electronic form of *L'Année Philologique*, the annual scholarly bibliography, as well as archeological information such as iconography, vase shapes and site plans.

The *TLG* has now entered more texts than any one classicist may ever be able to use, and David Packard has built two versions of a specialized computer called Ibycus, a mini and a personal, whose sole purpose is to manipulate the *TLG* texts and

---

to provide multilingual, scholarly wordprocessing. Between 1982 and 1985, while a graduate student at Harvard, one of the authors (Crane) wrote a set of search programs for the *TLG* which ran under UNIX. With the advent of CD ROM technology the *TLG* has become available on several different microcomputers,[2] and over three hundred copies of the *TLG* are now in use around the world.

As humanities computing expands into new areas, classics continues to keep pace and even lead in both teaching and research applications.The existence of electronic texts and the hardware and software with which to make use of them has been a motivating factor for other classicists either to enter more texts, for example in Latin, and to experiment with other computer applications in teaching and research. Much of the work has been a grassroots effort, begun by interested individuals who already had the technical skills or learned them in the process, and who then shared their results with the rest of the classics community.

None of this embarrassment of electronic riches would have had much effect on classicists had it not been able to greatly enhance their work. Students of classical literature must work with a paradoxical body of material. The five hundred volumes of the Loeb Classical Library—a good representation of the corpus of Greek literature—fit in two average bookcases. One can look at this collection of works and think that it is an easy corpus for one scholar to know well and to control. Yet they contain far more primary information than most specialists in Greek and Latin literature will ever be able to work through in detail. Although classicists have far less textual information than most humanists in terms of quantity—all Greek literature from Homer to Plato amounts to less than the letters and works of a single moderately prolific modern author or statesman—quantity is a crude measure. In modern humanistic studies, only a handful of scholars have studied each letter of Henry Adams, or read every volume of Sir Walter Scott. Only specialists in an area can closely examine the works that comprise it. But every word and every comma in every surviving Greek tragedy has not only been read but pored over, its meanings probed and its peculiarities systematically analyzed since at least the third century BC. Classicists have adapted to the narrow physical limits of their subject by pressing deeper into each work. Countless scholarly links tie the words and phrases of Greek together through commentaries, concordances, marginalia, books and articles. Classical scholarship has made a criss-cross of trails back and forth within the Greek texts. The number and density of these connections can overwhelm the graduate student whose task is to learn how to navigate through this network. Furthermore, these links are often indicated in arcane conventions that have been laid down over the centuries. Learning to use these is a task in and of itself.

And yet, for all the work that has been done on classical literature and civilization, much remains to be done. Knowledge leads to knowledge, and new connections only suggest more different combination of texts. Perhaps no single classicist can claim to have an intimate knowledge of Greek literature from Homer to Aristotle, and the body of Greek literature after Aristotle is much greater. The passage that sheds light on an idea in Sophocles may be hidden in a medical treatise by Galen or a Church Father. Classicists have always wanted to pursue the words and phrases of their languages as broadly as possible, but have had to depend in the past on their own memory and the few available printed tools and concordances. Within the limited domain of ancient literature, classicists seek absolutely every scrap of information relevant to a problem. Electronic databases allow them to augment their intellectual abilities, to explore their hunches and their hypotheses throughout a far wider range of literature than ever before.

But access to the texts is, even for the student of literature, only part of the puzzle. Classicists view information in a qualitatively different way than their colleagues in modern fields. The classicist faces problems very different from the student of Keats or even of Shakespeare. No living speakers of classical Greek survive—and thus no vivid nuances of their language. We spend lifetimes reconstructing the subtleties of Homeric diction or the critical turns of phrase of a Plato, but we are never sure of our knowledge, and a fifth century Athenian would surely find many of our conclusions bizarre or amusing. We do not know how to pronounce the language of Thucydides. Sometimes we cannot even determine what the original words of a text might have been, whether Sophocles actually wrote "*hybris* engenders the tyrant" *or* "tyranny engenders *hybris.*" Every classicist is not only a stranger in a strange land, but a stranger forbidden to speak or even to hear the language, forced to contemplate her subject silently from afar.

The desire to solve these textual difficulties and to pursue research into more and more texts is what inspired the developments in electronic databases that have taken place in classics up to this time. The *Thesaurus Linguae Graecae* began early because it answered one deep and long-standing need within the field: the ability to perform searches for word or phrases in the texts of the TLG brought data within reach of graduate students that had previously only been accessible to more mature scholars who had read through many texts. It also made it possible for anyone to collect more than enough data on the way words are used, and to pinpoint nuances of meaning that would otherwise remain elusive.

The textual difficulties are, however, only the beginning of the classicist's problems. Every Greek text needs to be placed in the full context of Greek society: religion, social practices, political trends, class consciousness. The evidence for all this comes from diverse sources. Paintings on Greek vases shed light on topics that may be of literary interest, such as Greek myth, but that also yield information on victory celebrations, on customs such as burial or marriage, and on the roles of the sexes. Architectural monuments show us the context in which tragedy and comedy were performed, public festivals carried out and even where individuals lived. Slides or videos of Greek landscape illustrate what terrain is mountainous and what flat—a critical piece of information for understanding the relationships between the many Greek cities. Two cities only a few miles apart as the crow flies may be separated by a several days' journey as the traveller moves around mountains. It is also possible to understand how the Greeks interacted with their physical environment, for example in the location of the cult centers of Delphi and Epidaurus. Without the full spectrum of information it is impossible to appreciate any one artifact properly, whether it be a text, a vase, or a building.

As more primary and secondary information accumulates, each of these categories of evidence has drifted into a different sub-specialty: textual criticism, connoisseurship, social history, topography. New trends and discoveries tend to be buried in specialized publications and not easily accessible to the researcher who is outside that specific area. It is difficult, for example, for the philologist to use architectural evidence without a great deal of preliminary effort, because she may not be familiar with the methodology of that subdiscipline. An iconographer is likely not to be comfortable with the problems of staging and meter in the plays of Aeschylus, because he may not have the background to work through the available literature. Each is in need of knowledge held by the other, but extracting the relevant information can often be an overwhelming effort. Each area of specialization has its own methodology, assumed background knowledge, vocabulary and reference works. This is the foundation on which a scholar builds original work. The non-specialist, lacking these tools, cannot easily roam through what is potentially relevant and useful material. Even using standard reference works efficiently can be so difficult that an interested person from outside the field, whether undergraduate, scholar or educated reader, cannot take advantage of it.

In many ways, the sub-disciplines of a field—in the case of classics, epigraphy, tragedy, architecture, topography, etc.—are like the provinces of a nation. Each has its own separate tradition and dialect, but all must share certain basic values and interests. Travelling from one province to another is much like moving from one subdiscipline to another: once they have arrived, travellers can begin to acquaint themselves with the local customs and ideas, but first they must make the journey. Classics is much like a nation in which travel from one province to another has grown extremely time consuming. Each year's publications push experts in one area further away from their colleagues in different ones—it is as if classics began as a tiny city state and had suddenly grown into a massive nation stretching thousands of miles. Every year it becomes harder to keep in touch with new developments in different sub-disciplines of the field. Customs and dialects have evolved in different and unconnected directions. As communication decreases and ignorance about what is happening elsewhere increases. there is less and less interaction, and fewer occasions in which an idea in one area can spark ideas elsewhere.

## The Perseus Project

Travel is one of the classic metaphors for learning—the Babylonian wanderings of Gilgamesh in search of knowledge are the first great epic tradition of which we know and the journey of Odysseus has become a topos in western literature. Hypermedia is analogous to the canals or railroads of the nineteenth century. A hypermedia database provides rapid and orderly linking of information, allowing scholars to move from one part of their field to another faster and with more precision than they otherwise could. Like railroads and canals, hypermedia links have predictable destinations. The user of a well designed hypermedia corpus can navigate in it with ease. Fruitful links are easy to discover and follow and interesting new domains easy to explore and master.

Hypermedia, with its ability to store and retrieve links between information in different media, has a special appeal for the overextended classicist, who is faced with a wide variety of information in textual, graphic and auditory form, and diverse cataloguing and indexing systems that traditionally give access to it. More conventional software tools and databases were originally welcomed by classicists to help them do better the work that they already were doing. Hypermedia systems can add to that, by helping scholars and students move into areas that are not easily approachable in the paper world.

Since the summer of 1987, the Perseus Project has been under development at Harvard University and at other collaborating institutions.[3] The project is working to create a hypermedia system for use in classics, and is concentrating on the accumulation, organization and storage of data so that it may be used by different audiences within the discipline, and by students and non-classicists. The decision to emphasize low cost and accessibility led to the adoption of Apple's *HyperCard* program as the environment of Perseus, since it runs on a computer that students and faculty can easily have on their desks. Therefore, Perseus will come with a set of pre-made links connecting the different types of information in it, and a limited ability for the reader to make her own links.[4]

Perseus is designed to support the breadth of information classicists need. To make the wide range of information in Perseus useful to all levels of reader, alternative views and access methods are possible. A simple way to approach this material is to read an English translation. (Figure 1) A student or a non-classicist using this mode can also look up names in the classical encyclopedia, or places on a map of Greece. (Figure 2) A reader who knows some Greek can concentrate on the adjacent Greek text. The student of Greek can click on any word, and see its morphological analysis. From that point, he or she may look it up in the Greek English Lexicon. Metrical analysis and some commentary makes Perseus useful in more advanced Greek classes as well. Students can also look up variant readings in an *apparatus criticus*. Perseus thus provides a series of smooth gradations from freshman translation course to graduate seminar. The data is the same in all cases: we simply arrange different views to suit changing needs.

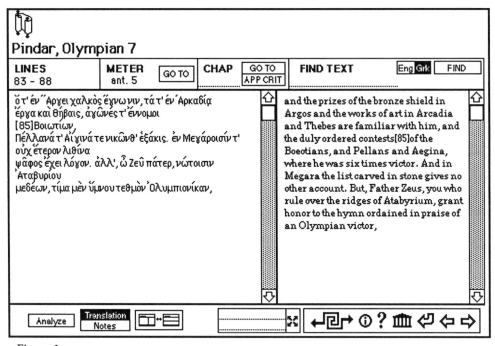

Figure 1

In addition to these more conventional applications, a reader of Perseus can explore other aspects of the same material. The student who is looking at the map of Greece above can go on to see a site plan of the site at Aegina. (Figure 3) By clicking on different places on the site plan, it is possible to see smaller areas in greater and greater detail. Each view is also linked to video images. (Figure 4) Clicking on a small arrow causes a video image to be displayed showing the view from that vantage point. An archeologist or art historian might want to start from the site plan,

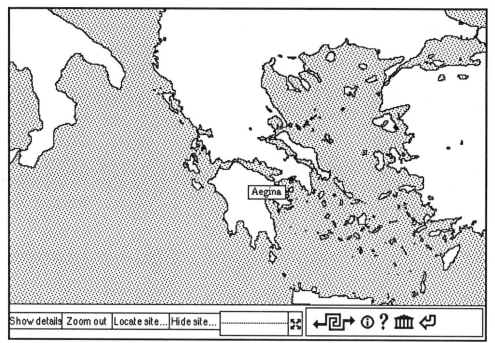

Figure 2

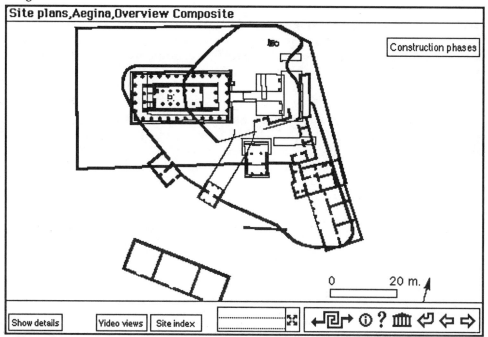

Figure 3

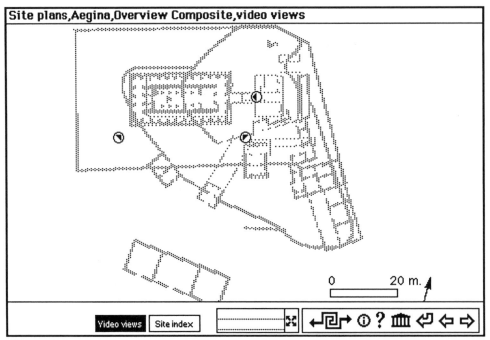

Figure 4

zoom in to the building level, (Figure 5) and then see a written entry on the building. A student who has gotten this far may need to look up architectural terms in the encyclopedia. In any case, it is possible to find other buildings of the same type, or to move over to the Vase or Coin Index and see what vases or coins come from Aegina.

Currently, Perseus has many more primary sources than it does secondary, so it has not yet filled in the intellectual links that will serve to bind all its contents together. However, more and more secondary material is being added, and the structure of the primary material is becoming better articulated, so the ability to move from one kind of information to another is constantly improving. Perseus contains an Overview of Greek History which was written especially for it by Thomas R. Martin, who teaches ancient history at Pomona College. The historical narrative is linked to primary sources in Perseus such as slides, maps and texts. This example of secondary material provides an alternative entry point into Perseus for the reader who needs the historical background to understand the primary evidence. (Figure 6)

# Aegina,ca. 500 B.C. Amphipoleion

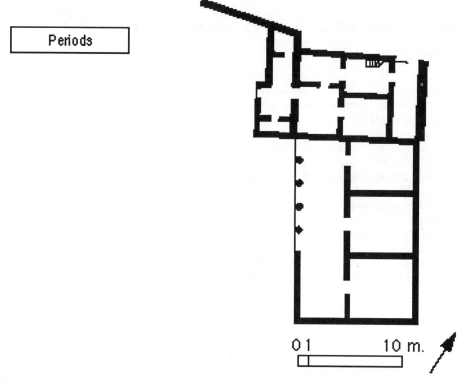

Periods

0 1          10 m.

Figure 5

The breadth of Perseus is one of its greatest strengths. but also presents a significant problem. In order to create a useful hypermedia database, we need to collect a critical mass of information. Perseus will contain most important texts that survive from Homer down to Plato. It will also have an atlas and maps of the major classical sites. It will contain images of art objects such as statues and vases that not only illustrate the major currents of artistic creation, but that cover iconography as well. Finally, it must contain some secondary material to help orient the non-specialist—a lexicon, a classical encyclopedia and a narrative overview of Greek history.

Simply collecting this much information in electronic form is a challenge; but structuring the data presents further problems. We cannot simply replicate the forms of printed reference works—nor should we want to. An art book can contain at most several hundred black and white images and several dozen good color prints, but a videodisc can store 54,000 color images on each side. One can have

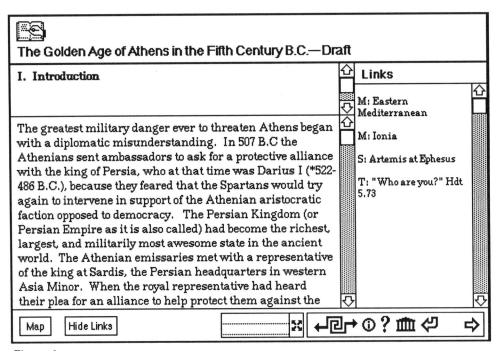

The Golden Age of Athens in the Fifth Century B.C.—Draft

**I. Introduction**

The greatest military danger ever to threaten Athens began with a diplomatic misunderstanding. In 507 B.C the Athenians sent ambassadors to ask for a protective alliance with the king of Persia, who at that time was Darius I (*522-486 B.C.), because they feared that the Spartans would try again to intervene in support of the Athenian aristocratic faction opposed to democracy. The Persian Kingdom (or Persian Empire as it is also called) had become the richest, largest, and militarily most awesome state in the ancient world. The Athenian emissaries met with a representative of the king at Sardis, the Persian headquarters in western Asia Minor. When the royal representative had heard their plea for an alliance to help protect them against the

**Links**

M: Eastern Mediterranean

M: Ionia

S: Artemis at Ephesus

T: "Who are you?" Hdt 5.73

Map    Hide Links

Figure 6

dozens of images for a major vase and illustrate every significant detail. An art historian can, with such a source of material, refer to dozens of pictures that focus on heads or torsos painted by the Berlin Painter and the Cleophrades Painter. A reader can apprehend subtle points of style much more quickly than if he were trying to discern the shape of a knee in a black and white picture of the vase. Again, a printed version of a text is fixed. It can contain text and translation, or just one of the two. It may or may not have commentary, and will certainly not have many images. Furthermore, extended commentary is usually printed in a separate volume. Using a hypermedia system like Perseus, a historian working on Thucydides can not only discuss the Pylos campaign with reference to the text, but can also include dozens of maps illustrating how this campaign unfolded, color pictures of the sites at which events took place and cross references to other texts included in the database that also shed light on this material.

Printed texts have helped arbitrarily segment the study of classics. Some books contain dramas, others contain vases, still others contain speeches or sculpture. Each document tends to focus on homogeneous material and most of its footnotes lead to other documents of the same type: books on vases point to other books on vases, a discussion of Aeschylus will allude primarily to other discussions of Aeschylus or (if it is broad in scope) may branch out to Sophocles and Euripides. The form of scholarly publication reinforces overspecialization and all its resulting narrowness.

Perseus is now at the beta testing stage. It consists of a CD ROM containing textual information and black-and-white images and a videodisc with about 12,000 still and moving color images. Although Perseus 1.0 will be ready in December 1990 as scheduled, it will remain in beta testing for the following academic year, and will be distributed officially in the fall of 1991 by a university publisher. Our original grant from Annenberg/CPB continues until 1993, and we will produce three more versions of Perseus, one each year. Perseus will continue to develop over this time. Once we have determined basic formats for primary sources such as texts and archeological objects, we will continue to add primary material, but will concentrate on adapting other conventional formats to our system.

The study of classics has been drifting in different directions in recent decades. The more secondary and primary information has become available, the harder it has become to master more than one small portion of the field. Of course, specialization does in some measure reflect an expansion of absolute knowledge, but it is also aggravated by logistical problems that are not intrinsic to that expansion. An expert in Aeschylus looking at a text of Aristophanes may not realize that an article relevant to this particular passage was published two years before, and he will be even less likely to know where to find the most recent excavation reports for a particular site. The computer cannot substitute for proper training—the scholar has to know how to use a text or how to evaluate the information in an excavation report—but the computer can reduce much of the legwork, by pointing out that a particular report exists. No computer will allow scholars to cover the complete range of information that illustrates the classical world, but even today's technology would allow scholars to cover far more ground than has heretofore been possible.

A new tendency is appearing in classics, as in other fields, to integrate other disciplines and techniques into classical scholarship. For example, the methodologies of anthropology, new historicism, women's studies are all being applied to traditional problems of classics.[5] These approaches are innovative, but they must build on the older philological methodologies in order to be valid. In addition, they tend to draw on data from more than one sub-specialty of classics in order to make their argument, since their purpose is to integrate previous knowledge into a new understanding of the classical world. Hypermedia, too, introduces an integrative approach to previously well delimited areas of knowledge. Its use as a tool in conjunction with the new methodologies can to serve to advance and reinforce them.

Once the quantity of information that a single publication can contain changes, the qualitative shape of that publication changes too. As the set of questions that a document can answer and the range of interests that it can serve expand, so do the responsibilities of the author. If one can link a text to an atlas and an atlas to a series of photographs, and the photographs to descriptive articles, the boundaries between each of these documents begin to blur. As Perseus develops, we have found that we must redefine the basic documents with which we have grown up. They now have to be of interest to a wider audience, with a scope that will embrace specialist and nonspecialist. Furthermore, because of the varied nature of the available data that may be incorporated into an article or document, authors can expand their range. So we see historians incorporating slides and video of sites in Greece into their research and teaching, and philologists making greater use of previously inaccessible vase paintings that portray mythological figures.[6]

Perseus places tragedies. maps, lyric poems, vases, histories, statues, coins, and other material in a single medium, and allows the user to move from one type of information to another. The student or researcher can easily examine a wider scope of material rather than focusing only on the relevant material that happens to appear in Greek comedy or in architectural plans. Furthermore, anyone creating an electronic "article" in Perseus must take advantage of as many different kinds of evidence as possible. Even if the Perseus editorial staff does not enforce this as a principle, some authors will start to take advantage of the full range of Perseus materials and their work will put pressure on the rest to follow suit. We cannot expect a change in established habits overnight, but we can expect to see a gradual evolution in which the study of classics incorporates more and more kinds of data, and asks more and different questions.

All humanists share the problems of the classicist. The canon of western culture has expanded at a dizzying rate over the past two centuries. A century ago, the study of modern Western literature had only barely begun to be a subject for serious academic discussion. Entire new media, such as film and video, have arisen and demand critical attention. Furthermore, we no longer have the luxury of a single cultural perspective. Chaotic and overwhelming as the roots of western culture may be, we have much to learn from ideas, art and literature that do not have European roots. The challenges of such types of study are being mitigated by current developments in the electronic tools that humanists use. Classics, which was in the forefront of traditional humanities computing, is using that advantage to open up in new directions. It has the background and experience to produce electronic tools that spearhead new scholarly trends.

**Notes**

1. Following the usage of this volume, "hypertext" refers to the electronic linking of blocks of text, "hypermedia" to the linking of texts with additional media such as graphics, video and sound.

2. The Ibycus PC SC was the first personal computer to handle the *TLG* compact disk. The Pandora program, developed under the leadership of one of the authors (Mylonas) at Harvard, runs on the Macintosh. Tony Smith, at Manchester University in the UK and Randall Jones at the University of California, Santa Barbara, are working on systems for the IBM PC.

3. Bowdoin College, Pomona College, University of Chicago, University of Virginia. For further information on Perseus see: Gregory Crane, "Challenging the Individual: The Tradition of Hypermedia," *Academic Computing* ( Jan. 1990): 22-3, 31-2, 34-8, and "Redefining the Book: Some Preliminary Problems," *Academic Computing* 2:5 (Feb. 1988); Elli, Mylonas, "Universes to Control: Classics, Computers and Education," in Phyllis Culham and Lowell Edmunds, eds. *Classics: A Profession in Crisis* (Lanham, MD: University Press of America, 1990); Elli Mylonas and Sebastian Heath, "Hypertext from the Data Point of View: Paths and Links in the Perseus Project," in *Hypertexts: Concepts, Systems, and Applications*, A. Rizk, N. Streitz and J. André eds. (Cambridge: Cambridge University Press, 1990); D. Neel Smith, "The Perseus Project," *New England Classical Newsletter and Journal* 17:4 ( May 1990): 10-22.

4. It would be fruitful to transfer it later to a more powerful, full featured hypertext system such as Xerox Notecards, or Brown University's Intermedia At present, however, the most important evaluation we can get of the use of a classics hypertext system is to have it used by as many classicists as possible. We hope to achieve this by making Perseus available on a machine that is already in widespread use among its potential audience.

5. The importance of these new trends in classics and their effect on the discipline as a whole is shown by the recent publication of the collection *Classics: A Discipline and Profession in Crisis?* This includes articles on new approaches to the study of classics such as anthropology, semiotics, and feminist criticism.

6. An excellent example of the incorporation of textual and visual information my be found in Prof. James Bierman's *Aristotle's Tragedy Construction Kit,* a piece of

*HyperCard* software that explains the *Poetics* of Aristotle. (Kinko's Academic Courseware Exchange, 1988)

7. "Docuverse": term now becoming current for for very large collections of electronically stored and linked information. See **Yankelovich**, "From Electronic Books to Electronic Libraries" in this volume.

# Linking Together Books: Experiments in Adapting Published Material into Intermedia Documents

Paul Kahn
Institute for Research in Information and Scholarship, Brown University

## The structure of literature and hypertext

Any text that is the object of study has a place in a body of literature, a context that is larger than the text itself, that fixes the text along a variety of axes including time, language, location, or theme. Each primary text has its structural properties: an author and date (even if the author is Anonymous and the date a range of conjecture); a line, paragraph, chapter, or book division. Each author has his or her biographical facts and resulting historical associations. And we can discover in each body of literature that we construct around that primary text an inherent structure built up from the structures of the texts themselves. This is particularly true of bodies of literature, such as Classical Chinese and Classical Greek, that have been the subject of critical study for hundreds of years, a criticism which focuses as much on the texts themselves as it does on the ideas these texts preserve. The scholarship which grows up around such a body of literature uses this structure to point at the text to which it refers. In the course of our scholarship we learn to navigate through the literature by using these structures, and we further propagate them as references in our work.

These associations among the discrete texts which make up a body of literature are fundamental to our understanding of the texts themselves. When we translate a body of literature and its secondary scholarship into electronic form we can exploit these structures to record and transmit these associations. A number of developments over the past decade have shown that electronic text can be manipulated and viewed in a much more fluid manner than can text printed on a page. One often cited example is the enormous collection of Classical Greek texts produced and distributed by *Thesaurus Linguae Graecae (TLG)* of the University of California at Irvine. In order to maintain the elaborate structures of Classical Greek scholarship, the *TLG* maintains a coding scheme for its electronic texts which identifies each line of each text in terms of the author, the work, and the chapter/verse location in that work. A number of hardware and software systems have been developed to provide scholars with access to these electronic texts.[1] All make use of this author/work/chapter/verse structure to identify to a scholar where a word has been found.

These first experiments demonstrate that scholarly tools for managing electronic text must go beyond the technology of locating patterns of characters in a stream of text; they must also allow us to record our trails of association. The scholar certainly needs control over primary texts such as the systems which access the *TLG* texts provide—concordance work and linguistic analysis are fundamental forms of scholarship. However, the scholar also needs electronic access to secondary literature. And as the scholar draws out the context in which a novel, play or poem exists it is the connections between literatures which take on increasing importance. To show a student the relationships between the work of contemporary writers, the scholar needs an electronic system, hypertext, that provides support for links between texts.

The basis of hypertext is the ability to create and follow persistent links between any two items, a concept traceable to the design of the Memex described by Vannevar Bush.[2] Bush's ideas, which we now know predate their first publication by over a decade,[3] focused on the problems of locating relevant information in the published record and recording how that information is intellectually connected. He recognized that the connectedness of the information was a matter of personal association, relying on the imperfect mechanism of human memory. Thus, the Memex (memory extender) would mechanically support that intellectual process. The trails of Bush's Memex have become the links in today's hypertext system. The discussion of these systems has largely dealt with how to create, maintain, represent, and navigate these links. I would like to focus here on the issue of where these links should be created, and specifically of how the structure of a body of literature can be used to generate a consistent set of objective links.

The links in a body of literature can be viewed as connecting two classes of associations: objective and subjective. Objective associations are those which derive from the structure of the texts themselves, the text as data. Subjective associations are those which derive from an interpretive understanding of the material.

Objective associations can be used to generate links between items in the data. In a body of literature, objective associations are to be found in the structural and linguistic properties of the text, and the properties of the author associated with the text. Many current printed reference works, which are already structured along these lines, contain the necessary information to create such objective hypertexts. A number of examples of this are given below, the simplest being the "See also" reference in an encyclopedia.

Subjective associations are located in the ideas which a scholar sees as represented by the text. Common examples in literature include commentaries on, or indications of, influences or similarities among authors or works. A commentator such as Arthur Cooper in *Li Po and Tu Fu*, a book of translations of these two great Chinese poets, freely explains a poem by Tu Fu in terms of a poem by Li Po on a similar theme. The two poems do not refer to each other directly, but Cooper conveys his own sense of association by directing the reader to "see poem on p. 61." Upon arriving on p. 61 the reader gets another view of the same theme and a broader context within which to appreciate both poems.

To offer an example of the contrast, the association of a text with information about the author of that text is an objective link (the authorship of a text is one of its properties); the association of an idea in one text with an idea in another text is a subjective link. The objective link is generated from the structure of the text itself, while the subjective link is the trace of a commentator's interpretation.

The scholarly apparatus of books and journals record both kinds of links in the existing printed media. As we move these same texts into an electronic system, how can we use hypermedia to support the same links? We are presented with the challenge of moving from a known communications media to a less familiar one, much like the transition early in this century from narrative fiction to film-making. How can we best exploit the new technology to present existing text? What new techniques equivalent to the quick cut, the montage, the zoom, can we discover?

I have used Intermedia, the hypermedia system under development at Brown University's Institute for Research in Information and Scholarship (IRIS), to explore these questions. With this tool I have taken representative selections from a body of published materials used for scholarly research and organized and presented this material electronically in ways that have proven to be equally or more useful than the printed form. I give examples of several kinds of documents unique to Intermedia which enhance the presentation of this kind of material in electronic form. I conclude with a set of principles, or rules, which can be used to organize similar collections of information using the Intermedia system.

## Moving Chinese literature into hypermedia

While composing an essay on the translations of Tu Fu done by the American poet Kenneth Rexroth,[4] I made use of a broad range of sources in the subject area of

Chinese Literature. Tu Fu (712-770), a major figure in traditional Chinese literature from the T'ang dynasty, is central to this golden age of Chinese poetry. Rexroth's translations of this poet are among the best in English. My research involved reference to over two dozen published books and a number of journal articles. The links within this set of material are precisely the kind of objective and subjective associations I am interested in expressing in hypermedia.

The initial research and writing of the essay were done before I had access to a hypertext system. But even without a hypertext system I found that the texts, translations, and commentaries I was studying lent themselves to intricate trails of association. Couldn't these disparate books and articles be better organized and navigated as an hypertext? To explore this question I created a hypermedia corpus of linked documents, called *Chinese Literature*.

My model includes selections from books rather than complete texts, due to practical constraints of text entry and copyright issues. A much richer corpus of material containing a complete library of books and journal articles could be created by expanding on this model. While the material currently in this corpus focuses on a few major poets, it is designed in an open-ended manner so that material on other writers can be easily added.

Unlike other sets of linked documents that have been created to support course work in Intermedia,[5] *Chinese Literature* consists entirely of material adapted from published books or journals. This means that it more closely resembles the kinds of materials used by graduate and post-graduate level researchers than the materials developed for undergraduate courses. The variety of types of books and the number of books involved are intended to represent the range of material needed for scholarly research. It also differs from previous Intermedia collections in that it was designed to support an open-ended area of inquiry and research rather than any specific college class.

Neither Intermedia nor any other hypermedia system currently available generates links based on document content or structure, though interesting experiments in this area have been recently carried out by Coombs[6]. More to the point, the CD WORD product[7] uses conventional chapter/verse references in Biblical commentaries to generate "virtual links" to the text and coordinated translations. This is a useful strategy where the conventions of reference are consistent and unambiguous, but it is difficult to generalize. While it is desirable to think of objective links being generated in some sense automatically as software "reads" the text, this is not yet possible. No electronic technology can "understand" all domains of human discourse sufficiently to accomplish such a task. However, much can still be learned by modeling these different kinds of links using the existing facility for manual authoring. The meta-issue of how to adapt printed structure to hypermedia structure remains the same. Using the tools provided by Intermedia, I have constructed the links in *Chinese Literature* entirely by hand. Based on this experience a set of rules are suggested for presenting published material in a hypermedia context.

## Intermedia tools

For a full operational description of earlier versions of the Intermedia system covering its design goals, its software architecture, and its basic functionality, see the papers co-authored by members of the Intermedia development team.[8] The work described here was done using version 3.0 of Intermedia running on the Apple Macintosh II under the A/UX operating system. The tools described below are designed to serve a variety of uses. While their capabilities are fixed, their application is quite open-ended.

### Desktop and folders

Intermedia documents are arranged in a desktop display similar to the display created by the Macintosh Finder. The top-level folder, which is always open, contains either documents or folders. Opening a folder reveals another window containing any combination of documents and/or folders. The folder name can be used to convey organizational information to the user. When opened, the folder name is expanded to include the name of each folder in which that folder is contained, reflecting the Unix path to that location in the file system.

### Document names

The name of a document may be up to 32 characters including blank spaces, similar to the naming conventions in the Macintosh operating system. This document name is always displayed at the top of the document window when the document is opened, and also appears in the Web View display (see below). The document name can be used to convey source and structure information concerning the contents of the document.

### InterWord

InterWord is a text processing application which supports the editing, displaying, and printing of formatted text, similar to Microsoft Word for the Macintosh. It

---

supports an abbreviated set of fonts, styles, and point sizes, as well as line spacing and margin controls. It can be used to create, edit and display text documents.

*InterDraw*

InterDraw is a structured graphics editor, similar in functionality to MacDraw. It can be used to create drawings consisting of rectangles, ovals, arcs, etc., filled or unfilled. It supports the entering and editing of text. Images such as line drawings, photographs, or maps can be scanned and pasted into InterDraw documents. This application can be used to display figures, illustrations, tables, or other mixtures of graphics and text.

*InterVal*

InterVal is a structured editor for creating and displaying vertical timelines. Labels for dates may consist of any combination of text and graphic elements.

*Anchors*

Any selectable element or group of elements in an Intermedia application can be defined as an anchor. Anchors serve as the source and destination point for links (see below). The definition of a "selectable element" depends on the application. In InterWord a selection can consist of any string of contiguous characters, which can be as small as the space between two characters or as large as the entire contents of a document. Typically an anchor will consist of a word or group of words. In InterDraw a selection can be any graphic or text element or group of elements. In InterVal a selection can be one or more events on the timeline. The position of an anchor in a document is updated each time the document is edited, so that the anchor as well as any links attached to that anchor persist from session to session.

*Anchor markers, property sheets, and explainers*

When the user creates an anchor, Intermedia adds an anchor marker to the display. The marker, consisting of a small rectangle containing a horizontal line, is positioned at the upper left corner of the anchor. When the anchor is linked to one or more other anchors, the horizontal line in the marker changes to an arrow. Each anchor has an associated "explainer" which is entered by the author. The anchor explainer is a string of text intended to identify the contents and/or context of the anchor. The anchor explainer may be displayed by selecting the anchor property sheet, but typically it is used as part of the link dialog box, as explained below.

*Links*

We have used the term "hypermedia" to emphasize that Intermedia allows you to make links between several media. In this case we use the term "media" to distinguish the three kinds of documents: text, graphics, and timelines. However, in the broader sense, Intermedia is intended to provide facilities for linking to reference collections such as dictionaries and on-line citation databases, video stills and sequences, audio, and animated graphics.

Intermedia allows the author to create a link between any two anchors. Links are bi-directional, so that the user can follow a link starting from either anchor. A single link marker (i.e. an anchor marker with an arrow) can represent any number of contiguous anchors linked to any number of anchors anywhere on the system. The user follows a link by selecting a link marker and picking the "Follow" menu command or by clicking twice on the marker with the mouse. If only one link emanates from the selected marker, the document containing the anchor at the other end of the link is opened in the foreground of the display and the view of that document is positioned so that the destination anchor is visible. The destination link marker and the extent of the associated anchor are highlighted. If there is more than one link emanating from the selected marker, or if the marker represents more than one anchor, the system presents the link dialog box. This dialog box contains a list of anchor explainers identifying the origin and destination anchors. Based on these explainers, the user selects the origin and destination anchors to indicate which link to follow.

*Web view*

Links in Intermedia exist within the context of a web, a collection of all the anchor and link information for a particular purpose, such as a course or research seminar.[9] *Chinese Literature,* like any other collection of material in Intermedia, consists of both a set of documents containing text and graphics and a web containing all the anchor and link information about these documents.

When beginning an Intermedia session, the user first selects and opens a web. The open web is represented in the web view document. The web view serves several purposes. It provides the user with a history of his movements and displays all documents linked to the current document. It also provides visual feedback as to which documents in the web relate to which links in the document. Selecting documents or links in the web view provides an alternate route to travel to documents that have already been visited or are linked to the current document.

Each document the user travels to is represented in the web view as an icon with a document name and a time-date stamp. Part of the icon indicates how the document was reached: by opening from the desktop, by selecting an already open document, or by following a link. If a link was followed, the anchor explainer of the destination link is displayed in addition to the document name.

The currently selected document is represented at the bottom of the web view, showing a map of all documents linked to the current document. When the user selects a link marker in the current document, the line or lines in this map between the current document and documents containing destination anchors for that link are highlighted. This visual feedback helps the user further identify where following a link would take him. In addition to helping the user see where he has been and what options he has for traveling from the current document, the web view also provides an alternate way to open documents—the user can open any document represented in the web view by double-clicking on it.

### Intermedia design principles

The tools in Intermedia reflect a number of fundamental design decisions. Because it is intended for use by multiple cooperating authors and readers, Intermedia is designed to support multiple users on a network of computer workstations accessing the same material simultaneously. While only one person can alter the contents of a document at a time, any number of people can view, create, or follow links to the same document. Creating and following links is made as simple as possible. Links are created interactively, and are immediately available upon creation. No distinction is made between an authoring and a reading environment; the same tools are available to all users. Instead of separating the two tasks, Intermedia provides control over who can do what by setting read, write, and annotate permissions on each document.

All the Intermedia applications are interactive, rather than batch, formatters. The user formats text and graphics by direct manipulation and selections from tool palettes and menus, rather than the insertion of codes into a text stream. The formatting of the resulting documents is intended to approach the graphic arts quality of the same kind of material presented on the printed page. Each document appears in its own scrolling window, and these windows are arranged on the display by the user in a manner analogous to arranging sheets of paper on a desktop similar to the interface first developed for the Xerox Star[10] and later the Apple Lisa and Macintosh computers. Like sheets of paper, document windows may overlap, and when they do, the top window covers any part of another document that lies beneath it. Intermedia assumes that a document's format has an integrity independent of either the document window or the display of link markers. The document is not reformatted when the size of a document window is changed; instead the document display is clipped to the size of the window. When links are made in a document, link markers are overlaid on top of the current format and are intended to be as unobtrusive as possible. Research done subsequent to the work described here on the application of graphic design to the layout of Intermedia screens is described in a conference paper.[11]

## The design of the Chinese literature corpus

Four common classes of published material form the basis of *Chinese Literature*: reference books, anthologies, monographs, and serials. Each class of publication has its own conventions for organizing and identifying its content. I will discuss in some detail how I have adapted reference books and anthologies, while mentioning the others only briefly. A description of the structure of two reference books and two anthologies follows, along with a description of how they are treated in Intermedia. These treatments are compared to other projects that have presented book materials in electronic form. I precede this with a discussion of how additional hypermedia documents, such as overview documents created with InterDraw and timeline documents created with InterVal, have been used to organize and enhance these published materials.

## New Intermedia documents

In "Reading and Writing the Electronic Book"[12] the designers of Intermedia discuss the relative strengths and weaknesses of printed and electronic books in some detail and point out the advantages electronic documents hold over their printed counterparts. Foremost among these is flexibility of organization and presentation. The order and format of material in a book is set at the time of publication. In a hypermedia system the same materials can be presented in many different ways, in many different combinations. Two examples of how Intermedia can be used to create multiple views of the same material are described here: overview and timeline documents.

---

*Overview documents*

George Landow, the first Intermedia author, developed the concept of a graphic "overview document" even before Intermedia became available for use in the experimental classroom at Brown. Also known as "wheel diagrams," these documents, created with InterDraw, display the relationships among elements in a manner similar to a flow chart. Unlike a flow chart, however, the intent of an overview document is to illustrate the interconnections among items or concepts related to the focus of the document. Landow developed the convention of creating an overview document for each author or movement studied in his survey of English Literature course. When a student is interested in finding material about Charles Dickens she locates the "Dickens" folder and opens the overview for that author, called "Dickens OV." (Figure 1) The graphic document displays a picture of the author in the center, connected by lines to labeled topics that relate to the author. Link markers attached to these labels then lead the student to the material of her choice.

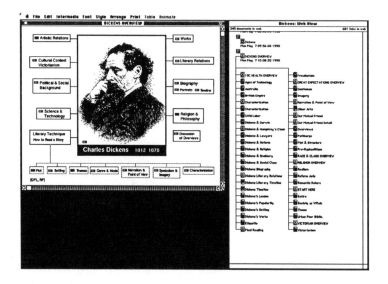

Figure 1: an author overview document from the *The Dickens Web* used to support an introduction to British Literature taught by George Landow. The basic graphic pattern, a central image of the author surrounded by rectangles labeled "Literary Relations," "Biography," "Religion and Philosophy," etc., is repeated for all authors taught in this course.

Like a table of contents, an overview document provides a useful entry point for the reader. When a user needs a place to start, an overview can serve the function of orienting and directing her. Unlike a table of contents, however, an overview document does not have to take a linear format, nor does it have to limit itself to pointing to material within a single "book." Several overviews of the same material can be developed, each focusing on a different theme or point of view, and with annotation privileges users can add their own.

Utting and Yankelovich discuss the need for graphical tools to help the user see how items are related in hypermedia systems.[13] Intermedia's web view is just such a tool, providing a local map showing how the current document is linked to the rest of the web. The similarities and differences between the overview document and this web view are worth commenting on at this point. Both of these documents graphically represent to the user all possible links from the current document. However, the web view currently does this in a generalized way, sorting the documents in one way (alphabetically by document name) and always representing them as document icons which branch off the "root" of the current document. The user gets this "for free," i.e., without any special effort on the part of the author beyond careful planning of links and document names. In contrast, the overview document must be drawn by hand using the graphics editing tools, but it gives the author an opportunity to present connections among groups of material in a variety of ways. Categories and hierarchies can be visually established by grouping labeled shapes. Precedence or influence can be expressed using position, lines, or arrows.

*Author and translator overviews*

Borrowing from Landow's convention, I created an author overview for Tu Fu. This document is intended to convey a high-level categorization of the printed sources available on the system. (Figure 2) One set of links leads to general notes on the poet in the encyclopedia and two anthologies. Another set leads to material concerned with the poet's historical context. At present this is limited to the two timelines discussed below. However, this could easily include additional information on the history of the T'ang dynasty and the events of the An-Shih rebellion which figure so heavily in Tu Fu's writing. Such material would be an excellent bridge from the study of literature to more substantial material focused on Chinese political history. A third set of links leads to translations. These are divided among major anthology appearances, pre-World War II and post-war studies and translations. A separate pointer leads to the index of translations of Tu Fu in *25 T'ang Poets* discussed below. A fourth set of links lead to the critical essays which focus on Rexroth's translations.

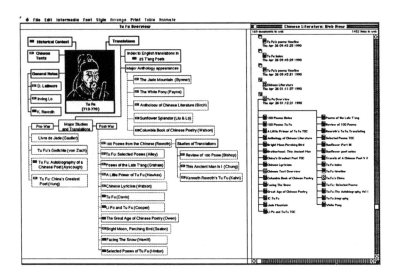

Figure 2: an overview document for the Chinese poet Tu Fu showing the organization of materials in *Chinese Literature* derived from books. The *Chinese Literature: Web View* on the right shows a map of the documents linked to the Tu Fu Overview. The labels in the overview diagram are organized in a hierarchy of topics while the documents in the web view map are arranged alphabetically.

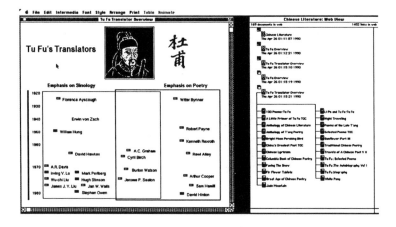

Figure 3: another overview for Tu Fu, organizing much of the same materials by translator along chronological and stylistic axes.

This overview document provides a good starting place for a reader entering the hypermedia corpus. The links all lead to the top of either the document containing the book or essay referenced or the section of that book relating to Tu Fu.

However, the same set of materials can be grouped very differently. A second overview of Tu Fu, containing just the names of his English translators, leads the reader to the same books. (Figure 3) In this case, however, the names of the translators are organized with their vertical position determined by chronology and their horizontal position expressing the style or orientation of their translations. In the first overview *Jade Mountain* and *Sunflower Splendor* are grouped as "major anthologies." In the second overview the translators of the same two books are distinguished as opposite in the categories of "Emphasis on Sinology" versus "Emphasis on English Poetry" as well as distant by some forty years. It is possible to create many different views of the same material because links in Intermedia are not hierarchical or strictly typed. The very neutrality of the linking mechanism can be used to great advantage.

Because so much material had been entered concerning Kenneth Rexroth, another overview document about this poet and translator seemed appropriate. This document indicates to the reader just how broad Rexroth's interests and influences were by listing his publications in terms of categories such as poetry, plays, essays, and translations. Such an overview can provide an excellent bridge between the material in Chinese Literature and other hypermedia collections to which the Rexroth overview would be linked, such as one on Japanese poetry or 20th century American literature.

*Text overview*

In addition to focusing on the work of a poet and a translator, the material in *Chinese Literature* can also support a focus on a particular literary text or group of texts. A poem such as "Lu yeh shu huai" is interesting aesthetically, formally, and linguistically and has inspired commentary in each of these areas. The overview document for this poem graphically organizes all the different approaches taken to this text. Annotated versions of the Chinese text from books by David Hawkes, Stephen Owen and Greg Whincup were scanned and arranged as InterDraw documents. The three versions of the poem differ in the form of romanization (Hawkes uses pinyin romanization, Whincup uses the Yale method, and Owen uses none) and the meaning assigned to each character. (Figure 4) Couplets in this poem are often cited in works on general Chinese poetics. This discussion of one such couplet in Cheng's *Chinese Poetic Writing* along with the accompanying grammar diagram was linked to the overview as well. Similar overview documents for other important poems could be created.

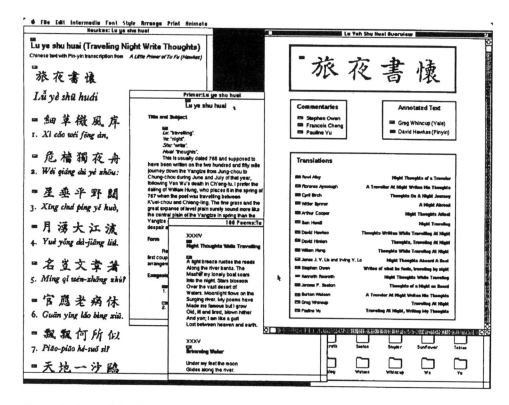

Figure 4: three of the documents concerning "Lu yeh shu huai" linked to the overview for that poem in the upper right—the Chinese text and pinyin transliteration by David Hawkes, the exegesis of the text by Hawkes, and the transliteration by Kenneth Rexroth. The overviews linked to three commentairies and sixteen translations.

*Timelines*

Timeline documents also offer a way of creating a variety of contexts within which to view the same material. Two timelines for this material were created using InterVal. The first was based on a brief chronology of events in Tu Fu's life that appears in A.R. Davis' literary biography. I created the second by combining the poem titles from the Tu Fu section of *25 T'ang Poets* with the dating of each poem found in William Hung's exhaustive study of the poet's life and writing. In the index to translations these poems are listed alphabetically by title. This second timeline allows the user to see the poems in chronological order, with each poem title linked to Hung's discussion and to the translation index. The two timelines viewed side by side provide a simple view of the poems in their historical context. (Figure 5)

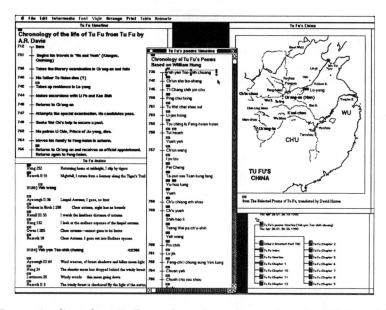

Figure 5: two timelines about Tu Fu—a chronology of events from the A.R. Davis biography alongside a list of poems arranged according to the chronology established by William Hung in *Tu Fu: China's Greatest Poet*, and a map showing geographical locations important to his life from David Hinton's *Selected Poems of Tu Fu*. The poems in the timeline based on Hung are linked to both the reference in Hung and the main index of translations shown on the lower left, which in turn is linked to each translation of that poem.

## Treatment of published materials

*Subject encyclopedia*

*The Indiana Companion to Traditional Chinese Literature* presents a good example of a subject encyclopedia. Completed in 1986 under the editorship of William H. Nienhauser, Jr. and published by Indiana University Press, it is a general reference work for this particular field of study, providing hundreds of brief articles on writers, works, genres, styles, groups, and movements in Chinese Literature before 1911. It consists of two parts: 10 survey essays and over 500 brief articles. Within the context of the encyclopedia itself, the subjects of these articles are cross-referenced in the text as described below. In addition, there are sections of bibliographic lists and indices for name, title, and subject.

This encyclopedia begins with ten general essays on major genres of Chinese Literature: Buddhist Literature, Drama, Fiction, Poetry, etc. Authors or works mentioned in an essay which are the subject of an article are marked with an asterisk to indicate a cross-reference. Articles are arranged alphabetically and consist of an essay and a brief bibliography listing editions, translations, and studies concerning the subject of the article. As with the general essays, authors or works mentioned in an essay which are the subject of another article are marked with an asterisk to indicate a cross-reference. The bibliography consists of two parts: a list of journal abbreviations, followed by a bibliography of works cited in the articles and a general bibliography of works on the subject. These are intended both for general reference and to decode abbreviations used in the articles.

The adaptation of an encyclopedia to electronic form has been done several times and many ways. An early prototype for a general encyclopedia is discussed by Weyer and Borning.[14] Their work emphasized the interactive possibilities of using graphics and simulations as well as text to create encyclopedia articles. The Grolier Academic American Encyclopedia (AAE), a full general encyclopedia, has been available in electronic form for several years, indexed as a full-text file on several systems. Most implementations of the AAE involve a boolean query front-end, using either a command language or a form. Several hypertext experiments have been done using the AAE. After Knowledge Retrieval System Inc. (KRS) produced the first CD ROM version of the AAE for the IBM PC, they demonstrated an experimental version which added "hot" buttons for all references to other articles.[15] Selecting a text label in one article would move to the top of another article. A more recent collaborative experiment by Apple, Grolier, and R. R. Donnelly, *The Grolier U.S. History Demonstration,* uses HyperCard to organize American History materials from the AAE.[16] This added a number of interesting features including access to bitmap graphics representing illustrations, maps, and flip-card animation, as well as sound. The TIES (The Interactive Encyclopedia System) and Hyperties programs developed at the Human-Computer Interaction Laboratory of the University of Maryland[17] are designed for the presentation of encyclopedia or museum exhibition materials. Hyperties provides links from a predetermined list of words to the top of corresponding articles. Like HyperCard, these links are uni-directional, the presentation of material is limited to screen-size chunks, and only one link can emanate from each active area.

Most recently, Josten's Learning Company has produced an electronic version of *The Compton's Encyclopedia* which integrates many of these same features.[18] Users may locate articles by title or by free-text searching. Cross-references are represented by margin icons, as are links to illustrations, audio, and animations. The user's research path is recorded and replayable within each session. Though the user cannot make cross-references, he can record bookmarks that allow him to return to a particular article at a later time.

All of these previous approaches differ from my treatment of the encyclopedia material in the *Indiana Companion* in several ways. First, links in both the KRS, Hyperties, and Compton's system are created in batch and cannot be interactively altered or added to. In contrast Intermedia has the author create each link interactively and links can be altered or added at any time. Second, and most importantly, the other encyclopedia implementations are closed systems of reference. Links are intended to lead only to other places in the encyclopedia, as there is no more general framework for integrating the encyclopedia articles with other materials. This is not the case with this electronic adaptation of the *Indiana Companion*, where the encyclopedia material is designed to be only part of a larger corpus of materials. Each document containing an article is linked to related articles and essays within the encyclopedia, following the editorial conventions of the published version and similar to these previous hypertext experiments. In addition, some text is also linked to material in other documents, representing connections to related books beyond the encyclopedia. In this way, a more general reference network is created.

Most of the examples chosen from the *Indiana Companion* relate to the extensive article by David Lattimore on Tu Fu, only because the content of *Chinese Literature* grew from a study of the work of this one writer. In the encyclopedia this article is referenced by one of the general essays and in turn refers to writers or works which are the subject of six other articles. These articles in turn refer to seven more articles.

To maintain a structure for the alphabetical organization of the articles and avoid unnecessary links I created a table of contents document containing the title of the general essay and the main entries for each article reproduced. In this way all articles were linked to the table of contents. All these documents were placed in a folder named *Indiana Companion*, and each document was given a name corresponding to the main entry preceded by "IC:" (i.e., "IC:Tu Fu" for the article on Tu Fu, "IC:Su Shih" for the article on Su Shih, etc.). This naming convention helped to identify the document as part of the encyclopedia in the web view. (Figure 6)

Wherever an asterisk in the text indicated a cross-reference within the body of an article, a link was made between the subject of another article and the top of the referenced article. (Figure 7) The top of each article was given an anchor explainer of the form "Li Po" and references to articles were given anchor explainers of the form "reference to Li Po." In this way the user can easily follow a reference within an article, as was intended by the editors of the encyclopedia. In addition, selecting the link marker at the top of an article displays all the places where the subject of that article is referenced elsewhere in the encyclopedia. The web view for any article shows all related articles as well as the Table of Contents document.

Placing articles in separate documents allows the user to follow references and still maintain visual contact with as many articles as display space will allow.. (Figure 8) The user can also select the link between the current article and any other document in the web view and see lists of anchor markers describing each link If the same material had been arranged as a single document these two advantages would have been lost. While Intermedia allows the user to create a link between anchors in the same document, these links are not reflected in the web view and following a link within the same document causes the user to lose visual contact with the source of the link.

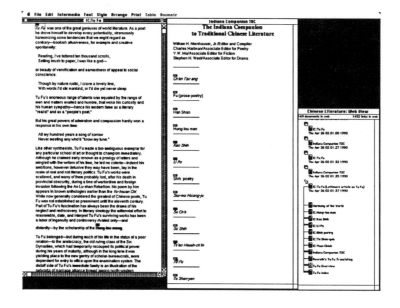

Figure 6: the top of the article in *The Indiana Companion* on Tu Fu open beside the table of contents, with the web view open on the right showing a list of all documents linked to this article. The documents whose name begins "IC:" are other articles from this subject encyclopedia.

In addition to these links between encyclopedia articles, I added what I have termed objective links to other material in *Chinese Literature*. The Tu Fu article mentions several poems by name. In the printed encyclopedia these poems are followed by citations to an edition of the Chinese text. In Intermedia each title is linked to an index of English translations described below. This provides the user with easy access to translations of and contextual information about specific works mentioned in the encyclopedia. The top of the Tu Fu article is also linked to the "general notes" section of an overview of the material on that poet, providing a trail to other general essays on the same subject in other anthologies. Thus, when viewing any particular article in the encyclopedia, the user has access through the web view to a list of related articles and other related documents and, through interaction with link markers in the document and the web view display, can judge which links lead to documents representing related articles and books. This network of associated documents can be easily extended and modified.

Rebellion. No poem by him appears in known anthologies earlier than the *Yu-hsüan chi* 又又 (dated 900). While now generally considered the greatest of Chinese poets, Tu Fu was not established as preeminent until the eleventh century. Part of Tu Fu's fascination has always been the drama of his neglect and rediscovery. In literary sinology the millennial effort to reassemble, date, and interpret Tu Fu's surviving works has been a labor of ingenuity and controversy rivaled only—and distantly—by the scholarship of the *Hung-lou meng.*

Tu Fu belonged—but during much of his life in the status of a poor relation—to the aristocracy, the old ruling class of the Six Dynasties, which had temporarily recouped its political power during his years of maturity, although in the long term it was yielding place to the new gentry of scholar-bureaucrats, more dependent for entry to office upon the examination system. The distaff side of Tu Fu's immediate family is an illustration of the networks of marriage alliance formed among northwestern aristocratic clans in the poet's day.

Tu Fu always referred to himself as a man of Ching-chao 京兆 (the prefecture including Ch'ang-an); of Tu-ling 杜陵, a place in the south of Ching-chao associated with Tu clans; or of Shao-ling 少陵, in Tu-ling. His ancestors served the southern courts through most of the Six Dynasties. Tu Fu's places of birth and education are unknown (the standard histories associate him with Hsiang-yang [modern Hupeh], probably an error due to the prominence of the Tu clan of that place). The family seems to have owned property at Tu-ling—in the neighborhood were many of their graveyard poplars (*Concordance*, p. 171)—and also at Yen-shih, burial-place of the great scholar-general Tu Yü, near the secondary capital, Lo-yang.

Tu Fu's many occasional poems, restored where possible to their original sequence, permit us to reconstruct much of the poet's detailed self-portrayal during and after the An Lu-shan Rebellion.

There is no comparable testimony regarding his earlier years. By his forties Tu Fu claimed to have written over 1,000 pieces, yet only 5-15 percent of them survive. Perhaps none of his poems antedates 735. It nevertheless seems clear that Tu Fu was groomed from an early age for the examination career—like that of his grandfather, Tu Shen-yen,* a *chin-shih* of 670—which could lead relatively quickly to literary and advisory posts in the capital, rather than for a more pedestrian career of provincial administration such as his father had entered, probably by hereditary privilege. The pattern thus set was to endure for life. When not living in retirement or engaged upon his restless travels, Tu Fu sought government employment only by examination or by submission of writings. His routine provincial appointments were limited to a minor police position, which he declined, and one in provincial education, which he quickly resigned. Unfortunately Tu Fu was no better suited to the advisory-admonitory posts he sought than to the ordinary administrative posts he avoided. His employment as Reminder under Emperor Su-tsung led within days to his arrest and trial for outspokenness (his message of thanks for pardon remained obdurately outspoken).

Tu Fu's adult life may be envisaged as a triptych, each panel representing a period with a different geographical center. The first period (c. 731-745), in the East and Southeast, was largely given over to his wanderings as a young bachelor devoted (by his account) to furs and silks, archery, falconry, and revelry. After travels down the coast as far as Chekiang, he journeyed to Ch'ang-an to take part in the *chin-shih* examination of 736. Despite his favorable position as an entrant of the capital prefecture, Tu Fu failed, for unknown reasons. Thereafter he traveled in the Northeast, perhaps at that time becoming family-head following his father's death. At Ch'en-liu 陳留 (modern Kaifeng) in 744 and the next year at Lu-chün 魯郡 south of T'ai-shan occurred the only actual meetings between the famous literary friends Tu Fu and Li Po.* What reality may have underlain the odd coupling of Li Po, the elder, Taoist "immortal of po-

Figure 7: a page from the printed version of the Tu Fu article. Note the asterisk beside the mention of Li Po indicating the presence of an article on that poet elsewhere in the encyclopedia.

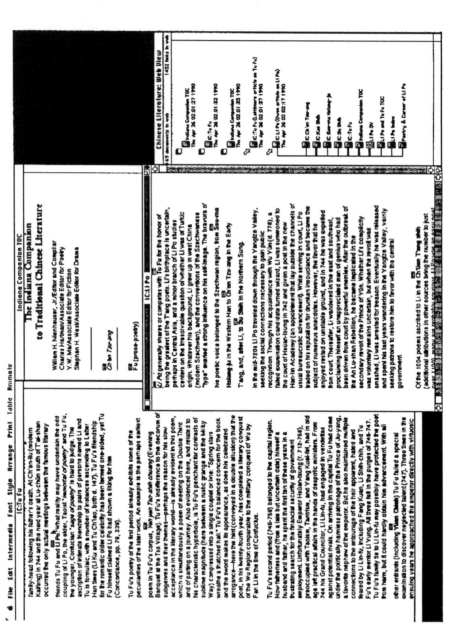

Figure 8: the same passage shown in Figure 7 in the Intermedia version of the Tu Fu article linked to the beginning of the Li Po article. Note the web view in the lower right showing the other articles also linked to the Li Po article.

*Index to translations*

*25 T'ang Poets: Index to English Translations* is a unique resource for the student of Classical Chinese literature. Sydney Fung and S. T. Lai have compiled a comprehensive index to English translations of poems by twenty-five poets from the T'ang dynasty published in book form up through 1981. The index is organized by poet, with each poem listed by first line or title according to Wade-Giles romanization.[19] (Figure 9) The listing of each title is followed by a short bibliographic reference to each book and page where it is translated (e.g., Alley IV:24) and the text of the first line of the translation. A full bibliographic reference for each book, expanding the abbreviated form (e.g., Alley IV: Alley, Rewi. Tu Fu: Selected Poems. Hong Kong: Commercial Press, 1962), is included in a separate bibliography at the beginning of *25 T'ang Poets*.

In addition to this primary method of accessing the index for each poem, several secondary indices are included in the book. There is an index of the first line of each English translation, as well as an index by translator broken down by translated poet. Each of these indices points to the sequence number of the poem in the main entry, which in turn points to the actual book and page location of the translation.

A reference book such as *25 T'ang Poets* which provides an index to other books is itself a kind of hypertext. It is a collection of non-sequential links, a set of "trails" to use Bush's sense of the word. As a printed book, such a reference work lacks the dynamics of a hypertext. Reference trails can be quite tedious and time consuming to follow, while many can lead only to omissions in a library's local holdings. The dedicated student can follow the trail offered by a printed index such as *25 T'ang Poets* by following the bibliographic tracks: from short reference on one page to long reference in another section of the book to a card catalog to a location in the library stacks to a page in another book. By the time she reaches the third basement level of the second library and finds the correct page in the correct edition, a researcher may have lost track of the original motivation for the search. Just as likely she may find the book removed from the shelf, individual copies of books being "single user" in design. She may find herself "lost in library space" trying to figure out how to get back to some productive workplace and frame of mind.

A hypertext treatment of the same kind of reference material gives the user the opportunity to immediately follow such trails. In the ideal system everything will be available on the system in a "multi-user" format, so that following a trail will not lead to a book that has been checked out. With this freedom of movement comes the issue of orientation. Hypertext designers are rightfully concerned about the problems of "getting lost in hyperspace" as the user navigates these trails and moves from one document to another.[20] While hypertext systems can be disorienting, the orientation of a user is as much the responsibility of the content designer, that is the author of the hypermedia collection, as it is the designer of the system tools. Landow (in this volume) discusses the need to develop a rhetoric that will support the comings and goings of complex hypertext. The conventions of footnotes, citations, and indices can provide a basis for Landow's "rhetoric of departure." We have come to expect that a number or symbol beside a word, a citation in brackets or figure reference is a cue to shift our attention elsewhere if we want to pursue related materials. However, when we follow a link and find ourselves in the midst of some essay or book chapter or confronted with a graphic illustration we have less of a tradition to draw on for the "rhetoric of arrival."

| 2826 | Lü yeh shu huai 旅夜書懷：細草微風岸 | | 4:2489 |
|---|---|---|---|
| | Alley V:135 | Thin reeds, and from the land A soft breeze | |
| | Ayscough II:190 | Fine grass, slight breeze from bank | |
| | Birch I:238 | Reeds by the bank bending, stirred by the breeze | |
| | —— in Wagner:19 | | |
| | Bynner I:152 | A light wind is rippling at the grassy shore | |
| | —— II:187 | | |
| | Clack III:488 | Some waving reeds, a light breeze off the shore | |
| | Cooper:237 | By bent grasses in a gentle wind | |
| | Fletcher I:99 | Some scattered grass. A shore breeze blowing light | |
| | Hart I:67 | Tufts of grass on the bank Stirred by the breeze | |
| | Hawkes:202 | By the bank where the fine grass bends in a gentle wind (P) | |
| | Herdan:246 | A faint wind through the fine grasses on the shore | |
| | Hung:256 | Between two shores of tender grass, in the slight breeze (P) | |
| | Liu (W) II:143 | A bank of fine grass and light breeze | |
| | Rexroth II:33 | A light breeze rustles the reeds Along the river banks | |
| | Tang:264 | A light wind ripples the tender grass on shore | |
| | 艸 Ting:54 | Blue stars flat wide field | |
| | Tsai (K):70 | A breeze blows gently on the grassy bank | |
| | Underwood II:144 | The light breeze brushes the grass-blue bank | |
| | —— II:201 | When grass is thin, When wet, soft winds of nights by seas drift in | |
| | Watson I:168 | Delicate grasses, faint wind on the bank | |
| | Yeh:38 | On the slender grass of the shore the wind gently blows | |
| 2827 | Lung-mên 龍門：龍門橫野斷 | | 4:2392 |
| | Davis II:23 | Lung-men makes a cleft across the countryside | |
| 2828 | Lung-mên chên 龍門鎮：細泉兼輕冰 | | 4:2296 |
| | Underwood II:69 | Little streams; thin ice | |
| 2829 | Lung-mên ko 龍門閣：清江下龍門 | | 4:2300 |
| | Davis II:133 | The clear river descends from the Dragon Gate | |
| | Underwood II:62 | Clear water runs and falls down from Lun-Mon | |
| 2830 | Man ch'êng êrh shou 漫成二首 | | 4:2439 |
| | (1) 野日荒荒白 | | |
| | Brace:40 | The sun's white rays illuminate the plain | |
| | Davis II:80 | The country sunlight is limitlessly bright | |
| | Underwood II:92 | The wilderness sun glows fallow, grows pale | |
| | (2) 江莫已仲春 | | |
| | Brace:40 | On my river-bank 'tis the second month of Spring | |
| | Davis II:81 | On the river bank it is already mid-spring | |
| | Underwood II:92 | On this river-bank Middle Spring has come | |
| | Watson I:166 | River slopes, already into the mid-month of spring | |
| | 艸 Wu:109 | With my face turned upward, I gazed and gazed at the birds | |

Figure 9: a page from *25 T'ang Poets: An Index to English Translations* showing the index for several poems by Tu Fu.

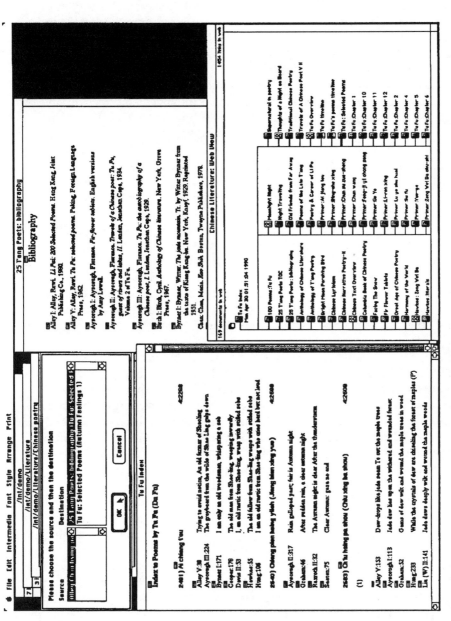

Figure 10: bibliographic material from *25 T'ang Poets* as Intermedia documents. Each abbreviated book source in the index is linked to the expanded book citation in the bibliography shown on the upper right. In this case selecting the linkmarker above "Alley V:153" in the lower left of the *Tu Fu Index* present the user with a dialog box from which to choose one of two destinations: the full citation for Alley's book (shown in the *Bibliography* document on the upper right) or the translation of "Autumn Feelings" in that book (not shown). The web view highlights these two document destinations with dark lines next to *25 T'ang Poets: bibliography* and *Tu Fu: Selected Poems* in the map.

Fung and Lai's comprehensive index to translations provided a good example of printed material to experiment with. The implementation for *25 T'ang Poets* as an electronic reference book was to create separate documents representing the index for each of the twenty-five poets and for the bibliography. I created a document containing merely a twentieth of the nearly one thousand Tu Fu poems listed in the index. I also created documents for several of the other poets in the index, in which material was be entered as time allowed. The secondary indices were not reproduced and instead were replaced by links in the documents themselves. A table of contents was created to represent an overview of the book as a whole. Entries in this document were linked to the top of each author index.

I entered the index for the poems by Tu Fu in the same format in which they appear in the printed book. Each citation was defined as an anchor and linked to an anchor containing the title of the translation to which it referred, as well as to an anchor containing the full citation for the book in the bibliography document. The anchor explainer for the citation consisted of the translator's name and the Wade-Giles romanization of the poem title (i.e. Alley:Lu yeh shu huai). Since *25 T'ang Poets* uses this romanization to identify each poem, I used the title of the translation and the title of the book in which it appeared as explainers for the destination of each link. In some cases I also linked the poem title at the top of the index entry to material about the poem in general, such as the Chinese text of the poem, mention of the poem in general notes on the poet, or an overview document about the poem. (Figure 10)

I entered the bibliography in a separate document, in form identical to the way in which it appears in the printed book. By making each bibliographic entry an anchor with an anchor explainer corresponding to the title of the book, I was able to link each citation to each place in the index where a translation in that book is referenced. This replaced the index of poems by translator with a dynamic index of poems by book. Selecting the link marker on a book in the bibliography produces a dialog box containing the title of the book as the source anchor and the Chinese title of each poem translated in that book as a choice of destinations. (Figure 11)

Another unique feature of this design is a view of all books containing translations of an individual poet. The web view of the Tu Fu index shows links to over fifty documents: other sections of *25 T'ang Poets*, books or sections of books containing the translations referred to in the index, overview graphic documents, documents containing Chinese text, or timelines. This design allows the user to follow a link from the index of all translations of that poem to any translation or related supporting material. Thus, *25 T'ang Poets* in this form serves the same purpose it was meant to serve as a reference book: it points to the location of each translation of each poem. The omitted indices of poems by first line and by translators is replaced and improved upon by three features of the web view. First, a glance at the web view indicates all the books which contain translations of a particular poet, as mentioned above. Second, the selection of the line in the web view map between the index and any particular document icon presents a full list of all the poems and corresponding translation titles in that document. Third, the selection of the link marker in the bibliography presents a list of all poems translated in that book.

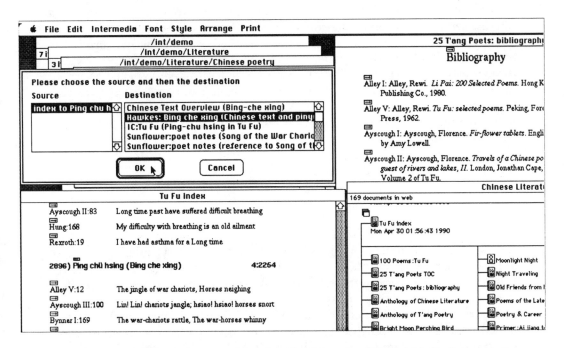

Figure 11: selecting the anchor containing the title of the poem "Ping chü hsing" presents the user with a dialog box containing a list of many links to follow, including the Chinese and pinyin text of the poem, mention of the poem in *The Indiana Companion* article on Tu Fu, and mention of the poem in the notes on the poet in the anthology *Sunflower Splendor*.

In addition, two important functions have been added. First, since Intermedia links are bi-directional, each translation also points back to the central index of translations of that poem. This means a user is also free to follow a trail from a translation of or direct reference to any poem to the index of all translations of that poem. This also improves on the index of first lines, the trail Fung and Lai left for a researcher to find the source poem for all indexed translations. Second, one of the most obvious advantages of an electronic book over its printed counterpart is that it can be easily modified. I was able in the course of my research to emend the

Intermedia version of the index to these poems to include translations published since 1981, as well as identifying the source poem of one unidentified translation, making this electronic version more current and accurate than the printed version.

This kind of emendation to a book brings up a number of unresolved issues: customizing, versioning, and filtering. How should alterations to a book be controlled? Hypermedia systems could provide us with a kind of public and private view of the same material by maintaining multiple versions of an electronic text and filtering out the appropriate version for each user. How should such filtering be accomplished? Such alterations would not be limited to additions and corrections to the text itself. We have all experienced the kind of customizing a library book goes through at the hands of a reader who thinks out loud with his pen or pencil. Marginal notes and underlining are a form of reading well suited, but not limited, to private book collections. While Intermedia does not yet provide tools to literally "scribble in the margins," it does allow multiple users to *annotate*, that is create links to and from a document they can not otherwise edit, links which can lead to their own notes. How should the sharing of notes and comments be managed? All of these are important questions for future research.

*Literary anthologies*

*Chinese Literature* contains selections from a number of literary anthologies. Typically such anthologies take the form of monographs containing translations from the work of several authors. These books share a similar structure. Translations are divided into chapters, which are organized by some combination of time period and author. Brief introductory material on each period and author may precede each section, though it is also common to gather background notes on writers into a separate section at the end of the book. Notes on individual poems are often placed in footnotes. A bibliography may be included as well.

The editors of an anthology provide two levels of pre-selection for the reader. First, they identify the important writers of a period. Second, they select representative works by those writers. Most anthologies, particularly large ones that cover a broad range of time periods, are designed so that sequential reading of the entire book is not necessary to understand the contents of each section. The reader of an anthology will typically use the table of contents or index to locate material from the period or by the writer of interest, read that material, and where necessary locate supporting material such as notes on a work or a writer elsewhere in the anthology.

There are selections from twelve large and small literary anthologies in

*Chinese Literature.* The structure of *Sunflower Splendor,* which contains selections from 3,000 years of Chinese poetry, is typical of the large anthologies. Tu Fu is one of fifty-three poets to be found in the chapter devoted to the T'ang dynasty. The poems included come from the work of a number of different translators. Notes on the poets appear in a separate section at the end of the book, while notes on individual poems are found in footnotes. By contrast *100 Poems From the Chinese* by Kenneth Rexroth exemplifies the small anthology collecting the work of a single translator. *100 Poems From the Chinese* covers nine poets from two time periods. Rather than being divided by chapter it is divided chronologically by poet. Notes on poets and poems are collected in a separate section at the end, followed by a short bibliography.

To represent *Sunflower Splendor* I created a table of contents document listing the titles of each part of the book, along with three other documents: one containing the Tu Fu translations from the T'ang chapter, one containing the notes on these poems, and one containing the general notes on Tu Fu by Irving Lo, one of the two editors of the anthology. I placed these documents in a folder called "Sunflower Splendor," gave each document a name beginning with "Sunflower" and linked the top of each document to the table of contents. I then made objective links within the text of the anthology. I linked the beginning of the section on Tu Fu to the notes on the author. Each mention of an individual poem in Lo's notes was linked to the translation of that poem in the anthology. I made additional links to connect the anthology materials with related work on the system, such as the index to translations, overview documents, and other appearances of the same translations. Within the document containing the translations themselves, the presentation differed from the printed book only in the case of footnotes. Instead of appearing below the text of the poem in the same document, these notes were placed in a separate document and linked to the text so that the user could select a link marker in the text of a translation and read the corresponding footnote in another window.

Hugh Stimson's translation of the long poem "Journey North" in this anthology is an interesting example of transforming seventeen footnotes into anchors and links. (Figure 12) In some cases the superscript indicating a footnote referred to the word it touched, while in other cases the note referred to the entire line or the relationship among words in a group of lines. In defining the anchor to link to a note, I was careful to define only that text which was commented on whenever the intention of the translator was clear. Using this method the user can also browse the notes and follow a link to the part of the poem being explained. Since Intermedia highlights the extent of the anchor for each link, I was better able to focus the user's attention on the appropriate text when a link marker was followed than was possible with the printed conventions of a superscript number beside a single word. (Figure 13)

The government armies ask to penetrate deeply;
their latent valor can be released all at once!
Then will you rise and open up Ch'ing and Hsü,
whirl your gaze, capture the Heng and the Chieh.[13]

A vast sky     piles up frost and dew
a corrective spirit     includes stern destruction
misfortune reversed     it's the year to destroy the Hu
the force is gathered     it's the month to take the Hu
Hu destiny     can it last for long?
The imperial strand     was never meant to be broken!     120

V

Recall how before, when     things got out of control,
matters were different from those of ancient times;
the vicious minister has been chopped to bits;
his companions in evil have since then been dispersed.
We do not hear that the Hsia and the Yin declined
because they themselves put Pao and Ta to death.[14]
Chou and Han achieved their reconstruction;
Hsüan and Kuang were indeed clear-sighted and wise.[15]
Martial, martial is General Ch'en,[16]
grasping his battle-ax, roused in his loyal zeal:
had it not been for you, all men would have ceased to be;
today, the nation still lives!     130

---

13 Ch'ing-chou occupies what is now Shantung; Hsü-chou, the adjacent state to the south. Heng Mountain and Chieh-shih Mountain recall another ancient state, northwest of Ch'ing-chou, near the homeland of the Hu, the heart of the rebel nation.

14 The Hsia and Yin (or Shang) dynasties fell because of the moral failings of their last rulers, reflected in their preoccupation with their beautiful consorts. Ta Chi, a concubine of the last ruler of Yin, was an accomplice in his unkingly revels and helped bring about the downfall of that dynasty. Pao Szu was a favored concubine and later queen of King Yu of the Chou dynasty, who was assassinated because of an instance when he catered to her whims.

15 The T'ang dynasty, like the dynasties of Chou and Han benefiting respectively from the efforts of reconstruction of King Hsüan and Emperor Kuang-wu, is destined to continue in civil peace.

16 During Emperor Hsüan-tsung's journey into exile at the time of An Lu-shan's rebellion, it was General Ch'en Hsüan-li who engineered the death of the minister Yang Kuo-chung and who persuaded the emperor to have Yang Kuei-fei executed.

Desolate     is Great Unity Hall
quiet, quiet     White Beast Gate
men of the capital     look for kingfisher splendor
as the auspicious spirit     moves toward the Golden Tower[17]
the parks and tombs     truly have their gods
are swept, sprinkled     often and without fail
bright, bright     the Great Founder's deed
his establishing     most broad and pervasive!     140
(CTS, PP. 1232–33)        (TR. HUGH M. STIMSON)

### Meandering River, Two Poems

[1]

A single petal swirling diminishes the spring.
Ten thousand dots adrift in the wind, they sadden me.
Shouldn't I then gaze at flowers about to fall before my eyes?
Never disdain the hurtful wine that passes through my lips.
In a small pavilion by the river nest the kingfisher birds;
Close by a high tomb in the royal park lie stone unicorns.
This, a simple law of nature: seek pleasure while there's time.
Who needs drifting fame to entangle this body?

[2]

Returning from court day after day, I pawn my spring clothes;
Every time I come home drunk from the riverbank.
A debt of wine is a paltry, everyday affair;
To live till seventy is rare since Time began.
Deep among the flowers, butterflies press their way;
The slow-winged dragonflies dot the water.
I'd whisper to the wind and light': "Together let's tarry;
We shall enjoy the moment, and never contrary be."
(CTS, P. 1309)        (TR. IRVING Y. LO)

---

17 The emperor, Su-tsung, on his return to the capital (Great Unity Hall and White Beast Gate) and his residence in the Golden Tower will, so Tu Fu hopes, bring good luck to the nation so that the imperial tombs can then renew their ritual lustrations, and the great work of the founder of the T'ang dynasty can be continued.

1 Following William Hung's reading of *feng-kuang* (*Tu Fu*, I, 129). This compound also means "scenery."

Figure 12: a section of the poem "Journey North" as it appears with footnotes in *Sunflower Splendor*.

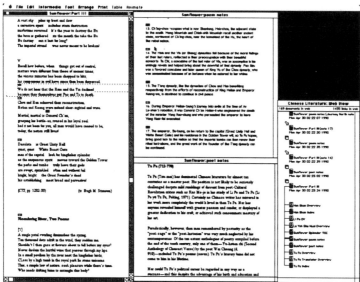

Figure 13: the same section shown in Figure 12 in an Intermedia document, linked to separate documents containing the footnote materials and the notes on the poet. Selecting the link marker for footnote 14 in *Sunflower: poem notes* highlights the two lines in the text to which the note refers.

---

Despite the difference in magnitude, the organization of *100 Poems From the Chinese* resembled that of *Sunflower Splendor*. Separate documents were created for a table of contents, introduction, translations of Tu Fu and two other poets, and notes on the poets. Poem titles were linked to notes on the poem, as the poems are all short and the book used endnotes without marks in the text of the poems themselves. Links were also made to other material on the system. Each poem title was linked to the index of translations. The web view of "100 Poems: Tu Fu" also shows a number of documents on the system which connected to these translations in particular. (Figure 14) Because Rexroth's translations figure heavily in three journal articles on the system, numerous links were made from specific lines to points in these essays. In this way the user is free to read the translations themselves or to follow these links to extensive commentary on the translations.

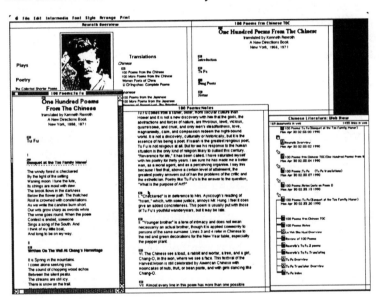

Figure 14: the Intermedia document containing the Tu Fu translations in *One Hundred Poems From the Chinese* by Rexroth, the *Rexroth Overview*, and separate documents containing the table of contents for the anthology and the notes on poets and poems. The web view on the right showing all the documents linked to Rexroth's translations.

Various methods are used to cite the Chinese source of each poem in these books.[21] If a definitive edition of each text in Chinese were identified and stored in electronic form, along the model of the *TLG* database of Classical Greek texts, such citations could be used to programmatically generate objective links. With such a database of texts it would be possible to make each reference to a Chinese source directly and unambiguously in electronic form. Such a system could generalize the kind of reference tool which *25 T'ang Poets* provides for a limited number of translations published in book form into an extensive network of translations, references, and commentaries all tied to a collection of source texts.

### Rules for authors

Landow in this volume  offers a set of rules derived from his experience in developing materials for *Context32*, in "The Rhetoric of Hypermedia." As he points out, hypermedia offers great promise not only for the presentation of educational materials for pedagogical purposes but also in support of traditional literary criticism and scholarship. It is all very clever and convenient to be able to follow links on a screen rather than searching out books in library stacks and shuffling papers on a desk, but as Landow suggests there is something more fundamental going on as well. A system like Intermedia "has the power to change the way we understand and experience the texts."

Landow's nineteen rules were derived from the development of *Context32*, an Intermedia corpus consisting primarily of original texts and graphic images. These rules reflect a concern for the integration of visual materials with text and the conveyance of relationships among disparate elements. In developing *Chinese Literature*, a collection of book materials with relatively few visuals, I have set down another set of rules. These rules are intended as suggestions toward a fuller set of rhetorical guidelines currently under development at IRIS for creating hypermedia materials. Many reflect technical issues, such as document naming and anchor explainers, which are specific to the Intermedia system.

1) The purpose of a link should always be to express connectivity between anchors. This connectivity can be explicit, such as a direct reference to another element of text or graphic, or implicit, such a connection between an element and a glossary explanation or illustration.

2) The text of anchor explainers should work with the name of the document that contains them. Anchor explainers appear in conjunction with the document name in the link dialog box and the web view. The explainer alone should describe the anchor content, while the explainer and document name in combination should explain the anchor context.

3) Use folders to group documents by author or topic. This minimizes the clutter of documents in a single folder window on the desktop display. Folder names also provide the user with a way to locate similar documents from the desktop.

4) When a document represents published material, make sure its document name identifies in some manner both the book it comes from and the part of the book it represents. When breaking a book up into multiple documents, find a simple convention for including some part of the overall book title and an identifier of the book part in the document name.

5) To provide basic navigation support for a book that is broken up into multiple documents, use links at the top of each document to connect the parts to a table of contents so that the web view will at minimum display connections of parts of a book.

6) Avoid links from one point in a document to another in the same document whenever possible. This can be done by dividing structural parts of a book into separate documents. Links within a document should be avoided because they offer two disadvantages: they do not appear in the web view in a fashion consistent with other links and following such a link removes visual contact with the source.

7) There is no need to imitate the book convention of footnotes. If the footnote is kept with the reference point, they should be placed close by without link markers so that scrolling past the reference will reveal the note. If footnotes are collected in a separate document, the text of each note should be linked to its reference point. This serves the purpose of the on-page note by allowing the user to maintain visual contact with the reference and reference point, but adds the flexibility of allowing the user to position the note wherever she wants.

8) Create overview documents to provide a point of focus for related materials and to express categories and directionality of connections. While any document may act as a directory in a sense, the creation of overview documents helps to express the connectivity and multiplicity of relationships to be found in the materials at hand.

With these rules in mind it is possible to create educational materials consisting of original text and graphics created with Intermedia tools as well as book materials adapted from printed formats. As additional media such as full-motion video, animation, and audio are added to the system, the strengths of a hypermedia system like Intermedia will grow enormously. However, regardless of how many new media are added to the environment, the enormous body of published materials will be the basis of scholarly research for decades to come. This experiment illustrates how the possibilities for adapting published material in Intermedia are open-ended and various.

## Sources of text and graphics included in *Chinese Literature*

The Chinese Literature Intermedia materials contains selections from the following published sources:

Alley, Rewi. *Tu Fu: Selected Poems.* Hong Kong: The Commercial Press, 1977.
Alley, Rewi. *Li Pai: 200 Selected Poems.* Hong Kong: Joint Publishing Co., 1980.
Ayscough, Florence and Amy Lowell. *Fir-flower tablets.* London: Constable, 1922.
Ayscough, Florence. *Tu Fu: the autobiography of a Chinese poet, I.* London: Jonathan Cape, 1929.
Ayscough, Florence. *Travels of a Chinese poet: Tu Fu, guest of rivers and lakes, II.* London: Jonathan Cape, 1934.
Birch, Cyril. editor. *Anthology of Chinese Literature: From early times to the fourteenth century.* New York: Grove Press, 1967.
Bishop, John L. "Review of 100 Poems From the Chinese by Kenneth Rexroth" in *Comparative Literature*, X, 1958.
Bynner, Witter, and Kang-hu Kiang. *The Jade Mountain.* New York: Knopf, 1929, in *Witter Bynner: The Chinese Translations.* New York: Farrar Straus Giroux, 1978.
Cheng, François. *Chinese Poetic Writing, with an Anthology of T'ang Poetry.* Bloomington: Indiana University Press, 1982.
Chung, Ling. "This Ancient Man Is I: Kenneth Rexroth's Versions of Tu Fu" in *A Brotherhood in Song: Chinese Poetry and Poetics.* Stephen C. Soong, editor. Hong Kong: Chinese University Press, 1985.
Cooper, Arthur. *Li Po and Tu Fu.* Suffolk: Penguin Books, 1973.
Cryer, James, and J. P. Seaton. *Li Po and Tu Fu: Bright Moon, Perching Bird.* Middletown: Wesleyan University Press, 1987.
Davis, A. R. *Tu Fu.* New York: Twayne Publishers, 1971.
Fung, Sydney S.K., and S.T. Lai, compilers and editors. *25 T'ang Poets: Index to English Translations.* Hong Kong: The Chinese University Press, 1984.
Graham, A.C. *Poems of the Late T'ang.* Suffolk: Penguin Books, 1965.
Graham, A.C. "The Hard Road to Shu" in *A Brotherhood in Song: Chinese Poetry and Poetics.* Stephen C. Soong, editor. Hong Kong: Chinese University Press, 1985.
Hamill, Sam. *Night Traveling.* Isla Vista: Turkey Press, 1985.
Hamill, Sam. *Banished Immortal: Visions of Li T'ai-po.* Fredonia, NY: White Pine Press, 1988.

Hamill, Sam. *Facing The Snow: Visions of Tu Fu*. Fredonia, NY: White Pine Press, 1989.

Hawkes, David. *A Little Primer of Tu Fu*. London: Oxford University Press, 1967.

Hawkes, David. *Classical, Modern and Humane: Essays in Chinese Literature*. Hong Kong: The Chinese University Press, 1989.

Hinton, David. *The Selected Poems of Tu Fu*. New York: New Directions Book, 1989.

Hung, William. *Tu Fu: China's Greatest Poet*. Cambridge: Harvard University Press, 1952.

Kahn, Paul. *Han Shan in English*. Fredonia, NY: White Pine Press, 1989.

Kahn, Paul. "Kenneth Rexroth's Tu Fu" in *Yearbook of Comparative and General Literature*, Vol. 37, 1990.

Kwock, C.H., and Vincent McHugh. *Old Friend From Far Away: 150 Chinese Poems from the Great Dynasties*. San Francisco: North Point Press, 1980.

Lattimore, David. *The Harmony of the World*. Providence: Copper Beech Press, 1980.

Levy, Dore. *Chinese Narrative Poetry: The Late Han through T'ang Dynasties*. Chapel Hill: Duke University Press, 1988.

Liu, Wu-chi, and Irving Yucheng Lo, co-editors. *Sunflower Splendor: Three Thousand Years of Chinese Poetry*. Bloomington: Indiana University Press, 1975.

Nienhauser, William H., Jr., editor and compiler. *The Indiana Companion to Traditional Chinese Literature*. Bloomington: Indiana University Press, 1985.

Owen, Stephen. *The Great Age of Chinese Poetry: The High T'ang*. New Haven: Yale University Press, 1981.

Owen, Stephen. *Traditional Chinese Poetry and Poetics: Omen of the World*. Madison: University of Wisconsin Press, 1985.

Payne, Robert, editor. *The White Pony: An Anthology of Chinese Poetry From the Earliest Times to the Present Day, Newly Translated*. London: John Day Company, 1947.

Pound, Ezra. *Cathay*. London, 1915.

Red Pine. *The Collected Songs of Cold Mountain*. Translated from Chinese by Red Pine. Port Townsend, Washington: Copper Canyon Press, 1983.

Rexroth, Kenneth. *One Hundred Poems From The Chinese*. New York: New Directions, 1956.

Rexroth, Kenneth. "The Poet As Translator" in *Window on the World: Selected Essays*. Bradford Morrow, editor. New York: New Directions, 1987.

Rexroth, Kenneth. "Tu Fu" in *Classics Revisited*. New York: New Directions, 1987.

Snyder, Gary. *Riprap & Cold Mountain Poems*. San Francisco: Four Seasons Foundation, 1969.

Tobias, Arthur. *The View From Cold Mountain: Poems of Han-shan and Shih-te*. Fredonia: White Pine Press, 1982.

Watson, Burton. *Cold Mountain, 100 Poems by the T'ang Poet Han-shan*. New York:

Columbia University Press, 1962.

Watson, Burton. *Chinese Lyricism*. New York: Columbia University Press, 1971.

Watson, Burton, editor and translator. *The Columbia Book of Chinese Poetry: From Early Times to the Thirteenth Century*. New York: Columbia University Press, 1984.

Whincup, Greg. *The Heart of Chinese Poetry: China's Greatest Poems Newly Translated*. New York: Anchor Press Doubleday, 1987.

Wu, Chi-yu. "A Study of Han-shan" in *T'oung Pao*, Volume XLV, 1957.

Yu, Pauline. *The Reading of Imagery in the Chinese Poetic Tradition*. Princeton: Princeton University Press, 1987.

## Acknowledgements

I wish to thank Karen Smith Catlin and James Nyce, whose comments on an earlier draft of this paper helped to clarify the discussion of objective and subjective links. George Landow's discussions of the rhetoric of hypertext have been invaluable to my own work, as have lengthy discussions with Marty Michel. Thanks are due to the dozen members of the Intermedia development team over several years led by Norm Meyrowitz, whose creativity and hard work has made these experiments possible. It was Sam Hamill who first suggested to me that I write something about Kenneth Rexroth's translations of Tu Fu. Half a megabyte of typing later, as Paul Simon once sang, I thank the lord for my fingers.

## Notes

1. See Linda Helgerson, "CD-ROM and Scholarly Research in the Humanities," *Computers and the Humanities* 22:2 (1988); and Paul Kahn, "Isocrates Project Final Report," IRIS Technical Report 87-2, 1987.

2. Vannevar Bush, "As We May Think," *Atlantic Monthly* ( July 1945).

3. James M. Nyce and Paul Kahn, "Innovation, Pragmatism and Technological Continuity: Vannevar Bush's Memex." *Journal of the American Association for Information Science* 40:3 (1989): 214-220.

4. "Kenneth Rexroth's Tu Fu," in *Yearbook of Comparative and General Literature* 37 (1990).

5. See George Landow, "Context32: Using Hypermedia to Teach Literature," *Proceedings of the 1987 IBM Academic Information Systems University AEP Conference;*

and Nicole Yankelovich, Bernard Haan, Norman Meyrowitz, and Steven Drucker, "Intermedia: The Concept and the Construction of a Seamless Information Environment," *IEEE Computer* 21 (January 1988): 81-96.

6. James H. Coombs, "Hypertext, Full Text, and Automatic Linking," *International Conference on Research and Development in Information Retrieval (SIGIR '90)*. September 5-7, 1990, Brussels, Belgium.

7. *CD WORD*. Dallas, Texas: CDWord Library, Inc., 1990.

8. L.N. Garrett, Karen E. Smith, and Norman Meyrowitz, "Intermedia: Issues, Strategies and Tactics in the Design of a Hypermedia Document System," *Computer-Supported Cooperative Work '86*. Austin, 1986; and Yankelovich et al., "Intermedia."

9. Norman Meyrowitz, "Intermedia: The Architecture and Construction of an Object-Oriented Hypermedia System and Applications Framework," *OOPSLA '86 Proceedings*, Portland, Oregon 1986.

10. David Canfield Smith, Charles Irby, Ralph Kimball, Bill Verplank, and Eric Harslem, "Designing the Star User Interface," *Byte* (April 1982): 242-282.

11. Paul Kahn, Julie Launhardt, Krzysztof Lenk and Ronnie Peters, "Design of Hypermedia Publications: Issues and Solutions." *International Conference on Electronic Publishing, Document Manipulations, and Typography (EP 90)*. September 18-20, 1990, Gaithersburg MD, 1990.

12. **See Yankelovich, Meyrowitz, and van Dam** in this volume.

13. Kenneth Utting and Nicole Yankelovich, "Context and Orientation in Hypermedia Networks," *ACM Transactions on Information Systems* 7:1 (1989): 58-84.

14. Stephen A. Weyer and Alan H. Borning, "A Prototype Electronic Encyclopedia," *ACM Transactions on Office Information Systems* 3:1 (1985): 63-88.

15. Tim Oren, Gary Kildall, and T. Rolander, "Experiences with Hypertext on CD ROM," unpublished paper.

16. The Apple Learning Disc: A HyperCard Collection for Education, project design and management, by Tim Oren, including selections from *The Whole Earth Learning Disc, The Grolier U.S. History Demonstration, Project Jefferson (USC), Perseus Project (Harvard and Bowdoin),* and *The Electric Cadaver (Stanford).*

---

17. Ben Shneiderman, "User Interface Design for Hyperties Electronic Encyclopedia," *Hypertext '87*, Chapel Hill, NC, 1987.

18. *Compton's Multimedia Encyclopedia*, Jostens Learning Corporation, 6170 Cornerstone Court, San Diego CA 92121.

19. A brief summary of how Chinese has been romanized: the Wade-Giles system was developed in the nineteenth century and has been used consistently in England and the United States to this day. Since the 1950s the government of the People's Republic of China (PRC) has used the pinyin system and, since the opening of China to the West, this system has gained greater acceptance everywhere, especially since it is now the system used in most Chinese language textbooks. For reasons of emotional politics and tradition, pinyin is rarely used in Taiwan and Hong Kong. A third system, Yale romanization, was developed and is used at Yale University for teaching Chinese. Wade-Giles is the most familiar to English readers and the least precise, Yale is the easiest for an English reader to sound out and the least commonly used, and pinyin is the most precise but makes use of consonant sounds unfamiliar to English readers. For example, the word for "star" is spelled *hsing* in Wade-Giles, *sying* in Yale, and *xing* in pinyin.

20. See Garrett et al., "Intermedia: Issues, Strategies and Tactics"; Jeff Conklin, "Hypertext: An Introduction and Survey," *IEEE Computer* 20: 9 (1987): 17-41; Frank G. Halasz, "Reflections on Notecards: Seven Issues for the Next Generation of Hypermedia Systems," *Communications of the ACM* 31:7 (1988).

21. *Sunflower Splendor* cites the source of each Tu Fu translation with a page number from the *Ch'üan T'ang shih* (reprint of the 1781 edition, 16 vols. Taipei, 1961), "Complete T'ang Poems" using the form "CTS p.1233." The index in *25 T'ang Poets* cites a different edition of the same book (Peking: Chung-hua shu-chu, 1960), identifying the volume number and page location using the form "4:233." Stephen Owen's studies cite the source of each poem he translates and discusses by number, use a Japanese edition of the "Complete T'ang Poems" (Hiraoka Takeo et al., comps., *Todai no shihen*, Kyoto, 1964-65) which assigns a unique sequence number to each poem of the form "*Todai* no. 11433."

# The Shakespeare Project:
# Experiments in Multimedia

Larry Friedlander
Department of English, Stanford University

Teaching lecture courses on drama and Shakespeare always left me feeling some-what frustrated. Not with the students, nor with the works, but with the futility of talking about something not there: the performance itself. In class, all we have to guide our discussion is a printed text; and no matter how rich and suggestive this text may be, it does not help us imagine the real experience of theater: communal, sensual, hallucinatory, fleeting as a dream.

In our tradition learning has basically meant the study of texts. From its beginnings, the classroom has been a place to talk about the printed word. So, there is little resemblance between the classroom and the strange space in which playing occurs, or between a group of note-taking students and an audience immersed in the unfolding world of a play. And nothing in the background of these English (or sometimes indeed physics) majors helps them to imagine the mysteries of the performer's art: the impact of the actor's presence, the excitement of virtuoso playing, and the moment when the audience forgets itself and passes from being spectator to participant in the story unfolding before its eyes.

About four years ago, I decided there must be some way to break out of the box; some way to way to bring the theater—as process, change, spectacle, event—to the student. Not to transform the classroom into a theater (one might as well just buy them a season's ticket to a good company), but rather to bring theater to them as a serious object of study.

I had long recognized the importance of letting students share in the process of theatrical creation. I remember, for example, once (when I was struggling to explain that the script is really very open and unstable, and that even when the staging has been set, small shifts in detail—the tone of a voice, the color of a light, the rhythm of a gesture—could transform the meaning of a moment on stage) I had invited two actor friends to do a scene for the class from Albee's *Zoo Story*.

In this play, a young disturbed drifter named Jerry mees Peter, a proto-yuppie seated on a Central Park bench, and proceeds to subtly woo and menace him. My friends worked on the moment when Peter is just beginning to sense something weirdly wrong with the conversation.

The actors did the scene competently enough, but there was something too predictable, too "Hollywood" about the way they played Peter's shift from trust to fear. As an exercise, I suggested that the actors retain the staging but think of themselves as animals: Peter, a penguin and Jerry, a panther. The result was electric. As Jerry slithered and glided about him, Peter reacted with a timid, waddling flaccidity which graphically suggested the paralyzing awakening of an animal to danger. The resulting moment was funnier, more menacing, and, above all, more surprising than the first try. It was fresh, different and, therefore, convincing; or, as actors say, "It worked."

What interested me as a teacher was how exciting it was for the students to watch how a play is made. They saw actors experiment with different ways to play a moment, and they saw how each new choice remade the event. In that small example, they effortlessly learned quite a lot about theater, things not visible in a text—that the outward performance is sustained and indeed controlled by the inward choices of the actor, that the same moment can be radically changed by small shifts in attention or feeling, and that the printed text in front of them with its fixed and seemingly authoritative structure is really just the starting point for the open-ended and playful exploration of possibilities.

The question I asked myself was whether I could make this process of experiment and choice visible to the students in some systematic way. This question was the beginning of work on what eventually became the Shakespeare Project (SP, from now on).

My many experiments over the years with trying to teach drama as performance had led to two basic solutions: one, get the students to watch plays, and two, get them to perform scenes themselves. However, while these both bring the reality of theater into the classroom, they leave some issues unresolved.

Obviously, it is important for students to see plays, and many fine performances, especially of Shakespeare, are available on film. But films are an awkward medium for instruction—clumsy to demonstrate with in the classroom, and cumbersome to handle for private study. A film conveys only a generalized impression of an event. We are in a passive relationship to the swiftly passing information, unable to examine the work in detail. Without some way to get into the event, it is difficult to develop criteria for judging and comparing the work. For film to work effectively as a medium of instruction, it must acquire the flexibility of text. In other words, we need to be able to see the event; select, repeat and analyze specific moments; compare different parts of the work; and intervene in and alter the work itself.

Moreover, films are of no help in teaching the *process* by which performances are built. Students watching Olivier play Hamlet have the privilege of watching a great, contained, and noble performance. However, Olivier's art as an actor conceals the hard work that underlies the performance. Watching the finished work, we are not privy to his choices of emphasis, characterization, and interpretation; nor do we see the hard work in rehearsal that led to those choices.

Finally, film presents us with a finished work which is apt to mislead the student into thinking that its version is authoritative, the only one possible. In fact, the script can, and is meant to, generate endless versions.

As an alternative to the passive viewing of films, I have had students (with no background in practical theater) stage scenes on their own. They thus experience the stage directly. Students love the experience, and it often transforms the world of plays for them. The problem, besides the time and expense necessary, is that after all theater is a high art, demanding great skill and experience. Students need to learn standards of excellence through exposure to the the best work available; educating students means, in part, stimulating their imagination and educating their eyes.

In 1984, I approached MaryLou Allen, then head of the Stanford Instructional Television Network, with a proposal to create a series of half-hour video tapes on theater, showing actors in rehearsal, alternate versions of scenes from Shakespeare, instruction on Elizabethan costume and language, and much else. MaryLou, in turn, instructed me in the wonders of videodisc and computer simulations. She and Michael Carter, head of IRIS, encouraged me to plunge into the alien waters of technology, and so I began the Shakespeare Project, a Stanford independent project initially developed with the help of SITN and IRIS.

I am not a child of the computer age. Until a few years ago, I would not even use a typewriter, much less a word processor. I resorted to technology only after I had exhausted all other avenues.

As I learned something about the powers of videodisc and computer simulation, I saw that this newly evolving technology might offer solutions I had been seeking. Videodisc is, first of all, an interactive medium which allows students to actively choose their course of study. This emphasis on choice seemed especially appropriate to theater.

Moreover, videodisc allows us to work with specific visual examples and problems. Videodisc can store and instantly retrieve large amounts of images, so students can both explore the experiential part of theater (i.e., the sensual and sensory spectacle created by sound, color, and movement) and use the visual database as a resource for their own work in staging and design. Videodisc allows easy movement through images, so that students can watch a great performance, and then compare that performance with other and differing versions of the same work, gaining insight into the choices made by a specific production. Finally, by combining the videodisc with computers, I realized I could create animation programs that allow students to design and stage their own versions of scenes and to learn about theatrical process in a relatively quick and inexpensive way.

The current system I am developing is the outgrowth of four years of experimentation. The technology is so new that it seems to change under one's feet. While my aims have remained fairly constant, I have been continually designing and redesigning. Because this kind of experimental development is costly, I have worked on little pieces at a time while pursuing further funding. First, I received a grant from FAD (the Faculty Author Development program) to develop a computer simulation program on staging called *The TheaterGame.* Then, using the IBM InfoWindow I created an interactive tutorial on the process of staging, called *From Page To Stage,* and an interactive annotated visual history of theater called *The Browser.*

During a conversation in spring 1987 with Bill Atkinson of Apple, I realized that with the new *HyperCard* program, under development at that time, I could do most of what I wanted quickly and inexpensively, and he agreed to let me work with a test version of the program. So the current form of the project is a multi-media system on *HyperCard* with a two-screen workstation linking a Mac Plus, a videodisc player, and a video monitor.

From the outset, I wanted to teach the full process of theater in an environment that would not reduce its richness, nor force the ambiguous contours of this complex art form into a procrustean bed of rules, prescriptions, and rigid judgments. I wanted students to develop their own standards of judgment through intimate and detailed contact with great performances. I hoped they could learn to watch theater with their whole selves—with mind, heart, and their deepest feeling for beauty. Above all, I wanted to avoid a rigid, linear presentation that would betray the astonishing openness of art.

---

My initial shopping list was designed to enable students to:

* imagine the full sensual reality of theater,
* see examples of the finest available work,
* study performances easily and flexibly,
* learn through partaking in the process of its creation,
* understand and experience the radical freedom of theater,
* uncover the range of choices concealed in the scripts, and
* develop an eye for visual experience.

I felt the center of the instruction should not be a series of right or wrong answers nor a mass of raw data, but a choice of diverse roads into theater. The system must feel playful and inviting, allowing students to relax into an open, flexible, and precise state of attention. Only in this way can students truly grasp and absorb complex experiences. I conceived the SP, therefore, not as a group of lessons but an assembly of different areas to explore.

The system combines the power of CAI with the visual resources of videodisc. Students sit facing two screens. On the video monitor they watch film and still images; on the accompanying computer screen, they can see text and graphics, as well as animations. Upon entering the program, students choose from a menu, called the *Playbill,* which lists the available areas. Students pace their own learning and are encouraged to move freely from one area to another.

The areas offer different kinds of activity as well as subject matter; that is, in some areas students watch scenes and read or write notes; in others, they write multi-media essays or design stages or stage scenes. In some areas they find structured tutorials; in others, they are free to browse through libraries of still images. All their responses and work are automatically saved for them in an electronic notebook. Later, they can use their notes to create essays or prepare class demonstrations.

I am not trying to teach any specific interpretation of a play, or of drama as a whole, but hoping to make information and concepts about theater visible and available. Though I supply notes and structured tutorials, the system allows instructors to write their own comments and lessons directly into the program.

These are the areas available (at least in this stage of the design):

**Performance.** Students can watch selected scenes from major Shakespearean plays in two or more versions, as well as scenes from important contemporary, experimental European theater pieces. As the film unrolls on the video screen, the computer offers a wide choice of accompanying annotations and study aids, any two of which can be viewed simultaneously. For example, while watching a scene students can read about the actors' performance choices, or the historical background of the production, or see variant versions of the text. In addition, the instructor or the students can write their own annotations. At any point, the user can switch to another version of the same scene. The application will move to the same place in the new version as in the original version.

**Study Area**. Students can take multimedia tutorials on basic concepts and theatrical tasks. The tutorials which introduce the students to the full range of collaborative skills necessary to mount a production are arranged according to the work done by actors, directors, designers. I have tried to make the tutorials as interactive as possible and to exploit the interplay of film, text, and graphics. Concepts are explained and demonstrated visually; then, the students are given a fresh example and the freedom to do their own analysis.

**Exploring.** A practice space is provided containing a library of illustrative examples which are keyed to the tutorials. If students need to work on a difficult concept, they can spend time here working out problems, comparing their solutions to mine.

**TheaterGame.** An animation program permits students to stage their own versions of a scene on a computer simulation program.

**Browsing**. This section contains a large collection of annotatcd images on theater with a dynamic index system. Students can organize and annotate their own series of images.

**Notebook**. Students can write multimedia essays, inserting visual quotes from film footage, images, and animations directly into the text. We have created special tools that allow students to capture and record film images and footage.

Each area is designed to illuminate specific issues, or to provide students with conceptual and practical tools, or hands-on experience. For example, viewing and comparing different productions of a scene in the **Performance** area vividly demonstrates how the performers' choices affect the final meaning of the work.

Consider the nunnery scene in *Hamlet*. From the text, it is clear that Hamlet is angry with Ophelia, since he tells her he does not love her and accuses all women of treachery. At the same time, however, he expresses his longing and love for her and accuses himself of unworthiness. What is going on? Does he or does he not love her? Why is he so angry, and so self-abusive? The text presents a problem with which any production of the play must deal. As we watch different solutions, we are astonished how radically free performers are to make their own meaning.

For example, in one version, Nichol Williamson plays Hamlet as rather seedy, lusting after an extremely lovely Ophelia. Here, a good deal of the scene takes place on a bed. The performers solve the illogicalities of the script by imagining that Hamlet is not angry, but is teasing Ophelia because he wants to seduce her.

In contrast, in a Russian version, a tortured, noble-looking Hamlet is discovered in a dark hallway by a fragile Ophelia whom he proceeds to humiliate and terrify. This Hamlet's illogical behavior is portrayed as stemming not from sexual teasing, but from the repressed violence of a man who both loves Ophelia and suspects her of treachery.

Both versions present appropriate, indeed compelling solutions to the same puzzle; yet, they are utterly different. By moving back and forth between the versions, students can see how the actors' choices have created quite different scenes from the same text.

Theater is a complex visual event; many kinds of information and action occur at the same moment. Students are often sophisticated about the complex movement of a poem, but they have little training in dealing with similar complexity when it is visual and swiftly passing. Students need training to grasp the many layers of action and choice compressed in one moment of action. Because students can study in detail the way each moment is staged in the **Performance** area, they begin to discern and isolate the precise means used to generate these large differences in meaning. In one version, a line is whispered insinuatingly; in another, the same line is accompanied with violent action as Hamlet thrusts Ophelia out of his way.

By watching, comparing, pausing, reading, and taking notes (they can even program the film to stop and display notes at places of their own choosing), they can learn: to see the intricate interconnections between sensual detail (the design of costumes, lights) and psychological detail (the actors' motives, gestures, tones); to retain swiftly passing visual impressions; to connect the staging of an early scene with a later one; and, in general, to become as familiar with visual motifs as they are with literary image and metaphor.

Students can move in and out of areas instantaneously. For example, if they are puzzled by an unfamiliar term, such as "actors' beats" or "interior monologues" in the annotations, they can ask for an explanation and be taken to the **Study Area** for a mini-tutorial on the subject. Further practice is available in the **Exploring** section, or they can browse through guided sequences of images on specific topics, such as Elizabethan life or the stage history of *Hamlet* for information or inspiration.

But it is practical work with concepts which particularly brings them to life. After studying examples of staging, and becoming familiar with the conceptual underpinnings of the subject, they can turn to *The TheaterGame* and make their own version of a scene.

This animation program was originally designed as a stand-alone computer application to teach the importance of stage action or, to use the theatrical term, "blocking." Blocking is fundamental to performance because it determines the placement of the players vis-a-vis each other and the audience and, therefore, controls how we view the unfolding action. To a very large extent, the script leaves these vital decisions to the performers, and much of rehearsal time is spent in working out the blocking, detail by detail, and moment by moment.

The importance of blocking to the final meaning of a scene cannot be overstated. Even the simplest scripts can be staged in widely diverse fashions. Take, for example, a straightforward bit of dialogue:

He: How are you today?
She: I am glad you asked.

Simple enough. But as soon as we try to stage it or "put it on its feet," as actors would say, we begin to see how our decisions will determine what the words mean. As readers of this text, we begin naturally by asking, "Who are these speakers?" Performers answer this question by asking concrete questions: Where are the characters and what are they doing? Are the characters looking at or away from each other? Do they move towards or away from each other? Are they sitting at a table? In bed? In a public place?

Compare two possible scenarios. In the first, "He" moves forcefully towards "She" before speaking, touching her perhaps, and then utters his line. "She" stares at him, turns away, goes to and looks out of a window, and then answers with her face averted. In the second, "He" is sitting in a chair and opening a newspaper when he talks; "She" responds by walking across to him, taking the paper out of his hands; then "She" sits down next to him, lights a cigarette, puts her head on his arm and finally says her line.

---

The stage actions create the illusion of narrative and psychological complexity. They create a little story for us about people we do not know. The blocking sets the tone of the action, establishes the psychological relations that govern the characters, and imparts mood, rhythm, and texture to the scene.

The exact same issues arise in staging great drama such as Shakespeare. Compare the above scenarios with the opening lines and moves of the nunnery scene from *Hamlet*:

Hamlet:      Soft you now,
             The fair Ophelia. Nymph, in thy orisons
             Be all my sins remembered.

Ophelia:     Good my lord,
             How does your honor for this many a day?

In the Williamson version mentioned above, Hamlet sees Ophelia lying on the bed, salaciously whispers to himself, "The fair Ophelia," then sidles up to her, kneels, and whispers the line in her ear. She languorously lifts her head from her book, smiles, and whispers her line back.

In the BBC Jacobi version, Hamlet is seated. Ophelia appears nervously in front of him. He jumps up, initially surprised and pleased to see her, and says "The fair Ophelia!"; then stops, looks at her suspiciously, stares at her book (which she is holding upside down!), grimaces, and, turning her book right side up, walks past her. Only as he is leaving does he sarcastically spit out the rest of his line. Ophelia, nearly crying, uses her line to try to stop him from going.

I hoped that *The TheaterGame* would open up the world of staging to students who have no access to practical theater, allowing them to sketch out the multiple possible stagings of a scene and to test how different blockings would actually look on a stage. The program is derigned to duplicate, as far as is possible on a microcomputer, the choices that have to be made in order to present a scene. Users must choose a stage, props, and costumed characters from a series of menus. Then, having designed their set, move the figures through a scene. Each movement is recorded and can be played back as a little film, either to be changed and edited, or to be stored in a file. The program is not tied to any one scene or play, and can work equally well with Shakespeare, Miller, or Ibsen.

The final program is a compromise between full-animation, which would give the student a passably realistic notion of how a scene might look but would be very

---

slow and memory-expensive, and a schematic simulation tool, which allows users to see the spatial connections painlessly. Animating characters for a Mac 512 took very fancy programming, and without the genial assistance of my programmer, Charles Kerns of IRIS at Stanford, this program would have died aborning.

The design was beset with many difficult choices: How to suggest the open space of the stage without having ludicrously small actors? How to choose between believable animation and speed? How to get the user to think with his eyes?

We knew we wanted the user to move the figures with the mouse, but could we control the positions of the body and head without resorting to the keyboard functions for up, down, side, thus diverting the user's attention from the stage? I wanted the user's attention focused on the screen, since I hoped students could develop some instinctive connection between what they saw on the screen and the idea they had about the meaning of a moment. Charles came up with a wonderful solution. All movement is controlled by clicking on the different parts of the figure. By clicking on the feet and dragging the mouse, the figure moves, automatically turning in the direction of the movement. Clicking on the waist and dragging the mouse in different directions makes the figure sit, kneel, or lie down. Clicking on the knees rotates the body, and clicking on the head turns the head. The system is visual and simple, and it helps keep the user kinesthetically connected to the moving figure.

The program can be used independently of the larger SP system. The instructor can demonstrate the way a scene might look, or assign a staging problem, and use the students' work as a starting point for class discussion.

Talking about staging leads into more general problems of interpretation. For example, here is an assignment I gave a class. In *Hamlet* there is a long scene in which Polonius, the advisor to the King, tries to tell the King and Queen that he thinks the reason Hamlet is mad is that he is in love with Ophelia, his daughter, and that she has rejected Hamlet on Polonius's orders.

Polonius takes an extraordinarily long time to get to the point, dithering about madness and kings like a character out of *Alice In Wonderland*. The classic question is, what kind of man is Polonius? Is he simply a silly fool in love with the sound of his own voice? In fact, Polonius is often played this way, in pompous and comic contrast to Claudius. But if he is such a buffoon, how did he rise to be Prime Minister? The class was asked to find other ways to conceive of him that yet make the scene work.

---

Using *The TheaterGame*, students developed various alternatives. In one, the court is seen as a very dangerous place indeed, bristling with soldiers, with the King and Queen seated upstage and removed from the courtiers. In such a militaristic, totalitarian court, Polonius's speech is risky, indeed potentially subversive. To show this, the student had soldiers drift down and surround Polonius as he begins to broach forbidden topics. In this staging, Polonius's hesitancy and baroque flourishes stem from his fear as he gingerly approaches explosive subjects.

Another student's solution is to place the focus on the Queen who, in this version, genuinely loves her son and is deeply distressed at his madness. Polonius is gentle and sympathetic to her, and so speaks haltingly and tactfully. She reacts by moving distractedly over the stage, unwilling to listen to the painful subject and dominating the action with her grief.

In the three versions, Polonius is successively a fool, a wary and vulnerable politician, and a gentle and considerate friend to the Queen. Students quickly see how by focusing attention on one character rather than another, or by re-imagining the location or the emotional atmosphere, they can control the effect of a moment.

Students can also use the materials they see as the basis for their written work. We all know how frustrating it is to discuss a visual experience and have no way to illustrate your point. Film reviewers can quote characters' lines, and describe the action and performance, but cannot show the moment directly to their readers. With the **Notebook** section, students can do just that—write a multimedia essay using not only text and graphics but bits of film, still images, and animation sequences.

This is how it works. Any time film is shown, users have access to a special "camera button." By clicking on the button and holding it down for as long as they wish, users capture and record footage creating a kind of "visual quote" or footnote. They can write accompanying notes and store the footage and the notes in special archives to be retrieved when they wish. The information is stored as an icon which can be freely moved about from files to the writing area and can be inserted directly into the text. When readers come upon an icon, they click it to open the film which then plays on the video screen, with or without accompanying notes. Students who have created scenes on *The TheaterGame* will be able to store the scene as an icon as well and later insert it into the essay.

So if students are asked to write on "Women in Shakespeare," they will be able to excerpt bits of scenes showing the differences between Cordelia and Lady Macbeth, or between two actresses' notion of Ophelia, and use the "quotes" to support or illustrate an argument. They can then display their version of the character or scene on *The TheaterGame*. Or they can, for example, browse through hundreds of slides, selecting and annotating ones that interest them and have the selections stored under appropriate titles, such as Women, Politics, Stage-Design, etc., and then create their own illustratcd articles on the topics.

## Generic tools for multimedia

Stanford's support for my work flows from the conviction that the kind of designing and programming we are doing in the SP will be of real importance to a wide range of fields. Essentially, we are trying to find ways that permit film to be handled as easily and flexibly as print. We seem to be succeeding. Working with film or images, we can control the rate of learning, stop and go back to look at another moment, compare one part of a work with another, make notes directly onto the images, combine and alter images, and shuttle back and forth from one visual record to another.

Theater of course is not the only complex event that is difficult to teach in the classroom. What I realized early on was that my work on the SP could be applied to a broad spectrum of subjects which have at their center visual and hard-to-record live events, be they intense sessions between psychologists and patients, or complicated maneuvers on the football field. When I convened a group of professors from such fields, it was generally agreed that a system which permitted controlled study of visual events would be valuable. In psychology, for example, students could watch and compare therapists working with the same patient or the same pathology. In sociology, films of public events would be accessible to detailed analysis and annotation.

We took care to develop our tools and programs in a generic way, so that they could be transferred with relative ease to other applications. For example, our performance shell, which allows the film to be linked to numerous stacks of information, can be used by anyone wanting to link text stacks and moving images. Our camera button, which allows the user to capture an image or film sequence, take notes on it, and store the information in a folder where it can be retrieved for inclusion in an essay or for presentation purposes, is also a tool that can be generally applied.

Stanford has established a multimedia lab to help professors use these and other tools to develop applications precisely suited to their needs. The idea of the Lab is to discover and solve teachers' real needs. Professors come forward with their problems and their 'wish list,' and they collaborate with skilled programmers on

---

appropriate solutions for their field. Applications in French, Human Biology and Medicine are being developed, all of which share in the excitement of bringing complex events into the classroom for study.

For example, Stanford is developing in conjunction with M.I.T. a program that lets students rent a Paris apartment. Students can wander through the rooms of an apartment, asking questions, talking with the owner, exploring the neighborhood. They can participate in a complex, realistic situation, and study it at their own pace.

An ambitious project on Human Biology is also under development, with faculty members serving as tour guides through a very rich series of interactive tutorials, exploring areas, and games. Students can, for example, browse through a kitchen, opening refrigerators and cupboards and select food for a meal. The computer then calculates the effects of the choice on the user's heart, and simulates the changes in capacity for that user trying to run up a flight of stairs.

## Some principles for designing applications

*The Shakespeare Project* uses the Macintosh and HyperCard linked to a videodisk player. However, the precise technology is not of central importance. New formats for delivery and programming will emerge. What seems important to me is to start developing guidelines for design that are truly useful in the classroom. Here are some principles I might suggest from my own experience:

*Involve the content expert from the very start, and let the design emerge from his or her real needs.*

Too often, educational programs are initiated by technological experts who say, 'Gee, we have these new gadgets, let's put them to use!' What may result is a fancy, over-designed application which no one wants to use. My project emerged out of my long time frustration with a specific pedagogical problem. I knew pretty clearly what I wanted videodisk to do for me. This clarity of focus on my part helped tremendously in the design process.

*The more material, information, and procedures, the simpler the basic organizational principle, i.e. a story, a trip, a museum, a set of interviews.*

Videodisk allows us to store and deliver tremendous amounts of material . It is easy to overload the design, emerging with a vast curio-shop of wares. The more material one works with, the simpler and more intuitive the design structure should be.

---

Find a simple 'spine,' and organize around it. Some ones that have worked well are: a trip through a museum or library, where information and activities are stored in appropriate rooms or galleries; maps of locales, cities, interesting spaces; using sets of experts, each of whom introduces and guides the user through a sub-set of the information.

*Let the user know what what to anticipate and what to expect. Provide an overview, a map, and firm guidance .*

The temptation is to make the system so free and interactive that users have complete control at every moment. While this is a praiseworthy goal, users can often feel bewildered and overwhelmed by choices and uncertainty. Striking a balance is a key to effective design.

Right at the start provide a clear sense of what the program is meant to accomplish, how long it may take to finish a section or complete a goal, and offer initial guidance. Offer comprehensive directories (and ways to navigate through them) and clear spatial maps of the structure of the program. For example, in *The Shakespeare Project* we offer first time users guided tours and short journeys through the materials.

*A good interface design is priority number one.*

Put yourself in the users' shoes. When they open the program, do they see a screen that is inviting, simple, reassuring? Can they intuit with ease how to navigate through the system, what buttons and icons mean, how to get help? Does the design tell the user what the program is about? what it is for? and how to proceed?

*Your design should not only be simple, informative, and efficient; it should appeal to the whole user, to the user's sense of beauty, curiosity, and fun.*

Learning is a form of enthusiasm, an excited reaching out towards the new. The more we are excited and stimulated and intrigued, the more energy we have to direct towards what is new and difficult. A good design allows us to relax and focus attentively on a subject.

Beauty is a form of positive attention; we look with delight and interest at what attracts us. We also like to be surprised, caught off guard, and amused. Humor wakes us up—as long as it is not cheap and patronizing. Put your whole self into the design. This leads to the next suggestion:

---

*Design for full-spectrum learning.*

Interactive media permits students to learn in many different ways, through seeing, hearing, reading, doing. Too often, we work out many ways for students to collect, link, and manipulate information, without exploiting the wide variety of ways they can confront, absorb, and shape that information.

We can read a play, hear it, see it, criticize it, report on it, and participate in it. All these activities are really different forms of learning about the same event. In *The Shakespeare Project*, we organize the material into different learning activities: watching, studying, organizing, writing, browsing, imitating, and creating. By encountering the same material in a variety of modalities, students grasp the richness and depth of the material. They also extend and refine their own capabilities, becoming better viewers, creators, and critics.

*Every discipline generates its own appropriate forms for learning. Art appreciation, psychology, and biology—all these require us to develop specific standards of judgment, specific criteria for truth. The program should enhance students ability to think in that discipline.*

Work at developing a format appropriate to your subject matter. Computer programs in the humanities, and in higher education as a whole, often fail because they try to fit all disciplines into a framework developed for use in mathematics or the experimental sciences.

For example, true or false questions are generally inappropriate to the study of a work of art. Skills needed for developing a sense of history are quite different from those needed to solve equations. When I teach theater, I need to encourage the students' willingness to make daring and unusual choices. Students need to learn not to imitate others, but to develop original and independent solutions to problems. My design should incite their daring, and reward their independence. I need to offer firm information while avoiding rigid categories of right or wrong.

*Don't do in videodisk what can be more gracefully done elsewhere.*

Only use the elaborate functions of multimedia to do what cannot be done otherwise. Don't, for example, have a user read large chunks of material on the computer, when they can digest this material much more efficiently and pleasantly in a book. Try to find the most economical and dramatic way of presenting and idea or fact. Like T.V., this is a medium with a short attention span.

# The Emblematic Hyperbook:
# Using HyperCard on Emblem Books

David Graham
Department of French and Spanish, Memorial University of Newfoundland

The emblem book, as it most often appeared in Europe from about 1531 to 1684,[1] was an assemblage of pictures and related short texts, the combination of which was usually somewhat enigmatic and almost always presented in such a way as to convey some moral lesson, whose point would be savoured all the more for being not instantaneously grasped. In recent years, interest in emblems, which for many years had been dormant, has undergone something of a revival, to the point that emblems have become almost a fashionable subject of study in scholarly circles, as Alison Saunders has pointed out in a recent article.[2] One effect of this surge in interest has of course been to provide even greater impetus to emblem study by revealing how much work remains to be done if the place of the emblem genre in the history of European thought is to be accurately assessed and if its inner workings are to be fully comprehended.

What makes the prospect of electronic access to emblem literature immediately exciting is the sheer difficulty one experiences in keeping track of the multiplicity of visual and textual motifs, repeated and echoed not only within individual emblems but from one emblem to another and from author to author. The mastery of this field displayed by Mario Praz must forever remain beyond the grasp of many emblem scholars whose knowledge of the emblem corpus—given its diversity, size and dispersal throughout European and American libraries—will be for the most part fragmentary and often limited to those books which have been the object of scholarly editions.

Particularly when working with emblem pictures, one is frequently struck by the cumbersome nature of the available bibliographic reference material. Consider, for example, the best current pictorial index to emblem material: Henkel and Schöne's *Emblemata*.[3] The value of this work, which reproduces all the emblems from several of the most influential emblem books together with a comprehensive index to their thematic subjects, has been incalculable to emblem scholars, and yet it has no shortage of drawbacks from a practical point of view. Its cost is so high—at over 800 DM—that few scholars indeed could hope to secure a copy for their own shelves, and thus would have to use the one in their university library, access to which may frequently be inconvenient or impossible.[4] Actual consultation of the work is a daunting task, since it weighs several kilos, and contains over 2000 large-format pages, each displaying a number of emblems with a translation of their text and cross-references to other emblems in the book. Consultation of the thematic index, followed by a search for individual emblems and then by their comparison, can be tedious, time-consuming, and frustrating, as one attempts to compare texts or pictures found several hundred pages apart, while simultaneously keeping one's place in the index. Despite its compendious bulk, the Henkel/Schöne catalogue contains only a fraction of the total number of pictures and texts in the entire emblem corpus, even if one accepts the contention recently advanced by Alison Saunders that the body of interesting and authentic emblem material is much smaller than has often been claimed.

In addition, the Henkel and Schöne catalogue has certain other disadvantages which are inextricably bound up with its existence *as a printed book*, the most obvious of which is that the contents themselves or the editorial disposition of those contents cannot be in any way modified by the reader.[5] For example, nothing can be added to the index itself or to the cross-references should one find them erroneous or wanting in some respect, except by writing in the book: reprehensible if one does not own the copy in question, and disfiguring even if one does. The emblems have been wrenched from their natural context, which is to say they are not in the order intended by their author; to facilitate a thematic comparison of material, they are grouped in subject categories devised by the editors. The German translations, should one prefer something different, cannot be easily replaced without reprinting the entire book. How much better things might be, one is led to speculate, if some computerized, visual emblematic database could be compiled and made available to emblem scholars, who could then modify it to suit the peculiar ends of their own research: with such a thought, the project described here, which may be summarized as an attempt to treat emblem material through the use of hypermedia, was conceived.

My first instinct in associating emblem books and the computer was simply to produce some kind of visual catalogue or database of emblem pictures, and so I began by investigating software such as *PictureBase*.[6] The more I worked on emblems, though, the more persuaded I became that it would be essential to keep pictures and text together, and that to rely on software or hardware which could not readily incorporate all the important elements of the emblematic structure would make nonsense of the entire project. For this reason, the release of *HyperCard* in August 1987 was an exciting development, as it was apparent from the start that *HyperCard* held considerable promise for a project such as the one which I envisioned. Having made a superficial reconnaissance of the program, I soon determined to begin by creating an "emblem stack", which would in effect be an entire emblem book in a *HyperCard* stack, with as many links as possible among pictures and text, and some rudimentary critical apparatus to permit searching and comparison of different emblems.

Figure 1.

The choice of Guillaume de La Perrière's *Le théâtre des bons engins* as the object of my first experiment was conditioned by a number of factors. To begin with, the extremely spare design of La Perrière's book relative to many other emblem collections is striking, and I assumed it would simplify my task: each emblem of *Le théâtre des bons engins* contains only one picture and one text, rather than two, three or four textual parts, as is often the case in other collections (see Figure 1). As well, La Perrière's work, the first vernacular French emblem book, is well-known and important enough in the field of French emblematics to justify its use as a *terminus a quo*, and the artistic quality of the illustrations is excellent. Finally, the illustrations themselves are of a reasonable size and may be clearly reproduced for scanning, and the individual texts are short ten-line poems.

To create my emblem stack, I realized I would have to perform a certain number of unfamiliar operations, none of which however seemed impossible or even particularly problematic at the time: I would have to design a background to receive the pictures, scan the pictures themselves and incorporate them into the stack, enter the text by typing it into a text field, and create such links among the cards as I wished. Brief experimentation showed that none of these operations would in itself be beyond me, despite my extremely limited background in any sort of programming, and so I pressed on, greatly encouraged by early success.

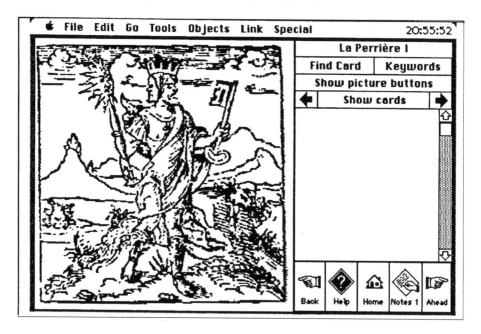

Figure 2: picture background

A series of fundamental decisions related to overall design had to be made early on. My first inclination had been to place picture and text on a single card, but I soon realized that this would be inadvisable: the card size, limited by the original

---

*The emblematic hyperbook*

Macintosh screen, was simply too cramped to permit such an arrangement without utterly sacrificing visual intelligibility.[7] I therefore separated pictures and text to some extent, placing them in separate backgrounds within my emblem stack, and soon found myself working with much more freedom. Given that each text would have its own card, I decided to scan La Perrière's emblems at twice original size (i.e. 4x area).[8] This meant that about half the available space on the cards of the picture background would have to be reserved for the pictures, with the remainder being mine to use as I chose for buttons, text fields and so forth. (Figure 2) Similarly, I quickly settled on a basic design for the text background wherein some 40% of the space would be given over to the text itself; this allowed me to include a reduced version of the picture (more or less actual size) as a visual aide-mémoire. (Figure 3) The larger than normal picture size afforded me a substantial increase in resolution, and I also realized that I could now place transparent buttons where I pleased on the picture surface and thus link any card to any other card by means of a keyword field.

This was a turning point in the history of the project, but it was probably at about this point that I began to have the feeling that I had perhaps bitten off more than I could easily chew. First of all, scanning the pictures[9] was taking far more time than I had anticipated: nearly ten minutes for each emblem once time spent adjusting the position of the paper was included. Second, I discovered that not only was *Hyper-Card* itself a glutton for internal computer memory, but editing the scanned pictures to remove extraneous scanned material and flaws introduced by the scanning process itself, pasting them into the picture background, scaling them back to original size[10] and pasting them a second time into the text background, caused such frequent out-of-memory crashes that I was compelled to purchase additional memory for my Macintosh Plus. Third, even with stack compression, each card in the picture background was occupying about 10K of disk space, and as a result my single unfinished emblem stack was very soon far too large to fit on a standard 800K diskette. I came to understand that if ever this project were to be useful to other emblem researchers, an alternative means of distribution would have to be found: either on hard disk, or (a more attractive solution) CD-ROM. While CD-ROM offered vast storage capacity, it was not erasable, and so the note fields which I had by this time thoughtfully included for my own and others' use would be rendered superfluous in that medium. It now seems to me that of the currently available technologies, erasable optical media are most likely to offer the best solution, but that by all accounts an improvement in disk access time will probably be required for performance levels to be acceptable to most users.

During this period of development, I experienced to the full both the frustra-tions and the exhilaration of working with *HyperCard*. Exhilaration because even I, a novice programmer, could fairly readily implement designs of my own making, and extend them as I managed to make the parts work; frustration because of untutored programming practices, but also because of shortcomings within *HyperCard* itself when used as a tool to accomplish work of the sort I was doing. So far the problems encountered had been entirely limitations of technology, but I was soon brought up against two further obstacles.

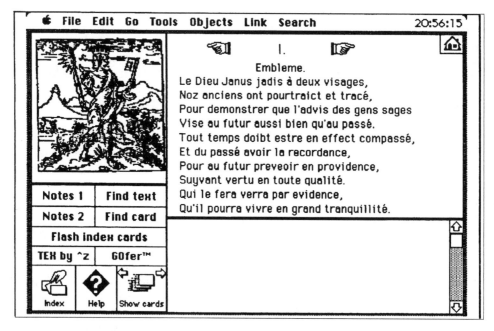

Figure 3: text background

The first of these was the fact that *HyperCard,* as originally released, had serious deficiencies in at least two areas of primary importance to this project, and indeed to any project attempting to use *HyperCard* as a hypermedia access tool. Although Andries van Dam has written that *HyperCard* "is beautifully engineered, and has a wonderful user interface, especially for hypertext-style linking", and despite the fact that certain types of links may be created semi-automatically, it seemed to me that *HyperCard's* native linking ability was generally inadequate, and that its search functions were extremely limited. In addition to these particular shortcomings, it seems fair to say that generally speaking, text-handling ability overall in *HyperCard* is not what it should be, despite some improvements in versions and promises of improvements in version 2.0.

Linking in particular is crucial to the definition of any project which claims to incorporate techniques of hypermedia, and I experienced a great deal of frustration as my work advanced, because it soon became apparent that links of the sort I had imagined would be far from trivial to implement. Any *HyperCard* button can of course contain a hard or soft link to any card, and of course links can be specified semi-automatically through the "Linkto" button in the "Button Info..." box; but it is important to notice that these links are unidirectional rather than reciprocal and that the semi-automatic linkages are limited to one per button. What I had envisioned was some means whereby links to any other card in the emblem database could be specified at will by any user, simply and intuitively, and subsequently modified, replaced or deleted as the need arose. As far as *HyperCard's* searching ability is concerned, the original release was quick but extremely rudimentary, and although subsequent versions have improved to some extent in their ability to specify more complex searches, this has been at some cost: the syntax to be used has become virtually impenetrable to the naive user, and I was assuming that users of my material would in all likelihood be virtually without *HyperCard* experience. As well, once again what I had in mind proved to be quite different from what was provided in native *HyperCard,* as I was anxious to provide some kind of visual search index to provide clues to the distribution of 'hits' within the stack.

It was therefore evident by this stage that certain supplementary searching and linking functions would have to be integrated into the stack if it were to be of real use, and I soon realized that if this were to be possible some additional programming would have to be done by me. Though I had of course at this juncture written numerous relatively short scripts, I began to discover that my ideas were always just ahead of my ability to implement them. This classic learning cycle, coupled with my almost entire lack of programming background or formal training meant that as a result I surely committed every elementary programming error, and doubtless was led to reinvent not only the wheel, but the axle, spoke, and tubeless tire as well, as I struggled with debugging unwieldy 'spaghetti code' produced by the kind of haphazard and freeform implementation which *HyperCard* tends to encourage in novice developers, and as some of my scripts grew to about 300 lines in length. Suffice it to say that the process of implementation using *HyperCard* proved feasible but considerably more tiresome than I had ever imagined it could be.

In its present form, the stack attempts to compensate for some of these shortcomings by providing a few features, in addition to the usual navigational possibilities common to all *HyperCard* stacks, which are either not present in unmodified *HyperCard* or which are not readily accessible to the average *HyperCard* user. The first of these features is the transparent button which can be placed on any picture to allow searching for visual elements for example, the key or the Janus face in Figure

2. While these buttons are normally invisible, to avoid interference with the visual material, any buttons present can be revealed by clicking the button marked "Show Picture Buttons".[11] A click on any transparent picture button launches a search of the other cards in the Picture Background for the next card containing the same visual element. When one is found, the search stops, the card is displayed, and if a button is present overlying the picture element, it is flashed on and off several times to show its location. The search function is enabled by linking each of the transparent buttons to a hidden list of keywords, which can itself be shown and used as the basis for a search for picture elements not represented by buttons. New keywords can of course be added to the list at any time, and new buttons can readily be added as well: the user is invited to click at the appropriate location and supply the name of the visual element to be identified, following which the button is automatically created and pasted over the specified area and the keyword is automatically added to the list of keywords.

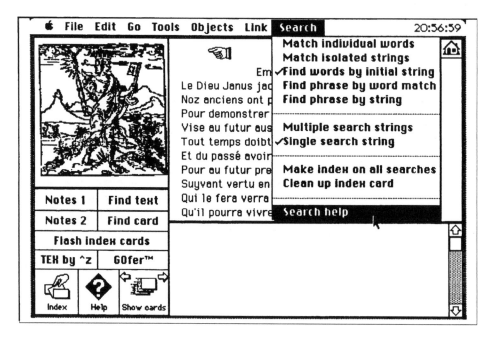

Figure 4: search menu

Each card of the picture background is of course cross-linked by buttons to a corresponding card in the text background, where the primary search functions are, predictably enough, oriented towards the emblem texts. Because the syntax of specifying the various options available in *HyperCard is* unlikely to be quickly mastered by the user less interested in *HyperCard* itself than in access to emblem material, a Search menu[12] has been provided in order to facilitate searches of the emblem text field. (Figure 4) Once a search option has been selected from the menu, the user has only to click anywhere in the text field for the underlying text to be selected and used as the basis for a search of the other cards. In addition, a button marked "Find Text" is provided, and leaves specification of the search string open for entry by the user.

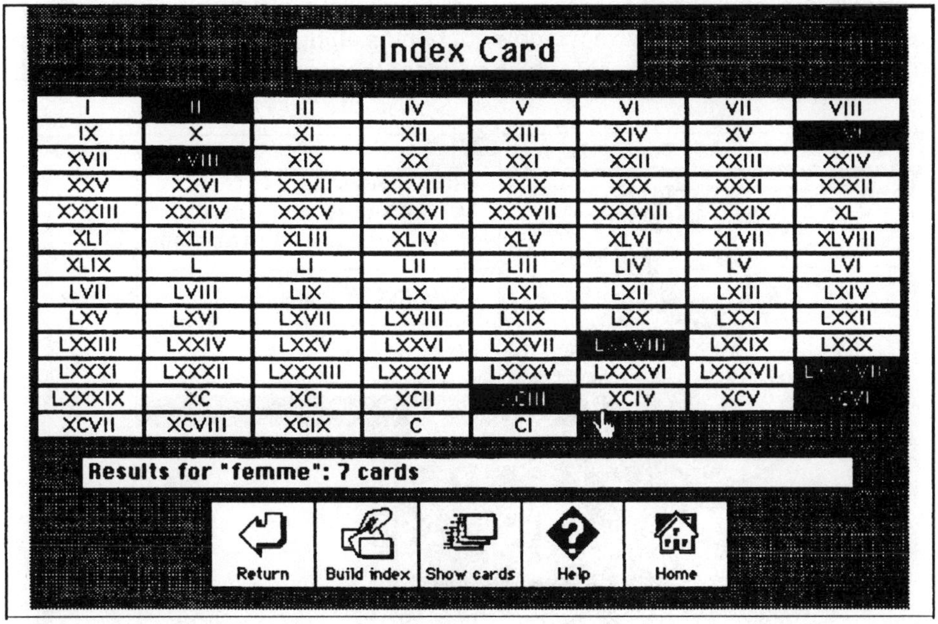

| Index Card | | | | | | | |
|---|---|---|---|---|---|---|---|
| I | II | III | IV | V | VI | VII | VIII |
| IX | X | XI | XII | XIII | XIV | XV | VI |
| XVII | VIII | XIX | XX | XXI | XXII | XXIII | XXIV |
| XXV | XXVI | XXVII | XXVIII | XXIX | XXX | XXXI | XXXII |
| XXXIII | XXXIV | XXXV | XXXVI | XXXVII | XXXVIII | XXXIX | XL |
| XLI | XLII | XLIII | XLIV | XLV | XLVI | XLVII | XLVIII |
| XLIX | L | LI | LII | LIII | LIV | LV | LVI |
| LVII | LVIII | LIX | LX | LXI | LXII | LXIII | LXIV |
| LXV | LXVI | LXVII | LXVIII | LXIX | LXX | LXXI | LXXII |
| LXXIII | LXXIV | LXXV | LXXVI | LXXVII | LVIII | LXXIX | LXXX |
| LXXXI | LXXXII | LXXXIII | LXXXIV | LXXXV | LXXXVI | LXXXVII | VII |
| LXXXIX | XC | XCI | XCII | CIII | XCIV | XCV | VI |
| XCVII | XCVIII | XCIX | C | CI | | | |

Results for "femme": 7 cards

Return   Build index   Show cards   Help   Home

Figure 5: the index background

The disadvantage of such a search procedure is that while it provides extremely rapid linear access to search strings, it does not automatically yield any useful information concerning the overall number of 'hits' or their distribution within the stack. Consequently, an index background is provided. (Figure 5) The user can specify whether or not an index is to be compiled on any search, or can launch a search directly from the index background. During compilation of the index, 'hits' are shown directly on the index card, and following completion of the search, some information is provided on the number of cards found containing the search string. Once an index has been compiled, any individual card can be viewed simply by clicking on its number on the index card, and the series of indexed cards can be viewed in succession for purposes of quick comparison.

Because *HyperCard* lacks sophisticated text-handling procedures, links are provided between the text background and two extremely useful text utilities. The first is GoFer,[13] a search utility with boolean specifications, fuzzy matching, and many other features absent from *HyperCard* at this point in its evolution. The second is *TEX*,[14] which is itself a *HyperCard* stack, though of a type very different from the emblem stack. *TEX* performs indexing and concordancing functions on any text file in an extremely intuitive way: the user clicks first on a word displayed as part of a frequency list, is then shown a window containing all the occurrences of that word in context, and can then choose to see each line in the context of the original text file.

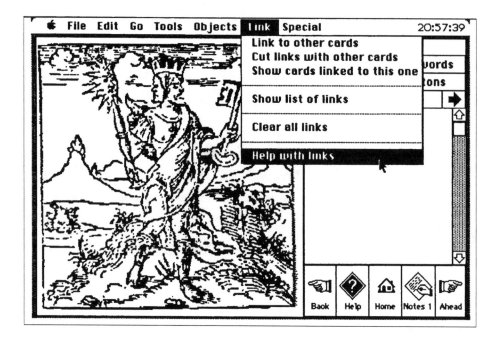

Figure 6: link Menu

To enable users to specify multiple linkages among cards, a Link menu has been added to the stack; (Figure 6) menu selections allow users to add links to other cards, delete or modify existing links, or view any card linked to the point of departure. The links themselves are specified by automatically inserting full pathnames into a hidden text field which can be revealed through menu selection; a click on any line of the field takes the user to the card whose pathname it contains. This part of the stack still requires the greatest amount of work to render it truly useful: at the moment, the links specified are not automatically made bidirectional, nor is it possible to add any information beyond the simple fact of the link. The user cannot note, as an integral part of the linking process, exactly why the link is being constructed, and while such information could be manually added to the text fields on the card which are provided for addition of notes, it would be preferable to include it as part and parcel of the link specification.

Many other features of this initial implementation would have to be revised or reconsidered before any distribution of the 'electronic emblem book' could take place. For a *HyperCard* emblem project to be of real use, several additional emblem stacks will have to be added to the one which now exists. This in turn will create additional problems of scale. Modifications and additions which will be doubtless be required would include such items as a "map" to enable users to avoid the "lost in hyperspace" phenomenon, diagrams of links among nodes, a separate stack to which cards could be copied for ready reference, and above all improved response time: this last will doubtless necessitate rewriting in their entirety several of the larger scripts.

Although my original reasons for undertaking this Project were exclusively practical, I now believe that there are valid theoretical grounds for favouring some sort of hypermedia approach to emblem literature. As Darrell Raymond and Frank Tompa have pointed out, most existing texts are not fragmentary, and so "the key problem in converting them to hypertext is the development of text fragments and links".[15] The emblem, however, is an inherently fragmentary genre, and so it is well suited to hypertextual treatment: not only does it normally present a mixture of texts and pictures, but the texts themselves are often broken into several parts in each emblem. The meaning generated by any individual emblem thus depends on the combined interpretation placed on the sum of the parts, which are thus inextricably linked by the process of reading, but remain far more typographically discrete than most textual forms. Raymond and Tompa go on to observe that

> From the point of view of document conversion, hypertext's main characteristic is fragmentation. Fragments are pieces of content or structure which are both discrete and independent. By discrete we mean that the distinction between components is explicit and well-defined; by independent we mean that components are capable of standing in multiple relations to one another. ( 873)

This description is almost a structural paradigm of emblem literature. Daniel Russell has described the process of reading an emblem text as one in which "one has to hold all the elements in mind to the end of the exposition and then place them together puzzle-wise to form the message."[16] Clearly, such a form of reading is likely to be considerably expedited by the kinds of linking and random access that hypermedia technology can provide.

Despite the inherent and necessary process of fragmentation and reassembly that is characteristic of emblematic composition and reading, and that is akin to what Claude Simon has called "bricolage", it seems clear that the emblems in any given collection are designed by the author and the engraver to present a reasonably coherent overall moral world view, and that this is done synchronically through the use of resemblances, echoes, allusions and reminders both in the pictures and in the text: "multiple relations", or links, if you will, created by the author but often left implicit and thus difficult to discover. Further, as numerous emblem scholars have demonstrated, the entire corpus of emblem literature is bound together by a tight diachronic web of allusion both textual and pictorial in nature: visual motifs and texts are repeatedly 'borrowed' by successive authors from their predecessors. Thus it is imperative, if the workings of the emblem are to be fully understood on any level, for the linking processes to be rendered as explicit as possible, and for each reader to be able to record the links which he or she believes most important. It is my hope that through some form of hypermedia approach the accomplishment of the emblem scholar's basic tasks will be simplified and accelerated, and the present *HyperCard* emblem project should be viewed as only the first and most tentative of many steps toward the realization of this goal.

---

## Notes

1. In other words, from the appearance of the first printed edition of Andrea Alciati's *Emblemata* to the publication of Claude-Francois Menestrier's *L'Art des Emblêmes*. While emblem books continued to be published during the eighteenth century, their conception, execution and intention were very different from earlier collections in that greater emphasis was placed on decoration and less on moral instruction and enigma.

2. "The Sixteenth-Century French Emblem Book: Writers and Printers," *Studi Francesi* 31 ( maggio-agosto 1987): 173-190. Emblem books and their place in the history of European mentality have been the subject of a number of first-rate studies in the last fifteen years. Particular attention should be paid to the classic work by Mario Praz, *Studies in Seventeenth-Century Imagery. Studi Eruditi* ( Edizioni di Storia e Letteratura, 1964) ; see also Barbara Tieman, *Fabel und Emblem: Gilles Corrozet und die franzosische*

---

*Renaissance-Fabel* (Munchen: Wilhelm Fink Verlag, 1974); and Daniel Russell, *The Emblem and Device in France.* (Lexington, KY: French Forum Publishers, 1985). At the original time of writing this article, I had not yet been able to examine the recent studies by Régine Reynolds-Cornell, *Witnessing an Era: Georgette de Montenay and the* Emblemes ou Devises Chrestiennes (Birmingham, Alabama: Summa Publications, Inc., 1987), and Alison Saunders, *The Sixteenth-century French Emblem Book: a Decorative and Useful Genre* (Geneva: Droz, 1988).

3. Arthur Henkel and Albrecht Schöne, eds. *Handbuch der Sinnbildkunst des XVI und XVII Jahrhunderts* (Stuttgart: J.B. Metzlersche Verlagsbuchhandlung, 1967).

4. The copy in my university library, for example, is part of the reference collection and so may not be taken from the building.

5. This account applies equally well, *mutatis mutandis,* to that other great printed tool of emblem scholarship, the multi-volume *Index Emblematicus* project directed by Peter Daly for the University of Toronto Press.

6. Ken Keller, Scott Shwarts, and Mark Moore. *PictureBase.* Symmetry Corporation, 1985, 1987.

7. *HyperCard* 2.0, due for release in late 1990, will remove this limitation by supporting larger screen displays.

8. The pictures in La Perrière's book measure about 52 mm by 54 mm in the original.

9. All pictures were scanned with a Thunderscan™, with the well-known advantage of low cost and the equally notorious drawback of slow speed, exacerbated by scanning at 200% magnification.

10. Two invaluable Desk Accessory programmes for this purpose were *Art Roundup* (Dubl-Click Software, 1986) and The Clipper™ (Solutions, Inc., 1987). The former is a useful and versatile tool for extracting pictures from their files; the latter is an extremely fine piece of software for cropping and scaling artwork.

11. An alternative method is for the pointer icon to change or oscillate whenever it is over an invisible button; this technique is used in **Delany & Gilbert's** *Joseph Andrews* stack.

12. Menus were added to the stack and their items implemented by means of the "NewMenu" XCMD © Nine to Five Software Co. and Michael Long.

---

13. David Spotts and Joel Reiser. *GoFer*. MicroLytics Inc., 1988.

14. Mark Zimmermann. *TEX*. Mark Zimmermann, 1988.

15. Darrell Raymond and Frank Tompa, "Hypertext and the Oxford English Dictionary," *CACM* 31 ( July 1988).

16. Russell, *The Emblem and Device*.

# HyperCard Stacks for Fielding's Joseph Andrews: Issues of Design and Content

Paul Delany and John K. Gilbert
Department of English, Simon Fraser University

When we started on our *Joseph Andrews* stacks early in 1988 we had two models, both developed at Brown University: *Isocrates* and *Context 32*. *Isocrates* is a searchable corpus of almost all surviving texts written in Greek before 700 A.D. Including the search software it takes up about 387 megabytes and is therefore distributed in a CD-ROM format. It is not primarily an instructional tool; rather, sophisticated researchers—classical scholars, in this instance—can use it to scan a comprehensive body of primary texts and zero in on passages relevant to preformulated queries. *Isocrates* also allows scholars to extract passages from the Greek corpus and paste them into articles as they are composed.[1]

*Context 32* was developed by George Landow of the Department of English at Brown, in cooperation with programmers from the Institute for Research in Information and Scholarship (IRIS).[2] Its authors have described it as "a corpus of linked documents" that makes students aware that "any particular phenomenon...[is] potentially multi-determined."(2) So, a master-screen or "Overview" for an individual author may be linked, directly or indirectly, to a large body of pertinent files. These might include explanations of historical background, genre or literary influence; in either textual or graphic form. Choosing an individual path through these files, the student is given an implicit model of how a mature critic undertakes literary analysis: out of a large and various body of knowledge, the critic makes complex associations and structures them into coherent interpretations of literary texts.

In our *Joseph Andrews* stacks we have tried to bring together some of the achievements of *Isocrates* and *Context 32* —though working on a much more restricted scale—but also to advance into new territory. Our unit runs on Apple's HyperCard, which we treat as, at its highest level, a control program for a diverse set of computer functions.[3] HyperCard can link documents, like *Context 32*, or search a database, like *Isocrates*; but such functions are conceptually subordinated to the control level of the program—which is not formally marked, but always implicitly active. The HyperCard interface, with its uniform display of buttons and linked windows, is more complex than it appears; for it can be used to invoke a varied repertoire of computer processes.

Consider, for example, the entry-screen for the *Joseph Andrews* stacks: (Figure 1)

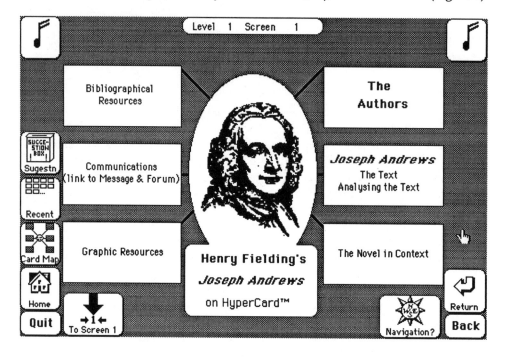

Figure 1.

Using the familiar WIMP interface (Windows, Icons, Mouse, Pointer), the user is asked to choose between buttons of uniform appearance; but they are far from uniform in function. We may recall one of Wittgenstein's metaphors for the operations of language:

> Think of the tools in a tool-box: there is a hammer, pliers, a saw, a screw-driver, a rule, a glue-pot, glue, nails and screws.—The functions of words are as diverse as the function of these objects....

Of course, what confuses us is the uniform appearance of words when we hear them spoken or meet them in script or print. For their application is not presented to us so clearly.[4]

Similarly, the buttons in our stack invoke differing functions. Many of them open windows containing illustrative text or graphics; these functions correspond to the familiar footnotes, cross-references or illustrations in the medium of the book. If the amount of text is no more than a page or two, it can easily be displayed in a scrolling window of appropriate size. If it is longer, however, we may want to have a button that both presents a text and activates a program that may extract and reorganize particular information from it. One button in our stacks opens the full text of *Joseph Andrews*—132,000 words—along with a minimal search capacity for single words and phrases. Another button invokes the full text accompanied by GOFER, a program that supports complex searches.

Other buttons take advantage of HyperCard's ability to control external programs and resources. For example, a bibliographic resource might be accessed in three different ways: it might be pasted directly into one of the *Joseph Andrews* stacks, it might be reached through a direct link with a CD-ROM player, or through a network connection to an external site. Some other resources that we have already implemented in our unit allow students to communicate by e-mail with an instructor and each other, to listen to a passage from the novel being read in a simulated eighteenth-century accent, to hear music from Handel's *Messiah* (which was first performed two months after the publication of *Joseph Andrews*), to have a text file read aloud, using a speech synthesizer, and to invoke an animated scheme of the novel's action. At present it may be cumbersome to shift from one resource to another, or to access more than one at once; we look forward to the time when multitasking and large monitors (17" or more) have become standard and we can run several programs simultaneously, each in their own window. A student might then be composing a term paper on *Joseph Andrews* in one window while having several others active: for example, the entry-screen of the *Joseph Andrews* stacks, the text of the novel, a dictionary, and the on-line catalogue of the university library. Chunks of information from any of these windows could easily be pasted into the essay as it progressed. Such an integrated environment for presenting and organizing knowledge gives us a challenging agenda for the 1990's.

### Designing the *Joseph Andrews* stack

In *Context32* the reader is mainly a browser, one who moves through a web of blocks and links, making his or her own interests the de facto organizing principle (or center) for the investigation at the moment. Each button or window links directly

---

to other relevant points in the corpus of documents, and the whole information structure will be continually re-focused or re-centered as the user wanders through it. This practice of "associative linking" and re-centering may be the best approximation of how a trained mind approaches a complex problem. Another kind of hypertext will put a classical linear text, with its order and fixity, at the center of the structure. The designer then links various supplementary texts to this center, including critical commentary, textual variants, and chronologically anterior and later texts. In this case, the original text, which retains its old form, becomes an unchanging axis from which radiate linked texts that surround and modify it.

*Joseph Andrews* is closer, in its design philosophy, to the second kind of hypertext (neither kind, we hasten to add, should be thought of as the one "right" way to use the medium). *Joseph Andrews* is not primarily designed for browsing, but rather for bringing to a focus various kinds of information that bear on a central and primary text. We have emphasized rapid and consistent navigation through the corpus, so that a student gets the information they need as efficiently as possible. In part, this emphasis made a virtue of necessity: HyperCard 1.2 only allows one card to be active at a time, and is restricted to a window the size of a small Macintosh screen. It would not be able to support the complex screens with overlapping windows and functions of *Context 32*.[5]

In hypertext design, we want the user to extrapolate from visual clues to grasp a more complete structure "behind" the single active screen. A critical design problem is that this assumed or "virtual" structure will vary with the user's choice of what links to follow between blocks of text. If the structure is completely open— that is, each block can link directly to all other blocks—a user will quickly become lost in the "bad infinity" of an excess of choice, where no structure has priority over any other. The *Joseph Andrews* stack keeps the user oriented by extensive reliance on fixed or hierarchical centers. The entry-screen to the stack remains as a privileged center, in two ways. First, this screen is a fixed point from which all subsequent screens descend. Second, the screen itself establishes a consistent visual metaphor, that of the hub and spoke, that is repeated on succeeding screens and guides the reader's responses to their contents. (Figure 2)

These hub and spoke templates are also *hierarchical:* what is at the end of a spoke at the entry level becomes a new hub when the user clicks on it and goes "down" to a finer level of organisational detail. When visualised in three dimensions, the stack becomes a series of tree structures, repeating a motif of *nodes, links,* and *levels.* At the top level, the master-screen is a control and distribution node leading to six sub-nodes at the next level down, each of which in turn controls a varying number of third-level functions. A screen invoked by a button always present called "Card

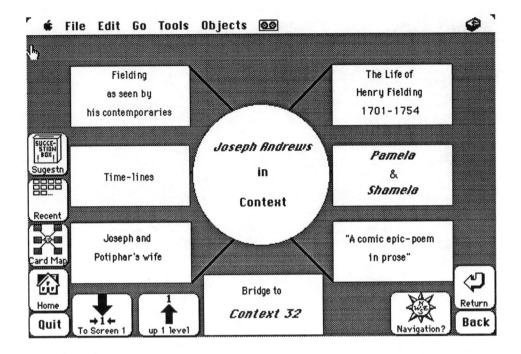

Figure 2.

Map" makes this tree structure explicit, and also allows the user to click on the map and go to a chosen node. (Figure 3)

The stack therefore works as a hierarchy of trees and sub-trees; to make a horizontal link at the second or third levels, one must go up a level to the next control node of the tree, then go back down to the destination function. This movement has been standardized by a built-in "up 1 level" button on most screens, which takes the user "up" to the relevant control node.

Because of the small Macintosh screen and the inability of HyperCard to display more than one card at a time, potential horizontal destinations are not visible from the active card. With a bigger screen and further development of HyperCard, we would want to have the next-level-up control node always displayed in an ancillary window (perhaps with active buttons included).

---

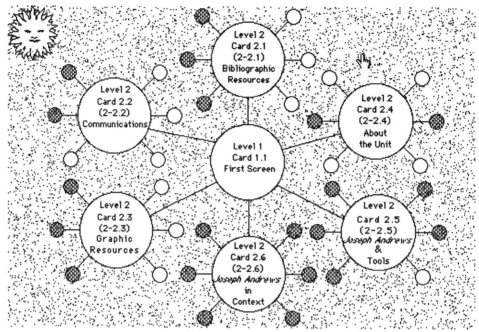

Figure 3.

We can compare our design to the British Inter-City rail system, a hub-and-spoke layout, in which all trains either start or finish in London (except that our structure has three dimensions rather than two). There are, for example, no direct trains from Oxford to Cambridge; instead, one must go from Oxford to London and then from London to Cambridge. The aims of the system are speed and economy; trains that go along the spokes are expresses with large passenger capacity, whereas a decentralized network would have to have many thousands of minor trains. But there is also a useful conceptual simplification for the train user, since all possible choices of route are reduced to two orientations: towards London, away from London. In HyperCard, there is no speed advantage in making a horizontal link by way of an intermediate node; rather, the advantages of our layout are that its logical structure is easily grasped, and that it can be easily expanded by adding levels and nodes either at the current top or bottom. If we wanted to add two more Fielding stacks—for example, on *Tom Jones* and *Jonathan Wild*—it would be simple to add a new top-level node controlling access to all three stacks.[6] Conversely, if we wanted to add more detail to the *Joseph Andrews* stack, we could simply go down one more level and add new nodes there. If all intermediate screens had six spokes, and all spokes at level seven had an information-delivery screen at the end, there would be 46,656 screens available. But because the program responds almost instantaneously when a user clicks on the "up 1 level" button, it would still be possible to go from the bottom to the top of a seven-level tree in a few seconds.

We recognize, however, that at the "information delivery level," as opposed to the "information organisation level," the hub-and-spoke template will cease to be appropriate. When information is delivered as text, for example, the structural metaphor will shift to the familiar scrolling window, with controlling functions built into the "frame." One such window contains the complete text of the novel, integrated with programs for searching and analysing the text. At this level, a block of the novel's text occupies the center, but does not have any spokes to other files or screens: (Figure 4)

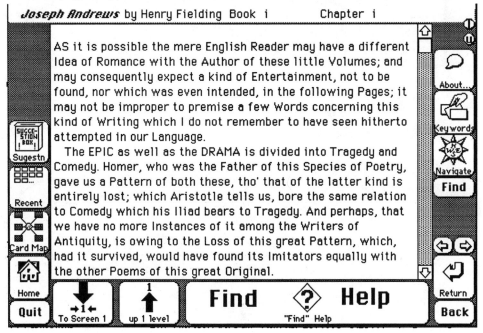

Figure 4.

Elsewhere, a delivery screen controls the reading of a passage from *Joseph Andrews* in an eighteenth-century English accent.

When *graphic* information is being delivered, a map will often provide the best center, with buttons linked to illustrations of places marked on the map. (Figure 5) And in "*Joseph Andrews* Live!" information is presented in four media at once—text, graphics, animation and sound—controlled by a schematic Plan of the Action. (Figure 6)

---

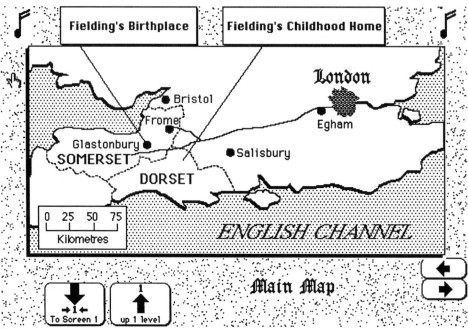

Figure 5.

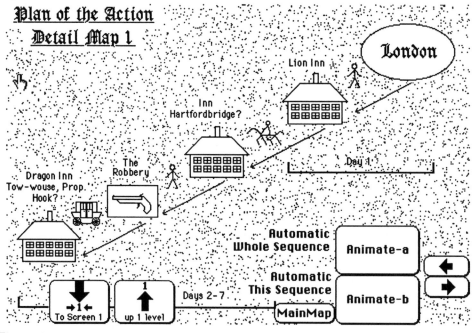

Figure 6.

The stack thus combines a strong and consistent structure at the level of hypermedia organisation, with a variety of modes of presentation at screens delivering information. This design has proved pleasing and effective to undergraduate students using the stack. We recognise, of course, the potential disadvantages of imposing any strongly centralised structure, whether it be a feudal administrative pyramid or the concentration of French government in Paris. Nonetheless, one can still wander freely through the *Joseph Andrews* stack, arriving eventually at any other node from the point of departure—though to do so, one must respect the hierarchical principle because there are no "horizontal" links.

## Hypermedia and the form of literary knowledge

A proven virtue of hypermedia is its ability to present an unfamiliar universe of reference for a literary text. Students reading a modern novel in which an automobile is mentioned will effortlessly invoke a mass of relevant knowledge. But in *Joseph Andrews* they probably will not know the logistics of travel on horseback, the difference between a stage-coach and a chaise, and so on; and such matters figure prominently in the novel's various journeys between London and Somerset. Hypermedia is a uniquely effective mode for presenting the sights, sounds, topography and everyday concepts of a distant historical era. When a new transit line is built between a city center and the suburbs, it has been observed that development will tend to begin at the far end of the line and move towards the center. With hypermedia, similarly, its advantages as an information resource seem to be proportional to the chronological distance of the material from the present day (or, more broadly, to the degree of unfamiliarity of the culture being represented).

When we move from information delivery to the higher levels of knowledge, theory and interpretation, hypermedia should perhaps be seen as a promising but still immature medium for criticism. Until now, *Context 32* has been the only substantial project on computerized knowledge representation for English studies. We accept its fundamental principle: that literary scholars do their work by building complex patterns of associative links between texts and contexts. What needs further exploration is our implicit structuring of these links. Sometimes we may make a simple link between, say, an archaic word and a dictionary definition of it; or between a historical event and a date. At the opposite extreme are complex "families" of links; for example, a feminist view of the Victorian novel. The central problem with such "families" is that they are variant ways of mapping a common textual field—and not just variant, but mutually incompatible. A Jamesian view of the novel cannot just be placed, as it were, "side by side" with a Tolstoyan one; they are rival systems of interpretation which seek to displace one another, in accordance

---

with the Nietzschean principle that "in order to build a temple, a temple must be destroyed." We suggested earlier that a literary interpretation involves first the situating of a master-node—say a feminist view of the novel—which is then a site for the convergence of theoretical propositions, and for the instantiation of those propositions in literary texts. In hypertext design, the interpretation that an experienced critic generates intuitively has to be formalized and reduced to a spatial metaphor of nodes, hierarchies, and shifting patterns of links. This whole network of data and interpretation (a distinction which is, of course, itself open to question) can be envisioned as a kind of cat's cradle, where varying patterns can be foregrounded successively.

The aims of *Joseph Andrews* are much less ambitious, and we realize that we are offering a simplified and somewhat inflexible model of literary inquiry. It is easy enough to provide files on the story of Joseph and Potiphar's wife in *Genesis,* or on Mandeville's sardonic version of sexual morality. What cannot yet be reproduced on a computer screen is how our minds explore large and fuzzy concepts, such as Fielding's whole vision of sexuality, religion, or the good life. If we wanted to add to our unit a truly adequate background corpus for such concepts, the problem of guidance would be increased by one or more orders of magnitude. A few relevant verses from the Bible can simply be presented in an appropriately embedded window; but for larger enterprises we need both the whole Bible, and some means of searching it. If we are to take advantage of the massive data resources made available by modern networks and CD-ROMs, we need to develop a "literary analysis machine": a front end that will mediate between fuzzy queries and the entire universe of literarily relevant data. Some elements of such a front end we have already, in moderately powerful search engines like SONAR; but others will test the limits of emerging expert systems theory.

In conclusion, we recall the double nature of HyperCard as a tool for computer aided instruction. In one aspect it is an efficient means of combining and delivering information in such media as text, database, sound, graphics, animation, and video. In its other aspect—as a control program or "knowledge front-end"—it can simulate various mental functions that we invoke when we approach a fuzzy corpus of knowledge with a more or less precise intellectual intention. In exploring the uses of hypermedia, we may be engaging in the most far-reaching union of technologies since the arrival of motion pictures with sound some fifty years ago.

**Notes**

1. Paul Kahn, "A Description of Isocrates: All of Greek Literature on a CD ROM," IRIS, July 1986.

2. Nicole Yankelovich, G. Landow and D. Cody, "Creating Hypermedia Materials for English Literature Students," *ACM SIGCUE OUTLOOK* 19 (1987): 12-25.

3. The *Joseph Andrews* unit was developed on a Macintosh SE with a 20MB hard drive, on which the unit itself occupies about 8MB. We also have successful mounted the program on five SEs simultaneously on a Waterloo MacJanet network; however, response time was slower than on a single machine—particularly for sound resources—and with present equipment we probably are restricted to less than ten SEs on a network.

4. Ludwig Wittgenstein, *Philosophical Investigations*, tr. G. E. M. Anscombe (Oxford: B. Blackwell, 1967), 6e.

5. At time of writing, HyperCard 2.0 had not yet been released; we will be revising our stack to take advantage of new features in this release.

6. However, we would then have to decide the placement of elements equally relevant to all three works—say, the file containing Fielding's biography. The solution could be either "vertical" or "horizontal." Elements common to the three works could be grouped at the next level below the top node; or, they could be reached from three different places at the level of individual works.

# Hypertext for the PC:
# The Rubén Darío Project

Joseph A. Feustle, Jr.
Department of Foreign Languages, The University of Toledo

Recent advances in computer technology have created new and exciting ways to approach the analysis and presentation of literature. Chief among these is hypertext, a computer program that sets before us completely different methods of organizing information and linking it together to form unique, electronic documents. In this sense, hypertext is as new as computers yet as traditional as the etymology of the word *text* itself: a *texture* of threads that reach out by means of the computer program and connect original works, critical studies, bibliographies, and historical backgrounds. With hypermedia we can also add photographs, drawings, and sound.

We generally associate text with paper, magazines, and books. A hypertext document frees text from the constraints that paper, page-size, and format have traditionally imposed. It is characteristically nonlinear and open in structure and offers many possible places to begin and end. The author of a hypertext document creates a context. The reader does not simply read from page one to the end but explores this context treating each component not in isolation but rather as part of a larger structure in which everything is connected. In a presentation on the baroque, for example, in addition to literature this context could include an overview of the history of the period, and examples of the baroque in art, architecture, and in music. This can be achieved in a single hypermedia document instead of having to deal with many individual books, records, audio tapes, photographs and slides. Also, in moving from one medium to another the user can better appreciate how the baroque arts were not born in isolation but were part of a larger, interrelated cultural context.

The non-linear organization of text is not exclusive to the world of computers. My work with hypertext frequently reminds me of Julio Cortázar's novel *62, modelo para armar* (1968); with its criss-crossing threads of events taking place in London, Vienna, and Paris, it is an excellent example of textured narrative prose. This novel, of course, was derived from earlier experiments in non-linear, open structure in his *Rayuela* of 1963. Through the use of texture and non-linear development Cortázar, as a novelist, sought to provoke new responses in his readers; we, as critics and teachers, may also effect in our readers and students a much deeper understanding of literature through the use of similar techniques: literature in context through hypertext.

Ted Nelson is the person generally regarded as the father of hypertext because of his work on the hypertext Editing System at Brown University in 1967 and 1968 and later on the even more expansive *Xanadu* project. His efforts have continued to evolve at Brown in the form of the Intermedia project at the Institute for Research in Information and Scholarship. George P. Landow has supervised the creation and continuing development of *Context32*, a corpus of 1,500 Intermedia documents joined by 2,600 bidirectional links that supports the teaching of English 32, *Survey of English Literature, 1700 to the Present*. During the first years of the project students used Intermedia on IBM RT PC workstations running UNIX 4.2. Since 1988, students have used Intermedia 3.0, which requires Macintosh II microcomputers and A/UX 1.1, Apple's version of UNIX. Similar hypermedia projects are being carried out at many other universities.

*Project Perseus* (**Crane and Mylonas**) and *Project Shakespeare* (**Friedlander**) are described elsewhere in this volume.[1]

Though it is designed for freshman English classes at the University of Southern California, *Project Jefferson* could well be used in any intermediate or advanced Spanish grammar and composition class. The goal of this project is to help the student cope with the problems created by "the fragmentation of knowledge into different disciplines and storage locations (and media) [that] creates many subtasks that need to be performed in doing research".[2] This is accomplished by bringing the many research media, sources, and tools together in a single hypertext environment. "Its ruling conceptual metaphor is that it is an Electronic Notebook with which students can gain access to a paper assignment on the U.S. Constitution. This access allows students to read a dictionary or encyclopedia for background information on Constitutional issues, download key ideas to their Electronic Notebook, search a database of bibliographic information; take notes, if need be; download a copy; and, finally, dump all this information into a Microsoft Word file as the raw materials of a research paper".[3]

Robert Alun Jones of the University of Illinois at Urbana-Champaign addresses the same problem of fragmentation in his article "Building a Hypermedia Laboratory," but from the scholar's point of view. Jones observes that "by drawing upon and integrating the otherwise isolated resources of scholarly experts, hypermedia promises to 'augment' the knowledge of the individual instructor and bring research and teaching closer together".[4]

Recently, the Giovanni Agnelli Foundation donated copies of *de Italia*, a hypermedia encyclopedia of Italian civilization on video disk that runs on Macintosh computers to sixteen universities, libraries, and museums in the United States. This program is made up of 20,000 photographs, 15,000 screens of text, and 500 graphs. The subject matter covers the history, economy, humanities, science, art, and architecture of Italy from the pre-Etruscan period to the present.

*Athena Muse* (more commonly known as *Project Athena*), is another ambitious hypermedia venture being developed at M.I.T. with funding from the Digital Equipment Corporation and IBM. *Muse* is designed to allow M.I.T. faculty to develop interactive video materials for their undergraduate courses based on combinations of text, graphics, video, and audio. Parts of this program are already in use on some of the four hundred fifty 32-bit graphics workstations on the M.I.T. campus, many of which are capable of combining full-motion digitized color video disk, cable television, digital audio, and high resolution graphics.

The *Muse* Spanish courseware is an interactive video narrative which creates situations in which students can develop a deeper understanding of the practical use and cultural extent of the language. Titled *No Recuerdo*, the story is set in Bogotá where the student must help a Spanish speaking scientist with amnesia to locate a vial containing a genetically engineered amnesia-causing micro-organism that poses a serious threat to all of Latin America. The program uses artificial intelligence to parse the questions and commands, and thereby determine the flow of the action.

There are many competing hypertext and hypermedia systems today. Among them are: *Hypergate, Hyper Pad, Hyperties, E.D.D.S., Vortex, K.M.S., Zoomracks, Knowledge Pro, ZOG, Marcon, gIBIS, Note Card, SuperCard, Plus, HyperCard* and *Guide*.[5] Of these, the latter two stand out. *HyperCard* is now supplied by Apple with every Macintosh computer that it sells.[6] *Guide*, by Owl International, has been written for both the Macintosh and IBM and IBM-compatible computers. In its European division, IBM packages *Guide* with each microcomputer that it sells.

The suggested minimal hardware configuration needed to run *Guide* is rather specific: an IBM-AT, AT-compatible or faster computer (PS/2 Models 50, 60, 70 or 80) with a minimum of 640K of internal memory, a mouse, and a hard disk. It is also desirable to have an EGA or VGA color monitor, some additional extended and/or expanded memory, and a **fast** 40 megabyte or larger hard disk. The reason for all this computing "horsepower" is that *Guide* runs under Microsoft *Windows*, an operating environment that uses icons, pull-down menus and a mouse, and that treats all material, text included, as graphics. While *Guide* will run on older model PC's, the speed with which it does is unacceptably slow.

---

The most recent version of *Guide,* 3.0, is accompanied by a well-written three hundred page instruction book that takes you through a series of sample and tutorial programs. This book also contains an extensive section on *LOGiiX,* a powerful new programming language that Owl International has added to version 3.0 of *Guide.* Owl also offers, at extra cost, a special reader with which others may use your hypertext materials but not alter them, and a program that converts files written in *Guide* on an IBM or compatible for use on a Macintosh and viceversa. Unless you already own version 2.03 (or more recent) of *Windows,* you will have to purchase a separate copy in order to run *Guide 3.0.*

*Windows* 3.0 is well on its way to establishing itself as the leading graphical user interface for the PC and PC-compatible computers. This most recent version has been optimized for the 80286 and 80386 microprocessors that are used in AT-class and faster computers to provide maximum speed and automatic memory management. It represents a substantial improvement over the earlier versions. In addition, it comes with a modest but adequate word processing program (*Windows Write*), a calculator, a paint program, and other enhancements, all of which can be used in conjunction with *Guide.* Besides *Guide,* there many other programs, such as *Paintbrush for Windows* by Z-Soft and *Windows "Draw!"* by Micrografx, that run in the *Windows* environment and provide valuable tools for preparing and enhancing materials ultimately destined for use in *Guide.*

Whether you are creating materials or using those written by others—"Guidelines" as Owl International calls them—the most characteristic features of *Guide* documents are their "buttons" or hot spots on the computer screen that bring about changes in the information displayed when you move the mouse pointer over one of them and click on it. With the exception of typing, all other actions are carried out by using the mouse to gain access to the appropriate commands in the pull-down menus. There is no programming language to be learned unless you specifically wish to avail yourself of the power of *LOGiiX. Guide* has four types of buttons: **expansion, reference, note** and **command**. When you move the mouse cursor over one of these buttons, it changes shape, as shown in Figure 1, to indicate the type of button that you have selected.

**Expansion** buttons appear on the screen in **boldface type** and are used to create the structure of a "Guideline." Clicking on one of them expands or replaces the button with text, graphics or more buttons. **Reference** buttons, *appearing in italics,* are linked to reference points either in the same document or in another one on your disk. **Note** buttons, <u>underlined text</u> on the screen, are used as a type of electronic "footnote." When you depress the mouse button and hold it over one of these, the "footnote" appears in a pop-up window and will remain on the screen as long as you

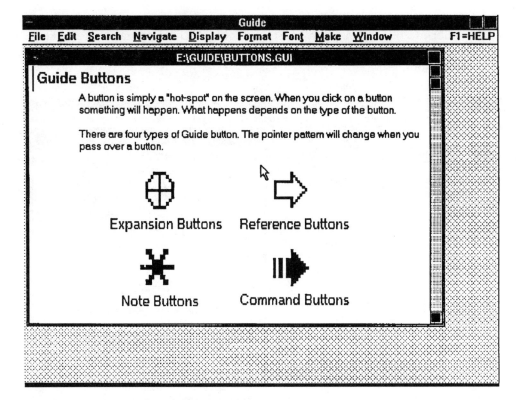

Figure 1

hold down the mouse button. These notes may contain text or graphics. **Command** buttons (see Figure 2) are a powerful new feature added to version 2.0 of *Guide*. They are used to control and gain access to information outside of *Guide*, such as a video disk player connected to the computer's serial port, or other programs, such as computer assisted drill material written in *PILOT*, or a word processor (*Windows Write*, for example) with which students can take notes or write essays and compositions based on what they have discovered in their explorations of the hypertext "Guidelines." One must write short scripts for each command button, but the format and language are straightforward. To run another program created in *PILOT*, you simply write a brief series of commands to (1) "Launch" the program, (2) have the current *Guide* screen reduce itself to an "icon" to make room for the new program about to appear, and (3) give the needed directions to the correct directory and subdirectory where the program is found. If the program, such as *PILOT*, is not a *Windows* program, it is necessary to create what is called a "PIF" (program information file) in *Windows*. This, too, is straightforward and easy. While *Guide* uses the text

---

formats for buttons that we reserve for other stylistic functions such as emphasis or designation of a title, we may continue to use bold, italicized, or underlined text (as is custom in our profession) thanks to the provisions that *Guide* makes in the way it handles buttons.

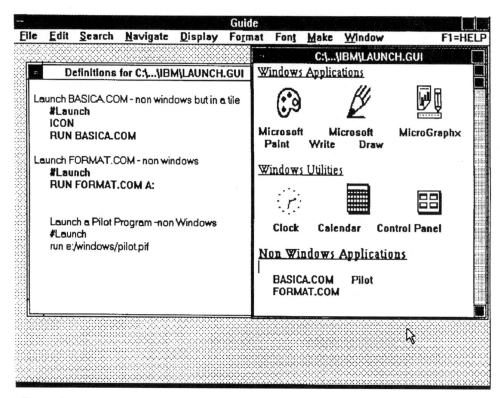

Figure 2

*Guide* contains some of the common features and functions of a word processor: insert and delete text, global search and replace, block movement and replacement of text. However, it is best to prepare text in the full-fledged word processor of your choice, where you have easy and familiar access to a full range of commands, and then save the text in ASCII format and read it into *Guide*. This method becomes even more important given the awkward way in which *Windows*, and therefore *Guide*, forces you to enter foreign language diacritical marks by holding down the ALT-key while you type the correct corresponding ASCII code number on the keyboard's number pad. For example: to obtain an "é", you must type ALT-130. Some word processors, *Nota Bene*, *PC Write* and *Xy Write* for example, use the ASCII format for all their files; others, like *Word Perfect*, may require you to run a file conversion program in order to produce the proper format. *Guide* will also accept text formatted in *Windows Write*, the word processor that comes with the complete version of *Windows*. If you prefer, you can configure *Windows* with a Spanish keyboard complete with dead-key accents when you first install it.

Likewise, although *Guide* allows you to crop and resize graphic images, I have found it preferable to prepare and revise them in a full-fledged graphics editor such as one of the *Paintbrush* series from Z-Soft or programs from Micrografx and other vendors that run in the *Windows* environment. Since these programs share the same operating environment with *Guide*, you can move an image from the graphics program to *Guide* by simply copying and pasting to and from the Clipboard that is part of *Windows*. There has, however, been one problem with this method: the size of the *Windows* Clipboard which, while adequate for most tasks, severely restricted the use of large color images. Version 3.0 of *Guide* solves this problem by allowing you to import graphics by "placing" them, a process that is very similar to the way in which some desktop publishing programs, *PageMaker* to cite one example, import graphic images. In this method, you simply need to choose "Place" from one of the pull-down menus, select your graphic file and then click in your "Guideline." Though not a *Windows* program, my own favorite graphics editor is *Hotshot Graphics* by Symsoft.

Making buttons and links in *Guide* is the easy part: a simple matter of moving the cursor with the mouse over the text to "mark" it and then executing the proper command from one of the pull-down menus. The challenge, as I discovered with my own project, is getting the text and graphics in the computer so that you can create a hypertext document with *Guide*.

### The Rubén Darío Project

My project is, in large part, a response to the continuing frustrations that I encounter each time I teach my course on Modernismo and have to try to bridge the ever-growing gap between that multi-media *fin de siècle* culture and ours. It began as a simple hypertext edition of Rubén Darío's *Prosas Profanas* and has now spread beyond those limits to include Darío's earlier prose and poetry and Modernismo in a much wider scope. The current version consists of over 1.6 megabytes of text, images and sound connected by more than 300 electronic links. I used it for the first time in the fall of 1989 in my advanced undergraduate / graduate class on Latin American poetry and I am continuing to expand it by adding the text from Darío's other major works, *Azul, Cantos de vida y esperanza, El canto errante, El oro de Mallorca*, his unfinished autobiographical novel, and Juan Valera's important «Carta-Prólogo» to

*Azul.* I have developed it simultaneously in *Guide* on an IBM PS/2 Model 80 with VGA color and a 70 megabyte hard disk and in *HyperCard* and *SuperCard* on a Macintosh SE kindly donated by Apple Computers. For the purpose of this article though, I will deal with the implementation in *Guide* only.

Imagine the situation that typical undergraduate students face with Darío's "Coloquio de los Centauros." In addition to the text of the poem, they will need a Spanish dictionary; an English dictionary to further explain the definitions of the unknown words; a high quality study of mythology; an illustrated history of art; several of the key studies on this poem taken from a bibliography on Darío; as well as whatever the particular edition of *Prosas Profanas* used may provide (even the excellent one by Debicki and Doudoroff).[7] It is also important that the student have a working knowledge of Darío's life and of Modernism in general so that he or she can appreciate the reasons why the poet seeks transcendence through woman, the real subject of the "Coloquio." The collection of materials required here is substantial, and the student must always have his or her finger on exactly the right page. With regular text this is laborious if not impossible, but with hypertext the task before the student is less onerous. Hypertext invites the students to explore and understand by automatically taking them to the right lines on the right pages of the most appropriate materials, something that *Guide* does very well. It reduces the fragmentation of related information that Chignell and Lacey correctly single out as an obstacle[8] and the time spent on secretarial tasks, saving it for the more important analysis and assimilation of prime material. Through the way hypertext links the materials, it can show the reader how the "Coloquio de los Centauros" is part not only of *Prosas Profanas* but of a much larger and interrelated cultural phenomenon, Modernism. Hypertext will do so, of course, only if the creator of the electronic document has carefully selected the files, and established the necessary links for the reader to explore.

Hypertext does not function in terms of pages, chapters, or volumes but rather of files and their links. One does not open hypertext and find the traditional table of contents with corresponding page numbers, as there are none. A more useful and correct beginning for a hypertext document, as Professor Landow suggests in his *Context32*, is a diagram of the major files and their links. Mine, for *Prosas Profanas*, up to its present state of development, is shown in Figure 3.

Readers may enter the document in any of the above files and examine any of the major blocks and their connections. They accomplish this on the computer screen by simply moving the cursor to the appropriate block and clicking the mouse. Each block in this diagram functions like the button on a radio: when you press one you may move from one station to another; here when you click on one of the buttons you are taken to the text, graphics, or other materials linked to that button or block.

---

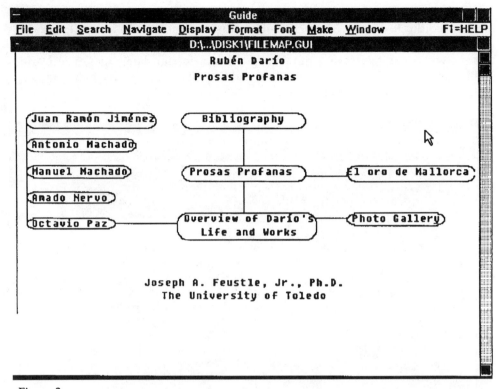

Figure 3

The largest single problem is getting the text and graphics into the computer. Estelle Irizarry has already written about scanning text with a Kurzweil scanner.[9] My own experiences produced mixed results. With a Hewlett-Packard *ScanJet* and *ReadRight*, the optical character recognition program by O.C.R. Systems, Inc. that I purchased with it, I could not scan the fifty-three poems that constitute *Prosas Profanas* with an acceptable degree of accuracy. Thus, I paid my oldest daughter to type them into the computer. The text that constitutes essays on an overview of Darío's life, works, and relationship to Modernism (20 typescript pages), on Juan Ramón Jiménez (18 typescript pages); Antonio Machado (18 typescript pages); Manuel Machado (4 typescript pages); Octavio Paz (20 typescript pages); and Amado Nervo (40 typescript pages), proved easier to scan than retype. I wrote several of these essays on the university's mainframe computer for a publisher who later changed directions and decided not to print them (others have been published in special collections and journals). As I no longer had the electronic files, and the manuscripts were all printed on paper in mono-space, 10-pitch type, I found that I could scan each

---

page into an electronic file with *ReadRight* in roughly 40 seconds and have a minimum of editing to do later. My version of *ReadRight* will not handle foreign language characters; however, O.C.R. System now markets *ReadRight International* which it claims will accurately scan a number of modern foreign languages. The Darío bibliography contains over five hundred and fifty citations and I have maintained it in electronic form for several years.

Figure 4

Once you discover the surprising ease with which you can add graphics to a hypertext document, it is hard to keep from including too many and thereby create a distraction from the pedagogical effectiveness of the document. The Hewlett-Packard *ScanJet* comes with an excellent graphics program called *Scan Gallery* that also runs in the *Windows* environment. Provided your computer has enough memory (the IBM PS/2 Model 80 that I use has 2 megabytes of extended memory), you can run the *Scan Gallery*, *Guide*, and several other programs in *Windows* at the same time and conveniently move information from one to another with the Clipboard. I decided to open my hypertext document with an image (see Figure 4)

---

that caught my attention in Madrid several years ago: the Rubén Darío stop on the metro. The irony struck me immediately (hopefully my students will come to feel it also): the poet's name sits atop a large advertisement for a commercial bank—Rubén Darío spent most of his years in Spain virtually penniless. When you click on this graphic you move next to the diagram of major files and their links.

Why bother with graphic images at all? In the case of Darío, Debicki and Doudoroff noted in their edition: "Unos doscientos pintores, grabadores, y escultores pasan por sus páginas, la mayor parte de ellos sólo nombrados una o dos veces y con poca o ninguna discusión".[10] A graphic image can vastly facilitate comprehension of an important idea, the theme of melancholy in Darío's poetry, for example. While one can explain concepts such as the relationship between melancholy, *desidia*, and *deseo*, average undergraduates may more easily understand melancholy if they could simply **see** it. For this purpose, I have scanned and included Albrecth Dürer's classic work *Melancholy*, whose angel's face conveys quite succinctly what would cost many words and much time to explain.[11] "En Chile, en busca de cuadros", the final prose section in *Azul,* offers even richer possibilities. Here, Darío paints with words in a series of short narratives titled *Acuarela* (Water Color), *Paisaje* (Landscape), *Aguafuerte* (Etching), *Retrato de Watteau* (Portrait by Watteau), *Naturaleza muerta* (Still life), and *Al carbón* (Charcoal). While the more cultured reader of Darío's age may well have been acquainted with this early form of multimedia, it is highly doubtful that even an advanced graduate student, highly specialized in Modernism, now would have even a superficial understanding of what Darío is attempting. Thus, I am using hypermedia to provide immediate examples of a Water Color (Jean-Auguste-Dominique Ingres, *L'Odalisque*), a Landscape (Vincent van Gogh, *Landscape with the Plains of the Crau*), a work by Watteau (*The Embarcation for Cytheria* or *Nymph Surprised by a Satyr*), a Still Life (Paul Cézanne, *Nature mort aux Pommes sur un Dressoir*), and a Charcoal (Francisco de Zurbarán, *Un fraile*). These same relationships can certainly be developed in hypertext treatments of the baroque or of surrealism, to cite two other possibilities.

Once you start including graphics, you quickly understand the need for the computing "horsepower" mentioned above. Cropping or resizing digitized graphic images requires lots of computer processing time. Also, scanned images can produce huge files, and space on the hard disk disappears quickly. The image of the Madrid subway entrance is a gray-scale reproduction of an 8 by 10 inch black and white print that I scanned in with the Hewlett- Packard. With the proper equipment, one can also include graphic images in color.

Most IBM and IBM-compatible computers offer EGA or VGA color as a matter of course. This translates into the ability to display between 16 and 256 colors simultaneously on the screen, which is usually enough to amaze most of us.[12] Color images can be taken from many sources: video tapes, television, video disks—most of the major museums have put copies of their collections on video disks—, and clip art (mostly black and white), ready-made drawings of all manner of things that are frequently used in desktop publishing. Getting color images into the computer can be as simple as placing a color slide into a device such as the Barneyscan[13] or Nikon slide digitizers or a picture from a magazine or book on a Howtek Scanmaster or Sharp flatbed scanner and watching it appear, seconds later, on the computer screen.[14] However, you should be aware that digitized color images average between four and five megabytes in size and thus require large and fast hard disks. One color photo that I recently scanned on a Howtek Scanmaster exceeded seven megabytes. The typical list price for one of these digitizers is between $8,000 and $9,000. While the Barneyscan, Howtek, Nikon and Sharp devices come with software programs, all require special interface cards such as the TARGA-16 (32,768 colors) at $1995, a special color monitor at $1500, and a minimum of 2 megabytes of additional computer memory at $300. While you may be tempted to write off color as too expensive, this technology is highly competitive, is seemingly changing each month, and is seeing prices fall as new competitors appear on the market. The Microtek 300Z scanner, which has recently appeared on the market, for example, produces 256 shades of gray or color, can be connected to a Macintosh or a PC, and is available at a university price of less than $1,900.[15]

The competition in the color market is keen not because of hypermedia but because of the potential that color has in desktop publishing. Though this is of little concern for hypermedia since the text and graphics are intended to remain in the computer and not be sent to print, it is precisely in the area of desktop publishing that you find most of the information and resources useful for hypermedia: text and image scanners, color interface cards and monitors, specialized graphics and utility programs, and other tools that make creating hypermedia easier. Two magazines oriented toward desktop publishing, *Publish!* and *Personal Publishing,* are excellent resources.

Hypermedia is labor-intensive. For a hypermedia project to be successful, like any other approach to scholarship, it must have its roots in a solid knowledge of the particular field in which it is destined to be used. It is not a substitute for the hard work that goes into the preparation of any serious piece of research; rather it offers the author opportunities to approach scholarship without having to worry about the usual limits that the format and the consequent costs of a book or a series of books would impose. The hypertext author may think in terms of the ideal work; not just the one that is financially possible at this time. Large hypertext documents are perfect candidates for distribution on CD-ROM's, whose capacity for text, video, and audio continues to grow.

Hypertext is not yet the death-knell for the book. But one would be foolish to condemn it as yet another "electronic page turner" and prematurely consign it to oblivion. It is an excellent repository for dissertations and, because of the facility with which it blends mediums, could become a prime tool for transcending the sometimes excessive specialization to which we fall prey. Hypertext is part of a larger technology that is gradually levelling some of the traditional distinctions between us. For the cost of the program and computer, one can be as competitive as any colleague at even the most prestigious university. Hypertext has quickly become the heart of one of the computer industry's most frequently used buzzwords: *multimedia*, a combination of text, graphics and sound for which most of the major companies are now readying special computers and programs in anticipation of selling this technology not just to institutions of higher education but also to corporate America, where the really big money is.

And what of the equipment, and which program to choose? My own opinion is that one should develop materials for the widest possible dissemination. Therefore, putting tremendous effort into programs that run on a limited number of workstations or microcomputers so sophisticated and expensive that only a few universities can afford them is counterproductive. One of the main advantages of this technology is its portability and, according to E.D.U.C.O.M. statistics, most of the microcomputers at universities in the United States are IBM and IBM-compatible brands. *Guide* is not the perfect program, but Owl International works continually on improvements and I have found their people most open to suggestions. You may also wish to look closely at *Plus* and *SuperCard* because, like *Guide*, they will be able to run your materials on either PC's or Macintoshes, or both.

Hypertext has been with us for over two decades, yet it is still possible, at this late date, to get in on the ground floor. *Guide* is an excellent program to start with while the doors and windows (not Microsoft) are still open. Now is the time to ENTER.

---

**Notes**

1. See also Gregory Crane, "Redefining The Book: Some Preliminary Problems," *Academic Computing* (February, 1988): 6-11; 36-41, and Judson V. Harward, "From Museum to Monitor: The Visual Exploration of The Ancient World," *Academic Computing* (May/June, 1988): 16-19; 69-71.

2. Mark H. Chignell and Richard M. Lacy, "Project Jefferson: Integrating Research and Instruction," *Academic Computing* (September, 1988): 12-17; 40-45.

---

3. Chignell and Lacey, "Project Jefferson," 45.

4. Robert Alun Jones, "Building a Hypermedia Laboratory," *Academic Computing* (November, 1988): 24-29; 43-44.

5. For reviews of several of these programs, see: Janet Fiderio, "A Grand Vision," *BYTE* 13 (October, 1988): 237-246; Mark Frisse, "From Text to Hypertext," *BYTE* 13 (October, 1988): 247-254, and Michael L. Begeman and Jeff Conklin, "The Right Tool for the Job," *BYTE* 13 (October, 1988): 255-267.

6. For information on *HyperCard*, see Mark D. Larsen, "Dealing Your Own Hand with *HyperCard*," *Hispania* 17 (May, 1988): 451-57.

7. Rubén Darío, *Azul. Prosas Profanas*. Edición, estudio y notas de Andrew P. Debicki y Michael J. Doudoroff (Madrid: Alhambra, 1985), 198-208.

8. Chignell and Lacey, "Project Jefferson," 15.

9. Estelle Irizarry, "Scanning with the Kurzweil," *Hispania* 71 (September, 1988): 733. Also, Joseph A. Feustle, Jr., "Electronic Text Scanning," *Hispania* 73 (March, 1990): 315-318. Please note that you must exercise the same caution regarding copyrighted material when scanning text as you do when making photocopies.

10. "Some 200 painters, engravers, and sculptors pass through his pages, the majority of them named once or twice and with little or no discussion." Debicki and Doudoroff, *Azul* 48.

11. Albrecht Dürer, *Das gesamte graphische Werk Druckgraphik* (München: Verlag Rogner & Bernhard, 1971): 1953. As with scanned text and photocopies, it is imperative that you exercise caution regarding copyrighted graphic materials. I make a point of including the full source citation as part of each screen image that I use.

12. The numbers and shades of color that can be displayed is a function of the number of bits assigned to each pixel (picture element) that makes up the computer screen. The simplest form is two-bit (no pun intended) color: either black or white. So called "true color" begins at 16 bits per pixel and really merits this name at 24 bits per pixel where it can display 224 or 16,777,216 colors.

13. I should like to express my thanks to Mr. Sparky Campinella of the Barneyscan Corporation for the lengthy demonstration of slide digitizing on a PC and a

Macintosh II in November of 1988 in Berkeley, California.

14. For a review of commercial scanners, see: Lauren Black and David Chalmers, "Image Scanners," *InfoWorld* (July 11, 1988): 41-52, and Richard Jantz, "Invitation to Quality," *Publish!* (August, 1988): 66-73.

15. Prices are approximate as of August 1990.

# Conceptualizing Hypermedia Curricula for Literary Studies in Schools

Alister Cumming
University of British Columbia

Gerri Sinclair
Simon Fraser University

The application of hypermedia to literary studies in schools promises to further educational goals of critical interpretation, sophisticated use of language, aesthetic appreciation, and awareness of cultural traditions. However, literary studies are less obviously "teachable" than other parts of the curriculum, where learning goals and instructional procedures may be more easily defined—and thus modeled readily in interactive software programs. Empirical research has found it notoriously difficult to understand how students learn from literature in school, providing only exploratory insights into this phenonemon.[1] Similarly, studies of the knowledge which teachers use to teach literature in schools reveal an array of complex, intuitive processes, which are probably too diverse to model explicitly.[2]

It is already evident that there are two fundamentally different approaches to the use of hypermedia for literary studies in schools. One approach preserves conventional instructional practices, but enhances them through computer-based interactive media; this choice may provide little which is new in the way of educational experience. The second approach entails a more radical reorganization of conventional curricula, especially interactions between students, following the lines proposed by Theodor Nelson.[3] This choice offers exciting potential, but may entail too radical a departure from current educational practices for general acceptance. In many respects, the two approaches of hypermedia implementation exemplify what Papert defines to be the "central question for educators...whether schools of the future will go on teaching the same curriculum, using computers to do the job better, or whether we'll see radical change in what is taught and what is learned in schools."[4]

The more radical approach to hypermedia implementation in schools requires the creation of "hyper-environments" for study and learning. Here, conventional classroom routines for rehearsing skills or reciting information are superseded by interactive communities of learners engaging in complex, dynamically linked tasks. The students themselves define the relevance of these tasks within a shared, computer mediated context. These hypermedia contexts provide access to relevant knowledge and facilities to integrate and develop new learning.

The present chapter develops a conceptual framework to guide and assess the implementation of hypermedia programs in schools. We review four projects which have recently developed innovative classroom applications of hypermedia for literary studies. Each project proves to have exploited the educational potential of hypermedia in unique ways. We consider these differences in view of distinctions, commonly made in curriculum analysis, between conceptions of learning, teaching, content, and social context.[5] These distinctions reveal different orientations to school curricula in each program, orientations which may significantly foster or constrain the benefits of hypermedia in educational practice.

It is worth noting that none of these programs conceives of learning in the rudimentary modes of drill-and-practice or simple skills rehearsal, which have featured in many programs for conventional micro-computers.[6] This may suggest that the technical complexity of interactive hypermedia tends to counter the reduction of learning to rote tasks, or it may be that the program designers who are adventurous enough to have attempted these innovations are, thus far, wary of such narrow conceptions of learning.

### Four exemplary programs

We have selected four exemplary hypermedia programs for analysis, drawing from among the few existing ones for literary studies in schools that we are aware of. At the time of writing, each program was in a preliminary stage of development. Future refinements are envisioned and, in most cases, are currently under way, some of which may make the present analysis out of date. We describe the principal features of each program, then assess their relation to the established curriculum. It is important to note that our analysis is restricted to information reported in written documentation on each program, not from our first-hand evaluations of the programs in use in schools. We have used a broad definition of hypermedia as a system which supports "non-sequential writing" or "online dynamic text" in multiple media.[7] Some of the programs do not adhere strictly to a narrower definition of hypermedia, requiring that all information in the system can be browsed through bidirectional links. But it is relatively easy to see how this could be achieved through modifications in the particular instances.

The four programs are:

- Grapevine

- Gulf Islands Novel Study Project

- CSILE Book Club

- Electronic-writer-in-residence

*Grapevine*[8] is an interactive array of multi-media material to supplement high school study of John Steinbeck's *Grapes of Wrath*. The HyperCard-based program incorporates more than fifty-four works, illuminating the "social and political history of the 1930s". These include: "books, films, television documentaries, still photographs, record albums and sound tapes, filmstrips, magazine and newspaper articles, and more" (159). Information relevant to the social context of the novel is indexed by thirty-three topics, making possible at least 1,836 links between topics like "dust bowl," "alien labor," or "New Deal," the novel itself, and the various media resources.

Annotations, suggested teaching activities, and references are provided, in addition to a system for "skimming through the material, browsing, searching, or studying it thoroughly" (60). The project provides extensive resources in different media for study of social issues relevant to the novel. It presumes that "a teacher deals with a novel not as an isolated piece of literature, but as one reflecting the times, the issues, and the author and other writers, artists, thinkers, and survivors" (60) of the historical period. Developments are presently under way to make the program user-adaptive by providing facilities like on-screen note pads and authoring systems for use by individual teachers or students.

The Gulf Islands Novel Study Project provides a generic format to guide children's analyses of novels, using print and graphics media.[9] It consists of hypermedia templates which, for any given novel, prompt students to: produce analyses of characters and plot; write critical reviews; prepare and integrate background information about an author; and answer hypothetical questions posed by a teacher (called "What if?"). For a specific book, students supply relevant information under each category using text, schematic, and pictorial forms. Links across media and topics are automatically established for users as they work with the program.

---

A demonstration version shows children's uses of the program to report on their interpretations of E.G. White's *Charlotte's Web* and George Selden's *The Cricket in Times Square*. Pedagogically, the program aims "to be simple enough for first-time student users to use, and for teachers to easily modify to suit their students' needs." Technically, the program is designed "to keep the stack small enough that it could be used with a minimum of storage space in a maximum number of hardware configurations." Students are expected to use the program to "actively interact to display their skills, ideas and understanding" (1, 3).

The CSILE Book Club is one aspect of a larger project developing and piloting computer-supported intentional learning environments (CSILE) for schools.[10] For literature study, grade 5 and 6 students prepare reviews of different novels and then enter their reviews into a collective data base. Chart facilities, linked to the text media, also permit students to create graphics to accompany their reviews. Books are chosen by the students; reviews are written to interest other students in reading the books. Students meet in groups to interpret, critically assess, and try to learn from one anothers' reviews.[11] Their discussions and interactions with the computer texts are prompted by on-screen cues guiding the children's thinking toward: high level questions; summaries of their existing knowledge; new insights; bases for agreement and disagreement; plans for further study; and so on.

Students append critical comments to the original reviews through on-screen notepads. Original drafts of the reviews are then revised by their authors, incorporating the peer feedback, to pass from a preliminary "candidate" status to a final "published" status, as judged by peer consensus. The completed reviews are then "catalogued" in the larger data base (by students) using a special propositional syntax (based on keywords and logical 'arguments' accessible to children). Students are also asked to determine principles for effective book reviewing, based on their assessments of their peers' collective work.

The computer's procedural supports for the discussion groups derive from earlier research on cooperative reading with children.[12] Students' thinking strategies while reading and discussing new texts were evaluated and modeled on adults' strategies. Pairs of students were assigned joint roles as "directors" or "actors"; directors aimed to draw out relevant knowledge, conceptual problems, and new learning from the actors. Based on analyses of these interactions, prompts were written to foster optimal thinking strategies, using the computer program to guide students' discussions, without adult support. The aims of the program are to foster "intentional learning,"[13] applying principles from recent research in cognitive science to direct children's development of higher order thinking and self-control.

The Electronic-writer-in-residence set up an on-line computer conference for poetry writing and commentary among grade ten students in Toronto, a poet in Vancouver, as well as other high school students in Vancouver and writers in other locations.[14] Drafts of poems were submitted by students and the "resident" poet, collectively critiqued, then revised for further display. The project lasted five months, compiling computer interactions which are catalogued and available for wider distribution by diskette. Above and beyond the fostering of creative writing, the rationale for the computer networking was to provide an "equity of use, placing students in control of what to write, when and where to 'send' it, and how to respond" (1). In evaluating the project, Owen & Kearns consider participants learned much about "human interaction, communication, publication (making our work public), and the nature of this strange and wonderful medium that connects us in such intimate ways across the continent." (8)

## Curriculum orientations

These applications of hypermedia are innovative in different ways, each devising very particular applications for specific issues in educational studies of literature. Though it is clear that hypermedia applications for literary studies in schools are still in a preliminary stage of development, the diversity of these few programs is, we think, instructive. A closer, comparative analysis of their curriculum orientations reveals much which might not be apparent from our previous outline of their principal features.

### Instruction

Instruction can be conceived as the *transmission* of information . This orientation is most evident in the Grapevine project, particularly in its early phases before the development of student personal notepads and individual authoring tools. Initial reports on Grapevine emphasize how hypermedia can enhance the potential to convey relevant data in different media to students. A second orientation is to consider instruction as the *transaction* of information. In the CSILE Book Club and the Electronic-writer-in-residence project, information is negotiated, through and around the hypermedia interface, by classroom participants. Instructional supports appear in CSILE's procedural prompts or the Electronic-writer-in-residence's feed-back. But this occurs in response to decisions established principally by students themselves. In the Novel Study Project, students' transactions of information occur outside of the hypermedia environment, while reading or researching information. Hypermedia is used later, to display students' achievements rather than to mediate or convey them. This might be called a *demonstrative orientation* to instruction, where tasks are completed for students to display information in the form of an achieved product.

*Content*

In the two projects which focus on the study of novels, the books themselves (i.e. Steinbeck's *Grapes of Wrath* or White's *Charlotte's Web*) provide concrete curriculum content, whereas in the Electronic-writer-in-residence the emphasis is on how students generate their own material (poems) as content. The CSILE Book Club divides its concerns between the processes of writing and revising book reviews and the study of various novels. Students' thinking strategies are thus given equal emphasis with the objects of study.

The modes for organizing curriculum content likewise differ. Grapevine and the Novel Study Project aspire toward an *encyclopedic organization* of content relevant to single novels. Thorough study of one literary item, and its related features, is aimed at. In contrast, the Electronic-writer-in-residence project and CSILE organize curriculum content in more of an *episodic mode*. Individual poems or book reviews produced by students serve to determine the curriculum content, creating a diverse, dispersed content for deeper analysis.

*Learning*

Different conceptions of students' learning underpin the four programs. In Grapevine, learning is considered to occur mainly through students' *compilation and integration of knowledge*. Hypermedia serve to foster students' bringing together of interrelated information into coherent conceptions. Though knowledge compilation does feature to some extent in CSILE, the Electronic-writer-in-residence, and especially the Gulf Islands Novel Study Project, these programs present goals for student learning which aim to *model higher orders of thinking* by providing developmental supports in complex tasks.

In CSILE, strategic supports for thinking are synthesized into procedural facilitations on the computer screen, which guide the social supports of peer discussions and self-analysis. Peer feedback likewise serves to foster reflective thinking and self-awareness of performance. In the Novel Study Project, a more general and conventional set of rhetorical organizers direct student performance on specific tasks and appear through the teachers' questioning about hypothetical situations. In the Electronic-writer-in-residence, the responses of an experienced poet and of peers to students' writing serve to model expert thinking in relation to their own work.

Except for the early versions of Grapevine, complex computer-based writing skills also feature as a substantial basis for learning, prompting student practice, analysis, and refinement of thinking. CSILE and the Electronic-writer-in-residence appear, however, to be the only two programs which provide a concrete basis for students' development of self-control over their own learning. The Novel Study Project presents task performance in the hypermedia environment as the end point of student activity, providing little support for learning to extend to other contexts or to be assessed strategically during the learning process.

*Social context*

One can approach this issue by distinguishing between hypermedia contents that are *program-generated*, *teacher-generated*, or *student-generated*. This distinction is important for issues like teacher adoption, preparation-time, and curricular flexibility.[15] Grapevine, for instance, has been developed as a resource containing massive quantities of information. Without the authoring system now being developed, its sheer quantity of information may make it difficult for teachers or students to use in classroom instruction. Similarly, CSILE provides a complex environment for learning and student interaction, such that teachers would find it difficult to integrate into existing routines for classroom study, without significantly reorienting conventional conceptions of student learning or instructional organization. For instance, Cumming's study of two experienced teachers using the program found that it took about six months for them to successfully intregrate CSILE into their teaching routines.[16] New systems of classroom management, interaction, and assignments had to be established. Concrete obstacles to adopting the "hypermedia curriculum" included: learning how to intregrate it with the conventional curriculum; having to account for students' achievements in new ways; and reallocating students' schedules to complete tasks.

In contrast, the Novel Study Project offers simple technical and pedagogical formulae, making it easily transposable from teacher to teacher, without requiring substantial modifications to conventional curricula. For the same reasons, though, it is unlikely that its introduction into classes would have much of an impact on changing the social context of learning in schools. This suggests that the other three projects come much closer to realizing the promise of hypermedia to offer genuine curricular restructuring.

CSILE and the Electronic-writer-in-residence are notable for foregrounding student input, decision-making, and interaction, thereby providing an environment for students to assess and advance their existing knowledge. The organizational structure of these two programs require that the hypermedia create environments for literary study which are self-sustaining and pedagogically interactive, without the need for teacher-dominated instruction usually conducted in schools.

This distinction marks the major issue in the development and implementation of hypermedia programs for literary studies in schools. The relationships of hypermedia to the social contexts of education suggest that a central factor in program design and implementation is the matter of who a program enables to make principal decisions about classroom study and learning — students, teachers, or the program? If the substantive content and uses of a program are largely pre-determined, as in off-the-shelf, commercially available hypermedia courseware packages, these may be difficult for teachers to adopt to their usual practices or students to integrate with their studies of other literature. If teachers are prompted to determine the content and uses of hypermedia, following conventional practices (as in the Novel Study Project), it is probable that the potential uses of hypermedia will be reduced to task routines which are not, fundamentally, unlike those now occurring in classrooms using less sophisticated media.

In view of these problems, it appears that the two projects (CSILE and Electronic-writer-in-residence) which require innovative restructuring of social relations among students, teachers, and the hypermedia may be the optimal means for attaining hypermedia's educational potential. Students are put in the position of making decisions about their own learning and social interactions — the hypermedia environments guiding them toward appropriate learning goals. From a teacher's viewpoint, however, these programs may be considered too time-consuming or unusual to manage within the routines of teaching they have already established. Practical issues like time allocation, the physical organization of the classroom, and students' work schedules need to be restructured and established anew.

## Summary and implications

The major issue which emerges from our analysis of the curricular impact of these innovative programs concerns the extent to which hypermedia programs might, or really can, reconceptualize approaches to literary studies in schools. The greatest promise to achieve this goal appears in programs, such as the CSILE Book Club or the Electronic-writer-in-residence, which use hypermedia environments to create functional contexts for learning and interaction far beyond those practiced in conventional classroom instruction. These programs come closer to realizing the profound changes in society's exchange of information envisioned in Nelson's *Literary Machines*. Hypermedia create educational contexts which differ qualitatively from ordinary schooling — supporting learning which is student-generated and transacted, directly linked to relevant expertise, episodically managed and integrated, and cognizant of its own emerging existence and terms of reference.

Alternatively, there are models for the development of hypermedia programs which conform more closely to conventional instructional practices — retaining their fundamental characteristics, but enhancing their presentation or multiplicity. In this sense, Grapevine functions much like a rapidly-accessed, topically-organized, multi-media library. The Gulf Islands Novel Study Project extends usual instructional formula for student assignments into hypermedia formats. In either case, literary studies are conceived mainly as the performance of routine analyses or the transmission of information, much as they usually are in schools. In these cases, hypermedia certainly provide a richer means of displaying student achievements or accessing multiple information sources. But expectations for student performance remain much as they would be without the hypermedia environment.

How can we expect these two routes to hypermedia implementation to fare in schools? Programs adhering to conventional curriculum models are likely to be well received. We can even expect them to emerge widely, in "grass roots" fashion, as innovative teachers adopt their usual practices to accommodate these new media.[17] Such hypermedia programs present predictable and orderly tasks, which can be organized and accomplished neatly by teachers and students with little deviation from usual policies.

At the same time, however, we can expect such hypermedia programs to miss the opportunities for learning available through the higher route designs. As recent research on the uses of micro-computers in classrooms has started to show, teachers as well as students tend to reduce the cognitive demands of classroom computer tasks in areas as diverse as: self-directed learning;[18] composing skills;[19] problem solving through Logo programming;[20] science projects;[21] and school-to-school networking.[22] Conventional curriculum models for educational computing quickly see computers come to function as "electronic work-sheets", having necessarily to fit into the usual organizational constraints and patterns of classroom instruction.[23]

On the other hand, the educational potential of the higher route hypermedia programs is enormous. We might see their value in their restructuring of the social contexts of learning so as to create a "mindfulness" in students which is capable of producing higher orders of thinking, access to expert knowledge sources, and self-control of learning processes.[24] But is a restructuring of educational contexts necessary to achieve such aims? Looking at the few case studies describing effective implementation of hypermedia in other settings, it would appear that this is so. At least, it has been reported as such for technical writing,[25] multilingual international networking,[26] university composition[27] or literature study.[28] In each instance, project reports have described how new patterns of organization, functional roles, and human dynamics have necessarily accompanied effective introduction of particular hypermedia into these instructional circumstances.

This makes us wonder how such restructuring might be feasible, on a broad scale, amid the conservative and conserving forces of schooling. Will teachers, students, school administrators, consultants, policy-makers, and parents support a nearly anarchistic organization of groups of learners pursuing individually-determined aims? What will the perceived achievements of learning be, and how could they be evaluated? How will forces of educational conservatism—competency tests, standard curricula, or established policies—confront such a radical departure? How could such restructuring be introduced equitably across socio-economic levels, given the costs, supports, and teacher development required?[29]

These questions, we believe, are the real challenge of hypermedia innovations for educators. None bear easy answers. Our analysis can, in closing, only offer several principles to guide hypermedia developments of more conventional curriculum models, gently toward the higher road—by suggesting they aim to provide students with:

• access to, and integration of, quantities and qualities of information not usually accessible through a single medium or conventional instruction;

• the means to engage purposefully in the transaction of information in relation to their existing knowledge and skills, above and beyond the transmission of new information and the display of achieved tasks;

• a functional learning environment around the computer interface, involving the allocation of shared responsibilities and goals among groups of users;

• supports to foster individual organization and decision-making leading to increased self-control;

• prompting of higher orders of thinking about literary material;

• opportunities to model peer and adult learning processes not usually offered in schools.

Ultimately, we find ourselves in agreement with Cynthia Solomon, who points out that "different computer environments give rise to different computer cultures." Solomon argues that "children and teachers who are learning to use computers need to develop an awareness of [these] different computer cultures, and they must blend these cultures to create their own."[30] We find it useful to substitute the term "hypermedia" for "computer" in Solomon's statement for, in fact, a hypermedia environment is one in which a computer drives and integrates the nonlinear interaction between learners and a variety of different information media. Within this context, we suspect that the most successful implementations of hypermedia programs in schools will be the ones in which teachers and students create their own cultures supported by non-traditional, "hyper-environments" for learning.

## Appendix

Technical aspects of the four programs are as follows:

The Gulf Islands Novel Study Project uses HyperCard stacks as templates, which are set at "scripting" to permit browsing and adaptations by users. Graphics are collected on MacPaint and FullPaint and can likewise be altered by users. CSILE was designed for UNISYS ICONS (for Ontario schools) but has recently been implemented on Mac II's and SUN workstations. A fileserver links 16 student stations equiped with their own RAM. Files are contained in a common root directory or users' home directories, forming a group database of (1) 'public' files accessible to all users and (2) 'private' files for individual users, which may be stored in either location. Prompts, icons, and keywords store data in textual and chart forms, as well as providing interfaces for users in specific environments like: "new learning", "planning", "questioning", or "timelines". The Grapevine project runs on a Macintosh Plus linked to a Pioneer 4200 videodisc player and monitor, using headphones for sound. HyperCard software controls the program, using a guide stack for browsing. Plans are underway to make the program available commercially. The Electronic-writer-in-residence project was set up as an online interactive computer conference which runs on the Simon Fraser University computer Network on an IBM 3081 mainframe under the MTS operating system. The computer conferencing software which runs under MTS is called *Forum. Participants (students, teachers, and poet) accessed the conference using a variety of microcomputers (Macintosh, IBM PCs and UNISYS ICONS) with many different communication software packages and 1200 baud modems.

**Notes**

1. P. Dias, *Making Sense of Poetry: Patterns in the Process* (Ottawa: Canadian Council of Teachers of English, 1986); J. Marshall, "The Effects of Writing on Students' Understanding of Literary Texts," *Research in the Teaching of English* 21 (1987): 30-63; J. Nespor, "Academic Tasks in a High School English Class," *Curriculum Inquiry* 17 (1987): 203-228; J. Squire, *The Responses of Adolescents While Reading Four Short Stories* (Champaign, Illinois: National Council of Teachers of English, 1964).

2. F. Elbaz, *Teacher Thinking: A Study of Practical Knowledge* (London: Croom Helm, 1983); R. McGregor and C. Meiers, *English Teaching in Practice* (Sydney: St. Clair Press, 1983).

3. T. Nelson, *Literary machines*. 5th ed. Swarthmore, Pa.: Project Xanadu, 1987.

4. S. Papert, "Logo as a Trojan Horse: Reflecting Logo Philosophy in the Context of Real School Experience." *Logo86 Conference Pre-Proceedings*. Cambridge, Mass.: MIT, 1986. xxxv.

5. J. Miller and W. Seller, *Curriculum: Perspectives and Practice*. (New York: Longman, 1985).

6. H. Mehan, "The Current State of Microcomputer Use in Schools," in H. Mehan and R. Souviney, eds., *The Write Help: A Handbook for Computers in Classrooms* (La Jolla, CA: Center for Human Information Processing, University of California, San Diego, 1984).

7. J. Conklin, "Hypertext: An Introduction and Survey," *IEEE Computer* 20:9 (1987): 17-41; T. Nelson, *Literary machines*.

8. R. Campbell, "(I Learned it) Through the Grapevine: Hypermedia at Work in the Classroom," *American Libraries* (March 1989): 200-205; R. Campbell and P. Hanlon, "Grapevine," in S. Ambron and K. Hooper, eds. *Interactive Multimedia: Visions of Multimedia for Developers, Educators, and Information Providers* (Redmond, Washington: Microsoft Press, 1988). 159-177.

9. K. Vine, *HyperCard in Literature: Applying HyperCard to a Grade Four Reading Program* (Ganges, B.C.: Saltspring Island Elementary School, 1988).

10. M. Scardamalia, C. Bereiter, R. McLean, J. Swallow, and E. Woodruff, "Computer-supported Intentional Learning Environments," *Journal of Educational Computing Research* 5 (1989): 51-68.

11. E. Woodruff and the CSILE research and technical group. *CSILE report noting progress to March 31, 1988* (Toronto: Centre for Applied Cognitive Science, Ontario Institute for Studies in Education, 1988).

12. J. Swallow, M. Scardamalia and W. Olivier, *Facilitating Thinking Skills Through Peer Interaction With Software Support*. Paper presented at the annual meeting of the American Educational Research Association, New Orleans, 1988.

13. C. Bereiter and M. Scardamalia, "An Attainable Version of High Literacy: Approaches to Teaching Higher-order Skills in Reading and Writing," *Curriculum Inquiry* 17 (1987): 9-30.

14. T. Owen, L. Kearns, et al. *Computers and Word Processing in the English Classroom*, 3 (1988). Riverdale Collegiate Institute, Toronto.

15. M. Riel and B. Miller-Souviney, "The Introduction of Microcomputers and the Possibility of Change," in H. Mehan and R. Souviney, eds. *The Write Help*, 35-55.

16. A. Cumming, "Change, Organization and Achievement: Teachers' Concerns in Implementing a Computer Learning Environment," *Journal of Educational Technology Systems* 7 (1988): 141-163.

17. T. Aoki, "Toward Understanding 'Computer Application'," *Journal of Curriculum Theorizing* 7 (1987): 61-71; M. Riel and B. Miller-Souviney, "The Introduction of Microcomputers"; T. Snyder, "Tools for Teachers," *The Computing Teacher* (August-September 1988): 8-16.

18. A. Cumming, "Change, Organization and Achievement."

19. C. Cazden, S. Michaels and K. Watson-Gegeo, *Final Report: Microcomputers and Literacy Project*. (Grant no. G-83-0051). Washington, D.C.: National Institute of Education, 1987; D.Dickinson, "Cooperation, Collaboration, and a Computer: Integrating a Computer into a First-second Grade Writing Program," *Research in the Teaching of English* 20 (1986): 357-378.

20. J. Hawkins, "The Interpretation of Logo in Practice," in R. Pea and K. Sheingold, eds. *Mirrors of Mind: Patterns of Experience in Educational Computing* (Norwood, N.J.: Ablex, 1987). 3-34.

21. L. Martin, "Teachers' Adoption of Multimedia Technologies for Science and Mathematics Instruction," in R. Pea and K. Sheingold, eds. *Mirrors of Mind*, 35-56.

22. M. Riel and B. Miller-Souviney, "The Introduction of Microcomputers."

23. H. Mehan, "The Current State of Microcomputer Use."

24. G. Solomon, "Information Technologies: What You See is Not (Always) What You Get." Research Report No. 3 (Tel Aviv: Tel Aviv University, 1986).

25. E. Barrett and J. Paradis, "The On-line Environment and In-house Training," in Edward Barrett, ed. *Text, Context, and Hypertext: Writing With and For the Computer* (Cambridge, Mass.: MIT Press, 1988). 227-249.

26. M. Cohen, J. Levin, M. Riel, *The World as Functional Learning Environment: an Intercultural Learning Network* (La Jolla, CA: Center for Human Information Processing, University of California, San Diego, 1985).

27. J. Slatin, "Hypertext and the Teaching of Writing," in Edward Barrett, ed. *Text, Context, and Hypertext*, 111-129.

28. W. Garrett-Petts, "Developing a Community of Readers: Computer Networking in the Freshman Literature Class," *English Quarterly* 21 (1988): 29-40.

29. K. Sheingold, L. Martin and M. Endreweit, "Preparing Urban Teachers for the Technological Future," in R. Pea and K. Sheingold, eds. *Mirrors of Mind*, 67-85.

30. C. Solomon, *Computer Environments for Children: a Reflection on Theories of Learning and Education* (Cambridge, MA: MIT Press), 13.

# Bibliography

This bibliography includes works relating to hypermedia and literary studies cited in this collection, with a few supplementary entries. For a more general, annotated bibliography on hypertext and hypermedia, see Jakob Nielsen, "Hypertext Bibliography," *Hypermedia* 1 (1989): 74-91.

Aegerter, William. "Change Control: A Structured Form of Hypertext." *Proceedings of Hypertext '87*. Chapel Hill: University of North Carolina, 1987.

Ambron, S., and Hooper, K., eds. *Interactive Multimedia: Visions of Multimedia for Developers, Educators and Information Providers*. Redmond, WA: Microsoft Press, 1988.

Backer, D., and S. Gano. "Dynamically Alterable Videodisk Displays." *Proc. Graphics Interface 82*. Toronto, May 17-21, 1982: 365-37.

Balkovich, E., S. Lerman, and R. P. Parmelee. "Computing in higher education: The Athena Project." *Computer* 18 (1985): 112-125.

Barrett, Edward, ed. *Text, Context, and Hypertext: Writing With and For the Computer*. Cambridge, MA: MIT Press, 1988.

_____, ed. *The Society of Text: Hypertext, Hypermedia, and the Social Construction of Information*. Cambridge, MA: MIT Press, 1989.

Barthes, Roland. "From Work to Text." In *Textual Strategies*. ed. Josue Harari. Ithaca: Cornell UP, 1979.

_____. *S/Z*. Trans. Richard Miller. New York: Hill and Wang, 1974.

Begeman, Michael L., and Jeff Conklin. "The Right Tool for the Job." *BYTE* 13 (October, 1988): 255-267.

Bender, W. "Imaging and Interactivity." *Fifteenth Joint Conf. Image Technology*, Tokyo, Nov. 26, 1984.

Bernstein, Mark. "The Bookmark and the Compass: Orientation Tools for Hypertext Users." *ACM SIGOIS Bulletin* 9 (1988): 34- 45.

Bierman, James. *Aristotle's Tragedy Construction Kit*. HyperCard software. Kinko's Academic Courseware Exchange, 1988.

Bolter, Jay D. "Beyond Word Processing: The Computer as a New Writing Space." *Language and Communication* 9 (1989): 129-142.

_____. *Writing Space: The Computer, Hypertext and the History of Writing*. Hillsdale, N.J.: Lawrence Erlbaum, 1990.

Brand, Stewart. *The Media Lab: Inventing the Future at MIT*. New York: Viking, 1987.

Brown, J. S. "Process versus Product: A Perspective on Tools for Communal and Informal Electronic Learning." In *Education in the Electronic Age: A Report From the Learning Lab*. WNET/Thirteen Learning Lab, New York, 1983: 41-58.

Burrows, J. F. *Computation into Criticism: A Study of Jane Austen's Novels and an Experiment in Method*. Oxford: Clarendon Press, 1987.

Bush, Vannevar. "As We May Think." *Atlantic Monthly* 176 (July 1945): 101-08.

Campbell, R. "(I Learned it) Through the Grapevine: Hypermedia at Work in the Classroom." *American Libraries* (March 1989): 200-205 .

Campbell, R. and P. Hanlon. "Grapevine." In S. Ambron and K. Hooper, eds. *Interactive multimedia: Visions of multimedia for developers, educators, and information providers*. Redmond, Washington: Microsoft Press, 1988. 159-177.

Catano, James. "Poetry and Computers: Experimenting with Communal Text." *Computers and the Humanities* 13 (1979): 269-275.

*CD WORD*. Dallas, Texas: CDWord Library, Inc., 1990.

Chignell, Mark H., and Richard M. Lacy. "Project Jefferson: Integrating Research and Instruction." *Academic Computing* (September, 1988): 12-17; 40-45.

Cohen, M., J. Levin, and M. Riel. *The World as Functional Learning Environment: An*

*Intercultural Learning Network*. La Jolla, CA: Center for Human Information Processing, University of California, San Diego, 1985.

Compton's Multimedia Encyclopedia. Jostens Learning Corporation, 6170 Cornerstone Court, San Diego CA 92121.

Conklin, Jeff. *A Survey of Hypertext*. MCC Technical Report STP-356-86. Austin, TX: MCC, 1986.

_____. "Hypertext: An Introduction and Survey." *IEEE Computer* 20 (1987): 17-41.

Coombs, James H. "Hypertext, Full Text, and Automatic Linking." *International Conference on Research and Development in Information Retrieval (SIGIR '90)*. September 5-7 1990, Brussels, Belgium.

Coombs, James H., Allen H. Renear, and Steven J. DeRose. "Markup Systems and the Future of Scholarly Text Processing." In *Communications of the Association for Computing Machinery* (November, 1987): 933-947.

Crane, Gregory. "Redefining The Book: Some Preliminary Problems." *Academic Computing* (February, 1988): 6-11; 36-41.

Dede, Christoper. "The Role of Hypertext in Transforming Information into Knowledge." *Proceedings NECC '88*. Dallas, Texas: 15-17 June 1988.

Delany, Paul. "Elements, Links and Structures in Hypermedia." Conference proceedings, "Communication Interactive: Instruments de Communication Evolués, Hypertextes, Hypermédias." Paris, May 15-17 1990.

DeRose, Steven J. "SGML and Hypertext." Paper presented at the Graphics Communications Association Conference, November 16-18 1988, Boston, Massachusetts.

_____. "Expanding the Notion of Links." *Proceedings Hypertext '89*. Pittsburgh, PA: Association for Computing Machinery, 1989. 249-257.

DeRose, Steven J., David G. Durand, Elli Mylonas, and Allen H. Renear. "What is Text, Really?" Paper presented to the Harvard Classics Department, 1986.

Dickey, William. "The Throats of Birds." "Zenobia, Queen of Palmyra." "Dick and Jane." "Statue Music." HyperCard poems. Available from the author: 1476 Willard St., San Francisco, CA 94117.

Doland, Virginia M. "Hypermedia as an Interpretive Act." *Hypermedia* 1 (1989): 6-19.

Douglas, Jane Y. "Beyond Orality and Literacy: Toward Articulating a Paradigm for the Electronic Age." *Computers and Composition* (August, 1989).

Edwards, Deborah M. and Lynda Hardman. "'Lost in Hyperspace': Cognitive Mapping and Navigation in a Hypertext Environment." In *Hypertext: Theory into Practice*. Ed. Ray McAleese. Oxford: Intellect,1989. 104-125.

Eisenstein, Elizabeth L. *The Printing Press as an Agent of Change: Communications and Cultural Transformations in Early-Modern Europe*. 2 vols. Cambridge: Cambridge University Press, 1979.

Engelbart, D.C., and W. K. English. "A Research Center for Augmenting Human Intellect." *Proc. FJCC* 33 (Fall 1968): 395-410.

Feiner, S., S. Nagy, and A. van Dam. "An Experimental System for Creating and Presenting Interactive Graphical Documents." *Trans. Graphics* 1 (1982): 59-77.

Fiderio, Janet. "A Grand Vision." *BYTE* 13 (October , 1988): 237-246.

Frisse, Mark. "From Text to Hypertext." *BYTE* 13 (October, 1988): 247- 254.

Garrett, L. Nancy, Karen Smith, and Norman Meyrowitz. "Intermedia: Issues, Strategies, and Tactics in the Design of a Hypermedia Document System." *Proceedings of the Conference on Computer-Supported Cooperative Work*. Austin, Texas. 3-5 December 1986.

Garrett-Petts, W. "Developing a community of readers: Computer networking in the freshman literature class." *English Quarterly* 21 (1988): 29-40.

Gibson, William. *Neuromancer*. New York: Ace Books, 1984.

Gore, Albert. "Remarks on the NREN." *EDUCOM Review* 25 (Summer 1990): 12-16.

Halasz, Frank G. "Reflections on Notecards: Seven Issues for the Next Generation of Hypermedia Systems." *Communications of the ACM* 31 (1988): 836-852.

Hammwöhner, Rainer and Ulrich Thiel. "Content Oriented Relations Between Text Units: A Structural Model for Hypertexts." *Proceedings Hypertext '87*. Chapel Hill, NC: Association for Computing Machinery, 1987. 155-174.

Harward, Judson V. "From Museum to Monitor: The Visual Exploration of The Ancient World." *Academic Computing* (May/June, 1988): 16-19; 69-71.

Helgerson, Linda. "CD-ROM and Scholarly Research in the Humanities." *Computers and the Humanities* 22 (1988).

Howard, Alan. "Hypermedia and the Future of Ethnography." *Cultural Anthropology* 3 (1988): 304-305,

*Hypermedia.* London: Taylor Graham, 1989-.

*Intermedia: From Linking to Learning.* Dir. Deborah Dorsey. Cambridge Studios and the Annenberg/Corporation for Public Broadcasting Project, 1986. 27-minute video on Intermedia project.

Jennings, Humphrey. *Pandemonium: the Coming of the Machine as Seen by Contemporary Observers, 1660-1886.* New York: The Free Press, 1985.

Jonassen, David H. and Heinz Mandl, eds. *Designing Hypertext/Hypermedia for Learning.* Heidelberg: Springer-Verlag, 1990.

Jones, Robert Alun. "Building a Hypermedia Laboratory." *Academic Computing* (November, 1988): 24-29; 43-44.

Joyce, Michael. "Siren shapes: Exploratory and constructive hypertexts." *Academic Computing* 3 (1988): 14.

Kahn, Paul D. "Isocrates: Greek Literature on CD Rom." In *CD ROM: The New Papyrus: The Current and Future State of the Art.* Ed. Steve Lambert and Suzanne Ropiequet. Redmond, Washington: Microsoft Press, 1986.

Kahn, Paul, Julie Launhardt, Krzysztof Lenk and Ronnie Peters. "Design of Hypermedia Publications: Issues and Solutions." *International Conference on Electronic Publishing, Document Manipulations, and Typography (EP 90).* Gaithersburg, MD: September 18-20 1990.

Kahn, Paul. "Kenneth Rexroth's Tu Fu." *Yearbook of Comparative and General Literature* 37 (1990).

Kahn, R.E., and V. G. Cerf. "The World of Knowbots." Draft report, Corporation for National Research Initiatives, 1988.

---

Kaye, A.R., and G. M. Karam. "Cooperating Knowledge-based Assistants for the Office." *Transactions on Office Information Systems* 5 (1987): 297-326.

Kozma, Robert. "Designing Cognitive Tools for Computers." Presentation at Hypertext Workshop. Intelligent Systems Branch, Air Force Human Resources Laboratory, Brooks AFB, Texas. 23 February 1988.

Lai, K., T. W. Malone and K. Yu. "Object Lens: A 'Spreadsheet' for Cooperative Work." *Transactions on Office Information Systems* 6 (1988): 332-353.

Landow, George P. "Hypertext in Literary Education, Criticism, and Scholarship." *Computers and the Humanities* 23 (1989): 173-198.

_____. "Context32: Using Hypermedia to Teach Literature." *Proceedings of the 1987 IBM Academic Information Systems University AEP Conference.*

_____. "The Rhetoric of Hypermedia: Some Rules for Authors." *Journal of Computing in Higher Education* 1 (1989): 39-64.

_____. "Relationally Encoded Links and the Rhetoric of Hypertext." *Proceedings of Hypertext '87*. Chapel Hill: University of North Carolina, 1987.

_____. "Ms. Austen's Submission." *IF*, 1 (1989).

Lanham, Richard A. "Convergent Pressures: Social, Technological, Theoretical." Conference on the Future of Doctoral Studies in English (Panel on Proposals for Change). Wayzata, Minnesota, April 1987.

_____. "The Electronic Word: Literary Study and the Digital Revolution." *New Literary History* 20 (1989): 265-90.

Larsen, Mark D. "Dealing Your Own Hand with *HyperCard*." *Hispania* 17 (1988): 451-57.

McAleese, Ray. "Navigation and Browsing in Hypertext." *Hypertext: Theory into Practice*. Ed. Ray McAleese. Oxford: Intellect, 1989. 6-44.

McLuhan, Marshall. *The Gutenberg Galaxy: The Making of Typographic Man*. Toronto: University of Toronto Press, 1962.

_____. *Understanding Media: The Extensions of Man*. New York: New American Library, 1964.

Meyrowitz, Norman K. "Networks of Scholar's Workstations: End-User Computing in a University Community." IRIS Technical Report 85-3, Inst. Research in
Information and Scholarship, Brown Univ., June 1985.

———. "The Missing Link: Why We're All Doing Hypertext Wrong." In *The Society
of Text: Hypertext, Hypermedia, and the Social Construction of Information.* Ed.
Edward Barrett. Cambridge, MA: MIT Press, 1989. 107-114.

———. "The Link to Tomorrow." *UNIX Review* 8 (1990): 58-67.

Miall, David S. *Humanities and the Computer: New Directions.* Oxford: Oxford University Press, 1990.

Morgan, Thaïs E. "Is There an Intertext in This Text?: Literary and Interdisciplinary
Approaches to Intertextuality." *American Journal of Semiotics* 3 (1985): 1-2.

Morrell, Kenneth. "Teaching with *HyperCard.* An Evaluation of the Computer-
Based Section in Literature and Arts C-14: The Concept of the Hero in Hel-
lenic Civilization." Perseus Project Working Paper 3. Cambridge, Mass:
Department of Classics, Harvard University, 1988.

Moulthrop, Stuart. "Containing Multitudes: The Problem of Closure in Interactive
Fiction." *ACH Newsletter* 10 (1988): 1,7.

———. "Hypertext and 'the Hyperreal'." *Proceedings Hypertext '89.* Pittsburgh, PA:
Association for Computing Machinery, 1989. 259-267.

———. "The Politics of Hypertext." (unpublished).

Nelson, Theodor H. "Replacing the Printed Word: A Complete Literary System." In
S. H. Lavington, ed. *Proceedings of IFIP Congress 1980.* North-Holland, 1980. 1013-
1023.

———. *Literary Machines.* P.O. Box 128, Swarthmore PA, 19091: Theodor Holm
Nelson, 1987.

Nielsen, Jakob. "The Art of Navigating Through Hypertext." *Communications of the
ACM* 33 (1990): 296-310.

Oren, Tim, Gary Kildall, and T. Rolander. "Experiences with Hypertext on CD
ROM." Unpublished.

---

Oren, Tim. The Apple Learning Disc: A HyperCard Collection for Education, including selections from *The Whole Earth Learning Disc, The Grolier U.S. History Demonstration, Project Jefferson (USC), Perseus Project (Harvard and Bowdoin),* and *The Electric Cadaver (Stanford).*

Owen, T., L. Kearns, et al. *Computers and Word Processing in the English Classroom 3.* Riverdale Collegiate Institute, Toronto, 1988.

Palaniappan, Murugappan, Nicole Yankelovich, and Mark Sawtelle. "Linking Active Anchors: A Stage in the Evolution of Hypermedia." *IRIS Technical Report 89-5.* Providence, R. I.: Institute for Research in Information and Scholarship, 1989.

Parunak, H. Van Dyke. "Hypermedia Topologies and User Navigation." *Proceedings Hypertext '89.* Pittsburgh, PA: Association for Computing Machinery, 1989. 43-50.

Pinsky, Robert. "A Brief Description of *Mindwheel." New England Review and Bread Loaf Quarterly* 10 (1987): 65.

Raymond, Darrell, and Frank Tompa. "Hypertext and the Oxford English Dictionary." *CACM* 31 (1988): 871-879.

Riel, M. and B. Miller-Souviney. "The introduction of microcomputers and the possibility of change." In H. Mehan and R. Souviney, eds. *The Write Help: A Handbook for Computers in Classrooms.* La Jolla, CA: Center for Human Information Processing, University of California, San Diego. 35-55.

Scardamalia, M., C. Bereiter, R. McLean, J. Swallow, and E. Woodruff. "Computer-supported intentional learning environments." *Journal of Educational Computing Research* 5 (1989): 51-68.

Shneiderman, Ben. "User Interface Design for Hyperties Electronic Encyclopedia." *Proceedings of Hypertext '87.* Chapel Hill: University of North Carolina, 1987.

Slatin, John M. "Text and Hypertext: Reflections on the role of the Computer in Teaching Modern American Poetry." In Miall, David S., ed. *Humanities and the Computer: New Directions.* Oxford: Oxford UP. 1990. 123-35.

———. "Hypertext and the Teaching of Writing." In Edward Barrett, ed., *Text, Context, and Hypertext.* Cambridge, MA.: The MIT Press, 1988.

Solomon, C. *Computer Environments for Children: A Reflection on Theories of Learning and Education.* Cambridge, MA: The MIT Press, 1988.

Sperberg-McQueen, Michael. "Structuring Text for Research." Paper presented at the Graphics Communications Association conference, November 16-18 1988, Boston, Massachusetts.

Stigleman, Sue. "Text Management Software." *Public Access Computer Systems Review* 1 (1990).

*Storyspace.* Eastgate Systems, P.O. Box 1307, Cambridge, MA 02238.

Suchman, Lucy A., and Randall H. Trigg. "A Framework for Studying Research Collaboration." *Proceedings of the Conference on Computer-Supported Cooperative Work.* Austin, TX. 3-5 December 1986.

Trigg, Randall H. *A Network-based Approach to Text Handling for the On-Line Community.* Ph.D. thesis. University of Maryland, 1983.

Trigg, Randall H., Lucy A. Suchman and Frank G. Halasz. "Supporting Collaboration in NoteCards." *Proceedings of the Conference on Computer-Supported Cooperative Work.* Austin, TX. 3-5 December 1986.

Utting, Kenneth, and Nicole Yankelovich. "Context and Orientation in Hypermedia Networks." *ACM Transactions on Information Systems* 7 (1989): 58-84.

Van Dam, A. "Keynote Address." *Proceedings of Hypertext '87.* Chapel Hill: University of North Carolina, 1987.

Van Dam, A., and D. E. Rice. "Computers and Publishing: Writing, Editing and Printing." In *Advances in Computers.* New York: Academic Press, 1970.

Vine, K. *HyperCard in Literature: Applying HyperCard to a Grade Four Reading Program.* Ganges, B.C.: Saltspring Island Elementary School, 1988.

Walter, Mark. "IRIS Intermedia: Pushing the Boundaries of Hypertext." *The Seybold Report on Publishing Systems* 18 (1989): 21-32.

Weyer, Stephen A., and Alan H. Borning. "A Prototype Electronic Encyclopedia." *ACM Transactions on Office Information Systems* 3 (1985): 63-88.

Woodruff, E. and the CSILE research and technical group. *CSILE report noting progress to March 31, 1988.* Toronto: Centre for Applied Cognitive Science, Ontario Institute for Studies in Education, 1988.

Yankelovich, Nicole, Bernard Haan, Norman Meyrowitz, and Steven Drucker. "Intermedia: The Concept and the Construction of a Seamless Information Environment." *IEEE Computer* 21 (1988): 81-96.

Yankelovich, Nicole, et al. "The Sampler Companion." IRIS Technical Report 85-1, Inst. Research in Information and Scholarship, Brown Univ., March 1985.

Yankelovich, Nicole, George P. Landow and David C. Cody. "Creating Hypermedia Materials for English Literature Students." *ACM SIGCUE OUTLOOK* 19 (1987): 12-25.

Zachary, G. Pascal. "Artificial Reality: Computer Simulations One Day May Provide Surreal Experiences." *Wall Street Journal* (23 January 1990): A1, A9.

Ziegfeld, Richard. "Interactive Fiction: A New Literary Genre?" *New Literary History* 20 (1989): 340-72.

# Notes on Contributors

**Jay David Bolter** is associate professor of Classics and adjunct professor of Computer Science at the University of North Carolina, Chapel Hill. He is author of *Turing's Man: Western Culture in the Computer Age*, and of *Writing Space: the Computer, Hypertext and the History of Writing*. With John B. Smith and Michael Joyce he has developed a hypertext system for the Macintosh called *Storyspace*.

**Gregory Crane** is an associate professor of Classics at Harvard University and is editor-in-chief of the Perseus Project. He has published a book on Homer and numerous articles both in the field of Classics and in computing in the humanities. He has worked extensively in full-text retrieval and hypermedia systems for the past eight years.

**Alister Cumming** is assistant professor in the Department of Language Education, University of British Columbia. His research concerns language and literacy learning, second language instruction, and curriculum evaluation.

**Paul Delany**, professor of English at Simon Fraser University, is author of *D. H. Lawrence's Nightmare: the Writer and his Circle in the Years of the Great War*, and of *The Neo-pagans: Rupert Brooke and the Ordeal of Love*. He has been involved with computers and the humanities for the past ten years, mainly in the fields of computers and composition and hypermedia. A former Guggenheim Fellow, he has also taught at Columbia University and at the University of Waterloo.

**Steven J. DeRose** served as a director of the FRESS hypertext system project at Brown University from 1979-1982, and as a design consultant for the recent CD Word biblical hypertext project. He has published papers on descriptive markup, hypertext, natural language processing, artificial intelligence, and other topics. He is now Senior System Architect at Electronic Book Technologies, a Rhode Island firm developing new technologies for large-scale electronic books.

**William Dickey** is professor of English and Creative Writing at San Francisco State University. He has published ten books of poetry, of which *Of the Festivity* appeared in the Yale Series of Younger Poets, with an introduction by W.H. Auden. The *Rainbow Grocery* received the Juniper Prize, and his most recent book, *The King of the*

*Golden River*, the Bay Area Book Reviewers award in poetry. He has edited a symposium, *The Writer and the Computer* for *New England Review/Bread Loaf Quarterly* (Autumn, 1987).

**Joseph A. Feustle, Jr.** is a professor of Spanish at the University of Toledo specializing in Latin American literature. He is the author of articles on Latin American novelists, poets, dramatists, and essayists from the Colonial Period to the present. His book on Rubén Darío, Juan Ramón Jímenez and Octavio Paz was published by the press of the Universidad Veracruzana in México. Dr. Feustle has also written on computer topics such as hypermedia, electronic text scanning, file transfer, telecommunications, and the application of this technology to teaching, research and administration at university level.

**Larry Friedlander** is professor of Drama at Stanford University and author of *The Shakespeare Project*.

**John K. Gilbert** is a graduate student in English at Simon Fraser University. His thesis deals with the application of computer technology to literary studies. He is also the potsmaster of the e-mail list PYNCHON (pynchon@sfu on bitnet or pynchon@cc.sfu.ca on internet), for the discussion of Thomas Pynchon and his works.

**David Graham** is associate professor of French and Head of the Department of French and Spanish at Memorial University of Newfoundland. His primary research interests lie in the fields of emblem study and hypermedia/hypertext. Since the article in this volume was written, he has completely revised the "Macintosh Emblem Project" and expanded it to include a current total of four emblem books.

**Terence Harpold** is a graduate student in Comparative Literature at the University of Pennsylvania. His publications include articles in *Studies in Romanticism* and *Literature and Psychology*. He is currently working on a doctoral dissertation on literary digression, hypertext and narrative theory.

**Paul Kahn** received a B.A. in English literature from Kenyon College in 1971, and has additional training in computer science, graphic design and Chinese language. In 1980 he was the recipient of a Poetry Fellowship from the NEH. He has published several books and articles in the fields of Mongolian and Chinese literature, including *The Secret History of the Mongols* (North Point Press 1984) and *Han Shan in English* (White Pine Press 1989). His writing on information and computer technology has appeared in *Byte, Publish, Optical Information Systems Journal, Journal of the*

*American Society of Information Science,* and the *Annual Review of Communications and Society,* as well as several computer science conference proceedings. Since 1985 he has been Project Coordinator at the Institute for Research in Information and Scholarship at Brown University, involved in the design and creation of hypermedia materials for education.

**George P. Landow** is professor of English and Art History at Brown University. In association with the Institute for Research and Information and Scholarship at Brown he developed *Context32.* Apart from his work on computing in the humanities he is author of many books and articles on Victorian literature, art and religion. A former Fulbright Scholar and Guggenheim Fellow, he has also taught at Columbia University, the University of Chicago, and Brasenose College, Oxford.

**Norman Meyrowitz,** Co-Director of Brown University's Institute for Research in Information and Scholarship (IRIS), has directed the Institute's hypertext and multimedia research since he helped found the Institute in 1983. Most recently, Meyrowitz has managed and been the principal architect of IRIS's Intermedia system, a networked, shared, multi-user hypermedia system for research and education. He was the keynote speaker at Hypertext '89 in Pittsburgh, PA. Meyrowitz's major research interests are in the areas of component software, next generation "desktop" environments, hypermedia, compound documents, text processing, user-interface design, and object-oriented programming. He has worked with a number of industrial partners on hypertext and multimedia research.

**Stuart Moulthrop** is assistant professor of English at the University of Texas at Austin. He received his PhD. from Yale in 1986 and has published articles on contemporary fiction, hypertext theory, and teaching with computers. He has recently finished a study of conspiracy novels of the seventies and eighties and is at work on a hypertext fiction called "Chaos."

**Elli Mylonas** is completing her Ph.D. in Classics at Brown University. She is currently a research associate in the Classics Department at Harvard University, and is the managing editor of the Perseus Project. She has published and spoken on hypertext, descriptive markup and literary texts and the use of computers in education. She is also on the Text Representation Committee of the Text Encoding Initiative.

**Gerri Sinclair** is adjunct professor in the Faculty of Education, Simon Fraser University, where she directs the EXCITE centre. She consults internationally on interactive media and computer networking.

---

**John M. Slatin,** associate professor, is Director of the English Department's Computer Research Lab at the University of Texas at Austin. He is the author of *The Savage's Romance: The Poetry of Marianne Moore* (1986) and several earlier essays on hypertext.

**Andries van Dam** is a professor of Computer Science at Brown University where he has been on the faculty since 1965, and was one of the Department's founders and its first Chairman, from 1979 to 1985. His research has concerned computer graphics, text processing and hypermedia systems, and workstations. He has been working for over 20 years on the design of "electronic books," based on high-resolution graphics displays, for use in teaching and research. Van Dam helped to found and was an editor of Computer Graphics and Image Processing from 1971 to 1981, and was an editor of ACM's Transactions on Graphics from 1981 to 1986. In 1967, Professor van Dam co-founded ACM's SIGGRAPH. The widely used reference book *Fundamentals of Interactive Computer Graphics*, co-authored with J.D. Foley, was published in 1982; its greatly expanded successor, *Computer Graphics: Principles and Practice*, co-authored with J.D. Foley, S.K. Feiner, and J.F. Hughes, was published in 1990. *Pascal on the Macintosh: a Graphical Approach*, co-authored with David Niguidula, was published in 1987. In 1974 van Dam received the IEEE Centennial Medal; in 1988 the State of Rhode Island Governor's Science and Technology Award; and in 1990 the National Computer Graphics Association's Academic Award. He is past Chairman of the Computer Research Board, and Senior Consulting Scientist at Prime Computer and Bloc Development.

**Nicole Yankelovich,** a founding member of the Institute for Research in Information and Scholarship (IRIS), currently holds the position of Project Coordinator. She has participated in the design and development of Intermedia from the inception of the project, contributing most heavily to the user interface specifications. She has published many articles about Intermedia and its use, and is active in the hypermedia field. She served as the editor for ACM Press' HyperCard stackware *Hypertext on Hypertext*, is a member of the editorial board of *Hypermedia*, a British journal published by Taylor Graham, and has served on the conference Planning and Program Committees for Hypertext '87 and Hypertext '89. Prior to working for IRIS, Yankelovich was a research assistant under Andries van Dam in Brown's Computer Science Department, where she authored a hypermedia maintenance manual using Brown's Electronic Document System. She received an A.B. in Political Science from Brown University in 1983.

# Index

The MIT Press, with Peter Denning as general consulting editor, publishes computer science books in the following series:

**ACM Doctoral Dissertation Award and Distinguished Dissertation Series**

**Artificial Intelligence**
Patrick Winston, Founding editor
Michael Brady, Daniel Bobrow, and Randall Davis, editors

**Charles Babbage Institute Reprint Series for the History of Computing**
Martin Campbell-Kelly, editor

**Computer Systems**
Herb Schwetman, editor

**Explorations with Logo**
E. Paul Goldenberg, editor

**Foundations of Computing**
Michael Garey and Albert Meyer, editors

**History of Computing**
I. Bernard Cohen and William Aspray, editors

**Information Systems**
Michael Lesk, editor

**Logic Programming**
Ehud Shapiro, editor;  Fernando Pereira, Koichi Furukawa, Jean-Louis Lassez, and David H. D. Warren, Associate editors

**The MIT Press Electrical Engineering and Computer Science Series**

**Research Monographs in Parallel and Distributed Processing**
Christopher Jesshope and David Klappholz, editors

**Scientific and Engineering Computation**
Janusz Kowalik, editor

**Technical Communication**
Ed Barrett, editor